Approaching the Millennium

THEATER: Theory/Text/Performance

Enoch Brater, Series Editor
University of Michigan

Approaching the Millennium
Essays on *Angels in America*

Deborah R. Geis and Steven F. Kruger, Editors

Ann Arbor

The University of Michigan Press

2000   1999   1998   1997   4   3   2   1

A CIP catalog record for this book is available from the British Library

Library of Congress Cataloging-in-Publication Data

Approaching the millennium : essays on Angels in America / edited by
    Deborah R. Geis and Steven F. Kruger.
      p.   cm. — (Theater—text/theory/performance)
    Includes bibliographical references (p.   ).
    ISBN 0-472-09623-0 (alk. paper). — ISBN 0-472-06623-4
(pbk. : alk. paper)
      1. Kushner, Tony. Angels in America.   2. AIDS (Disease) in
literature.   3. Homosexuality and literature—United States—
History—20th century.   4. Politics and literature—United States—
History—20th century.   I. Geis, Deborah R., 1960–   .
II. Kruger, Steven F.   III. Series.
PS3561.U778A8532   1997
812'.54—dc21   97-33750
                                                           CIP

Acknowledgments

This book would not have been possible without the energy and commitment of many individuals. At the University of Michigan Press, we would like to thank LeAnn Fields for believing in and guiding this project; Laurie Clark for her generous assistance every step of the way; Mary Meade, Kristen Lare, Elizabeth Gratch, and the rest of the production and marketing staff for all of their efforts on behalf of the volume. Our thanks as well to the anonymous readers who offered comments and suggestions in their evaluations of the manuscript for the Press. For their support and advice on early stages of this project, we thank Enoch Brater, Hersh Zeifman, Toby Silverman Zinman, Robert Vorlicky, and Diana Fuss. For their assistance with the Robert Altman interview, we thank Charles Maland, the Directors' Guild of America, Johnny Planco, and Signe Corriere. Many thanks, of course, to the writers who contributed essays to this volume, all of whom deserve applause for their scholarly inspiration, creativity, patience, and humor.

For their continuing support, we would like to thank our colleagues and staff members at Queens College and at the Graduate School and University Center, City University of New York, especially Rosalie Barberi, Gerry Beckerman, Barbara Bowen, Patricia Clough, Nancy Comley, Evelyn Diaz, Jill Dolan, Kimiko Hahn, Bill Kelly, Charles Molesworth, Anthony O'Brien, Janice Peritz, David Richter, Michael Sargent, Richard Schotter, Amy Tucker, Bette Weidman, and John Weir, as well as all of our students.

There are many others to whom we extend our gratitude for their support and friendship throughout the course of this project, and we apologize to any whose names have been omitted here. Deborah Geis would particularly like to thank David J. Weiss, Anthony Barone, Kathleen Moore, Karen Vrotsos, Beth Baldwin, Janet Pennisi, Mary E. Papke, Allen Dunn, and Chris Holmlund. Steven Kruger especially thanks Judith Raiskin, Mary Wood, Rita Copeland, David Wallace, Robert S. Tilton, Rita Connolly-Tilton, Joan Nestle, Naomi Holoch, and Meryl Siegman. We would both like to thank our parents (Dorothy Geis and the late Norman Geis; Alice S. Kruger and Stanley I. Kruger), siblings (Nancy Bardgett and Sarah Geis Moore; Susan D. Kruger and Joshua D. Kruger), and other family members. Special thanks to our partners, from Deborah Geis to Stanton B. Garner, Jr. and from Steven Kruger to Glenn Burger, for their love and sustenance.

Finally, we pay special tribute to three writers—David B. Feinberg, Charles Ludlam, and Melvin Dixon—who are among the many people whose lives ended too soon due to AIDS; their vision, talent, and "fabulousness" serve as ongoing sources of inspiration, and this book is dedicated to their memory.

Portions of this book appeared previously in other publications, and we thank the editors and publishers for their permission to include these works in the present volume. Michael Cadden's "Strange Angel: The Pinklisting of Roy Cohn" was first published in *Secret Agents: The Rosenberg Case, McCarthyism, and Fifties America*, edited by Marjorie Garber and Rebecca L. Walkowitz (Routledge, 1995), copyright © 1995 by Routledge. David Román's "November 1, 1992: AIDS/*Angels in America*" was adapted from his book *Acts of Intervention*, copyright © 1997 by Indiana University Press. One section of Gregory W. Bredbeck's "'Free[ing] the Erotic Angels': Performing Liberation in the '70s and '90s" was adapted from his article "The Ridiculous Sound of One Hand Clapping: Placing Ludlam's 'Gay' Theatre in Space and Time," which appeared in *Modern Drama* 39, no. 1 (spring 1996): 64–83, copyright © 1996 by University of Toronto Press. David Savran's essay "Ambivalence, Utopia, and a Queer Sort of Materialism: How *Angels in America* Reconstructs the Nation" was first published in *Theatre Journal* 47, no. 2 (May 1995): 207–27, copyright © 1995 by The Johns Hopkins University Press. Nicholas de Jongh's "Representing Sex on the British Stage: The Importance of *Angels in America*," © 1996 by Nicholas de Jongh, is reproduced by permission of the author, c/o Rogers, Coleridge and White Ltd., 20 Powis Mews, London WI1 1JN, England. Our thanks to Tony Kushner for the quotations *passim* from *Angels in America: A Gay Fantasia on National Themes, Part One: Millennium Approaches* (Theatre Communications Group, 1993), copyright © 1992, 1993 by Tony Kushner, and *Part Two: Perestroika* (Theatre Communications Group, 1994), copyright © 1992, 1994 by Tony Kushner. For the photographic reproduction of Raphael's "Transfiguration" that accompanies James Miller's essay, we thank Photo Alinari. For production photographs, we thank Ken Friedman, Louis Palomares, and the American Conservatory Theater; Jay Thompson, Craig Schwartz, Nancy Hereford, and the Mark Taper Forum.

Contents

Apocalyptic Imaginations: Kushner's Theater of the Millennium

Theater of the Fabulous: *Angels* in Performance Contexts

Introduction

Tony Kushner's complex and demanding play *Angels in America* has been, in the words of John M. Clum, "the most talked about, written about, and awarded, play of the past decade or more," "a turning point in the history of gay drama, the history of American drama, and of American literary culture."[1] Harold Bloom included Kushner's play in his "Western canon" alongside Shakespeare and the Bible, and John Lahr wrote in the *New Yorker,* "Not since [Tennessee] Williams has a playwright announced his poetic vision with such authority on the Broadway stage."[2] While we might be wary of the instant canonization that these critics (and many others) have conferred upon the play, clearly, *Angels in America* is an important work, honored by the Pulitzer Prize, thought worthy of recognition by spectators from diverse backgrounds at the same time that it has been embraced, and rejected, for its politics. Ultimately, and perhaps inevitably, the sometimes hyperbolic praise of the play has itself become a site of controversy.[3]

Although *Angels in America* has received extensive coverage in the popular media, scholars have just begun to examine the play, and we feel that the time is right for a fuller critical assessment. In *Approaching the Millennium: Essays on Angels in America* we bring together a wide-ranging and challenging series of essays by scholars with a variety of interests—from dramaturgy to queer theory, from AIDS activism to Brechtian epic theater. Approaching *Angels in America* as theatrical text, as literary work, as popular cultural phenomenon, as political reflection and intervention, these essays begin to mine the complexity of the play (its structure, its themes, its explicit and implicit arguments) and to place it in its particular, conflicted historical moment, a moment when, indeed, "millennium approaches," when, with a sense of an impending ending, global politics stands between the Cold War and its vaguely glimpsed sequel, when the domestic political scene is embroiled in a contentious debate over "identity," and particularly over the relations of race, gender, sexuality, and class to an overarching "national identity," when the AIDS crisis has rewritten a sense of the past, present, and future.

Bringing together an impressive array of characters (female and male; gay, straight, and bisexual; black and white; Jewish, Mormon, and WASP; angelic and human; historical and fictional)—complicated by their portrayal by only eight actors—Kushner's epic vision places itself explicitly in the current American conflict over identity politics yet also situates that debate in a broader historical context: the American history of McCarthyism, of immigration and of the "melting pot," of westward expansion, of racist exploitation. And at a time when stars wear red ribbons to awards ceremonies but the AIDS crisis is woefully underrepresented theatrically, *Angels* (like its predecessors *As Is, The Normal Heart,* and *Zero Positive*) claims its space on the stage—not, we would hope, as a token gesture but more as a movement into activism. By taking on AIDS as a topic, the play takes part in the volatile struggles of the AIDS crisis, struggles themselves interconnected with the politics of sexuality, gender, race, and class. *Angels'* constructions of the future—pointing perhaps toward an apocalyptic, cataclysmic ending, perhaps toward the negotiated ending of "perestroika"—clearly express uncertainty about where the politics of the current moment might take us; visions of human possibility couched in the terms of a problematized angelic revelation, they constitute a certain argument about the dangers and potentials inherent in this current moment and urge us to a particular kind of action, "a kind of painful progress. Longing for what we've left behind, and dreaming ahead."[4] One challenge undertaken by the writers in this collection, then, is to wrestle (as Prior and the Angel do) with some of the interlocking political arguments and questions brought forward in Kushner's play. These acts of engagement (or combat) include examining how the play approaches issues of identity politics and the politics of AIDS; how it presents history; how the evocation of a "millennial" future resonates with the play's consideration of present, urgent "national themes"; how the play may, or may not, constitute an effective intervention in ongoing scenarios of bigotry, homophobia, and political repression.

Integral to the politics of *Angels* is its status as a *dramatic* work—its literariness and theatricality, its place in dramatic traditions, the history of its productions, and its remarkable reception. Kushner's play, implementing a "new" genre that he calls Theater of the Fabulous, enacts what might be termed a postmodern American epic style in the theater. This style is reflected in the play's two-part (eight-act, seven-hour) form; in the complexity of its narrative structure; in its mixing of everyday experience with the stuff of dreams and fantasy, its interruption of the realistic mode by the "angelic" and the metadramatic; in its commingling of dialogue with monologue, diatribe, poetic and vatic voices. While *Angels* clearly stands in some ways in the modernist tradition of American poetic realism (Eugene O'Neill, Tennessee Williams), it also draws on other traditions: the politically didactic, comic, and metadramatic theater of Bertolt Brecht (Kushner, also an adapter of Brecht's plays, has commented frequently on this indebtedness); the narrative structures of Shakespeare's plays (particularly the late romances); the British drama of the "New Left" (Caryl Churchill, David Hare, Edward Bond) and its outspoken socialist commitments; the traditions of genderfuck and camp of Charles Ludlam's Theatre of the Ridiculous.

The ambitiousness of *Angels* and the variety of modes in which it works, of course, mean that its production poses some particularly difficult issues: how to present settings as diverse as Prior's hospital room and Harper's Antarctic fantasy; how to handle the sometimes lightning-fast scene changes, the split and interwoven scenes that cross one another on the stage, often overlapping and competing for our attention; how to stage the meeting of human and angelic realms; how to follow Kushner's own direction that "the moments of magic—the appearance and disappearance of Mr. Lies and the ghosts, the Book hallucination, and the ending—are to be realized as bits of wonderful *theatrical* illusion" so that, even if "the wires show," "the magic . . . [is] at the same time . . . thoroughly amazing" (1:5). *Angels* has received a number of productions—in Los Angeles, New York, San Francisco, London, Avignon, Frankfurt, Tel Aviv, to name only a few—providing a rich basis for discussion of its production challenges, including the cultural shifts required in its "translation" from one stage to the next. And the multiple productions of Angels and its wide popularity enable a consideration, despite the play's recent date, of its reception. Why, among all the plays, novels, and poems written out of the current moment of gay and lesbian activism, and out of the experience of the AIDS crisis, has Kushner's work particularly struck a chord of response? Does the imminent "canonization" of the play necessarily imply a diminishing of its potential as a call for political activism?

The first group of essays in this book, "Reagan's Children: *Angels,* Politics, and American History," examines the play's efforts at responding to a variety of charged and conflicted historical moments and at speaking within a particular political context. David Savran, reviewing the remarkable American reception of *Angels,* asks why, despite its "radical" claims, it has been so popular. He reads the play's "theory of history and utopia"—based both in Walter Benjamin's theologically inflected historical materialism and in the expansionist and communitarian movement of Mormonism—as providing at least a partial answer. For Savran, Kushner's play fits an Enlightenment tradition that believes in "progress," and it also participates in a tradition of classic American literature that presents a politics of "dissension" only finally to affirm the possibility and desirability of consensus. Savran argues that the eager reception of *Angels in America* ultimately marks a recognition of the play's position within a comfortable and dominant tradition of liberal pluralism; where it is most oppositional is in the realm of sexual politics.

Both David Román and James Miller begin their considerations of Kushner's play by evoking moments of the play's production that were particularly charged politically: for Román, the eve of the 1992 presidential election; for Miller, the day after the Stonewall 25 march in the summer of 1994. Román uses the postponement of the Los Angeles opening of *Angels*—from before the election to after—as an occasion for reflecting on the construction of theater history and the ways in which the promulgation of an "official account" erases or simplifies lived experience. He suggests further that the construction of an authoritative or authorized history of AIDS performs work similar to that done in determining theater history. Kushner's play itself, Román argues, "calls into question the concept of an official history," challenging us to "bring forth into the public sphere" those parts of lived experience left out of official historical documentation.

James Miller's essay is, like Román's, particularly concerned with situating *Angels in America* in relation to the history of the AIDS crisis. Linking Kushner's play both to AIDS activism and to an opposed, Apollonian movement of "anagogy," an impulse toward spiritual transcendence of the suffering of life and death in the world, Miller argues that *Angels* should be placed among "a new group of unusually complex and challenging works that cannot be easily labelled 'activist' or 'aesthetic' responses to AIDS because they are oddly neither—or both at once." Though Kushner's play participates in an anagogic movement, it does so without leaving the conflicts and failures of worldly life behind.

Michael Cadden's essay considers Kushner's treatment of the figure of Roy Cohn, in the context of a process of posthumous "outing" that Cadden calls "pinklisting." Cadden reads Kushner's treatment of Cohn as an attempt "to reclaim Roy Cohn from a homophobic discourse that parades itself as political analysis." This reclaiming is complex and difficult, given Cohn's own disavowals of gayness and of AIDS and his implication in McCarthyism; Kushner does not cover over Cohn's "evil." Even so, Cohn can, if unwillingly and only through others' acts of claiming, forgiveness, and memory, participate in a queer "movement toward a new community based on a solidarity across both new and old lines of group identification."

Ron Scapp focuses on the moments of hope embodied in the closing scene of *Perestroika,* reading these moments as an allegory for historical American fantasies of democracy and self-determination. As his essay suggests, behind the rhetoric of such fantasies is always an ideological construct of "progress" as a historically shaped "American" ideal. Drawing upon the speeches of figures as diverse as Ronald Reagan, Thomas Paine, and Malcolm X, Scapp argues that Prior's rejection of stasis/death in favor of "the unity offered to him and his friends through the fantasy of democracy" might also be read as a reminder of the crucial distinction between accepting the "narrative of homogeneity" and expressing a "courageous" vision of political solidarity.

The second part of the book, taking the Angel of America's multiple "I"s as its cue, is entitled " 'I I I I': Identities in *Angels.*" Here several scholars take on the problems of essentialism and identity politics in Kushner's play. In a speech delivered at the March on Washington for Gay and Lesbian Rights in April 1993, Kushner speaks of his dream image of the Black Other and its importance to him in his own "embrace of [his] status as a pariah."[5] While Kushner could be accused here of participating in an eroticizing or fetishizing of racial alterity, it is also clear that he allows for some degree of interrogation of this trope in his complex representation of Belize in *Angels.* Framji Minwalla, using the encounters (collisions) between Belize and Louis in *Millennium Approaches* and between Belize and Roy in *Perestroika* as his points of emphasis, looks at the representations of race and gender identity positions within the play. As Minwalla points out, "an anxiety about ethnicity, cultural heritage, and otherness . . . saturates . . . [the] imaginative space" of *Angels.* Belize becomes the "cipher," the "blankness," the screen onto which other characters project their racial anxieties. The question remaining, says Minwalla, is whether—in an American culture that fetishizes and yet pretends to have dissolved racial differences—Prior's final visionary claim for universalized citizenship is indeed possible.

Much has been made of *Angels* as a "Jewish" drama, but Alisa Solomon's essay draws affirmative connections between the play's Jewishness and its queerness, suggesting that the two gay Jews at its center—Louis Ironson and Roy Cohn—need to be explored in ways that transcend their stereotyped antecedents of Jewish sissy boy or power-hungry villain. Solomon cites a number of conservative reviewers' negative reactions to the play in order to point out that *Angels* demonstrates the continual efforts on the part of the Right to persuade the public of the linked "threats" of Judaism and homosexuality. Kushner uses the character of Louis not as the simple author surrogate some have seen him as, argues Solomon, but, rather, to create a more complex critical portrait. With both Louis and Roy, Kushner never loses sight of the crucial irony that even allows him—in such moments as Roy's abrupt, shticky awakening after Ethel's deathbed lullaby—to turn the audience's capacity for easy sentimentality back on itself.

Allen J. Frantzen also focuses attention on Kushner's treatment of ethnicity, looking at the play's construction of Prior Walter as a WASP (White Anglo-Saxon Protestant). Frantzen particularly directs attention to how Kushner associates stasis with Anglo-Saxon heritage, making Prior the appropriate recipient of the Angel's imperative to "stop moving." A stable WASP identity is contrasted to the mobility of other American ethnic groups, but all racial identity is, in Frantzen's reading, finally posed against the political and the possibility this provides for transformation. Here Frantzen sees Kushner as working in a tradition of Anglo-Saxonism closely related to the American doctrine of Manifest Destiny: though he makes a politically, rather than racially, unified people—gay people—the "chosen people" of his narrative, he continues, like the advocates of Manifest Destiny, to envision their entry into a "promised land."

Steven F. Kruger considers Kushner's treatment of identity more broadly, asking how the notion that identities might be changed or converted operates in *Angels in America*. While the play depicts a variety of changes in its characters' sense of themselves, it also moves to question whether "real" changes have occurred. Kruger looks in particular at how this double movement functions in the depiction of Joe Pitt, who "comes out" as a gay man but who may remain essentially untransformed. Kruger suggests that one of Kushner's central concerns is whether real conversions of self are possible, how these might occur, and how they might be implicated in the attainment of lasting political change.

Contemporary culture is saturated with images of the millennium, evident in everything from the names of hotels to popular songs to religious pamphlets. In part 3, "Apocalyptic Imaginations: Kushner's Theater of the Millennium," three writers take on the play's treatment of the end of an era—an end that seems to promise some sort of revelation, that is undoubtedly informed by the presence of AIDS and the Cold War, but that is also always accompanied by a queer and resistant irony (Prior's "*Very* Steven Spielberg" as the Angel crashes through the ceiling). Stanton B. Garner Jr. situates *Angels in America* in relation to apocalyptic thinking and to a post-modernism "deeply informed by the rhetoric and psychosocial preoccupations of Cold War millenarianism" but also deeply skeptical of "ideas of finitude and conclusion." Kushner's postmodernist play evokes an apocalyptic discourse of closure at the same time that it problematizes it, cultivating "indeterminacy and deferral." As Garner argues, then, the play contests stigmatizing versions of millenarianist rhetoric that have been particularly volatile and dangerous in relation to AIDS and (homo)sexuality, but it, nonetheless, does not reject historical and even apocalyptic thinking, instead reconfiguring these in a "counterhistorical" movement intended to challenge the exclusions and violences of dominant historical narratives.

Martin Harries looks at the spectacular, "angelic" side of *Angels,* suggesting that the play's anti-Brechtian "return to the supernatural" is nonetheless ultimately Brechtian in impact: recognizing how Brechtian demystification has become conventional and mystified, Harries suggests that Kushner moves to demystify demystification itself. Harries also considers Kushner's revision of Walter Benjamin's "angel of history," focusing on the problem of "the accurate representation of history," which Harries sees as equally crucial for Benjamin and Kushner. While Harries reads Kushner's account of history as concerned with taking apart the ideological fantasies of the Reagan years, he also suggests that Kushner's theater "concoct[s] a countermagic that not only disenchants but also has its own sacred force."

Deborah R. Geis examines how *Angels in America* links insanity and prophecy, both modes of "inhabit[ing] the in-between spaces" of society. Situating the play at a particular postmodern moment, Geis focuses on Harper and Prior, the two characters most consistently associated with the "threshold of revelation." She argues that the play shows both characters coming to terms with "the uncontrollable realm of the Imaginary, the insane," in such a way as not to deny but to foreground history, memory, theatricality. And Geis sees the theatricality of Kushner's play as closely linked to the kind of "insane" imaginative work that its characters do: the play's most theatrical moments serve not to deny "the real" but to encounter it in a way that might enable it to be seen anew, seen in a particularly *revealing* way.

In the final part of *Approaching the Millennium,* "Theater of the Fabulous: *Angels* in Performance Contexts," we turn to recent and future stagings (and adaptations) of Kushner's play, examining both its production history and the challenges these productions have raised as others continue to work with (or against?) the text of *Angels.* Arnold Aronson is concerned with pragmatic problems of staging *Angels* and with how those problems are integrally related to the production of meaning for the play's audiences. Aronson compares the scenography of London, Broadway, and Los Angeles productions, examining how these different productions present the idea of America. He notes the play's relative scarcity of specific, easily identifiable locales, and he argues that *Angels in America* is best set "on an essentially empty stage." This evokes not only a certain American "every-town" but also postmodern ideas of "nonlinear, nongeometric, disjointed, juxtapositional" space that Aronson sees the play, in its "layering of scenes and transpositions of characters," as enacting.

In the interview "On Filming *Angels*" (conducted 20 November 1995) director Robert Altman discusses his plans for a movie version of Kushner's play. Though Altman is reluctant to predict how things will "turn out" in the filming, it becomes clear that he has a strong reading of the play—one that will emphasize social and political contexts; deromanticize the Angel of America; stress the fantastic, and personal, qualities of fantasy, while at the same time making clear its social shaping. Seeing the play as already "cine-matic," Altman is particularly concerned with how, in filming it, to keep it from becoming "just a movie." It should be noted that in 1997 Altman decided not to participate in the filming of *Angels,* having agreed—in coop-eration with Tony Kushner—that the project should be passed on to P. J. Hogan, the director of *Muriel's Wedding.* We have included the interview, however, for its visions of Kushner's text, which are perhaps all the more tantalizing when accompanied by the knowledge that this is, after all, a glimpse of what might have been from one of the great filmmakers of our time.

The following two essays, by Janelle Reinelt and Art Borreca, provide different perspectives on the issue of Kushner's appropriation and transfor-mation of Brechtian epic theater: Reinelt focuses on two American pro-ductions of the play, while Borreca uses the London version as a point of departure. Like David Savran, Reinelt critiques Kushner's political stance, suggesting that he "drift[s] away from socialist themes" and that the play fails to provide "alternatives to bourgeois individualism." She, however, also recognizes a certain Brechtian, epic, potential in the play. For Reinelt the status of the epic play depends upon both its "provisional positing of a dif-ferent way of organizing social life" and the formation of "a Brechtian tri-angle of speculation and critique, aesthetic pleasure and political engage-ment," among spectators, actors, and play. A play can only be "epic," then, in certain situations of production, and she goes on to analyze the 1993 New York and 1994 San Francisco productions, looking at scenography, set design, audience preparation and reception, to "establish the different potentialities of the play" as an American version of Brechtian epic theater.

Like Reinelt, Art Borreca is particularly concerned with how to stage the play's complex "social and theatrical dialectics": as he suggests, *Angels in America* is dialectical not just thematically but also stylistically. Thus, in Borreca's view Kushner deploys realistic narratives and a Benjamin-influenced "anti-Brechtian spectacle" in dialectical relation to each other. With Declan Donnellan's London production—its scenography, its treatment of the play's stylistic montage—providing examples of one successful mining of the play's energies as epic theater, Borreca develops a dramaturg's protocol for a staging of the play, a production that would do justice to the play's complex dialectical movements, place it in its social and political contexts, and stimulate audiences into dialogue with the play's ideas.

Nicholas de Jongh also takes the London production of *Angels* as his focus, paying particular attention to the significance, for British theater, of Kushner's refusal to separate the representation of sexuality from the consideration of social and political questions. In insisting on this linkage between sex and politics, *Angels* intervenes strongly in a British theatrical tradition averse to representations of sexuality. As de Jongh suggests, its presentation at a state-sponsored theater represents an important turning point for the dramatic representation of (homo)sexuality in England.

Finally, Gregory W. Bredbeck's discussion of *Angels* reinvokes some of the political issues raised in the earlier parts of this collection at the same time that it situates the play in the context of key moments in queer performance history. Bredbeck's concern is with the play's connection to a sometimes troubled tradition of the drama of liberation; using early radical gay theater by way of comparison, Bredbeck turns to Charles Ludlam's Theatre of the Ridiculous, particularly *Bluebeard,* to show a certain liberatory potential that Ludlam's Stonewall-era works claimed for themselves. The text of *Angels,* Bredbeck argues, manages to emphasize the ambivalences and contradictions that characterize both "gay liberation theory" and "gay and lesbian civil rights"; it displays the "fissure between these two discourses . . . as one of its objects of performance." The result, to return to the topic of history, is a postmodern critique of hegemonic narrative as Kushner "liberates history from its illusory pose as a unified and determining trajectory." With that liberatory impulse—and, of course, with Prior's benediction that we are "fabulous creatures, each and every one" (2:148)—we open the curtains for these essays on *Angels in America.*

NOTES

1. John M. Clum, *Acting Gay: Male Homosexuality in Modern Drama,* rev. ed. (New York: Columbia University Press, 1994), 313, 324.

2. Harold Bloom, *The Western Canon* (New York: Harcourt, Brace, 1994); John Lahr, "Earth Angels," *New Yorker,* 13 December 1993, 133.

3. See, for example, Gordon Rogoff, "Angels in America, Devils in the Wings," *Theater* 24 (1993): 21–29.

4. Tony Kushner, *Angels in America: A Gay Fantasia on National Themes. Part Two: Perestroika* (New York: Theatre Communications Group, 1994), 144. Subsequent references to *Perestroika* and to part 1 of *Angels—Angels in America: A Gay Fantasia on National Themes. Part One: Millennium Approaches* (New York: Theatre Communications Group, 1993)—will be given parenthetically in the text.

5. Tony Kushner, "Copious, Gigantic, and Sane," in *Thinking about the Longstanding Problems of Virtue and Happiness* (New York: Theatre Communications Group, 1995), 50.

Reagan's Children:
Angels, Politics, and
American History

Ambivalence, Utopia, and a Queer Sort of Materialism: How *Angels in America* Reconstructs the Nation

David Savran

Critics, pundits, and producers have placed Tony Kushner's *Angels in America: A Gay Fantasia on National Themes* in the unenviable position of having to rescue the American theater. The latter, by all accounts, is in a sorry state. It has attempted to maintain its elite cultural status despite the fact that the differences between "high" and "low" have become precarious. On Broadway increasingly expensive productions survive more and more by mimicking mass culture, either in the form of mind-numbing spectacles featuring singing cats, falling chandeliers, and dancing dinnerware or plays like *The Heidi Chronicles* or *Prelude to a Kiss,* whose style and themes aspire to "quality" television. In regional theaters, meanwhile, subscriptions continue to decline and with them the adventurousness of artistic directors. Given this dismal situation, *Angels in America* has almost singlehandedly resuscitated a category of play that has become almost extinct: the serious Broadway drama that is neither a British import nor a revival.

Not within memory has a new American play been canonized by the press as rapidly as *Angels in America*.[1] Indeed, critics have been stumbling over one another in an adulatory stupor. John Lahr hails *Perestroika* as a "masterpiece" and notes that "not since Williams has a playwright announced his poetic vision with such authority on the Broadway stage."[2] Jack Kroll judges both parts "the broadest, deepest, most searching American play of our time,"[3] while Robert Brustein deems *Millennium Approaches* "the authoritative achievement of a radical dramatic artist with a fresh, clear voice."[4] In the gay press, meanwhile, the play is viewed as testifying to the fact that "Broadway now leads the way in the industry with its unapologetic portrayals of gay characters."[5] For both Frank Rich and John Clum *Angels* is far more than just a successful play; it is the marker of a decisive historical shift in American theater. According to Rich, the play's success is in part the result of its ability to conduct "a searching and radical rethinking of the whole esthetic of American political drama."[6] For Clum the play's appear-

13

ance on Broadway "marks a turning point in the history of gay drama, the history of American drama, and of American literary culture."[7] In its reception *Angels*—so deeply preoccupied with teleological process—is itself positioned as both the culmination of history and as that which rewrites the past.

Despite the enormity of such claims, I am less interested in disputing them than in trying to understand why they are being made—and why *now*. Why is a play featuring five gay male characters being universalized as a "turning point" in the American theater and minoritized as the preeminent gay male artifact of the 1990s? Why is it both popular and "radical"? What is the linkage between the two primary sources for the play's theory of history and utopia—Walter Benjamin and Mormonism? And what does this linkage suggest about the constitution of the nation? Finally, why has queer drama become *the* theatrical sensation of the 1990s? I hope it's not too perverse of me to attempt to answer these questions by focusing less on the construction of queer subjectivities per se than on the field of cultural production in which *Angels in America* is situated. After all, how else would one practice a queer materialism?

The Angel of History

The opposite of nearly everything you say about *Angels in America* will also hold true: *Angels* valorizes identity politics; it offers an antifoundationalist critique of identity politics. *Angels* mounts an attack against ideologies of individualism; it problematizes the idea of community. *Angels* submits liberalism to a trenchant examination; it finally opts for yet another version of American liberal pluralism. *Angels* launches a critique of the very mechanisms that produce pathologized and acquiescent female bodies; it represents yet another pathologization and silencing of women. A conscientious reader or spectator might well rebuke the play, as Belize does Louis: "you're ambivalent about everything."[8] *Angels'* ambivalence, however, is not simply the result of Kushner hedging his bets on the most controversial issues. Rather, it functions, I believe—quite independently of the intent of its author—as the play's political unconscious, playing itself out on many different levels: formal, ideological, characterological, and rhetorical (Frank Rich refers to this as Kushner's "refusal to adhere to any theatrical or political theory").[9] Yet the fact that *ambivalence*—or *undecidability*—is the watchword of this text (which is, after all, *two* plays) does not mean that all the questions it raises remain unresolved. On the contrary, I will argue that the play's undecidability is, in fact, always already resolved because the questions that appear to be ambivalent have in fact already been decided consciously or unconsciously by the text itself. Moreover, the relentless operation of normalizing reading practices works to reinforce these decisions. If I am correct, the play turns out (*pace* Frank Rich) to adhere all too well to a particular political theory.

Formally, *Angels* is a promiscuously complicated play that is very difficult to categorize generically. Clum's characterization of it as being "like a Shakespearean romance" is doubtlessly motivated by its rambling and episodic form, its interweaving of multiple plot lines, its mixture of realism and fantasy, its invocation of various theological and mythological narratives, as well as its success in evoking those characteristics that are usually associated with both comedy and tragedy.[10] Moreover, *Perestroika's* luminous finale is remarkably suggestive of the beatific scenes that end Shakespeare's romances. There is no question, moreover, but that the play deliberately evokes the long history of Western dramatic literature and positions itself as heir to the traditions of Sophocles, Shakespeare, Brecht, and others. Consider, for example, its use of the blindness/insight binary opposition and the way that Prior Walter is carefully constructed (like the blind Prelapsarianov) as a kind of Tiresias, "going blind, as prophets do."[11] This binarism, the paradigmatic emblem of the tragic subject (and mark of Tiresias, Oedipus, and Gloucester), deftly links cause and effect—because one is blind to truth, one loses one's sight—and is used to claim Prior's priority, his epistemologically privileged position in the text. Or consider the parallels often drawn in the press between Kushner's Roy Cohn and Shakespeare's Richard III.[12] Or Kushner's use of a fate motif, reminiscent of *Macbeth,* whereby Prior insists that Louis not return until the seemingly impossible comes to pass, until he sees Louis "black and blue" (2:89). Or Kushner's rewriting of those momentous moral and political debates that riddle not just classical tragedy (*Antigone, Richard II*) but also the work of Brecht and his (mainly British) successors (Howard Brenton, David Hare, Caryl Churchill). Or the focus on the presence/absence of God that one finds not just in early modern tragedy but also in so-called absurdism (Beckett, Ionesco, Stoppard). Moreover, these characteristics tend to be balanced, on the one hand, by the play's insistent tendency to ironize and, on the other, by the familiar ingredients of romantic comedies (ill-matched paramours, repentant lovers, characters suddenly finding themselves in unfamiliar places, plus a lot of good jokes). Despite the ironic/comic tone, however, none of the interlaced couples survives the onslaught of chaos, disease, and revelation. Prior and Louis, Louis and Joe, Joe and Harper, have all parted by the end of the play, and the romantic dyad (as primary social unit) is replaced in the final scene of *Perestroika* by a utopian concept of (erotic) affiliation and a new definition of family.

Angels in America's title, its idea of utopia, and its model for a particular kind of ambivalence are derived in part from Benjamin's extraordinary meditation, "Theses on the Philosophy of History," written shortly before his death in 1940. Composed during the first months of World War II, with fascism on its march across Europe, the darkness (and simultaneous luminosity) of Benjamin's "Theses" attest not only to the seeming invincibility of Hitler but also to the impossible position of the European Left, "stranded," as Terry Eagleton notes, "between social democracy and Stalinism."[13] In this essay Benjamin sketches a discontinuous theory of history in which "the services of theology" are enlisted in the aid of reconceiving "historical materialism."[14] Opposing the universalizing strategies of bourgeois historicism with historical materialism's project of brushing "history against the grain" (257), he attempts a radical revision of Marxist historiography. Suturing the Jewish notion of Messianic time (in which all history is given meaning retrospectively by the sudden and unexpected coming of the Messiah) to the Marxist concept of revolution, Benjamin reimagines proletariat revolution not as the culmination of a conflict between classes, or between traditional institutions and new forms of production, but as a "blast[ing] open" of "the continuum of history" (262). Unlike traditional Marxist (or idealist) historiographers, he rejects the idea of the present as a moment of "transition" and instead conceives it as *Jetztzeit,* "time filled by the presence of the now" (261), a moment in which "time stands still and has come to a stop" (262). Facing *Jetztzeit,* and opposing all forms of gradualism, Benjamin's historical materialist, then, is given the task not of imagining and inciting progressive change (or a movement toward socialism) but of "blast[ing] a specific era out of the homogeneous course of history" (263).

The centerpiece of Benjamin's essay is his explication of a painting by Paul Klee, which becomes a parable of history, of the time of the Now, in the face of catastrophe (which for him means all of human history):

> A Klee painting named "Angelus Novus" shows an angel looking as though he is about to move away from something he is fixedly contemplating. His eyes are staring, his mouth is open, his wings are spread. This is how one pictures the angel of history. His face is turned toward the past. Where we perceive a chain of events, he sees one single catastrophe which keeps piling wreckage upon wreckage and hurls it in front of his feet. The angel would like to stay, awaken the dead,

and make whole what has been smashed. But a storm is blowing from Paradise; it has got caught in his wings with such violence that the angel can no longer close them. This storm irresistibly propels him into the future to which his back is turned, while the pile of debris before him grows skyward. This storm is what we call progress. (257–58)

In Benjamin's allegory, with its irresolvable play of contradictions, the doggedly well-intentioned angel of history embodies both the inconceivability of progress and the excruciating condition of the Now. Poised (not unlike Benjamin himself in Europe in 1940) between the past, which is to say "catastrophe," and an unknown and terrifying future, he is less a heavenly actor than a passive observer, "fixedly contemplating" that disaster which is the history of the world. His "Paradise," meanwhile, is not the site of a benign utopianism but a "storm" whose "violence" gets caught under his wings and propels him helplessly into an inconceivable future that stymies his gaze.

Benjamin's allegory of history is, in many respects, the primary generative fiction for *Angels in America*. Not only is its Angel clearly derived from Benjamin's text (although with gender reassignment surgery along the way—Kushner's Angel is "Hermaphroditically Equipped"), but so is its vision of Heaven, which has *"a deserted, derelict feel to it,"* with *"rubble . . . strewn everywhere"* (2:48; 121). And the play's conceptualizations of the past, of catastrophe, and of utopia are clearly inflected by Benjamin's "Theses," as is its linkage between historical materialism and theology. Moreover, rather than attempt to suppress the contradictions that inform Benjamin's materialist theology, Kushner expands them. As a result, the ideas of history, progress, and paradise that *Angels in America* invokes are irreducibly contradictory (often without appearing to be so). Just as Benjamin's notion of revolution is related dialectically to catastrophe, so are *Angels'* concepts of deliverance and abjection, ecstasy and pain, utopia and dystopia, necessarily linked. Kushner's Angel (and her/his Heaven) serve as a constant reminder both of catastrophe (AIDS, racism, homophobia, and the pathologization of queer and female bodies, to name only the play's most obvious examples) and of the perpetual possibility of millennium's approach, or in the words of Ethel Rosenberg (unmistakably echoing Benjamin), that "history is about to crack wide open" (1:112). And the concept of utopia/dystopia to which s/he is linked guarantees that the vehicle of hope and redemption in *Angels*—the prophet who foresees a new age—will be the character who must endure the most agony, Prior Walter, suffering from AIDS and Louis's desertion.

Within the economy of utopia/dystopia that *Angels* installs, the greatest promise of the millennium is the possibility of life freed from the shack-
les of hatred, oppression, and disease. It is hardly surprising, therefore, that
Roy Cohn is constructed as the embodiment and guarantor of dystopia.
Not only is he the paradigm of bourgeois individualism—and Reaganism—
at its most murderous, hypocritical, and malignant, but he is the one with
the most terrifying vision of the "universe," which he apprehends "as a kind
of sandstorm in outer space with winds of mega-hurricane velocity, but
instead of grains of sand it's shards and splinters of glass" (1:13). It is, however, a sign of the play's obsessively dialectical structure that Roy's vision of
what sounds like hell should provide an uncanny echo of Benjamin's "storm
blowing from Paradise." Yet even this dialectic, much like the play's
ambivalences, is deceptive insofar as its habit of turning one pole of a binarism relentlessly into its opposite (rather than into a synthesis) describes a
false dialectic. Prior, on the other hand, refusing the role of victim, becomes
the sign of the unimaginable, of "the Great Work" (2:148). Yet, as with
Roy, so Prior's privileged position is a figure of contradiction, coupling not
just blindness with prophecy but also history with an impossible future, an
ancient lineage (embodied by Prior 1 and Prior 2) with the millennium yet
to come, and AIDS with a "most inner part, entirely free of disease" (1:34).
Moreover, Prior's very name designates his temporal dislocation, the fact
that he is at once too soon and belated, both that which anticipates and that
which provides an epilogue (to the Walter family, if nothing else, since he
seems to mark the end of the line). Prior Walter also serves as the queer
commemoration of the Walter that came before—Walter Benjamin—
whose revolutionary principles he both embodies and displaces insofar as he
marks both the presence and absence of Walter Benjamin in this text.[15]

Throughout *Angels in America* the utopia/dystopia coupling (wherein
disaster becomes simultaneously the marker for and incitement to think
Paradise) plays itself out through a host of binary oppositions:
Heaven/Hell, forgiveness/retribution, communitarianism/individual-
ism, spirit/flesh, pleasure/pain, beauty/decay, future/past, homosexual-
ity/heterosexuality, rationalism/indeterminacy, migration/staying put,
progress/stasis, life/death. Each of these functions not just as a set of
conceptual poles in relation to which characters and themes are worked
out and interpreted but also as an *oxymoron,* a figure of undecidability
whose contradictory being becomes an incitement to think the impossible: revolution. For it is precisely the conjunction of opposites that
allows what Benjamin calls "the flow of thoughts" to be given a "shock"
and so turned into "the sign of a Messianic cessation of happening"

(262–63). The oxymoron, in other words, becomes the privileged figure by which the unimaginable allows itself to be imagined.

In Kushner's reading of Benjamin the hermaphroditic Angel becomes the most crucial site for the elaboration of contradiction. Because her/his body is the one on which an impossible—and utopian—sexual conjunction is played out, s/he decisively undermines the distinction between the heterosexual and the homosexual. With her/his "eight vaginas" and "Bouquet of Phalli" s/he represents an absolute otherness, the impossible Other that fulfills the longing for both the maternal and paternal (or, in Lacanian terms, both demand and the Law). On the one hand, as the maternal "Other," s/he is constituted by "demand . . . as already possessing the 'privilege' of satisfying needs, that is to say, the power of depriving them of that alone by which they are satisfied."[16] On the other hand, "as the law of symbolic functioning," s/he simultaneously represents the "Other embodied in the figure of the symbolic father," "not a person but a place, the locus of law, language and the symbolic."[17] Being the impossible conjunction of the maternal and the paternal, s/he provides Prior with sexual pleasure of celestial quality—and gives a new meaning to safe sex. At the same time, s/he also fills and completes subjectivity, being the embodiment of and receptacle for Prior's "Released Female Essence" (2:48).

Although all of these characteristics suggest that the Angel is constructed as an extratemporal being, untouched by the ravages of passing time, s/he comes (quite literally for Prior) already culturally mediated. When s/he first appears at the end of *Millennium,* he exclaims, "*Very* Steven Spielberg." Although his campy ejaculation is clearly calculated as a laugh line, defusing and undercutting (with typical postmodern cynicism) the deadly earnestness of the scene, it also betrays the fact that this miraculous apparition is in part the product of a culture industry and that any reading of her/him will be mediated by the success of Steven Spielberg and his ilk (in films like *Close Encounters of the Third Kind* and *E.T.*) in producing a particular vision of the miraculous (with lots of bright white light and music by John Williams). To that extent the appearance of the Angel signals the degree to which utopia—and revolution!—have now become the product of commodity culture. Unlike earlier periods, when utopia tended to be imagined in terms of production (rather than consumption) and was sited in a preceding phase of capitalism (e.g., in a preindustrial or agrarian society), late capitalism envisions utopia through the lens of the commodity and—not unlike Walter Benjamin at his most populist—projects it into a future and an elsewhere lit by that *"unearthly white light"* (1:118), which represents, among other things, the illimitable allure of the commodity form.[18]

Although the construction of the Angel represses her/his historicity, the Heaven s/he calls home is explicitly the product (and victim) of temporality. Heaven is a simulacrum of San Francisco on 18 April 1906, the day of the Great Earthquake. For it is on this day that God "abandoned" his angels and their Heaven *"and did not return"* (2:51). Heaven thus appears frozen in time, *"deserted and derelict,"* with *"rubble strewn everywhere"* (2:121). The Council Room in Heaven, meanwhile, *"dimly lit by candles and a single great bulb"* (which periodically fails), is a monument to the past, specifically to the New Science of the seventeenth century and the Enlightenment project to which it is inextricably linked. The table in the Council Room is *"covered with antique and broken astronomical, astrological, mathematical and nautical objects of measurement and calculation."* At its center sits a *"bulky radio, a 1940s model in very poor repair"* (2:128), on which the Angels are listening to the first reports of the Chernobyl disaster. Conflating different moments of the past and distinct (Western) histories, Heaven is a kind of museum, not the insignia of the Now, but of *before,* of an antique past, of the obsolete. Its decrepitude is also symptomatic of the Angels' fear that God will never return. More nightmare than utopia, marooned in history, Heaven commemorates disaster, despair, and stasis.

Because of its imbeddedness in the past, the geography of Heaven is a key to the complex notion of temporality that governs *Angels in America.* Although the scheme does not become clear until *Perestroika,* there are two opposing concepts of time and history running through the play. First, there is the time of the Angels (and of Heaven), the time of dystopian "STASIS" (2:54) as decreed by the absence of a God, who, Prior insists, "isn't coming back" (2:133). According to the Angel, this temporal paralysis is the direct result of the hyperactivity of human beings: *"YOU HAVE DRIVEN HIM AWAY!"* the Angel enjoins Prior, *"YOU MUST STOP MOVING!"* (2:52), in the hope that immobility will once again prompt the return of God and the forward movement of time. Yet this concept of time as stasis is also linked to decay. In the Angel's threnody that ends the council scene, s/he envisions the dissolution of "the Great Design, / The spiraling apart of the Work of Eternity" (2:134). Directly opposed to this concept is human temporality, of which Prior, in contradistinction to the Angel, becomes the spokesperson. This time—which is also apparently the time of God—is the temporality connected with Enlightenment epistemologies; it is the time of "Progress," "Science," and "Forward Motion" (2:132; 50). It is the time of "Change" (2:13) so fervently desired by Comrade Prelapsarianov and the "neo-Hegelian positivist sense of constant historical progress towards happiness or perfection" so precious to Louis (1:25). It is the promise fulfilled at the end of *Perestroika,* when Louis, apprehending "the end of the Cold War," announces, "the whole world is changing!" (2:145). Most important, the time of "progress, migration, motion," and "modernity" is also, in Prior's formulation, the time of "desire," because it is this last all-too-human characteristic that produces modernity (2:132). Without desire (for change, utopia, the Other) there could be no history.

Despite the fact that this binary opposition generates so much of the play's ideological framework, and that its two poles are at times indistinguishable, it seems to me that this is one question on which *Angels in America* is not ambivalent at all. Unlike the Benjamin of the "Theses on the Philosophy of History," for whom any concept of progress seems quite inconceivable, Kushner is devoted to rescuing Enlightenment epistemologies at a time when they are, to say the least, extremely unfashionable. On the one hand, *Angels in America* counters attacks from the pundits of the Right, wallowing in their post–Cold War triumphalism, for whom socialism, or "the coordination of men's activities through central direction," is the road to "serfdom."[19] For these neoconservatives "we already live in the millennial new age," we already stand at "the end of history," and, as a result, in Francis Fukuyama's words, "we cannot picture to ourselves a world that is *essentially* different from the present one, and at the same time better."[20] Obsessed with "free markets and private property," and trying desperately to maintain the imperialist status quo, they can only imagine progress as regression.[21] On the other hand, *Angels* also challenges the orthodoxies of those poststructuralists on the Left by whom the Marxian concept of history is often dismissed as hopelessly idealist, as "a contemptible attempt," in Aijaz Ahmad's words, to construct "grand narratives" and "totalizing (totalitarian?) knowledges."[22]

In the face of these profound cynicisms *Angels* unabashedly champions rationalism and progress. In the last words of *Perestroika*'s last act Harper suggests that, "in this world, there is a kind of painful progress. Longing for what we've left behind, and dreaming ahead" (2:144). The last words of the epilogue, meanwhile, are given to Prior, who envisions a future in which "we," presumably gay men, lesbians, and persons with AIDS, "will be citizens." *"More Life,"* he demands (2:148).

Kushner's difference with Benjamin—and the poststructuralists—over the possibility of progress and his championing of modernity (and the desire that produces it) suggest that the string of binary oppositions that are foundational to the play are perhaps less undecidable than I originally suggested. Meaning is produced, in part, because these oppositions are constructed as interlocking homologies, each an analogy for all the others. And, despite the fact that each term of each opposition is strictly dependent on the other and, indeed, is produced by its other, these relations are by no means symmetrical. Binary oppositions are always hierarchical—especially when the fact of hierarchy is repressed. *Angels* is carefully constructed so that communitarianism, rationalism, progress, etc., will be read as being preferable to their alternatives: individualism, indeterminacy, stasis, etc. ("the playwright has been able to find hope in his chronicle of the poisonous 1980s").[23] So, at least as far as this string of interlocked binary oppositions is concerned, ambivalence turns out to be not especially ambivalent after all.

At the same time, what is one to make of other binarisms—most notably, the opposition between masculine and feminine—toward which the play seems to cultivate a certain studied ambivalence? On the one hand, it is clear that Kushner is making some effort to counter the long history of the marginalization and silencing of women in American culture generally and in American theater, in particular. Harper's hallucinations are crucial to the play's articulation of its central themes, including questions of exile and of the utopia/dystopia binarism. They also give her a privileged relationship to Prior, in whose fantasies she sometimes partakes and with whom she visits Heaven. Her unequivocal rejection of Joe and expropriation of his credit card at the end of the play, moreover, signal her repossession of her life and her progress from imaginary to real travel. Hannah, meanwhile, is constructed as an extremely independent and strong-willed woman who becomes part of the new extended family that is consolidated at the end of the play. Most intriguingly, the play's deliberate foregrounding of the silencing of the Mormon Mother and Daughter in the diorama is symptomatic of Kushner's desire to let women speak. On the other hand, *Angels* seems to replicate many of the structures that historically have produced female subjectivity as Other. Harper may be crucial to the play's structure, but she is still pathologized, like so many of her antecedents on the American stage (from Mary Tyrone to Blanche DuBois to Honey in *Who's Afraid of Virginia Woolf?*). With her hallucinations and "emotional problems" (1:27), she functions as a scapegoat for Joe, the displacement of his sexual problems. Moreover, her false confession that she's "going to have a baby" not only reinforces the link in the play between femininity and maternity but also literally hystericizes her (1:41). And Hannah, despite her strength, is defined almost entirely by her relationship to her real son and to Prior, her surrogate son. Like Belize, she is given the role of caretaker.

Most important, the celestial "sexual politics" of the play guarantees that the feminine remains Other. After his visitation by the Angel, Prior explains that "God . . . is a man. Well, not a man, he's a flaming Hebrew letter, but a male flaming Hebrew letter." In comparison with this masculinized, Old Testament-style, "flaming"(!) patriarch, the Angels are decidedly hermaphroditic. Nonetheless, the play's stage directions use the feminine pronoun when designating the Angel, and s/he has been played by a woman in all of the play's various American premieres. As a result of this clearly delineated gendered difference, femininity is associated (in Heaven at least) with "STASIS" and collapse, while a divine masculinity is coded as being simultaneously deterministic and absent. In the play's pseudo-Platonic—and heterosexualized—metaphysics, the "orgasm" of the Angels produces (a feminized) "protomatter, which fuels the [masculinized] Engine of Creation" (2:49).

Moreover, the play's use of doubling reinforces this sense of the centrality of masculinity. Unlike Caryl Churchill's *Cloud 9* (surely the locus classicus of genderfuck), *Angels* uses cross-gender casting only for minor characters. And the crossing of gender works in one direction only. The actresses playing Hannah, Harper and the Angel take on a number of male heterosexual characters, while the male actors double only in masculine roles. As a result, it seems to me that *Angels,* unlike the work of Churchill, does not denaturalize gender. Rather, masculinity—which, intriguingly, is always already queered in this text—is produced as a remarkably stable, if contradictory, essence that others can mime but which only a real (i.e., biological) male can embody. Thus, yet another ambivalence turns out to be always already decided.

The American Religion

The nation that *Angels in America* fantasizes has its roots in the early nineteenth century, the period during which the United States became constituted, to borrow Benedict Anderson's celebrated formulation, as "an imagined political community, . . . imagined as both inherently limited and sovereign."[24] For not until the 1830s and 1840s, with the success of Jacksonian democracy and the development of the ideology of Manifest Destiny, did a sense of an imagined community of Americans begin to solidify, due to a number of factors: the consolidation of industrialization in the Northeast, the proliferation of large newspapers and state banks, and a transportation revolution that linked the urban centers with both agricultural producers and markets abroad.[25]

It is far more than coincidence that the birth of the modern idea of America coincided with what is often called the Second Great Awakening (the first had culminated in the Revolutionary War). During these years, as

Klaus Hansen relates, "the old paternalistic reform impulse directed toward social control yielded to a romantic reform movement impelled by millennialism, immediatism, and individualism." This movement, in turn, "made possible the creation of the modern American capitalist empire with its fundamental belief in religious, political, and economic pluralism."[26] For those made uneasy (for a variety of reasons) by the new Jacksonian individualism this pluralism authorized the emergence of alternative social and religious sects, both millennialist evangelical revivals and new communities like the Shakers, the Oneida Perfectionists, and, most prominently and successfully, the Mormons.[27] As Hansen emphasizes, "Mormonism was not merely one more variant of American Protestant pluralism but an articulate and sophisticated counterideology that attempted to establish a 'new heaven and a new earth.'" Moreover, "both in its origins and doctrines" Mormonism "insisted on the peculiarly American nature of its fundamental values" and on the identity of America as the promised land.[28]

Given the number and prominence of Mormon characters in the play, it should come as little surprise that Mormonism, at least as it was originally articulated in the 1820s and 1830s, maintains a very close relationship to the epistemology of *Angels in America*. Many of the explicitly hieratic qualities of the play—the notion of prophecy, the sacred book, as well as the Angel her/himself—owe as much to Mormonism as to Walter Benjamin. Even more important, the play's conceptualization of history, its millennialism, and its idea of America bring it startlingly close to the tenets of early Mormonism. Indeed, it is impossible to understand the concept of the nation with which *Angels* is obsessed (and even the idea of queering the nation!), without understanding the constitution of early Mormonism. Providing Calvinism with its most radical challenge during the National period, it was deeply utopian in its thrust (and it remains so today). Indeed, its concept of time is identical to the temporality for which *Angels in America* polemicizes. Like *Angels,* Mormonism understands time as evolution and progress (in that sense it is more closely linked to Enlightenment epistemologies than Romantic ones) and holds out the possibility of unlimited human growth: "As man is God once was: as God is man may become."[29] As part of a tremendous resurgence of interest in the millennium between 1828 and 1832, Mormonism went far beyond the ideology of progress implicit in Jacksonian democracy (just as *Angels'* millennialism goes far beyond most contemporary ideologies of progress).[30] Understood historically, this utopianism was in part the result of the relatively marginal economic status of Joseph Smith and his followers, subsistence farmers and struggling petits bourgeois. Tending "to be 'agin the government,'" these early Mormons were a persecuted minority and, in their westward journey to Zion, remained the subjects of widespread violence, beginning in 1832, when Smith was tarred and feathered in Ohio.[31] Much like twentieth-century lesbians and gay men—although most contemporary Mormons would be appalled by the comparison—Mormons were, throughout the 1830s and 1840s, attacked by mobs, arrested on false charges, imprisoned, and murdered. In 1838 the governor of Missouri decreed that they must be "exterminated" or expelled from the state. In 1844 Smith and his brother were assassinated by an angry mob.[32]

The violent antipathy toward early Mormonism was in part the result of the fact that it presented a significant challenge to the principles of individualist social and economic organization. From the beginning Mormonism was communitarian in nature and proposed a kind of ecclesiastical socialism in which "those entering the order were asked to 'consecrate' their property and belongings to the church." To each male would then be returned enough to sustain him and his family, while the remainder would be apportioned to "every man who has need." As Hansen emphasizes, this organization represents a repudiation of the principles of laissez-faire and an attempt "to restore a more traditional society in which the economy was regulated in behalf of the larger interests of the group."[33] This nostalgia for an earlier period of capitalism (the agrarianism of the early colonies) is echoed by Mormonism's conceptualization of the continent as the promised land. Believing the Garden of Eden to have been sited in America and assigning all antediluvian history to the Western Hemisphere, early Mormonism believed that "the term (New World) was in fact a misnomer because America was really the cradle of man and civilization."[34] So the privileged character of the nation is linked to its sacred past, and, as with Benjamin, history is tied to theology. At the same time, this essentially theological conceptualization of the nation bears witness to the "strong affinity," noted by Anderson, between "the nationalist imagining" and "religious imaginings."[35] As Timothy Brennan explains it, "nationalism largely extend[s] and modernize[s] (although [does] not replace) 'religious imaginings,' taking on religion's concern with death, continuity, and the desire for origins."[36] Like religion, the nation authorizes a reconfiguration of time and mortality, a "secular transformation of fatality into continuity, contingency into meaning."[37] Mormonism's spiritual geography was perfectly suited to this process, constructing America as both origin and meaning of history. Moreover, as Hans Kohn has pointed out, modern nationalism has expropriated three crucial concepts from those same Old Testament mythologies that provide the basis for Mormonism: "the idea of a chosen people, the emphasis on a common stock of memory of the past and of hopes for the future, and finally national messianism."[38]

This conceptualization of America as the site of a blessed past and a millennial future represents, simultaneously, the fulfillment of early-nineteenth-century ideas of the nation and a repudiation of the ideologies of individualism and acquisitiveness that underwrite the Jacksonian marketplace. Yet, as Sacvan Bercovitch points out, this contradiction was at the heart of the nationalist project. As the economy was being transformed "from agrarian to industrial capitalism," the primary "source of dissent was an indigenous residual culture," which, like Mormonism, was "variously identified with agrarianism, libertarian thought, and the tradition of civic humanism." These ideologies, "by conserving the myths of a bygone age" and dreaming "of human wholeness and social regeneration," then produced "the notion of an ideal America with a politically transformative potential." Like the writers of the American Renaissance, Mormonism "adopted the culture's *controlling* metaphor—'America' as synonym for human possibility," and then turned it against the dominant class. Both producing and fulfilling the nationalist dream, it "portray[ed] the American ideology, as all ideology yearns to be portrayed, in the transcendent colors of utopia."[39] As a form of dissent that ultimately (and contradictorily) reinforced hegemonic values, Mormonism reconceived America as the promised land, the land of an already achieved utopia, and simultaneously as the land of promise, the site of the millennium yet to come.

I recapitulate the early history of Mormonism because I believe it is crucial for understanding how *Angels in America* has been culturally positioned. It seems to me that the play replicates both the situation and project of early Mormonism with an uncanny accuracy and thereby documents the continued validity of both a particular regressive fantasy of America and a particular understanding of oppositional cultural practices. Like the projects of Joseph Smith and his followers, *Angels* has, from the beginning, on the levels of authorial intention and reception, been constructed as an oppositional, and even radical, work. Structurally and ideologically, the play challenges the conventions of American realism and the tenets of Reaganism. Indeed, it offers by far the most explicit and trenchant critique of neoconservatism to have been produced on Broadway. It also provides the most thoroughgoing—and unambivalent—deconstruction in memory of a binarism absolutely crucial to liberalism, the opposition between public and private. *Angels* demonstrates conclusively not only the constructedness of the difference between the political and the sexual but also the murderous power of this distinction. Yet, at the same time, *not despite but because of these endeavors*, the play has been accommodated with stunning ease to the hegemonic ideology not just of the theatergoing public but of the democratic majority—an ideology that has become the *new* American religion: liberal pluralism.[40]

The old-style American liberalisms, variously associated (reading from Left to Right) with trade unionism, reformism, and competitive individualism, tend to value freedom above all other qualities (the root word for liberalism is, after all, the Latin *liber,* meaning "free"). Taking the "free" individual subject as the fundamental social unit, liberalism has long been associated with the principle of laissez-faire and the "free" market and is reformist rather than revolutionary in its politics. At the same time, however, because liberalism, particularly in its American versions, has always paid at least lip service to equality, certain irreducible contradictions have been bred in what did, after all, emerge during the seventeenth century as the ideological complement to (and justification for) mercantile capitalism. Historically, American liberalism has permitted dissent and fostered tolerance, within certain limits, and guaranteed that all men in principle are created equal (women were long excluded from the compact as were African-American slaves). In fact, given the structure of American capitalism, the incommensurability of its commitment both to freedom and equality has proven a disabling contradiction, one that liberalism has tried continually, and with little success, to negotiate. Like the bourgeois subject that is its production and raison d'être, liberalism is hopelessly schizoid.

The new liberalism that has been consolidated in the United States since the decline of the New Left in the mid-1970s (but whose antecedents date back to the first stirrings of the nation) marks the adaptation of traditional liberalism to a post–welfare state economy. Pursuing a policy of regressive taxation, its major constituent is the corporate sector; all others it labels "special interest groups" (despite certain superficial changes, there is no fundamental difference between the economic and foreign policies of Reagan/Bush and Clinton). In spite of its corporatism, however, and its efficiency in redistributing the wealth upward, liberalism speaks the language of tolerance. Unable to support substantive changes in economic policy that might in fact produce a more equitable and less segregated society, it instead promotes a *rhetoric* of pluralism and moderation. Reformist in method, it endeavors to fine-tune the status quo while at the same time acknowledging (and even celebrating) the diversity of American culture. For the liberal pluralist America is less a melting pot than a smorgasbord. He or she takes pride in the ability to *consume* cultural difference—now understood as a commodity, a source of boundless pleasure, an expression of an exoticized Other. And yet, for him or her, access to and participation in so-called minority cultures is entirely consumerist. Like the new, passive racist characterized by Hazel Carby, the liberal pluralist uses "texts"—whether literary, musical, theatrical or cinematic—as "a way of gaining knowledge of the 'other,' a knowledge that appears to replace the desire to challenge existing frameworks of segregation."[41]

Liberal pluralism thus does far more than tolerate dissent. It actively enlists its aid in reaffirming a fundamentally conservative hegemony. In doing so, it reconsolidates a fantasy of America that dates back to the early nineteenth century. Liberal pluralism demonstrates the dogged persistence of a *consensus politic that masquerades as dissensus.* It proves once again, in Bercovitch's words, that

> the American way is to turn potential conflict into a quarrel about fusion or fragmentation. It is a fixed match, a debate with a foregone conclusion: you must have your fusion and feed on fragmentation too. And the formula for doing so has become virtually a cultural reflex: you just alternate between harmony-in-diversity and diversity-in-harmony. It amounts to a hermeneutics of laissez-faire: all problems are obviated by the continual flow of the one into the many, and the many into the one.[42]

According to Bercovitch, a kind of dissensus (of which liberal pluralism is the contemporary avatar) has been the hallmark of the very idea of America—and American literature—from the very beginning. In this most American of ideologies an almost incomparably wide range of opinions, beliefs, and cultural positions are finally absorbed into a fantasy of a utopian nation in which anything and everything is possible, in which the millennium is simultaneously at hand and indefinitely deferred. Moreover, the nation is imagined as the geographical representation of that utopia, which is both everywhere and nowhere. For, as Berlant explains, "the contradiction between the 'nowhere' of utopia and the 'everywhere' of the nation [is] dissolved by the American recasting of the 'political' into the terms of providential ideality, 'one nation under God.'"[43] Under the sign of the "one" all contradictions are subsumed, all races and religions united, all politics theologized.

Dissensus and the Field of Cultural Production

It is my contention that the play's mobilization of a consensual politic (masquerading as *diss*ensual) is precisely the source not only of the play's ambivalence but also of its ability to be instantly recognized as part of the canon of American literature. Regardless of Kushner's intentions, *Angels* sets forth a project wherein the theological is constructed as a transcendent category into which politics and history finally disappear. For all its commitment to a historical materialist method, for all its attention to political struggle and the dynamics of oppression, *Angels* finally sets forth a liberal pluralist vision of America in which all, not in spite but because of their diversity, will be welcomed into the new Jerusalem (to this extent it differs sharply from the more exclusionist character of early Mormonism and other, more recent millennialisms). Like other apocalyptic discourses, from Joseph Smith to Jerry Falwell, the millennialism of *Angels* reassures an "audience that knows it has lost control over events" not by enabling it to "regain . . . control" but by letting it know "that history *is* nevertheless controlled by an underlying order and that it has a purpose that is nearing fulfillment." It thereby demonstrates that "*personal* pain," whether Prior's or that of the reader or spectator, "is subsumed within the pattern of history."[44] Like Joseph Smith, Tony Kushner has resuscitated a vision of America as both promised land and land of infinite promise. Simultaneously, he has inspired virtually every theater critic in the United States to a host of salvational fantasies about theater, art, and politics. And he has done all this at a crucial juncture in history, at the end of the Cold War, as the geopolitical order of forty-five years has collapsed.

Despite the success of the 1991 Gulf War in signaling international "terrorism" as the successor to the Soviet empire and justification for the expansion of the national security state, the idea of the nation remains, I believe, in crisis (it seems to me that terrorism, being less of a threat to individualism than communism, does not harness paranoia quite as effectively as the idea of an evil empire). If nothing else, *Angels in America* attests both to the continuing anxiety over national definition and mission and to the importance of an ideological means of assuaging that anxiety. In *Angels* a series of political dialectics (which are, yet again, false dialectics) remains the primary means for producing this ideological fix, for producing dissensus, a sense of alternation between "harmony-in-diversity and diversity-in-harmony." The play is filled with political disputation—all of it between men, since women, unless in drag, are excluded from the public sphere. Most is centered on Louis, the unmistakably ambivalent, ironic Jew who invariably sets the level of discussion and determines the tenor of the argument. If with Belize he takes a comparatively rightist (and racist) stance, with Joe he takes an explicitly leftist (and antihomophobic) one. And, while the play unquestionably problematizes his several positions, he ends up, with all his contradictions, becoming by default the spokesperson for liberal pluralism, with all *its* contradictions. Belize, intriguingly, functions unlike the white gay men as an ideological point of reference, a kind of "moral bellwether," in the words of one critic.[45] Because his is the one point of view that is never submitted to a critique, he becomes, as David Román points out, "the political and ethical center of the plays." As the purveyor of truth, "he carries the burden of race" and so seems to issue from what is unmistakably a "white imaginary" ("this fetishization," Román notes, "of lesbian and gay people of color as a type of political catalyst is ubiquitous among the left").[46] He is also cast in the role of caretaker, a position long reserved for African Americans in "the white imaginary." Even Belize's name commemorates not the Name of the Father but his status as a *"former drag queen"* (1:3), giving him an identity that is both performative and exoticized. He is the play's guarantee of diversity.

The pivotal scene for the enunciation of Louis's politics, meanwhile, is his long discussion with Belize in *Millennium,* which begins with his question "Why has democracy succeeded in America?" (1:89), a question whose assumption is belied by the unparalleled political and economic power of American corporatism to buy elections and from which Louis, as is his wont, almost immediately backs down. (His rhetorical strategy throughout this scene is to stake out a position from which he immediately draws a guilty retreat, thereby making Belize look like the aggressor.) Invoking "radical democracy" and "freedom" in one breath and crying "fuck assimilation" (1:89–90) in the next, he careens wildly between a liberal discourse of rights and a rhetoric of identity politics. Alternating between universalizing and minoritizing concepts of the subject, he manages at once to dismiss a politics of race (and insult Belize) and to assert its irreducibility. Yet the gist of Louis's argument (if constant vacillation could be said to have a gist) is his disquisition about the nation:

> this reaching out for a spiritual past in a country where no indigenous spirits exist—only the Indians, I mean Native American spirits and we killed them off so now, there are no gods here, no ghosts and spirits in America, there are no angels in America, no spiritual past, no racial past, there's only the political. (1:92)

For Louis America hardly exists as a community (whether real or imagined). Rather, for this confused liberal America is defined entirely by its relationship to the "political." With characteristic irony Kushner chooses to present this crucial idea (which does, after all, echo the play's title) in the negative, in the form of a statement that the rest of the play aggressively refutes. For, if nothing else, *Angels in America*—like *The Book of Mormon*—demonstrates that there are angels in America, that America is in essence a utopian and theological construction, a nation with a divine mission. Politics is by no means banished insofar as it provides a crucial way in which the nation is imagined. But it is subordinated to utopian fantasies of harmony in diversity, of one nation under a derelict God.

Moreover, this scene between Louis and Belize reproduces millennialism in miniature, in its very structure, in the pattern whereby the political is finally subsumed by utopian fantasies. After the spirited argument between Louis and Belize (if one can call a discussion in which one person refuses to stake out a coherent position an argument), their conflict is suddenly overrun by an outbreak of lyricism, by the intrusion, after so much talk about culture, of what passes for the natural world:

> *Belize:* All day today it's felt like Thanksgiving. Soon, this . . .
> ruination will be blanketed white. You can smell it—can you
> smell it?
> *Louis:* Smell what?
> *Belize:* Softness, compliance, forgiveness, grace. (1:100)

Argumentation gives way not to a resolution (nothing has been settled) but to the ostensible forces of nature: snow and smell. According to Belize, snow (an insignia of coldness and purity in the play) is linked to "softness, compliance, forgiveness, grace," in short, to the theological virtues. Like the ending of *Perestroika,* in which another dispute between Louis and Belize fades out behind Prior's benediction, this scene enacts a movement of transcendence whereby the political is not so much resolved as left trailing in the dust. In the American way contradiction is less disentangled than immobilized. History gives way to a concept of cosmic evolution that is far closer to Joseph Smith than to Walter Benjamin.

In the person of Louis (who is, after all, constructed as the most empathic character in the play), with his unshakable faith in liberalism and the possibility of "radical democracy," *Angels in America* assures the (liberal) theatergoing public that a kind of liberal pluralism remains the best hope for change.[47] Revolution, in the Marxist sense, is rendered virtually unthinkable, oxymoronic. Amid all the political disputation there is no talk of social class. Oppression is understood in relation not to economics but to differences of race, gender, and sexual orientation. In short: *an identity politic comes to substitute for Marxist analysis.* There is no clear sense that the political and social problems with which the characters wrestle might be connected to a particular economic system (Comrade Prelapsarianov is, after all, a comic figure). And, despite Kushner's avowed commitment to socialism, an alternative to capitalism, except in the form of an indefinitely deferred utopia, remains absent from the play's dialectic.[48] Revolution, even in Benjamin's sense of the term, is evacuated of its political content, functioning less as a Marxist hermeneutic tool than a trope, a figure of speech (the oxymoron) that marks the place later to be occupied by a (liberal pluralist?) utopia. *Angels* thus falls into line behind the utopianisms of Joseph Smith and the American Renaissance and becomes less a subversion of hegemonic culture than its reaffirmation. As Berlant observes, "the temporal and spatial ambiguity of 'utopia' has the effect of obscuring the implications of political activity and power relations in American civil life."[49] Like "our classic texts" (as characterized by Bercovitch), *Angels* has a way of conceptualizing utopia so that it may be adopted by "the dominant culture . . . for its purposes." "So molded, ritualized, and controlled," Bercovitch notes (and, I would like to add, stripped of its impulse for radical economic change), "utopianism has served . . . to diffuse or deflect dissent, or actually to transmute it into a vehicle of socialization."[50]

The ambivalences that are so deeply inscribed in *Angels in America,* its conflicted relationship to various utopianisms, to the concept of America, to Marxism, Mormonism, and liberalism, function, I believe, to accommodate the play to what I see as a fundamentally conservative and paradigmatically American politic—dissensus, the "hermeneutics of laissez-faire." Yet it seems to me that the play's ambivalence (its way of being, in Eve Sedgwick's memorable phrase, "kinda subversive, kinda hegemonic")[51] is finally less a question of authorial intention than of the peculiar cultural and economic position of this play (and its writer) in relation to the theater, theater artists, and the theatergoing public in the United States. On the one hand, the Broadway and regional theaters remain in a uniquely marginal position in comparison with Hollywood. The subscribers to regional theaters continue to dwindle, while more than half of Theatre Communications Group's sample theaters in their annual survey "played to smaller audiences in 1993 than they did five years ago." Moreover, in a move that bodes particularly ill for the future of new plays, "workshops, staged readings and other developmental activities decreased drastically over the five years studied."[52] On the other hand, serious Broadway drama does not have the same cultural capital as other forms of literature. Enmortgaged to a slew of others who must realize the playwright's text, it has long been regarded as a bastard art. Meanwhile, the relatively small public that today attends professional theater in America is overwhelmingly middle-class and overwhelmingly liberal in its attitudes. Indeed, theater audiences are in large part distinguished from the audiences for film and television on account of their tolerance for works that are more challenging both formally and thematically than the vast majority of major studio releases or prime-time miniseries.

Because of its marginal position, both economically and culturally, theater is a privileged portion of what Pierre Bourdieu designates as the literary and artistic field. As he explains, this field is contained within a larger field of economic and political power while, at the same time, "possessing a relative autonomy with respect to it." It is this *relative autonomy* that gives the literary and artistic field—and theater in particular—both its high level of symbolic forms of capital and its low level of economic capital. In other words, despite its artistic cachet, it "occupies a *dominated position*" with respect to the field of economic and political power as a whole.[53] And the individual cultural producer (or theater artist), insofar as he or she is a part of the bourgeoisie, represents a "dominated fraction of the dominant class."[54] The cultural producer is thus placed in an irreducibly contradictory position—and this has become particularly clear since the decline of patronage in the eighteenth century and the increasing dependence of the artist on the vicissitudes of the marketplace. On the one hand, he or she is licensed to challenge hegemonic values insofar as it is a particularly effective way of accruing cultural capital. On the other hand, the more effective his or her challenge, the less economic capital he or she is likely to amass. Because of theater's marginality in American culture, it seems to be held hostage to this double bind in a particularly unnerving way: the very disposition of the field guarantees that Broadway and regional theaters (unlike mass culture) are constantly in the process of having to negotiate this impossible position.

What is perhaps most remarkable about *Angels in America* is that it has managed, against all odds, to amass significant levels of both cultural and economic capital. And, while it by no means resolves the contradictions that are constitutive of theater's cultural positioning, its production history has become a measure of the seemingly impossible juncture of these two forms of success. Just as the play's structure copes with argumentation by transcending it, so does the play as cultural phenomenon seemingly transcend the opposition between economic and cultural capital, between the hegemonic and the counterhegemonic. Moreover, it does so, I am arguing, by its skill in both reactivating a sense (derived from the early nineteenth century) of America as the utopian nation and mobilizing the principle of ambivalence—or, more exactly, dissensus—to produce a vision of a once and future pluralist culture. And, although the text's contradictory positioning is to a large extent defined by the marginal cultural position of Broadway, it is also related specifically to Tony Kushner's own class position. Like Joseph Smith, Kushner represents a dominated—and dissident—fraction of the dominant class. As a white gay man, he is able to amass considerable economic and cultural capital despite the fact that the class of which he is a part remains relatively disempowered politically (according to a 1993 survey, the average household income for self-identified gay men is 40 percent higher than that of the average American household).[55] As an avowed leftist and intellectual, he is committed (as *Angels* demonstrates) to mounting a critique of hegemonic ideology. Yet, as a member of the bourgeoisie and as the recipient of two Tony Awards, he is also committed, if only unconsciously, to the continuation of the system that has granted him no small measure of success.

A Queer Sort of Nation

Although I am tempted to see the celebrity of *Angels in America* as yet another measure of the power of liberal pluralism to neutralize oppositional practices, the play's success also suggests a willingness to recognize the contributions of gay men to American culture and to American literature in particular. For, as Eve Sedgwick and others have argued, both the American canon and the very principle of canonicity are centrally concerned with questions of male (homo)sexual definition and desire.[56] Thus, the issues of homoeroticism, of the anxiety generated by the instability of the homosocial/homosexual boundary, of coding, of secrecy and disclosure, and of the problems around securing a sexual identity, remain pivotal for so many of the writers who hold pride of place in the American canon, from Thoreau, Melville, Whitman, and James to Hart Crane, Tennessee Williams, and James Baldwin—in that sense the American canon is always already queered. At the same time, however, unlike so much of the canon, and in particular the canon of American drama, *Angels in America* foregrounds explicitly gay men. No more need the reader eager to queer the text read subversively between the lines, or transpose genders, as is so often done to the work of Williams, Inge, Albee, and others. Since the 1988 controversies over National Endowment for the Arts funding for exhibitions of Mapplethorpe and Serrano and the subsequent attempt by the endowment to revoke grants to the so-called NEA Four (three of whom are queer), theater, as a liberal form, has been distinguished from mass culture in large part by virtue of its queer content. In the 1990s a play without a same-sex kiss may be entertainment, but it can hardly be considered a work of art. It appears that the representation of (usually male) homosexual desire has become the privileged emblem of that endangered species, the serious Broadway drama. But I wonder finally how subversive this queering of Broadway is when women, in this play at least, remain firmly in the background. What is one to make of the remarkable ease with which *Angels in America* has been accommodated to that lineage of American drama (and literature) that focuses on masculine experience and agency and produces women as the premise for history, as the ground on which it is constructed? Are not women sacrificed—yet again—to the male citizenry of a (queer) nation?

If Kushner, following Benjamin's prompting (and echoing his masculinism), attempts to "brush history against the grain" (257), he does so by demonstrating the crucial importance of (closeted) gay men in twentieth-century American politics—including, most prominently, Roy Cohn and two of his surrogate fathers, J. Edgar Hoover and Joseph McCarthy. By so highlighting the (homo)eroticization of patriarchy, the play demonstrates the always already queer status of American politics and, most provocatively, of those generals of the Cold War (and American imperialism) who were most assiduous in their denunciation of political and sexual dissidence. Moreover, unlike the work of most of Kushner's predecessors on the American stage, *Angels* does not pathologize gay men. Or, more exactly, gay men as a class are not pathologized. Rather, they are revealed to be pathologized circumstantially: first, by their construction (through a singularly horrific stroke of ill luck) as one of the "risk groups" for HIV; and, second, by the fact that some remain closeted and repressed (Joe's ulcer is unmistakably the price of disavowal). So, it turns out, it is not homosexuality that is pathological but, rather, its *denial*. Flagrantly uncloseted, the play provides a devastating critique of the closeted gay man in two medicalized bodies: Roy Cohn and Joe Pitt.

If *Angels in America* queers historical materialism (at least as Benjamin understands it), it does so by exposing the process by which the political (which ostensibly drives history) intersects with the personal and sexual (which ostensibly are no more than footnotes to history). Reagan's presidency and the neoconservative hegemony of the 1980s provide not just the background to the play's exploration of ostensibly personal (i.e., sexual, marital, medical) problems but the very ground on which desire is produced. For, despite the trenchancy of its critique of neoconservativism, *Angels* also demonstrates the peculiar sexiness of Reagan's vision of America. Through Louis it demonstrates the allure of a particular brand of machismo embodied by Joe Pitt: "The more appalling I find your politics the more I want to hump you" (2:36). And, if the Angel is indeed "a cosmic reactionary" (2:55), it is in part because her/his position represents an analogue to the same utopian promises and hopes that Reagan so brilliantly and deceptively exploited. Moreover, in this history play questions of male homosexual identity and desire are carefully juxtaposed against questions of equal protection for lesbians and gay men and debates about their military service. Louis attacks Joe for his participation in "an important bit of legal fag-bashing," a case that upholds the U.S. government's policy that it's not "unconstitutional to discriminate against homosexuals" (2:110). And, while the case that Louis cites may be fictional, the continuing refusal of the courts in the wake of *Bowers v. Hardwick* to consider lesbians and gay men a suspect class, and thus eligible for protection under the provisions of the Fourteenth Amendment, is anything but.[57] Unilaterally constructing gay men as a suspect class (with sexual identity substituting for economic positionality), *Angels* realizes Benjamin's suggestion that it is not "man or men but the struggling, oppressed class itself [that] is the depository of historical knowledge" (260). More decisively than any other recent cultural text, *Angels* queers the America of Joseph Smith—and Ronald Reagan—by placing this oppressed class at the very center of American history, by showing it to be not just the depository of a special kind of knowledge but by recognizing the central role that it has had in the construction of a national subject, polity, literature, and theater. On this issue the play is not ambivalent at all.

NOTES

My thanks to Rhett Landrum, Loren Noveck, John Rouse, and Ronn Smith, for their invaluable contributions to this essay.

1. Joseph Roach has suggested to me that the closest analogue to *Angels* on the American stage is, in fact, *Uncle Tom's Cabin,* with its tremendous popularity before the Civil War, its epic length, and its skill in addressing the most controversial issues of the time in deeply equivocal ways.

2. John Lahr, "The Theatre: Earth Angels," *New Yorker,* 13 December 1993, 133.

3. Jack Kroll, "Heaven and Earth on Broadway," *Newsweek,* 6 December 1993, 83.

4. Robert Brustein, "Robert Brustein on Theatre: *Angels in America,*" *New Republic,* 24 May 1993, 29.

5. John E. Harris, "Miracle on 48th Street," *Christopher Street* (March 1994): 6.

6. Frank Rich, "Critic's Notebook: The Reaganite Ethos, with Roy Cohn as a Dark Metaphor," *New York Times,* 5 March 1992, C15.

7. John Clum, *Acting Gay: Male Homosexuality in Modern Drama* (New York: Columbia University Press, 1994), 324.

8. Tony Kushner, *Angels in America: A Gay Fantasia on National Themes. Part One: Millennium Approaches* (New York: Theatre Communications Group, 1993), 95. All further references will be noted in the text.

9. Frank Rich, "Following an Angel for a Healing Vision of Heaven and Earth," *New York Times*, 24 November 1993, C11.

10. Clum, *Acting Gay*, 314.

11. Tony Kushner, *Angels in America: A Gay Fantasia on National Themes. Part Two: Perestroika* (New York: Theatre Communications Group, 1994), 56. All further references will be noted in the text.

12. See, for example, Andrea Stevens, "Finding a Devil Within to Portray Roy Cohn," *New York Times*, 18 April 1993, sec. 2, pp. 1, 28.

13. Terry Eagleton, *Walter Benjamin, or Towards a Revolutionary Criticism* (London: Verso, 1981), 177.

14. Walter Benjamin, "Theses on the Philosophy of History," in *Illuminations*, ed. Hannah Arendt, trans. Harry Zohn (New York: Schocken Books, 1969), 253. All further references will be noted in the text.

15. Tony Kushner explains: "I've written about my friend Kimberly [Flynn] who is a profound influence on me. And she and I were talking about this utopian thing that we share—she's the person who introduced me to that side of Walter Benjamin. . . . She said jokingly that at times she felt such an extraordinary kinship with him that she thought she was Walter Benjamin reincarnated. And so at one point in the conversation, when I was coming up with names for my characters, I said, 'I had to look up something in Benjamin—not you, but the prior Walter.' That's where the name came from. I had been looking for one of those WASP names that nobody gets called anymore" (David Savran, "The Theatre of the Fabulous: An Interview with Tony Kushner," in *Speaking on Stage: Interviews with Contemporary American Playwrights*, ed. Philip C. Kolin and Colby H. Kullman [Tuscaloosa: University of Alabama Press], 1996, 305).

16. Jacques Lacan, "The Signification of the Phallus," in *Ecrits: A Selection*, trans. Alan Sheridan (New York: Norton, 1977), 286.

17. Elizabeth Grosz, *Jacques Lacan: A Feminist Introduction* (London: Routledge, 1990), 74, 67.

18. Benjamin maintained a far less condemnatory attitude toward the increasing technologization of culture than many other Western Marxists. In "The Work of Art in the Age of Mechanical Reproduction," for example, he writes of his qualified approval of the destruction of the aura associated with modern technologies. He explains that because "mechanical reproduction emancipates the work of art from its parasitical dependence on ritual, . . . the total function of art" can "be based on another practice—politics," which for him is clearly preferable (Benjamin, "Work of Art in the Age of Mechanical Reproduction," 224).

19. Although one could cite a myriad of sources, this quotation is extracted from Milton Friedman, "Once Again: Why Socialism Won't Work," *New York Times*, 13 August 1994, 21.

20. Krishan Kumar, "The End of Socialism? The End of Utopia? The End of History?" in *Utopias and the Millennium*, ed. Krishan Kumar and Stephen Bann

(London: Reaktion Books, 1993), 61; Francis Fukuyama, *The End of History and the Last Man,* quoted in ibid., 78.

21. Friedman, "Once Again: Why Socialism Won't Work," 21.

22. Aijaz Ahmad, *In Theory: Classes, Nations, Literatures* (London: Verso, 1992), 69. Ahmad is summarizing this position as part of his critique of poststructuralism.

23. David Richards, "'Angels' Finds a Poignant Note of Hope," *New York Times,* 28 November 1993, 2:1.

24. Benedict Anderson, *Imagined Communities: Reflections on the Origin and Spread of Nationalism* (London: Verso, 1991), 6.

25. See Lawrence Kohl, *The Politics of Individualism: Parties and the American Character in the Jacksonian Era* (New York: Oxford University Press, 1989).

26. Klaus J. Hansen, *Mormonism and the American Experience* (Chicago: University of Chicago Press, 1981), 49–50.

27. See Ernest R. Sandeen, *The Roots of Fundamentalism: British and American Millenarianism 1800–1930* (Chicago: University of Chicago Press, 1970), 42–58.

28. Hansen, *Mormonism,* 52.

29. Joseph Smith, quoted in Hansen, *Mormonism,* 72.

30. See Richard L. Bushman, *Joseph Smith and the Beginnings of Mormonism* (Urbana: University of Illinois Press, 1984), 170.

31. Hansen, *Mormonism,* 119.

32. For a catalogue of this violence, see Jan Shipps, *Mormonism: The Story of a New Religious Tradition* (Urbana: University of Illinois Press, 1985), 155–61.

33. Hansen, *Mormonism,* 124–26.

34. Ibid., 27, 67.

35. Anderson, *Imagined Communities,* 10–11.

36. Timothy Brennan, "The National Longing for Form," in *Nation and Narration,* ed. Homi K. Bhabha (London: Routledge, 1990), 50.

37. Anderson, *Imagined Communities,* 10–11.

38. Hans Kohn, *Nationalism: Its Meaning and History* (Princeton: Van Nostrand, 1965), 11.

39. Sacvan Bercovitch, "The Problem of Ideology in American Literary History," *Critical Inquiry* 12 (Summer 1986): 642–43, 645.

40. Despite the 1994 Republican House and Senate victories (in which the Republicans received the vote of only 20 percent of the electorate) and the grandstanding of Newt Gingrich, the country remains far less conservative on many social issues than the Republicans would like Americans to believe. See Thomas Ferguson, "G.O.P. $$$ Talked; Did Voters Listen?" *Nation,* 26 December 1994, 792–98.

41. Hazel Carby, "The Multicultural Wars," in *Black Popular Culture,* a project by Michele Wallace, ed. Gina Dent (Seattle: Bay Press, 1992), 197.

42. Bercovitch, "Problem of Ideology in American Literary History," 649.

43. Lauren Berlant, *The Anatomy of National Fantasy: Hawthorne, Utopia, and Everyday Life* (Chicago: University of Chicago Press, 1991), 31.

44. Barry Brummett, *Contemporary Apocalyptic Rhetoric* (New York: Praeger, 1991), 37–38.

45. Lahr, "Theatre: Earth Angels," 132.

46. David Román, "November 1, 1992: AIDS/*Angels in America,*" from *Acts of*

Intervention: Performance, Gay Culture, and AIDS (Bloomington: Indiana University Press, 1997). This essay is also contained in the present volume.

47. This is corroborated by Kushner's own statements: "The strain in the American character that I feel the most affection for and that I feel has the most potential for growth is American liberalism, which is incredibly short of what it needs to be and incredibly limited and exclusionary and predicated on all sorts of racist, sexist, homophobic and classist prerogatives. And yet, as Louis asks, why has democracy succeeded in America? And why does it have this potential, as I believe it does? I really believe that there is the potential for radical democracy in this country, one of the few places on earth where I see it as a strong possibility. It doesn't seem to be happening in Russia. There is a tradition of liberalism, of a kind of social justice, fair play and tolerance—and each of these things is problematic and can certainly be played upon in the most horrid ways. Reagan kept the most hair-raising anarchist aspects of his agenda hidden and presented himself as a good old-fashioned liberal who kept invoking FDR. It may just be sentimentalism on my part because I am the child of liberal-pinko parents, but I do believe in it—as much as I often find it despicable. It's sort of like the Democratic National Convention every four years: it's horrendous and you can feel it sucking all the energy from progressive movements in this country, with everybody pinning their hopes on this sleazy bunch of guys. But you do have Jesse Jackson getting up and calling the Virgin Mary a single mother, and on an emotional level, and I hope also on a more practical level, I do believe that these are the people in whom to have hope" (Savran, "Theatre of the Fabulous: An Interview with Tony Kushner," 305–6).

48. See Tony Kushner, "A Socialism of the Skin," *Nation*, 4 July 1994, 9–14.

49. Berlant, *Anatomy of National Fantasy*, 32.

50. Bercovitch, "Problem of Ideology in American Literary History," 644.

51. Sedgwick used this phrase during the question period that followed a lecture at Brown University, 1 October 1992.

52. Barbara Janowitz, "Theatre Facts 93," insert in *American Theatre* (April 1994): 4–5.

53. Pierre Bourdieu, "The Field of Cultural Production, or: The Economic World Reversed," *The Field of Cultural Production: Essays on Art and Literature,* ed. Randal Johnson (New York: Columbia University Press, 1993), 37–38.

54. Editor's intro., Bourdieu, *Field of Cultural Production,* 15.

55. *Gay and Lesbian Stats: A Pocket Guide of Facts and Figures,* ed. Bennett L. Singer and David Deschamps (New York: New Press, 1994), 32.

56. See Eve Kosofsky Sedgwick, *Epistemology of the Closet* (Berkeley: University of California Press, 1990), 48–59.

57. It is not the subjects who constitute a bona fide suspect class (like African Americans) that are suspect but, rather, the forces of oppression that produce the class. For an analysis of the legal issues around equal protection, see Janet Halley, "The Politics of the Closet: Towards Equal Protection for Gay, Lesbian, and Bisexual Identity," *UCLA Law Review* (June 1989): 915–76.

November 1, 1992:
AIDS/*Angels in America*

David Román

We must speak for hope as long as it doesn't mean
suppressing the nature of the danger.
                —Raymond Williams, *Resources of Hope*

November 1, 1992

It's Sunday, November 1, 1992, and I am in Los Angeles at the Mark
Taper Forum for the opening marathon performances of *Millennium
Approaches* and *Perestroika,* the two plays that comprise Tony Kushner's
Angels in America: A Gay Fantasia on National Themes. I am with four friends.
We are all quite thrilled. We are five gay men of the theater at the theater:
Jim is a playwright, Matthew is a director, Tim is a solo performer, Michael
is a singer, and I am a professor. We are five gay men who have lived to be
thirty years old and beyond, an accomplishment we never lose sight of these
days. We have anticipated today's marathon for some time now. It's an
arrival of sorts, although we are not sure what it is that we will experience
today. What we do know is this: we are about to partake in a full day and
evening marathon. *Angels in America* is a two-part work that held its world
premiere in San Francisco at the Eureka Theatre in May 1991. At the
Eureka part 1, *Millennium Approaches,* was presented in a fully staged form,
and part 2, the then incomplete draft of *Perestroika,* was presented in a staged
reading as a work-in-progress. The Mark Taper production will be the first
time *Perestroika* will be fully staged and the first time both parts of *Angels in
America* will be seen together as a complete and fully staged work performed
in marathon and in repertory. We have brought along water, fruit, candy,
medications, and cigarettes. Some of these things we will be sharing, but not
all of us smoke, nor do we all have AIDS. The plays have been previewing
in repertory for the past weeks, and the buzz is big and loud.

We arrive at the Taper in clusters. Matthew, Michael, and I are the
first ones to arrive a little before noon. While we are waiting for the others, Michael shows us his foot, which is bloated and discolored; he's

undergoing chemo treatment for his lesions. Michael has been living with AIDS for over a decade and, for all practical purposes, has had a concurrent career as a longtime survivor. Michael Callen is one of the founders of the People with AIDS Coalition, has published books and essays on surviving AIDS, and has spoken about AIDS everywhere, from daytime talk shows to the United States Congress. He is one of the people I most respect in the world. We wonder out loud how comfortable he will be sitting in the theater for such a long time. We have been told that the plays can last over seven hours. We speculate on Clinton's chances of beating Bush out of the White House. The elections are on Tuesday. None of us feel we can endure four more years of a Republican administration's lousy record on AIDS. It's not clear who will win, but some of us have hope. Tim and Jim show up next. We all exchange hugs and kisses and display the goods that we have brought along for the marathon. It's a gorgeous day in Los Angeles.

Once inside the theater and before the houselights dim completely, the actor Kathleen Chalfant takes to the stage cross-dressed as Rabbi Isidor Chemelwitz and begins the first scene of *Millennium Approaches*. Rabbi Chemelwitz is presiding over the funeral of Sarah Ironson. Sarah Ironson is, according to the Rabbi, "not a person but a whole kind of person."[1] Like the old rabbi himself, she was a Jewish immigrant who "carried the old world on her back across the ocean" and who now, in October 1985, the month in which the play's action commences, is dead. "You can never make that crossing that she made, for such Great Voyages in this world do not any more exist. . . . Pretty soon . . . all the old will be dead" (1:10–11), the Rabbi prophesies. It's an exhilarating moment in the play. Chalfant's perfectly complex reading of the scene at once satirizes the grandiosity of the speech and dares us to imagine our own lives in such terms.

Angels in America opens with an exit, a ceremonial closure for Sarah Ironson. The Rabbi, aware of his own mortality and perhaps because of this, insists upon performing a ritual to render her life history official; he sets out to instruct Sarah Ironson's clan of her remarkable journey, one that he mundanely demonstrates was typical. Now that she is dead, the rabbi must also offer a type of tribute to her life. This despite him having minimal contact with her. ("She preferred silence," he offers; "So I do not know her and yet I know her" [1:10].) He introduces one of Kushner's central themes of the play, the idea of the journey, and contextualizes the dead woman's life in relation to history and community. The Rabbi's invocation of Sarah's journey (and, by extension, his own) announces *Angels in America* as a play concerned with the problematic concept of an official history. Fearing his pending extinction, the rabbi admonishes his listeners to take note of the spectacular realities of their unrecorded lives.

Kushner's ambitious and remarkably successful play invites audiences, particularly gay male audiences, to identify throughout the play with these moments. Recall *Angels in America* is subtitled a *"gay* fantasia on national themes." Kushner sets out to exploit this fact by offering gay men in the midst of plague an occasion to continue to interrogate what it means to be part of a community in these difficult times. His project, as rendered in the cultural practices of the theater, demands that as gay men we persevere in locating and claiming our agency in the constructions of our histories. Kushner insists that we recognize that the procedures of our lives in response to AIDS not only matter (the subject of traditional AIDS plays) but that these procedures also hold insight and concern into the current U.S. political landscape—again, subtitled a "gay fantasia on *national* themes." *Angels in America* calls into question the concept of an official history. The play asks us to make distinctions between official and lived history, to notice what is documented and to bring forth into the public sphere what is not. In this sense Kushner puts pressure on the naturalization process imbedded in official history. Theater histories also involve questions of official documentation. The language used to describe the process of theatrical production, while familiar, if not seemingly fundamental, requires critical interrogation. Raymond Williams, the Marxist cultural critic, has taught us that ostensibly foundational terms are actually imbedded with specific ideological meanings. His book *Keywords* has provided a critical model that has been imported by AIDS cultural theorists to demystify some of the foundational terms of dominant AIDS discourse.[2] Jan Zita Grover, for example, has written about the ways that the keywords of AIDS are "primarily the property of the powerful" and situates her project "to identify and contest some of the assumptions underlying our current knowledge [about AIDS]" in the spirit of Raymond Williams's cultural theories and in conjunction with AIDS activists, including people living with AIDS.[3] To map the limits of official theater historiography as it pertains to AIDS performance, I follow Grover's example by turning to some of the keywords used to describe and/or mark the run of a theatrical production.

Keywords: *Opening, Premiere; Performance, Production*

In theater parlance the opening night of a production signals an arrival; as such, it serves multiple needs and functions. An opening night, unlike a

Ellen McLaughlin (the Angel) and Stephen Spinella (Prior) in the 1992 Mark Taper Forum production of *Angels in America,* directed by Oskar Eustis and Tony Taccone. *(Photo by Jay Thompson, courtesy Mark Taper Forum.)*

rehearsal or a preview, brings together various elements of the production process through the ritual of arrival. For the artists involved in the production an opening night is an opportunity to honor all the behind-the-scenes work of the production. Actors, directors, and designers, for example, exchange cards and gifts; friends, spouses, and supporters of the artistic team are invited to attend and usually bring flowers or other tokens of support. The presenting theater or performance space invites patrons and donors to participate in the event as well. From these customs two things become apparent: first, an opening night is a type of exchange ritual that recognizes the support systems of the theater; it calls attention to the idea of a community composed of artists and producers, theater staff and management, sponsors and patrons, and a select spectator who has some involvement with any of these people. Second, an opening night calls attention to the selective audience of the event; the audience is never arbitrary or random. The majority of the audience is composed of spectators already invested in the success of the production. Sometimes, in fact, depending upon the goals of the production, future producers and presenters also are invited to the opening night in the hope that the play will be produced elsewhere in the future. Given these two components, one can reasonably assert that opening nights are spectacles of communal investment and hope. Opening nights, inevitably given these conditions, call attention to the labor of production. If the performance at an opening is constructed as the culmination of the artistic process, the "opening" itself displays the theatrical apparatus of production, including the various and often competing social relations that "link the artistic and economic activity" of theatrical production.[4] In other words, an opening night foregrounds the investments of those involved with the production of theater.

Despite the profound symbolic significance of these factors, the primary construction of an opening night is to mark the entrance of a production into an official theater history. The language of theatrical production explicitly addresses this process of entering into theater history. And yet, given the precision of this language, key dates in the process of production are often confused and conflated. Thus, it may prove helpful to mark the distinctions between the terms *preview, press night, opening, performance,* and *production.* Opening night announces the arrival of the production into history; it is the night that theater critics—who are barred from previews where the production may still be in development—are invited to review the performance. Productions, however, may also hold press nights. Press night performances generally precede opening night. These performances are also previews, performances in which the artistic team fine-tunes the production in front of a paying audience. In the trajectory toward opening night producers can "freeze" a production in previews in order for critics to begin attending performances for review. These frozen previews are called "press nights" and allow theater critics and reviewers a certain flexibility in scheduling their theatergoing and in meeting their deadline schedules. Once the production is frozen the artistic team must refrain from making substantive changes in the production. Generally speaking, the professional ethics of the print and media theater review process demands that a play not be reviewed before it officially "opens." This is a courtesy extended by the press to the theater, reciprocated by the theater to the press in the complimentary tickets to the opening night or press night. Critics and reviewers are invited to attend the opening night in order to maintain its construction as an official arrival and in order to confirm their own participation in the construction of a theater history. Many, however, attend press nights and bypass the actual official opening. Reviewers in the daily print media, for example, often have their reviews written *before* the opening night, although these reviews are not published until the play officially opens. Thus, the theater reviews that we read in the popular press are not necessarily reviews of the opening night performance. For theater historians these reviews in the popular press are often the main documentation of the entire production's process and reception.[5]

A world premiere, much like an opening night, also announces an official arrival. A world premiere claims that the performance you are watching will be the first official performance of the play anywhere in the world. It assumes authenticity and originality. Furthermore, a world premiere, unlike simply any opening night—except, of course, the opening night of a world premiere—presupposes historical significance. It assumes that somewhere at some time the play will be restaged. Once that happens the production is forced to comply with more modest claims: the West coast premiere, the Broadway premiere, the West End premiere, the Chicago premiere, etc. It also positions the play for revival, as in the fiftieth-anniversary production or the restored or complete production. A world premiere can also signal the significance of the playwright, the director, or even the producing theater. In all these cases to call a performance a world premiere assumes a genealogy for the play that begins at the opening night of a world premiere. But, in truth, such genealogies obscure the materiality of the production's history—from its development to its opening performance. Moreover, these genealogical narratives conflate the unique and dynamic experience of any given performance with an absolute reading of a production; in this system the opening night performance *becomes* the production and thereby erases the distinct features between them and the process by which this occurs. The language of official theater historiography—*openings, premieres*—conflates performance with production and sets up the fantasy that production and reception stop after the opening night performance.

I offer this diversion into keywords of the theater in order to call attention to the challenges faced by theater historians in constructing what Marxist theater historian Bruce McConachie explains as "a more complete historical sociology of the theater" that "would require extensive empirical and theoretical investigations into the sociohistorical conditions necessary for the emergence of various kinds of theatre, the relations between historical forms of theatrical expression and the dominant ideology of a historical period, and the functions of theatre in reproducing, modifying, or contradicting hegemonic relations of production."[6] For the theater of AIDS such a project provides the methodological means and the political inspiration for viewing plays and performances as critical practices that shape our understanding of AIDS.

AIDS and Theater Historiography

One of the reasons I highlight the differences between *premieres* and *openings, production* and *performance*—keywords that while relational are not coterminous—is to put pressure upon the officializing history already in place in the critical reception of Kushner's play. With the mainstream and critical success of *Angels in America* it becomes necessary to question the ideological assumptions of the individuals and media producing official critical reviews and pronouncements on the plays. I also want to call attention to the totalizing narratives naturalized as official histories both in the theater and in our understanding of AIDS. "Narrativity," as theater historian Thomas Postlewait explains, "is not merely a technique, borrowed from literature, but instead a condition of our temporal understanding of individual and social experience."[7] And not just for theater history. In many ways the discourses of theater history resemble the medical discourses of AIDS.

The term *AIDS* for "acquired immune deficiency syndrome," Jan Zita Grover explains, "was officially adopted by the Centers for Disease Control (CDC) in 1982."[8] Grover offers a concise explication of the medical profession's process of identifying the various symptoms, diseases, and invading organisms, for example, that led to the official CDC adoption of *AIDS* as a term in 1982. But certainly, as Grover suggests, people were dying from the opportunistic infections we now associate with AIDS before the official arrival of the term *AIDS*. In this sense AIDS predates the official 1982 record of the CDC. Moreover, people who died before the official CDC definition died of complications due to AIDS, despite there being no such thing as AIDS before 1982.[9] The point here is that AIDS existed before its official entrance into the historical register; while the specific cultural practices that produced the term *AIDS* may not have taken effect until 1982, viruses and infections were debilitating and killing many people before this date.[10]

A fragile genealogy of these events, in fact, can be constructed from lesbian and gay publications, medical journals, and the mainstream press. The first article in the gay press to refer to what we now know as AIDS was reported in the 18 May 1981 edition of the *New York Native;* the first writings in a medical journal appeared in the *Morbidity and Mortality Weekly Report* of 5 June 1981; and an article in the 3 July 1981 edition of the *New York Times* was that newspaper's first account of the epidemic. Each of these articles registers the epidemic's official entrance into historical consciousness and establishes the seemingly foundational basis for a print media history. But these media occasions in and of themselves do not necessarily construct a history of AIDS. Like the theater review process, which is based upon the logic of opening night performances, these reports can only mark their own participation and location in the process and production of HIV and AIDS. Indeed, the notion of a theater opening as an official arrival relies on the same narrative construction as such key dates for HIV and AIDS as "day of diagnosis," "day of first opportunistic infection," or "day of test results." The apparent stability of these constructions is belied, however, by the larger ambiguities of HIV infection and status. To test positive on one day does not necessarily mean that one was "negative" the day before; to test negative, moreover, does not automatically mean that one has not been exposed to HIV. And HIV test results cannot trace the date of transmission or guarantee one's immunity in the future. Just as the idea of a theater opening obscures the performance history of any given production by positing the fallacy of first arrival, so too do these dates of HIV- or AIDS-related medical occasions pronounce and perform the signature of history on the body and thereby eradicate the process(es) of HIV and AIDS; theater openings and premieres pitched as official arrivals signal the language of medical origins, and vice versa. Each is based on a logic of sequential ordering that is both selective and self-serving and ideologically constructed as unmarked.

Insofar as AIDS is rendered an official historicizing vis-à-vis the dates of the body's responses to diagnostic procedures and tests, and insofar as a print genealogy of AIDS overdetermines the arrival of AIDS and obscures the process(es) of AIDS, AIDS will continue to be understood within the confines of these narratives of origin. Narratives of AIDS are always problematic, whether they arise from science or the media. Narratives of AIDS are always representations of AIDS, and, as Cindy Patton makes clear, "representations of AIDS at every level—in the media, in the science, in the cultural assumptions manifest in the effects of institutional process—are multiple and discontinuous."[11] And, while much could be said of the necessity of these official dates for organizing a personal response to HIV and AIDS, it is important to recognize that the information gathered from the official occasions of HIV and AIDS may discipline us into certain responses.[12] When physicians read the body they put into language an interpretation that is rendered definitive; these interpretations are naturalized as certainties under the muscle of science. No wonder, then, that so many people affected by HIV and AIDS now speak the discourse of this discipline and offer sometimes differing interpretations of the body. Consider Michael Callen, my November 1, 1992 theater companion, who, after being officially diagnosed with AIDS in 1982, introduced a different way of thinking about AIDS— most notably, the then radical and for many presumptuous concept of "long-term survivor" and the violently contested and revolutionary concept of "safe sex." In *Surviving AIDS* he writes: "Discovering a different way of thinking about AIDS at such a crucial turning point in my life provided a framework for me to justify believing that I might survive my disease. It was a life raft that kept me afloat in a sea of doom and gloom."[13] Gay men beginning in the early 1980s offered other gay men tactics for survival not always accepted or even acknowledged within the official narratives of AIDS. This is true among accounts written by gay men as well.

Among the most significant of Cindy Patton's points in her tremendously valuable book *Inventing AIDS* is her admonishment of the "amnesia surrounding the history of activism between 1981–1985."[14] Patton's concerns regarding revisionist AIDS histories serve as the basis for my comments here. And, while Patton's points are specific to AIDS service organizations, safe sex campaigns, and other early efforts within the lesbian and gay community to challenge government neglect, it is possible to extend her analysis to the history of artistic and cultural responses to AIDS. In this regard the historiographic narrative that positions *The Normal Heart* and *As Is,* both produced in 1985, as the earliest responses to AIDS in the theater is not only inaccurate; it also does a grievous disservice to such artists, playwrights, and theater collectives as Robert Chesley, Jeff Hagedorn, Rebecca Ranson, and San Francisco's *AIDS Show* collaborators, among others, whose AIDS performances were produced as early as 1983.

A theater history around plays and performances that address AIDS therefore must avoid the tendency to offer an official AIDS theater history as a totalizing narrative. In fact, I would argue that among the goals of the AIDS theater historian should be to construct a model of analysis that cautions against the officializing rhetorical tendencies of theater history in general. Such a project would be consistent with other projects on AIDS that describe the encounter with discourse about HIV and AIDS as overwhelming and perhaps unknowable in its totality:

> Inscribed since its appearance as profoundly unimaginable, as beyond the bounds of sense, the AIDS epidemic is almost literally unthinkable in its mathematical defeat of cognitive desire.
>
> But already we have here begun to make sense of AIDS, even if only in noting how it defeats our usual academic practices of careful, inclusive analysis. And we have also here assumed AIDS as an ongoing event, as something that moves within a history that is only partially *its* history. The mathematical sublime thus quickly gives way in the case of AIDS to what we might call the historical sublime, for even more than the mathematical, the historical sublime marks reading—and our stake in it—as an activity framed equally by demand and defeat, as the ground on which we are condemned to negotiate the difference between that which can be comprehended by the capacities of the intellect and that which can only be apprehended as beyond, in excess, or pitted against such capacities.[15]

These are Thomas Yingling's words to describe the incommensurabilities between what we know and what lies beyond the reach of our cognition. Yingling's focus on the challenges that AIDS poses for our "usual academic practices" informs the problems faced when constructing an AIDS theater historiography.

Aware that our project is framed by demands and defeats, an AIDS theater history should question the positivism imbedded in traditional theater history.[16] This is not to say that we should abandon projects that attempt to recuperate an AIDS theatrical past; rather, our efforts to do so must acknowledge that a complete history of AIDS theater is now improbable. We need to continue to document the theater's responses to AIDS, collect and publish the various materials of people who have died of AIDS, and interview the living. But we also need to accept as axiomatic that the nature of a theatrical performance itself involves a sense of loss; performances are not repeatable. And it is this loss of the performance that fuels the practice of theater history. As in all aspects of AIDS and history the task at hand for the theater historian interested in AIDS plays and performances is to call attention to the overdetermined components that construct these official histories in the first place. I think we need to deconstruct more carefully these theater histories and see our own critical practice as an act of intervention in the emerging institutionalization of an official AIDS theater history. Once again I quote Cindy Patton to make this point. Patton is discussing a disturbing trend among historical accounts of AIDS activism that privileges the political actions of ACT UP, the direct action group that emerged in 1987, at the expense of early AIDS organizing, and the revisionist history this type of historicizing engenders:

> These types of analysis of AIDS activism deny not only the immediate response of the gay male community to the AIDS epidemic in the early 1980s, but erase even more of the historical involvement in AIDS work of gay liberationists. . . . [The] implication that gay men sat around doing nothing but being "in rage" until 1987 ignores the radical roots of many of the current ASOs [AIDS service organizations], and the radicalism of people working inside what has become "the system." This is not to underestimate the differences and conflicts between ACT UP and the ASOs, but outside observers and increasingly, activists who have been told nothing of the early days of AIDS organizing, misunderstand the important place of each in the fight against AIDS. One reason for this rapid revision of AIDS organizing history is the reality that many of the early organizers are now dead.[17]

For my purposes and argument the truth that many of the early playwrights and performers whose work dealt in one form or another with AIDS are now dead, and that so many of the artistic collaborators, producers, theater staff, and spectators who participated in these productions and performances are also dead, and therefore may leave no record of the events, already points to the futility of constructing an accurate or total AIDS theater history. Many early performances around AIDS were simply that, performances without opening nights, world premieres, and the critical review process that invites their official registration into theater history. But this is still the case for many performances and productions throughout the United States. Likewise, many people with AIDS are still unaccounted for by the CDC, AIDS service organizations, and other institutions set up to minister to the needs of people with AIDS.

Even an AIDS play as celebrated and seemingly well documented as *Angels in America* demonstrates the problems of these officializing practices.

Angels in America was commissioned in 1987 by Oskar Eustis, who at the time was the artistic director of the Eureka Theatre in San Francisco. The first reading of *Angels in America* took place in November 1988 at the New York Theater Workshop. When Eustis accepted a position as resident director at the Mark Taper Forum, Gordon Davidson, the Taper's artistic head, struck a deal with the Eureka Theatre: "the Taper would develop the play on its own, but the Eureka would stage the world premiere."[18] At the Taper *Angels* broke into two parts. In the spring of 1990 a workshop production of *Millennium Approaches* was staged. One year later *Angels in America* held its world premiere at the Eureka. *Millennium Approaches* was presented in a fully staged form and accompanied by a staged reading of a draft of *Perestroika* as a work-in-progress. On November 1, 1992 the Mark Taper was set to host the Los Angeles opening of *Millennium Approaches* and *Perestroika,* the first official performances of the complete fully staged *Angels in America.* Even though *Perestroika* received its first fully staged production at the Mark Taper Forum, the Taper—because of contractual obligations to the Eureka Theatre—was not able to claim a world premiere for *Perestroika.* The idea of an opening and a premiere, as this brief production history suggests, is in some ways a misnomer. By the time the complete *Angels In America* was presented at the Taper thousands of people had already experienced some version of either or both parts.

The opening of *Angels in America* scheduled for November 1, 1992 was actually postponed. For various reasons the plays were withheld for review by critics for a week. Thus, the accounts of *Angels in America* in the popular press—in the *New York Times,* the *Los Angeles Times, Time, Newsweek,* for example—were based upon the performances beginning on November 8, 1992, the week *after* the national elections. The performances of November 1, 1992—which were followed by a reception and party attended by the playwright, actors, director, and artistic staff of *Angels;* the management and staff of the Mark Taper; various other playwrights, actors, and artists; and the many friends of all these people—escaped the critical process of review. Despite the opening festivities, these performances on the eve of the elections were not entered into theater history as official. One could argue, perhaps, that this postponement was yet another tactic to call attention to the demands of production, a Brechtian estrangement-effect extending beyond performance and production to include historical reception. Given Tony Kushner's admitted admiration for Brecht, such an assertion is not without its merits. A postponement in the theater, such as this one, cannot help underscoring the material conditions of theater production. As such, the informal and unofficial opening of *Angels* on November 1, 1992 became a rehearsal for the official press opening of November 8, 1992. So what, then, of November 1, 1992 other than its Brechtian gestus?

The eve of the national elections held profound promise for lesbians and gay men and all people involved in the fight against AIDS. As of October 31, 1992—the day before the originally scheduled opening of the Taper's production of *Angels in America*—245,621 cases of AIDS had been reported in the United States alone.[19] These people, needless to say, were all diagnosed with AIDS during the Reagan and Bush administrations. In the one week between November 1 and November 8—the week between the opening night and the official press opening of *Angels in America*—an estimate of nearly 1,000 people in the United States would be diagnosed with AIDS. Over 171,890 people officially died of AIDS-related causes in the United States alone by the time of Bill Clinton's January 1993 presidential inauguration.[20] Such numbers, or rather the deaths of so many people with AIDS, underscored the high stakes of the election; electing Bill Clinton, if nothing else, would put into relief the utter despair of twelve years of government neglect.

AIDS, up through 1992, emerged within and was determined by the sociopolitical institutions in the United States whose effects, in Judith Butler's phrasing, "produce and vanquish bodies that matter."[21] Butler's insistence upon making intelligible the cultural forms that produce and vanquish bodies that matter speaks directly to the work of AIDS activists in the United States who relentlessly pursued the presidential candidates during the earliest days of the primaries—"AIDS is a primary issue!"—and who tirelessly pressed Clinton and Bush to address AIDS from a national platform. Fueled by the reprehensible politics of the 1992 Republican convention and inspired by Clinton's gestures toward lesbian and gay people, those of us engaged in the fight against AIDS saw the 1992 election as a potential turning point in U.S. cultural politics surrounding AIDS. Revising the cultural psyche around AIDS has always been one of the foundational missions of AIDS activists, from the earliest efforts of people with AIDS to redress the morphology of "AIDS victim" to more current efforts to reposition AIDS centrally in the political sphere.[22] In these attempts to revise the cultural psyche, when people with AIDS and their supporters contest the regimes of power sustaining AIDS, hope emerges as a political means to bring about social change. To watch *Angels in America* on the eve of the elections was to participate in a public ritual of hope.

On one level this hope materializes through our identification with

Prior Walter's journey with AIDS, from his fear and despair in *Millennium Approaches* to his newfound power in *Perestroika*. And on the eve of the elections the hope of *Perestroika,* rekindled in the play through love and kinship, announced a shift from the utopic to the possible. On another level the expulsion of evil in *Perestroika* thematized by the death of Roy Cohn and the ritual forgiveness and banishment initiated and performed by Belize, Cohn's nurse and Prior's best friend—along with Louis Ironson, Sarah's grandson and Prior's ex-lover, and the ghost of Ethel Rosenberg, Roy Cohn's most famous casualty—enacted a ritual for us in the audience as well. "A particular evil can be at once experienced and lived through," Raymond Williams explains in *Modern Tragedy,* an insight that informs the place of Cohn in the plays and of the Republican administration in our lives.[23] The recital of Kaddish by Belize, Louis, and the ghost of Ethel Rosenberg for Cohn's spirit signaled an end to an era that in the play occurs in early 1986 yet took on new symbolic meaning when performed on November 1, 1992. In the play the scene of Roy Cohn's death and the Kaddish prayer that follows is pivotal; it moves the play from the despair and paralysis of part 1 to the hope and agency of part 2. The scene brings the characters and their audiences to the recognition of evil, as embodied by Cohn, "as actual and indeed negotiable."[24]

That Roy Cohn, who as a key figure of the regulatory regime instrumental in producing and vanquishing bodies that matter, would himself die an AIDS death is a Foucauldian irony but also a tragic one. "A queen can forgive her vanquished foe," Belize instructs in *Perestroika,* a reminder in the play of the AIDS activist claim that all people with AIDS are innocent.[25] From Belize's perspective Cohn, no matter how execrable, cannot be "blamed" for his own illness. Such rituals of atonement and forgiveness can only be politically efficacious when accompanied by a recognition of the negotiable structures of evil. (This is not to say we disavow our anger: the scene of the Kaddish prayer for Roy Cohn, while entrenched in feelings of love and forgiveness, ends with Louis and Ethel Rosenberg both exclaiming, "You sonofabitch" [2:126].) Political agency, according to Raymond Williams, emerges when a shift in the social structures of oppression makes possible a new system of feelings and ideas. This potential for change, emanating from the lived experiences of people in the public world, is what has escaped the official theater historiography of *Angels in America.* Yet, for many of us at the Mark Taper Forum on the eve of the presidential elections, such a shift in the national AIDS ideology seemed possible on November 1, 1992.

NOTES

This essay is part of a longer chapter on *Angels* that appears in my book *Acts of Intervention: Performance, Gay Culture, and AIDS* (Bloomington: Indiana University Press, 1997). Thanks to Sue-Ellen Case, Michael Mayer, Bob Vorlicky, Cindy Patton, Don Shewey, Tim Miller, Matthew Silverstein, and Richard Meyer for their generous and insightful comments. Thanks also to Tony Kushner for inviting me to attend the Taper production of *Angels* on November 1, 1992. This essay is dedicated to James Carroll Pickett and Michael Callen.

Epigraph from Raymond Williams, *Resources of Hope: Culture, Democracy, Socialism* (London: Verso Books, 1989), 322.

1. Tony Kushner, *Angels in America: A Gay Fantasia on National Themes. Part One: Millennium Approaches* (New York: Theatre Communications Group, 1993), 10. Further references will appear in the text.

2. Raymond Williams, *Keywords: A Vocabulary of Culture and Society,* rev. ed. (New York: Oxford University Press, 1983).

3. Jan Zita Grover, "AIDS: Keywords," in *AIDS: Cultural Analysis/Cultural Activism,* ed. Douglas Crimp (Cambridge, Mass.: MIT Press, 1987), 18. But see also her essay "AIDS, Keywords, and Cultural Work," along with the discussion following the essay in *Cultural Studies,* ed. Lawrence Grossberg, Cary Nelson, and Paula Treichler (New York: Routledge, 1992), 227–39.

4. Bruce A. McConachie, "Historicizing the Relations of Theatrical Production," in *Critical Theory and Performance,* ed. Janelle G. Reinelt and Joseph R. Roach (Ann Arbor: University of Michigan Press, 1992), 169.

5. Thomas Postlewait explains the problems of such evidence in his essay "Historiography and the Theatrical Event: A Primer with Twelve Cruxes," *Theatre Journal* 43 (May 1991): 157–78.

6. McConachie, "Historicizing the Relations of Theatrical Production," 170.

7. Postlewait, "Historiography and the Theatrical Event: A Primer with Twelve Cruxes," 177.

8. Grover, "AIDS: Keywords," 19.

9. One needs only to remember that even with the official adoption of AIDS by the CDC in 1982, the definition of AIDS—opportunistic infections, T-cell count, etc.—has been the subject of debate. Only in 1993 did some of the opportunistic infections specific to women with HIV officially register an AIDS diagnosis. Consider too that someone with a T-cell count of under 200 and with no opportunistic infections was not diagnosed with AIDS until that same year.

10. Douglas Crimp makes this point in "How to Have Promiscuity in an Epidemic," in *AIDS: Cultural Analysis/Cultural Activism,* esp. 249–50 and n. 11.

11. Cindy Patton, *Inventing AIDS* (New York and London: Routledge, 1990), 1.

12. I am thinking not only of treatment options, clinical trials, and insurance policies that depend upon this information to take effect but also such issues as sexual options and decisions, support networks, and the various structures of feeling associated with information regarding personal health.

13. Michael Callen, *Surviving AIDS* (New York: HarperCollins, 1990), 6.

14. Patton, *Inventing AIDS*, 19.

15. Thomas Yingling, "AIDS in America: Postmodern Governance, Identity, and Experience," in *Inside/Out: Lesbian Theories, Gay Theories*, ed. Diana Fuss (New York: Routledge, 1991), 292.

16. Bruce A. McConachie outlines this positivist approach with three points: "(1) The belief that only objective truths can be counted as knowledge; (2) The assumption that only facts, dispassionately observed, can provide the basis for significant truth; and (3) A commitment to a 'theory free,' inductive process of arranging the facts so that they yield objective explanation. Armed with this method, the positivist investigator believes he can describe 'how it was' and explain 'how it happened'" ("Towards a Postpositivist Theatre History," *Theatre Journal* 37 [December 1985]: 467).

17. Patton, *Inventing AIDS*, 139.

18. Bruce Weber, "*Angels*' Angels," *New York Times Magazine*, 25 April 1993, 48.

19. The January 1992 issue of *HIV/AIDS Surveillance*, published through the U.S. Department of Health and Human Services, reported 206,392 cumulative cases of AIDS in the United States through December 1991 (*HIV/AIDS Surveillance*, 8). The number of cases between 1 January 1992 and 31 October 1992, according to the *Morbidity and Mortality Weekly Report* (41:44 [November 1992]: 840), was 39,229; adding these two figures brings me my total of 245,621. Although the *Morbidity and Mortality Weekly Report* is published weekly, it does not report AIDS cases on a week-by-week basis; consider, however, that, in the month of November 1992, 3,749 cases of AIDS were newly reported (*Morbidity and Mortality Weekly*, 1 December 1992).

20. As reported in the year-end edition of *HIV/AIDS Surveillance* ([February 1993]: 17). The numbers, reflecting deaths through December 1992, are reported as "case fatality rates" and divided into two groups: 169,623 adults and 2,267 children.

21. Judith Butler, *Bodies That Matter: On the Discursive Limits of "Sex"* (New York and London: Routledge, 1993), 14.

22. See, for example, Robert Rafsky's "An Open Letter to Bill Clinton," published on the eve of the elections (*QW* [8 November 1992]: 21–22). But see also Jeffrey Schmaltz, who writes one year later, "Whatever Happened to AIDS?" *New York Times Magazine*, 28 November 1993, 56–60, 81, 85–86. Both of these writers died of complications due to AIDS. While there is no record of Clinton's response to Rafsky other than his comments to him during a confrontation in New York at the time of the presidential primaries, Clinton centered his December 1, 1993 World AIDS Day address on Schmaltz's essay.

23. Raymond Williams, *Modern Tragedy* (Stanford, Calif.: Stanford University Press, 1966), 60.

24. Ibid.

25. Tony Kushner, *Angels in America: A Gay Fantasia on National Themes. Part Two: Perestroika* (New York: Theatre Communications Group, 1994), 124. Further references will appear in the text.

Heavenquake: Queer Anagogies in Kushner's America

James Miller

> With august gesture the god shows us how there is
> need for a whole world of torment in order for the
> individual to produce the redemptive vision.
> —Friedrich Nietzsche, *The Birth of Tragedy*

If Prior Walter is the unlikely individual chosen to produce a redemptive vision of AIDS in *Angels in America,* Tony Kushner is the august gesturer behind the scenes who shows us how there is need for a whole world of torment in order for his audience (as well as his characters) to make some painful progress beyond it. But does Kushner play this Nietzschean "god" for laughs?

This question troubled me as I emerged from the Broadway production of *Perestroika* the day after the Stonewall 25 march in the summer of 1994. Though the old showtune "Heaven, I'm in Heaven!" was still vibrating in my memory, no upbeat Broadway melody could drown out the ironic resonances of the philosopher's downbeat dictum in the playwright's dire "Gay Fantasia on National Themes." Exhausted from having laughed hard for three hours through my embarrassingly copious tears, I wondered whether I had just witnessed the birth of gay tragedy from the spirit of musicals (at last) or the comic death of the aestheticism-activism debate sparked in the late 1980s by the AIDS Coalition to Unleash Power (ACT UP), now much maligned.[1]

"Hell, You're in Hell!" had been the cynical undersong of much activist chanting against the official AIDS world for the past seven years, including the otherwise festive day of the Stonewall Anniversary. Prior, who was no cynic, would surely have enjoyed the exultant spirit of the march. It had passed near his beloved Bethesda Fountain—where Kushner perversely strands him in the bleak midwinter of 1990. If Prior had lived to see the hot June sun of our Sunday in the Park with RuPaul, I mused, would he have marched with the defiantly raggle-taggle warriors of ACT UP?

He would certainly not have been out of place at the head of the parade with the dauntless drag queens whose immortality as "Stonewall Veterans" was proclaimed by RuPaul from a large stage erected above the dust clouds on the Great Lawn in Central Park. Their feisty aesthetic spirit, reflected in Prior's Gloria Swanson dream self, had gloriously survived the feverish darkness of the epidemic as well as the flaring light of activism. Realizing this, I found it difficult to separate the queerness of Prior's electrifying climb up the neon ladder into Heaven in the fourth act of part 2—an anagogy that springs from Nietzsche's infamous declaration about the death of God—from the collective drive toward a redemptive vision of gay life that thousands upon thousands of us felt beneath our tawdry sequins and rainbow regalia as we marched into Central Park to hear Liza Minnelli sing an anthem for our liberation.

Though the crowds cheered to see her decked out in one of her mother's old dresses—showering "Judy realness" upon us, as one observer snidely put it—happily Liza resisted the temptation to belt out "Somewhere over the Rainbow." Instead, she favored us with the Big Number from *Kiss of the Spider Woman:*

> Someday we'll be FREE,
> I promise ya we'll be FREE.[2]

Free of AIDS, of course, but also free of the angry God worshiped by the religious Right. "God Hates Fags!" proclaimed one of the blunter fundy placards brandished at the Stonewall marchers near the corner of 59th and First.[3] If that God were dead, there'd be a statue of Kushner contemplating the bust of Nietzsche in every gay ghetto in the country.

Very Steven Spielberg

When Nietzsche was meditating on the need for showing a world of torment in order to produce a redemptive vision, the specific god he had in mind as the overseer of this tragic process was the Apollonian Christ who floats over the mountaintop in Raphael's "Transfiguration." In the shadowy lower half of this painting, completed in 1520, a crowd of villagers begs Christ's lesser disciples to drive an evil spirit out of an epileptic boy whose demented eyes are cast upward at a miraculous scene unfolding on a nearby mountain. Since the disciples below the mountain lack sufficient faith to conduct an exorcism on their own, Raphael depicted their confusion as a bewildering tangle of bodies and sight lines.

The disciples up on the mountain, by contrast, awaken to the astonishing but certain truth that Jesus has received a visitation from the Old Testament prophets Moses and Elijah. What we behold through the newly opened eyes of faith is a raising of ancestral Jewish spirits from the dead (as from the Inferno at the Harrowing) into the hallowed air around the Redeemer. This unearthly scene is paralleled on the ground by the raising of the bodies of Peter and John from sleep—as they will be raised from death at the Last Judgment—while the spirits of two future saints materialize at the dark edge of the picture as pious witnesses to the miracle.

The face of Jesus shines like the sun over their heads. His garments glow with an intense bluish-white light as if bleached by angelic radiance. To be thus transfigured is to be illumined from within by divine energy so that all without is brilliantly illuminated or cast into deepest shadow. Where Christ simply stood with the prophets in the biblical accounts of the Transfiguration, Raphael's Saviour levitates with anagogic vigor above them, his mantle floating heavenward in the charismatic wind, his arms extending triumphantly toward God, his divinity revealing itself in a mandorla of luminous clouds.

According to Nietzsche, this majestic figure represents the "naively Apollonian artist," exemplified by Raphael himself, who sustains through aesthetic illusion the ancient Athenian fantasy that humanity can be "entheos"—literally "engodded," lifted to a divine state of happiness or at least obliviousness to suffering—through the painful enlightenments of tragedy. Somewhere over the rainbow is not quite where Raphael's Christ is yearning to fly, but he's way up high on the apocalyptic updraft of Old Testament prophecy, and there's no dragging him down to the human level of the biblical Jesus, whose transfiguration is decidedly low-key by comparison.

Opposed to the dreamlike illusions of the Apollonian artist are the maddening realities intuited by the Dionysian agonist whose soul boldly confronts the tectonic substrates of pain and cruelty upon which the temple of Western civilization has been built.[4] In the gaping yet direly beautiful boy possessed by demons, Nietzsche saw a perfect representative of the bacchic seer whose wild eyes can gaze upon the aesthetic uplift of the Apollonian spirit without being fooled by its groundless promises of redemption. As an alternative to anagogy, the boy offers the philosophical spectator a kind of "hypogogy," a frightening immersion in the chaos and bewilderment of life in the earthbound body. A world of torment opens up around his flailing limbs, made intensely visible through the dramatic use of chiaroscuro in the tangled configurations of villagers and disciples. We must be shown a frozen

Raphael's *Transfiguration. (Courtesy Photo Alinari.)*

instant of their shadowy world in all its confusion if the Apollonian artist is to persuade us that the cool luminous rationality emanating from the god will ultimately triumph over the madness down in the dark.

Nietzsche's sympathies, of course, were all with the demented boy. Through his untransfigured gaze the painting becomes a symbolist mirror for the philosopher's own psychic torments, reflecting his struggle to shatter the cherished illusions of Christian morality through the prophetic apprehension of hard Dionysian truths.

If Kushner comes out as a gay Nietzschean in his "Fantasia on National Themes," it may be in his prophetic shattering of the aesthetic illusion that the world of torment, the cruel theater of the AIDS crisis, exists primarily to show us the need for divine transcendence of our fallen human state. Kushner's sympathies are clearly all with the ex–drag queen who *refuses* to be transfigured by his ascent into Heaven. When Prior rejects Apollonian anagogy in favor of a Dionysian hypogogy back into the spooj-splattered world of time, the play reaches its queer climax as a Nietzschean renunciation of aesthetic naïveté. Kushner may call for "a shower of unearthly white light" (reminiscent of the aura around Raphael's Christ) to flood Prior's bedroom as the Angel breaks through the ceiling in the final heart-stopping moments of *Millennium Approaches,* but the wonder of this transfiguring sight is swiftly dispelled by Prior's queeny response to all heavenly special effects. "God Almighty . . . ," he gasps, as his chiaroscuroed arms flail up to shield his crazed eyes from the light of divine reason, "*Very* Steven Spielberg!"[5]

From a Nietzschean angle the aestheticism-activism debate over the representation of AIDS in the arts would appear to be simply another variation on the ancient theme of the culture clash between Apollonian illusionism and Dionysian rage. Advocates of gay aestheticism (like Edmund White and Andrew Holleran) have assumed the role of the disciples on the mountaintop: their gaze is fixed on the transfiguration of AIDS from a worldly crisis into an otherworldly climax in the tragic unfolding of human destiny.[6] The activists, by contrast, belong in the lower half of the picture, down in the murky shadows with the sick boy and the bewildered crowds. Their perplexing engagement with the messy physical and political realities of the epidemic leaves them no time for contemplating (except as a vain transcendentalist fantasy) the sunny paradises into which the AIDS dead habitually rise in memorial service hymns, elegiac portraits, Hollywood movies, and the apocalyptic panels of the Quilt. In their sacrilegious hearts the activists tend to despise the triumphant apotheosis of AIDS saints, just as Nietzsche despised the pious exaltation of the god who augustly gestures to the whole world of human torment without feeling its sting.[7]

The Abnormal Heart

The aestheticism-activism debate first erupted as AIDS drama in 1984 with Larry Kramer's *The Normal Heart*. Ironically, in Kramer's fulminations against the politicization and consequent aestheticization of "promiscuity" in New York gay culture of the 1970s, Kushner may well have found a few prophetic hints for Prior's anagogic discovery of heaven. "We were a bunch of funny-looking fellows who grew up in sheer misery and one day we fell into orgy rooms and we thought we'd found heaven," Kramer has a rueful gay libber, Mickey, recall as the turmoil of the AIDS crisis confounds his dreams of erotic freedom, "And we would teach the world how wonderful heaven can be."[8] That was then. This is now: for Kramer's activist alter ego, Ned Weeks, falling into an orgy room might as well be falling into a grave.

The sexual high of the 1970s disgusts Ned because of its vertiginously inverted outcome: the fatal hypogogy of the 1980s. Though Kramer has been unstinting in his dramatic and dogmatic efforts to resist the facile "memento mori" moralizations of the epidemic, his activist initiatives have failed to slow the momentum of immortal longings and heavenly aspirations in AIDS drama. It is a popular wish-fulfilling momentum Kushner goes along with, camps up, accelerates. Miraculously, Prior remains hopeful and still heavenbent at the play's end, in the Bethesda Fountain epilogue, even after he's discovered (and taught the world) just how awful a paradise regained can be.

Is Kushner a hyperactivist with a Nietzschean will to power who vastly expands the original force field of ACT UP by unleashing the heavenly forces hymned by his ideological foes? Or is he the herald of an aesthetic counterreformation, a postactivist with Holleranesque éclat who blasts the Kramerized vision of deliverance from the AIDS Holocaust by exposing its latent apocalypticism in absurdly literal stage images? His position in the aestheticism-activism debate is impossible to determine without first addressing the question of the Angel's identity as a minister of divine justice. Her manifestation in the theater is so spectacular, so visually embodied, that the wires holding her up only seem to confirm her reality as a necessary presence in the audience's communal meditation on the cultural repercussions of the epidemic. To regard such a wished-for presence as merely a stage device, or as a hallucination caused by some kind of collective AIDS hysteria, seems like an easy way to beg the play's toughest theological question: is she the Angel of Death or the Messenger of Hope?

Prior is the Jacob who must wrestle with this question and eventually with the Angel herself. Fortunately, his physical frailty is offset by a spiritual toughness reminiscent of the fighting spirit of the drag queens who kicked off the Stonewall Riots in 1969. In 1985, however, it's not a troop of riot police whom Prior must fight off but the viral legions of Death whose Angel has left her "wine-dark kiss" (1:21), a KS lesion, on his skin as a liebestod-ish omen of what he will suffer as a gay PWA (person with AIDS) abandoned by his lover. From such suffering there will be no liberation through a Stonewall-style movement for social justice.

If Kushner's position in the aestheticism-activism debate is initially hard to determine, this may be due in part to his careful dating of the play: most of the plot takes place in 1985–86, when Reagan's America was reeling from the first shock waves of AIDS phobia in the wake of Rock Hudson's death. Reagan himself, as the activists have long pointed out, was scandalously unshaken by the sudden springing of the epidemic to public attention. Though Kushner spares no punches in his satiric revelations about "Reagan's children" (1:74), he leaves the contentious social arena of Ned Weeks and company severely alone. New York clearly has room for only one activist Jeremiah crying in the theatrical wilderness, and Kushner is evidently too respectful of Kramer the playwright (not to mention Kramer the PWA) to steal his thunder.

When I saw part 1 on Broadway in 1993, however, I recall feeling oddly anxious that Kushner was evincing no anxiety of influence—as if he had a moral obligation to acknowledge somewhere in his work the profound political impact of that other gay Jewish Reagan-hating playwright from New York on all serious AIDS drama produced in the second decade of the epidemic.[9] Could Prior, the angelically appointed prophet of gay New York, be a shiksa parody of Ned Weeks or of Kramer himself? If so, then Kushner's aesthetic rapprochement to Kramer amounts to a theological reductio ad absurdum.

None of Kushner's characters has anything like a "normal heart" stirred by the righteous indignation of activism. Their pre-activist world is strategically innocent of ACT UP, as is Prior's decidedly abnormal heart. The beating of angel wings sweeps Kushner's New York clean of all the rubble left over from the contextualist attacks on formalist transcendentalism in the art world of the late 1980s.[10] His version of the AIDS apocalypse seems to proceed on a relentlessly aestheticizing course as if no sparks had ever flown between Larry Kramer and Douglas Crimp, as if no tempers had ever flared at the Gay Men's Health Crisis, as if no crowds had ever blocked traffic on the Brooklyn Bridge to protest the tardiness of drug trials, as if no silence had ever equaled death for the bewildered survivors at Ground Zero.

In an early interchange between Prior and his faltering lover, Louis, the

Apollonian vision of the AIDS crisis as a manageable justice issue to be resolved reasonably through the democratic process is bewilderingly expanded and cynically debunked as a nostalgic theodicy:

> *Prior:* . . . Tell me some more about justice.
> *Louis:* You are not about to die.
> *Prior:* Justice . . .
> *Louis:* . . . is an immensity, a confusing vastness. Justice is God.
>
> (1:39)

But God is dead for Louis, whose theological ramblings amount to no more than hollow sophistries. Inevitably, these fail to sustain Prior's frail fantasies of containing the plague through the law (or the Law): if justice is God indeed, then both are dead in Louis's bleakly cynicized worldview. His subsequent unfaithfulness to his sick lover confirms his faithlessness in a deeper sense. He cannot believe in any world ordered by law or love in which the death sentence of AIDS is meted out to poor "innocent" souls like Prior while "guilty" reprobates like himself survive the viral Holocaust.

Louis, appropriately, never sees an angel in his America. "There are no angels in America," he flatly declares in one of his typical Job-like rants against the Land of the Free (1:92). The play sets out to prove him wrong—at the literal level of thaumaturgical stage machinery. The magnificently troublesome spirit who plummets into Prior's bedroom shortly after Louis's dispiriting denial of her existence proves to be not just an angel in America but the Angel of America. If the illusion of her visitation is not convincingly created and sustained with every magic trick in the backstage book, Kushner warns (1:5), the aesthetic point of Prior's ultimate renunciation of it will be lost.

The formalist urge to impose a unifying structure on the "confusing vastness" of the theological as well as epidemiological crisis of the plague years is expressed by Louis (ironically) in his vain efforts to console Prior before their breakup. To Louis's Edmund Whitish argument that "it should be the questions and shape of a life, its total complexity gathered, arranged and considered, which matters in the end," Prior responds with a putdown worthy of Larry Kramer: "I like this; very zen; it's reassuringly incomprehensible and useless. We who are about to die thank you" (1:38–39). If, as Kushner implies, Louis is the Caesar to Prior's gladiator in the AIDS arena, then the tragically noble effort to view at a glance the total complexity of life, to achieve a divine degree of aesthetic distance, merely reflects Louis's unacknowledged presumption of superiority to the suffering masses of humanity. Aesthetic distance is not only an imperialist illusion, as left-wing critics of formalism have long argued. It is also the illusion of a naively Apollonian artist.

Prior's proto-activist plea for a culturally useful response to AIDS does not dispel the illusion, however, for Louis simply denies that his lover is gravely ill—"You are not about to die," he twice declares—as if Caesar were flashing a thumbs-up signal to his favorite gladiator. It's the ultimate speech act of a self-aggrandizing fool: you will live because I decree it with an august gesture that shows you the need for a whole world of torment. Prior has no choice but to topple Louis off his high seat, to drag him down into the physical agony and spiritual suspense of the arena by ending his argument with an incontestably ugly fact: "My butt is chapped from diarrhea and yesterday I shat blood" (1:39).

How can sweet dreams of aesthetic transcendence survive immersion in the infernal flux of bodily fluids that is Prior's daily reality? Why bother with aesthetics when it's anesthetics that Prior needs to dull his pain?

Faced with the absurd challenge of making something artistic out of bloody diarrhea, Kushner might have opted for a surrealist inversion of aestheticism. Like Georges Bataille snorting like a pig before the shit-stained undershirt pictured in Salvador Dali's *Lugubrious Game,* Louis could have exorcised his Apollonian horror of the plague by reveling with Prior in a sub-Nietzschean cult of ugliness, foulness, cruel anality.[11] It might have been cathartic (in its original laxative sense) for a dirty scene or two. But the play of ironically intersecting social and sexual contexts that Kushner sets up in part 1 would have rapidly deteriorated into a lugubrious game for which there could be no part 2.

Just when the split between the lovers threatens to divide the restless philosophical current of part 1 into a cynical repudiation of aesthetic solace, on Louis's side, and a meandering drift toward activist martyrdom, on Prior's, Kushner sends the Angel crashing through the ceiling of their old bedroom into the confusion of their old debate. Surely now it will be resolved through divine intervention, an *angelus ex machina.*

Hark, the Herald Angel comes with "a great blaze of triumphal music" (1:118) to celebrate the imminent victory of transcendental aestheticism over the ugliness of the plague. Holleranesque fantasies of the gods "bursting with beauty" on the ceiling of a gay Sistine Chapel are miraculously realized in 3-D over Prior's night-sweaty bed.[12] Or so at first it seems. In part 2 Prior discovers that the Angel cannot cure him with illuminated books, baroque trumpet concerti, or flaming Michelangelesque tableaux.

Ironically, it is Prior who is summoned into Heaven to save the Angelic Hierarchs from the plague of mortality, the "Virus of TIME" (2:49).

By firing Prior up with prophetic zeal, restoring his defunct libido, and liberating him from the mundane prison of the status quo, the Angel reveals herself in a shocking new light. As the driving force behind the Sexual Revolution in America, she must also be the tutelary spirit of the Stonewall Generation, to which Prior and Louis and all their plague-stricken friends belong. Far from floating above the action like Raphael's Christ or like the spiritual intercessors in traditional elegiac allegories of salvation, she plunges into it with ferocious energy as if she were Larry Kramer with wings. She knows what it takes to make faggots angry. She knows how to fan the flames of rage. Prior must wrestle with her (literally) as a flying contradiction "in actu" as well as "in verbo"—a beautiful yet terrible synthesis of activist spunk and aesthetic spirituality.

Ecology of Delusions

The unstable relationship of Prior and Louis is paralleled on the straight side by the faltering marriage of Joe and Harper. Despite his "mega-butch" appearance, Joe is instantly spotted as a closet case by Louis when the two chance to meet in the office washroom. Though sexually naive, Joe's wife has also psyched out the truth about him and in her anguish turns to Valium as a temporary escape route from her loveless marriage. She thus becomes the bitter pill-popping bacchanal of the 1980s—the female counterpart of the gay PWA who swallows AZT capsules every four hours to ward off the Angel of Death.

The cruel Dionysian momentum of the epidemic breaks the neat Apollonian symmetry of the two couples when Louis, fleeing his responsibilities with Prior, finds temporary solace in the relatively easy seduction of Joe. Prior and Harper are both left in the lurch, their domestic illusions dashed, their defenses down. Time for the devils in America to raise some hell.

The Angel's infernal counterpart in the play is Roy Cohn, a monster dredged up from the darkest undercurrents of the American Dream. Like his historical namesake, Kushner's Roy is a pernicious closet case whose self-loathing has fueled a lifetime of political aggression against homosexuals, whom he defines with brutal bravado as men who "have zero clout" (1:45). He is Nietzsche's very un-American Superman metamorphosed into a wheeling-dealing, telephone-tentacled slimebag from the McCarthyite abyss.

"I wish I was an octopus, a fucking octopus," he gleefully fantasizes in his opening speech: "Eight loving arms and all those suckers" (1:11). Loving arms indeed, for at least two of them are aching to embrace the haplessly attractive Joe and suck him down into the maelstrom of homo horrors. Joe is swiftly "possessed" by his devil in a professional sense, but, unlike Nietzsche's exultant version of Raphael's demented boy, he fails to shake off his erotically naive vision of where his salvation lies.

Roy's "salvation" lies in lying. Though diagnosed with AIDS in the first act of part 1, he refuses to be outed as a gay man by the stigma of the plague. This denial of his "diseased" sexual identity will persist to the end of his life, and even beyond, as revealed in part 2. Officially, he has liver cancer. Equating death with homosexuality as fervently as the activists will equate it with silence, he loudly threatens to destroy the career of anyone (starting with his long-suffering doctor, Henry) who might jeopardize his public image as a perfectly straight and invincibly healthy *Übermensch*.

An epidemic of lies and cover-ups thus afflicts the lives of the five leads quite as grievously as the AIDS epidemic itself, which functions through both parts of the play as an almost infinitely extendable metaphor for the weakening of the law, the family, the church, the workplace, the government, and all other traditional defense systems of American democracy. Like an oracle of millenarian chaos, Harper gazes through drug-crazed Dionysian eyes at "old fixed orders spiralling apart" and "systems of defense giving way" under the extreme pressure of the multiplying crises of the epidemic under the Reagan Misadministration (1:16–17).

One system that gives way without much resistance is Harper's Mormon Family Values. With Joe away on suspiciously long walks in Central Park, she dreams up a sexy travel agent who truthfully (if paradoxically) identifies himself as "Mr. Lies." While he is obviously an allegorical embodiment of the mendacious Reagan-era Zeitgeist, his menacing role as a musical illusionist—he'll lure Harper with a phallic oboe in part 2—is clearly a demonic variation of Nietzsche's Apollonian artist. By whisking her away to "a very white, cold place, with a brilliant blue sky above," he provides her with a pseudo-anagogic escape from the shadows of the City of Man. For a brief interlude the ascetic desert of her Antarctic visionscape seems like heaven. "No sorrow here," Mr. Lies tells her truthfully, "tears freeze" (1:101).

The tragic enlightenment born of his hallucinatory fictions results in a chilling (not a purging) of the powerful emotions welling up from Harper's agonized psyche. If her trip to the South Pole starts off as an escapist erotic fantasy, it ends up being an encounter session with her worst theological nightmare: she discovers that the ozone layer, her image of angelic perfection enveloping the earth, is not just perilously reduced but ominously ruptured by the blinding Apollonian sun. The "delicate ecology" of her delusions is threatened by an imperious rationality that will compel her to feel nothing for herself or her husband as it forces her to rise, in her imagination at least, above the painful tangle of their doomed marriage (1:102).

During another Valium vacation she turns up unexpectedly in one of Prior's nostalgic drag dreams (1:31–32). The intersection of their fantasy lives establishes a fragile bond of sympathy between the play's two main prophets. Like his female alter ego, Prior receives what medieval mystics used to call the gift of "discretio spirituum" (the suprarational ability to see spirits and hence to judge the future) as compensation for his sufferings as an abandoned lover.

Meanwhile, as the tectonic plates of painful Dionysian reality shift and grind and vibrate in the after shocks of AIDS, the other characters cross one another's paths along the social and racial fault lines of New York with the frenetic energy of Raphael's overlapping villagers. When Louis leaves Prior, he hangs out with his predecessor in Prior's affections, Belize, a black ex–drag queen turned male nurse, who counters the Jewish intellectual's utopian theorizing of immigrant experience with the hard truths of racial injustice in America. The multiple doubling of roles (e.g., the same actor plays Belize and Mr. Lies) contributes to the effect of overlapping confusions. While Roy, attracted by Joe's cowboyish charms, tries to lure him into the all-male world of power politics as a Washington "royboy," Louis, repelled by Roy's corrupting world of neo-con careerism, succeeds in luring Joe back to his apartment after cruising him in the Rambles.

Histories of various overlapping kinds—personal, sexual, medical, racial, national, biblical—are Kushner's prevailing concern in *Millennium Approaches*. Despite its prophetic title, part 1 is intensely retrospective in character: as an extended prelude to angelic intervention, it links up the panic scene of the AIDS crisis with earlier calamities in Western sociomedical history through a series of typological connections and ancestral parallels between contemporary and historical characters. The Dionysian substrate seems to buckle and erupt with the accumulated agonies of the past. Prior, for instance, awakens from nightmares on two different nights to discover the hovering presences of two ancestors also named Prior, the Angel's unlikely heralds, whom plagues had carried off in earlier centuries. With the august gesture of Nietzsche's Apollo, Kushner shows us a whole world of torment opening up on the dark frontiers of American history. His characters are compelled (which compels us) to recall the poverty and racism endured by antebellum slaves and their African-American descendants; to relive the hazardous journey of Jewish immigrants through the stormy waters of the twentieth century; and to recoil from the nightmarish revival of McCarthyism in the politically orchestrated outbreak of mass hysteria and mobilized prejudice in the Age of AIDS.

Painful Progress

Though the typological synthesis of histories in part 1 certainly continues in part 2, especially in the Mormon Diorama scenes, the prevailing visionary character of *Perestroika* is radically forward-looking in an individualistic sense rather than tribally or ethnically retrospective.[13] While part 1 is chiefly concerned with justice or its apparent absence in the social theater of epidemic cruelties, part 2 struggles to transcend the vanity-of-vanities world of the law by fusing the cosmic power of love with the social power of forgiveness. As Kushner constantly suggests in the play's biblical allusions, its two parts are bound together in contentious concord like the Old and New Testaments.

While the five acts of *Perestroika* cover only two months of calendar time, January–February 1986, they are set against a limitless expanse of theorized future evoked by "the World's Oldest Living Bolshevik," a blind prophet of Marxist utopianism identified as Aleksii Antedilluvianovich Prelapsarianov (2:13). As his mock-theological name suggests, his archaic views predate the Fall of Soviet-style communism and are therefore innocent of the momentous political implications of Gorbachev's reconstructive rise to power in the mid-1980s. These ironies aside, Prelapsarianov wisely deplores the obsessive nostalgia and shrinking prospects of the Americans caught up in the disillusioning Age of AIDS. They are too concerned with the practical task of day-to-day survival. They either lack vision in a prophetic sense or so distrust the imagination as a source of healing power that their fantasies of a cure fail to raise their spirits above the bewilderments of the diseased present. "You who live in this Sour Little Age," he harangues the audience, "cannot imagine the grandeur of the prospect we gazed upon: like standing atop the highest peak of the mighty Caucasus, and viewing in one all-knowing glance the mountainous, granite order of creation" (2:14). Recognizable in Prelapsarianov's grand prospect, despite its grounding in Marxist materialism, is the old mystical illusion of omniscience fostered by Apollonian aestheticism. Raphael's Christ has floated over the same mountain range, viewed the same rocky order of creation from the self-aggrandizing heights of spiritual detachment.

If, as Kushner suggests, the Bolshevik's majestically anagogic but morally naive vision of a grimly unitary materialism is indeed lost, it is surely for the better: who could stand living in so purely an Apollonian (not to mention Caucasian) universe anymore? There may be lots of time for change in it, but it leaves no room for the intractably complex realities like racial difference and sexual destiny that the epidemic, for better or worse, has brought to the fore in contemporary struggles for justice and health. What happens after the ultra-Apollonian prologue in the play's racially and sexually diversified scenes is a more Dionysian celebration and certainly a more spiritually rousing experience of postlapsarian disunity (amounting to cosmic disintegration) than the inflexible order of Prelapsarianov's merely theoretical creation could ever tolerate.

"The world's coming to an end," Harper cried in part 1 (1:28). In part 2 she will learn that some old worlds are better ended than endured, while others are so new in their visionary reconstruction of heaven that they are best entered into blind. If the Sour Little Age of AIDS is not sweetened much in part 2, it is at least broadened and deepened for all the main characters. Harper escapes once again to the emotional deep-freeze of her imaginary Antarctica with the cunning Mr. Lies, who tries to lure her soul beyond sexual depression into metaphysical despair—the bitter end of all Apollonian rationalizations of Dionysian disintegration—with the bewitching bluenotes of his tragic oboe (2:19). She resists him, however, and the magic Antarctic sky fades into the ordinary background of a winter's night in the allegorically appropriate setting of Prospect Park. Though far from sane—the police soon find her there chewing on a pine tree, a maenadic symptom of Dionysian possession—she has scored an important victory over the top-down pressures of egocentric deceit and escapist denial that have taken over America as Reagan's Washington allows the epidemic to happen.

The police escort her back to her apartment, where Joe's eminently sane mother, Hannah, newly arrived in New York from Salt Lake City to save her son's marriage, takes charge of Harper with a calming stalwartness. Having rejected the fantasy world of Antarctica, Harper proceeds with critical alacrity to see through the homophobic "Family Values" construct of reality promoted by her morally conservative yet mystically heterodox church. She literally sees through it as a transparent fantasy, a falsely promising vision of America as a heaven on earth for latter-day saints, by staring at the flashy hologram of a pioneer family heading west to the sterile shore of a lifeless lake in Utah projected onto the stage in the Diorama Room at the Mormon Visitor's Center. When Hannah brings her daughter-in-law to the center to keep an eye on her while she works as a volunteer, Harper sits for hours before the Diorama transfixed by the bitterly ironic analogy between her sham marriage and its illusory Mormon model. Hallucinating, she confuses the Good Father in the religious mirage with Joe. To reject this second fantasy world, then, she must lose her faith along with her husband.

Bravely she abandons both, as her soaring arc through the play carries her away from her miserable past toward a wildly open-ended (queer?) future in San Francisco. As the unlikely prophetess of the AIDS apocalypse, the visionary pioneer who can cross the plains of illusion to the thresholds of revelation in the Heavenly City by the Bay, she is granted (without a trace of camp irony) the play's most Dionysian vision of heavenly healing—a vision worthy of Nietzsche's demented boy. It is Harper's heaven that is healed, not her fallen world, but the healers turn out to be the souls of worldlings who have suffered death through war, famine, or pestilence, the traditional weapons of the Horsemen of the Apocalypse.

Her anagogic dream is recounted in an ecstatic soliloquy, since no stage machinery, however magical, could possibly pull off the necessary special effects. "Souls were rising," she recalls at thirty-five thousand feet aboard a jumbo jet bound for the West Coast (2:144). After forming a great net by joining hands like skydivers, the souls were transformed by their participation in this delirious cosmic dance ("wheeling and spinning") into ozone molecules absorbed into the outer rim of the troposphere to repair the damaged ozone layer. "Nothing's lost forever," she concludes, with the rustic simplicity of a born-again Democrat: "In this world, there is a kind of painful progress." No blues for the death of God here: her high fantasy of resurrection as an ecofeminist recycling project is a tough-get-going American answer both to Prelapsarianov's wordy theory of material creation and to the wordless descent into apathy and despair anticipated by the oboe-wailed riffs of Mr. Lies.

Apocalyptic resolution meets pastoral regeneration in Harper's dream, ending her painful progress through the play on a note of exultant hope. But, for all that, is her upbeat inversion of ACT DOWN (which is what skydivers normally do) to be taken seriously? Should her tranquilizing dream be discounted as a Valium flashback?

If *Perestroika* is full of such up-in-the-air visionary moments, its main action back at ground level surprisingly consists in the rejection of all divine revelations. Even as Harper must reject the lies imbedded in her cold pastoral of Antarctica, so her male counterpart, Prior, must reject the revelations of universal entropy and angelic fatalism recorded in his blazing Book of Prophecy. In the second scene of act 2 this peculiar text (hot off the heavenly press) is delivered to him by the orgasmic Angel of America. Hilariously, the ex–drag queen finds himself reliving the supremely serious moment in nineteenth-century American history when the Angel Moroni threw the Book at the Mormon prophet Joseph Smith. Like Joseph, Prior even gets a nifty pair of stone spectacles to help him read the blindingly bright pages of celestial scriptures. When the Angel presses the Book against Prior's chest, they experience an ineffable climax together comparable only to the obscure fusion of sexuality and textuality heralded in the 1590s by Theresa of Avila and in the 1970s by Roland Barthes and other French literary theorists. This odd "jouissance" is so intensely untheoretical, however, that Prior promptly swoons, and the Angel has to lower him in her arms to the ground.

"The sexual politics of this are *very* confusing," admits the newly initiated prophet in a critical aside to Belize that few attentive audience members would care to dispute (2:49). The comedy of confusion abounds in the play as a satiric comment on the politics of certainty: just when many Middle Americans thought that Reaganite conservatism (like McCarthyite nationalism before it) was the straight and narrow way to a bright future because the Moral Majority was brazenly justifying it on the revelation of God's Law through the Scriptures, lo and behold, along comes a *très gai* counter-prophet with some all-American revelations of his own that will throw everything into confusion, including heaven, which suffers a calamitous "heavenquake" at the very progressiveness of the twentieth century's various immoral minorities (2:50).

Thresholds of Revelation

The second decade of the epidemic has seen the emergence of a new group of unusually complex and challenging works that cannot be easily labeled "activist" or "aesthetic" responses to AIDS because they are oddly neither—or both at once. *Angels in America* is the most notable example of this fusion (or confusion) of first-decade categories in the theater, as Paul Monette's *Halfway Home* is in prose fiction and John Greyson's *Zero Patience* is in film. That these works should be full of miraculous breakthroughs, magical empowerments, supernatural solicitings, clairvoyant dreams, apocalyptic revelations, and special effects in a holy as well as a Hollywood sense is not surprising in light of their religious function as antidotes to the poisonous gloom on the medical front. Their impact on cultural perceptions of AIDS is bound to be medically provocative—not to mention theologically controversial—if only because their creators insistently work against the current of dire prophecies issuing relentlessly from the oracles of medicine. They look beyond the tentative short-term prognoses offered to trembling patients by their physicians, beyond the kind of diagnosis scene dubiously immortalized in the 1985 TV melodrama *An Early Frost*. Poor Michael, the sensitive piano-playing hero in this mortality tale, had only Chopin to turn to when his doctor informed him that he had AIDS.[14] If he were a character in one of these new transfigurative works, he would be told by a spirit to ready himself for an ecstatic remission from the ironies of the sero-positive life or else be pushed along with all the anxious readers of long-range epidemiological forecasts from the World Health Organization ("ten million infected worldwide by the end of the millennium!") toward a prophetic reading of the epidemic *sub specie aeternitatis*.

By challenging the recent political tendency to regard the epidemic as a rather embarrassing hangover from the last administration, a bureaucratic morass, a lost cause, the religious design of these new works also blasts the double complacency of the permanently despondent and the puritanically smug. Radically experimental, dialectically explosive, they offer escape routes from the entropic battle of the activists and the aesthetes. Besides breaking impasses, they also break through the thick walls of disdain and distrust separating "Us" from "Them" on the basis of gender, race, class, religious affiliation, sexual orientation, and serostatus. As established religions (including the positivist faith in Science and Medicine) continue to flounder in their divisive reactions to the epidemic, traditional views of salvation are evidently failing to unite the ranks of the faithful or to boost the morale of the plague weary. Turning from the altars to the arts for hope, the bereaved and the bewildered are finding a new set of prophets to reinvent heaven in bold transfigurative visions of the harrowing of AIDS.

The term *transfigurative* implies more than *transformative* here, though the prophetic visions of Kushner, Monette, and Greyson do serve to transform the popular image of the epidemic as a gay plague by reshaping perceptions of the gay PWA as a vice-driven pariah or a paragon of heroic virtue. What these artists do in their morally harrowing works, besides rejecting all facile moralizations of the plague, is to intensify personal involvement with its perplexities at levels far deeper than the early frosting of Michael (who was chiefly concerned with his family's "shame"). The wintry deepening of bewilderment does not lead to a truly religious transfiguration of the crisis, however, unless it is followed by a springing of renewed desire that elevates what would otherwise be a depressing activist critique of "the AIDS tragedy" into something like a divine comedy.

Transfigurative art satisfies the high fantasy of permanent remission from the plague of mortality itself. It is produced in periods of extreme personal suspense and violent cultural fragmentation, when artists find themselves facing not only the internal breakdown of their own physical and spiritual immunities against sickness or despair but also the external collapse of traditional systems of defense in the state or the church. Raphael, for instance, painted his *Transfiguration* in the final feverish months of his life, when the Black Death was still ravaging Italy in periodic outbreaks and the first stentorian trumpets of the Reformation were sounding in Catholic ears like the Doom.

Countering Nietzsche's severely binarized reading of the painting as an Apollonian illusion "triumphing" over Dionysian reality, I'm inclined to view it triadically as an emblem of the integration of apotropaic, animistic, and anagogic visions in transfigurative art of any period, including the Age of AIDS. The shadowy lower scene with the demented boy and his anxious exorcists illustrates the ancient apotropaic function of religious art: the ritual "warding off" or "driving away" of demons, monsters, evil spirits, or anything else perceived as harmful to the health or harmony of society. The high plateau of dreams and revelations in the middle of the painting, in turn, is where the spirits of the dead are raised for the edifying amazement of the living. This site brings to mind the animistic function of religious art, comparable to the operation of a medium at a séance. Finally, amid the clouds of glory in the top third of the painting Christ himself reveals the anagogic function of artistic visions that effectively "lead or guide" the viewer up beyond the shadows of mortality to contemplate the state of the blessed from the mystical heights of divine understanding and happiness.[15]

After all the blazing alephs and spectral conjurations and midair angelic somersaults Kushner provided, I'm left wondering whether he wholeheartedly transfigures the AIDS crisis for us in the end. Or does he simply refigure it as a postactivist trip down the Yellow Brick Road to theological disillusionment?

The mystical upturn in part 2 seems to end in a bathetic rejection of the very possibility of anagogy (queer or otherwise) in the AIDS crisis. If Prior qualifies as a Nietzschean hero, it's because he heroically chooses to go back inside the theater of viral cruelties—even when he's offered a painless apotheosis in the style of Raphael's Christ. The Hereafter is simply too imaginary, too illusory, for a demented boy who prefers the immigrant realities of the Here and Now. Far from being paradigmatic of eternal ideals in a Christian or Neoplatonic sense, Prior's heaven inevitably disappoints him as a palely static image of the historical San Francisco before its hedonistic transformation in the 1970s into a Gay Mecca. Like an old photograph of the city, its dull lusterless projection into the Beyond seems disturbingly unreal—and dangerously retro as a nostalgic fantasy of pre-AIDS serenity.

"Imagination is a dangerous thing," Prior confesses to Harper in the Diorama Room. "It can blow up in your face," she concurs (2:70). So much for cherished Romantic notions of the imagination as inspired reason or as a font of healing optimism for the dejected psyche. Prior is too campily ironic and critically ill to buy that old literary line.

The collapse of his anagogic fantasy is hardly surprising from a Christian perspective, since the outsider universe of the play has a strongly Judaic "feel" to it right from the rabbinical oration that opens part 1. Considering that Kushner's Jewish identity is as strong a shaping influence on the play's diaspora of a plot as his proud-under-pressure gay identity, I'm not surprised by the conspicuous absence of a Christ figure in his Mormonized Old Testament history of the plague, despite its impressive crowd of true and false prophets. Jesus of Philadelphia, Tom Hanks's messianic role, wouldn't cut it in Kushner's New York. Though Prior does finally throw off his Moses drag for a plain overcoat in the Bethesda epilogue, he never makes it or tries to make it as a camp Miss Jesus in the style of Paul Monette's ex-Catholic drag queen, Tom Shaheen.[16] Perpetual migration without eternal transcendence is a traditional theme in Jewish lamentation that reaches its climactic expression in part 2 in the recitation of the Kaddish by a surprised and supernaturally prompted Louis over the body of his arch-enemy, Roy Cohn.

As Prior's spiritual antithesis, Roy appropriately experiences an anagogy in reverse. As Prior is descending from heaven, he catches sight of the demonic lawyer "standing waist-deep in a smoldering pit, facing a volcanic, pulsating red light" (2:138).[17] This final confinement of his malevolent energies in what looks like a traditional inferno appears to be the ultimate in poetic justice for a vicious closet case: it is his eternal contrapasso-like closeting in the volcano of his repressed and tormenting desires. Yet, from the transfigurative angle of Kushner's "Divine" (in the camp sense) Comedy, Roy's new location might also be seen as a purgatory or even as a paradise for the soul of an incorrigible barrator. It is his new law office, and he's hard at work on a new case, the greatest of his career: defending God, who's of course "guilty as hell" (2:139), against the calumnies leveled at him by his heavenly offspring. Like the good gay, the bad gay lives on, in his own way, past hope.

The parting glance at Roy's damnably comic bravado in the afterlife ironically revives the anagogic impulse in Prior's life with AIDS back on earth in the play's epilogue, which is dated "February 1990." Four years have passed since his heavenly ascent, and yet he remains, perversely clinging to life. Sitting with Belize, Hannah, and Louis on the rim of the

Bethesda Fountain, the erstwhile prophet of the AIDS apocalypse has his friends explain the historical and prophetic significance of the Angel Bethesda, who is represented in stone at the top of the fountain. While Louis and Belize look back to the days of the Second Temple, when the angel created a healing fountain in the temple square by touching the earth with her feet, a fountain that would not run dry until the Romans destroyed Jerusalem, Hannah looks forward to the millennium, when the fountain will flow again and the sick will be healed by bathing in its purifying waters. No one is chanting ACT UP slogans or reciting the Kaddish around this pastoral site of apocalyptic piety, in the bleak midwinter of suspended hope, when the City of Man has cut the water supply (as it has cut its public health budget) to the pipes of the mystical "fons vitae."

Kushner does finally play Nietzsche's augustly gesturing god for laughs, since tragedy is an aesthetic illusion of enlightenment ultimately rejected by the survivors of the Angel's visit. From the epilogue's distinctly postactivist perspective there is no media-hallowed AIDS tragedy to act up over and no action left for Prior and his stoic friends but waiting. Waiting for the miraculous cure: imagining one is just too exhausting and dangerous because it raises hell, raises ghosts, raises angels. Imaginary angels are likely to blow up in your face when they turn out to be rather more than Apollonian illusions.

"I like them best when they're statuary," Prior admits in a sly repudiation of the statue scene in *The Winter's Tale:* "They commemorate death but they suggest a world without dying" (2:147).[18] Behind this ironic admission, with its heartfelt yearning for immortality without immobility, lies Kushner's complex answer to the aestheticism-activism debate along with his Nietzschean response to the illusion of anagogic transfiguration.

NOTES

Friedrich Nietzsche, *The Birth of Tragedy and The Genealogy of Morals,* trans. Francis Golffing (Garden City, N.Y.: Doubleday, 1956), 33–34.

1. For a philosophical discussion of the issues involved in the aestheticism-activism debate, see my article "AIDS and Aesthetics," in *Encyclopedia of Aesthetics,* ed. Michael J. Kelly (New York: Columbia University Press, 1998). I have incorporated some of my remarks on Kushner's aestheticism from this article into the present essay. Parodic allusion to musicals is a sure sign of aesthetic leanings in gay playwrights who deal with AIDS. Lerner and Loewe's *My Fair Lady* turns up in Paul Rudnick's *Jeffrey;* Jerome Kern's *Show Boat* is echoed in Larry Kramer's *The Destiny*

of Me; and Irving Berlin's *Top Hat* underscores the search for Gay Heaven in *Perestroika.*

2. "The Day after That," lyrics by Fred Ebb, music by John Kander (1990). On Liza's appropriation of this jailhouse ballad from *Kiss of the Spider Woman* as an inspirational anthem for World AIDS Day, see my article "Raising Spirits: The Arts Transfigure the AIDS Crisis," in the *1995 Medical and Health Annual* (Chicago: Encyclopaedia Britannica, 1994), 127–28. My discussion of Kushner in "Raising Spirits" (145–49) has been expanded in the present essay.

3. The day after the march, reading Janny Scott's frontpage report "Gay Marchers Press ahead in 25-Year Battle," in the *New York Times* (27 June 1994, B2), I discovered the source of this theological pronouncement: the infamous "Reverend" Fred Phelps of the Westboro Baptist Church, Wichita, Kansas.

4. I have borrowed the term *agonist* from Kushner, who uses it in the afterword to *Perestroika* ("With a Little Help from My Friends"). See *Angels in America: A Gay Fantasia on National Themes. Part Two: Perestroika* (New York: Theatre Communications Group, 1994), 150. Further references will appear in the text.

5. Tony Kushner, *Angels in America: A Gay Fantasia on National Themes. Part One: Millennium Approaches* (New York: Theatre Communications Group, 1993), 118. Further references will appear in the text.

6. The case for aestheticism as the "proper" gay response to the epidemic received its most eloquent expression in Edmund White's "Esthetics and Loss," *Artforum* 25 (January 1987): 68–71. For a satiric treatment of the traditional elegiac theme of the consolation of beauty, see Andrew Holleran's essays "Tragic Drag" and "Beauty NOW," *Ground Zero* (New York: Plume, 1988), 91–100, 131–44.

7. Leo Bersani has panned *Angels in America* by dismissing Kushner's religiously American allegorization of gay identity. "The enormous success of this muddled and pretentious play," sneers Bersani in *Homos* (Cambridge: Harvard University Press, 1995), 69, "is a sign, if we need still another one, of how ready and anxious America is to see and hear about gays—provided we reassure America how familiar, how morally sincere, and particularly in the case of Kushner's work, how innocuously full of significance we can be." I fail to see why Kushner would bother to "out" Roy Cohn onstage if his dramatic aim was to make gay identity seem morally sincere or innocuously full of significance to (straight?) Americans. If the "confusing vastness" of the play lacks the clarity of French neoclassical tragedy, it is not because Kushner is a muddled and pretentious tragedian, a Racine manqué, but because, like Nietzsche, he has strategically renounced the tragic *éclaircissements* of Apollonian dramaturgy. For Kushner's razzy reaction to *Homos,* see his essay "On Pretentiousness," *Thinking about the Longstanding Problems of Virtue and Happiness* (New York: Theatre Communications Group, 1995), 72–77.

8. Larry Kramer, *The Normal Heart* (New York: New American Library, 1985), 103. When Gay Heaven is not found in an orgy room, it is often located on a beach as in the anagogic endings of the films *Longtime Companion* and *Philadelphia.* On the theological significance of these littoral readings of heaven, see my article "Dante on Fire Island: Reinventing Heaven in the AIDS Elegy," in *Writing AIDS: Gay Literature, Language, and Analysis,* ed. Timothy F. Murphy and Suzanne Poirier (New York: Columbia University Press, 1993), 297–303.

9. Ironically, in his afterword to *Perestroika* (2:157–58) Kushner acknowledges

a bad attack of influence anxiety in the presence not of Larry Kramer but of Harold Bloom, author of *The Anxiety of Influence*.

10. The model for theoretically informed discussions of official AIDS discourse remains *AIDS: Cultural Analysis/Cultural Activism,* ed. Douglas Crimp, *October* 43 (Winter 1987).

11. Georges Bataille, "'The Lugubrious Game,'" in *Visions of Excess: Selected Writings 1927–1939,* ed. and trans. Allan Stoekl (Minneapolis: University of Minnesota Press, 1985), 28.

12. In "Snobs at Sea: 1983" (*Ground Zero* [New York: William Morrow, 1988], 35) Andrew Holleran can hardly contain his aesthetic reverence for the men at the old Everard Baths: "They were as improbable and beautiful lying in their rooms in their Jockey shorts and towels as the gods Michael had painted on his ceiling on Seventh Street—a burst of beauty, fantasy, art—in the midst of a nightmare reality. The thrill of homosexuality is finally an aesthetic thrill."

13. Despite Kushner's socialist animadversions against American individualism in the afterword to *Perestroika* (2:150), the main characters in part 2 work out their destinies in a painfully individualistic way. Forming a left-wing collective to take "direct action against the AIDS Crisis," as ACT UP posters would have commanded in 1990, seems like the last thing the wobbly little coterie of survivors is inclined to do in the Bethesda epilogue.

14. For a critical discussion of the diagnosis scene in *An Early Frost,* see Paula A. Treichler, "AIDS Narratives on Television," in *Writing AIDS,* ed. Murphy and Poirier, 172.

15. For further examples of apotropaic, animistic, and anagogic responses to the epidemic, see my article "Raising Spirits," *Medical and Health Annual,* 139–43.

16. While Miss Jesus cannot levitate like Raphael's Christ, Tom Shaheen does make a triumphant ascent in a simple literal sense that foreshadows the complex miracle of anagogy. He climbs a beach house staircase daily after his siesta on the sand. For the spiritual outcome of this physical ascent, see Paul Monette, *Halfway Home* (New York: Crown, 1991), 37ff.

17. This brief scene was cut from the Broadway production of *Perestroika,* a directorial decision apparently intended to speed up the action and heighten the comic impact of the play's concluding scenes for the New York audience.

18. This comparison was suggested to me by my partner, John Stracuzza, a die-hard Italian aesthete who only cries in the theater when statues come to life.

Strange Angel:
The Pinklisting of Roy Cohn

Michael Cadden

When Ned Weeks, the thinly disguised autobiographical hero of Larry Kramer's *The Normal Heart,* learns from a friend that he has been removed from the Board of Directors of the play's fictional version of the Gay Men's Health Crisis, he responds defensively by naming names—the members of a group even more important to him than the one he founded:

> I belong to a culture that includes Proust, Henry James, Tchaikovsky, Cole Porter, Plato, Socrates, Aristotle, Alexander the Great, Michelangelo, Leonardo da Vinci, Christopher Marlowe, Walt Whitman, Herman Melville, Tennessee Williams, Byron, E. M. Forster, Lorca, Auden, Francis Bacon, James Baldwin, Harry Stack Sullivan, John Maynard Keynes, Dag Hammarskjold . . . These are not invisible men. . . . The only way we'll have real pride is when we demand recognition of a culture that isn't just sexual. It's all there—all through history we've been there.[1]

Without stopping to argue cases with a fictional character, I want to label the mode of performance Ned engages in as "pinklisting." The subtitle of Martin Greif's *The Gay Book of Days* defines my genre wittily if not succinctly: *An Evocative Illustrated Who's Who of Who Is, Was, May Have Been, Probably Was, and Almost Certainly Seems to Have Been Gay during the Past 5,000 Years.*[2]

For the most part pinklisting in the hands of gay and lesbian writers is as celebratory as it is speculative. Perhaps especially for a person of my generation and those older than me (I'm fortysomething), books like *The Gay Book of Lists, Lavender Lists, Lesbian Lists,* and *The Big Gay Book* serve the function of collecting in print all the dish that went into the epic catalogues of our oral tradition in the years before Stonewall. Their subject headings suggest the hope that sheer numbers will end centuries of heterosexist lies, secrets, and silence: "19 Famous Gay and Lesbian Relationships," "14 Men Who Loved Boys," "17 Lovers of Natalie Barney," "50 Gay and Lesbian Authors Who Have Won Major Mainstream Awards," "22 People Who

Confronted the Military." Gay and lesbian pinklisting sees itself as providing role models and suggests, however problematically, the continuity of a gay and lesbian presence (and usually struggle) across the borderlines of time and place.

In *The Gay Book of Lists* Leigh W. Rutledge extends the genre into more dangerous terrain, listing "3 Men the Gay Movement Doesn't Want to Claim"[3]—Francis Cardinal Spellman, J. Edgar Hoover, and Joseph R. McCarthy. None of these men, you will note, make Larry Kramer's Hall of Fame. Nor does a gay man who was friends with all three and is the subject of this article, Roy Cohn. As a rule, when Cohn is subjected to the phenomenon of pinklisting, the performance is not produced by gay writers interested in community pride. The standard pinklisting of Roy Cohn appears in what passes for the liberal press in the United States. Both homophobic and heterosexist, liberal pinklisting usually has far more to do with blacklisting, a genre Cohn understood well, than with the celebration of a gay presence in history. Take, for example, these poisonous lines from Robert Sherrill's review of Nicholas von Hoffman's biography *Citizen Cohn*,[4] a review that appeared in the *Nation:*

> Cohn was rumored to have humped, or been humped by, [David] Schine, his colleague of the McCarthy days, but von Hoffman says there is no evidence of such a relationship. Ditto the rumors that he humped, or was humped by, his dirt-supplying pal J. Edgar Hoover. Ditto the rumors that he humped, or was humped by, Cardinal Spellman (who reputedly was hot for choirboys)—all very, very close friends of Cohn, to be sure, but by von Hoffman's reckoning they serviced one another only in political ways.[5]

Sherrill's over-the-top review is a classic example of the homophobic pinklisting of Roy Cohn that has characterized much of the liberal press since Cohn's death from AIDS in 1986. Proscribed by both their own journalistic code of ethics and Cohn's legendary litigiousness from yelling "fag" in print while he was still alive, reporters have taken every postmortem opportunity to avenge themselves against this right-wing icon and his cronies, often in the same inquisitorial style that they helped make infamous. Here's Sherrill, in the role of latter-day Joe McCarthy, on the fact that Cohn had ties to a so-called lavender Mafia, a group of closeted gay men in the Reagan administration: "This seems to be a line of investigation that von Hoffman was too lazy to pursue. Roughly how many men does he mean? How close to the White House do these rumors take us? How high do they go?" One almost expects Sherrill to insist that von Hoffman "name names."

Sherrill caps his performance with a moralizing literary gloss on von Hoffman's description of Cohn's deathbed, pinklisting him as a victim less of AIDS than of another fin-de-siècle syndrome first identified by Oscar Wilde—DGS: "To his death he denied that he was homosexual, but the Dorian Gray scene of his dying of AIDS said it all: 'Roy . . . lay in bed, unheeding, his flesh cracking open, sores on his body, his faculties waning' and with a one inch 'slit-like wound above [his] anus.'" (No doubt it was not till they had examined the rings that they recognized who he was!) It is all too easy to assume what the unspoken "all" that Sherrill assumes this scene "says" actually is; his narrative forges the links between closeted cause and corporeal effect. I can only respond to Sherrill's use of Cohn's hideous death as the fitting narrative closure to a life he disapproved of with the words that Joseph Welch, Cohn's chief adversary at the Army-McCarthy hearings, once aimed at Cohn's employer: "Have you no sense of decency, sir, at long last? Have you no sense of decency?"

Decency is in low supply when the subject is Roy Cohn and the venue is the mainstream press. In the weeks before his death he was the subject of both a "60 Minutes" report, which focused on the illness he insisted was liver cancer, and a Jack Anderson/Dale Van Atta column that published both the real nature of his disease and the details of his treatment. Of course, neither of these pieces flouted the conventions of doctor-patient and governmental confidentiality because they were interested in Cohn's illness; they were interested in what that illness might allow them to say about the sexuality Cohn had chosen to keep hidden. AIDS gave them a final opportunity to out Cohn and thus shatter his immunity from journalistic gossipmongering. As Andy Rooney succinctly put it: "[Cohn] denied he was a homosexual suffering from AIDS. Death was an effective rebuttal to that last denial."[6]

Before the body was cold the *New York Times* weighed in with headlines whose tongue-in-cheek campiness barely contained a hysterical glee: on the front page, "Roy Cohn, Aide to McCarthy and Fiery Lawyer, Dies at 59"; and, inside, "Roy Cohn, McCarthy Aide and Flamboyant Lawyer, Is Dead."[7] "Fiery"? "Flamboyant"? As Eve Kosofsky Sedgwick has remarked, "why not say 'flaming' and be done with it?"[8] The obituary itself moves quickly to the causes of death—one primary, "cardio-pulmonary arrest," and two secondary, "dementia" and "underlying HTLV-3 infections," in order to establish its real interest in the infected body of Roy Cohn: "Most scientists believe the HTLV-3 virus is the cause of AIDS, or acquired immune deficiency syndrome, the fatal disease that cripples the body's immune system and is statistically most common among homosexual men and intravenous drug users." One can almost hear the entire editorial board in the background, gloating, "Got 'im."

The obituary goes on to sketch what the *Times* obviously means to be the profile of an archetypal gay man but one whose sexuality their own house ethics enjoined them from disclosing. Alvin Krebs, the writer, helpfully informs us that "[Cohn's] parents, particularly his mother, doted on their only child, bragging about how clever he was"—the kind of detail presumably so generic that it goes missing from obituaries of "normal" men but is retained here to evoke a very 1950s notion of the dire consequences of doting motherhood. Another woman, in this case a political enemy of Cohn's, is again called in to do the dirty work when the obituary finally turns to the articulation of its homosexual subtext:

> There were sneering suggestions that [Cohn, Schine, and McCarthy] were homosexuals, and attacks such as that by the playwright Lillian Hellman, who called them "Bonnie and Bonnie and Clyde."
>
> Years later Mr. Cohn denied that he was "ever gay inclined" and pointed out that Mr. McCarthy got married and had a son and that "David Schine married a former Miss Universe and had a bunch of kids."

A killer transition oozing with cheap irony indicates that nobody at the *Times* was taken in by Cohn's denial: "Nonetheless, it was Mr. Cohn's intense devotion to Mr. Schine at the time they were working for the McCarthy committee that got them both into serious trouble." Finally, just in case the reader has failed to get the unspeakable point of this obituary, a few well-chosen "lifestyle" items are added to complete the picture of Roy C:

> Mr. Cohn was a short, ungainly man with thinning hair and blue eyes, which were often bloodshot, perhaps because he kept late hours at fashionable discotheques such as Studio 54 and the Palladium, although he said he "adored" the sun. He also admired animals, chiefly dogs, and his office contained an extensive collection of stuffed animals.

Here even Cohn's verbs require the quarantine of quotation marks. A *Times* man dare risk nothing more stylistically daring than the decidedly less theatrical *admired* for fear of contamination by this gay, conservative, nocturnal life.

Let me make it clear at this point that I am no fan of Roy Cohn. I have no problem with the way he is memorialized in the AIDS Quilt, for example— "Bully. Coward. Victim."—especially if that last noun is allowed to resonate as fully as possible. I have no problem with the demonization of Roy Cohn; as a liberal in good standing, I consider Cohn as something like evil incarnate, but for his politics, not for his sexual identity. Krebs's *Times* obituary, like Sherrill's review, paints Cohn as a pathological freak—a latter-day version of the Robert Walker character in Hitchcock's *Strangers on a Train*. Instead of an ideological critique of a very ideological man, they luridly suggest, but never logically argue for, the connections between Cohn's sexual identity, right-wing politics, and death from AIDS. They rejoice in the fact that, as a diseased member of the American body politic, Roy Cohn has been lopped off.

A number of works by contemporary gay male artists have attempted to reclaim Roy Cohn from a homophobic discourse that parades itself as political analysis—pinklisting as a form of blacklisting. Instead of dismissing Cohn as the enemy, these artists see him as a figure who can be valuably deployed to raise important questions about definitions of gay identity and gay community. Robert Mapplethorpe's portrait of Cohn, for example, shows a disembodied head floating in blackness, more death mask than record of a living human being. This is John the Baptist as imaged and imagined by Samuel Beckett, though, of course, it is Mapplethorpe himself who has played the role of Salome and beheaded Cohn with a single queer photographic gaze. Uncharacteristically, however, Mapplethorpe does not in any way fetishize the queerness of this particular queer subject, choosing to emphasize, instead, Cohn's isolation not only from the body politic he might have identified with but also from his body itself. Divorced from either corporeal or community context, Cohn is simply seen, as it were, "giving good head."

In another gay appropriation of Cohn, Ron Vawter's two-part performance piece *Roy Cohn/Jack Smith* (1992) juxtaposes the performance artist's recreation of an outrageously campy, Salome-like solo by avant-garde cult figure Jack Smith with Gary Indiana's version of what a pro-family, anti-gay dinner speech by Roy Cohn might have sounded like. In his introduction to the evening Vawter explained why, as a gay New Yorker who is HIV positive, he was drawn to these two men, who shared with him a city, a sexual orientation, and a probable cause of death. As he later explained in an interview:

> I thought the two placed together would make for an interesting spectrum of male homosexuality. . . . I was interested in how these two very different people reacted and responded to a society that set out to repress their sexuality. . . . In my mind they were the farthest extremes

one could be, and I was afraid of both of them. Quite frankly, I was afraid that behaving homosexually required one either to be like a Jack Smith or like a Roy Cohn, and both positions were scary.[9]

It is this same variety of subject positions within male homosexuality in the United States that informs the work I want to focus on, Tony Kushner's two-part epic *Angels in America: A Gay Fantasia on National Themes*. Like Vawter, Kushner places Cohn at the center of his examination of gay identity and community. But, while Vawter investigates two ends of a discrete spectrum, Kushner works from the assumption that Cohn's identity, and gay identity in general, is at the center of contemporary American life. Kushner's Cohn also raises questions about the nature and purpose of pinklisting and about its value for a new queer politics.

In his program notes for the Royal National Theatre of Great Britain's production, Kushner notes how his own multiple identifications during a Southern boyhood led him to Cohn: "Cohn was homosexual, and so am I. He was also Jewish, but there were lots of great Jews to read about, and nearly no gay men (this was Louisiana, 1968); when one came along, my attention was fixed."[10] Kushner later took a "grim satisfaction" in Cohn's death from AIDS, but, according to an interview with Arthur Lubrow in the *New Yorker,* he was "jolted out of his enjoyment" by the aforementioned *Nation* article written by Robert Sherrill, which, in Kushner's eyes, "equated Cohn's corrupt political life with his sleazy sex life." Kushner was fascinated by the fact that it was Cohn, not McCarthy, who was the usual target of anticonservative venom: "People didn't hate McCarthy so much— they thought he was a scoundrel who didn't believe in anything. But there was a venal little monster by his side, a Jew and a queer, and this was the real object of detestation."[11] In the program note for the National Theatre, Kushner indicates what, for him, the case of Roy Cohn might mean: "AIDS is what finally outed Roy Cohn. The ironies surrounding his death engendered a great deal of homophobic commentary, and among gay men and lesbians considerable introspection. How broad, how embracing was our sense of community? Did it encompass an implacable foe like Roy? Was he one of us?"

Kushner's play answers with what I take to be an uncomfortable yes— and that yes is precisely the distance between a first-generation AIDS play like *The Normal Heart* and a second-generation work like *Angels in America.* If Kramer's play is about how the health problems of a relatively homogeneous minority have been ignored or dismissed by American majoritarian culture, Kushner's play reflects a new gay self-recognition about the ways in which the oppression of gay men and lesbians, like the oppression of other minority groups, has been integral to majoritarian self-recognition, especially during the Reaganite 1980s, when antihomosexuality served many of the same purposes that anticommunism did in the 1950s. In *The Normal Heart,* when Ned Weeks complains about the silence of his associates at the fictional version of the GMHC (Gay Men's Health Crisis), he is complaining about the lack of big mouths at the margins of American life. The silence and denial of Roy Cohn took place center stage in American power politics and takes center stage in Kushner's refiguration of the American political landscape. For Kramer AIDS is about the fate of the gay community; for Kushner AIDS, while retaining a gay-specific identity, is about the fate of the country.

Like all discourse surrounding AIDS, *Angels in America* is about definitions of identity. Part 1 of the play, *Millennium Approaches,* begins with many definitions at least superficially in place. A rabbi eulogizes the values brought from the old country and laments the passing of a generation of Russian Jewish immigrants to America: "How we struggled, and how we fought, for the family, for the Jewish home, so that you would not grow up *here,* in this strange place, in the melting pot where nothing melted." Indeed, nothing is melting in the opening scenes; conservatives stick with conservatives, gay men with gay men, Mormons with Mormons. The society of the play is fractured into groups with their own labeled identities. The label no one claims is "American"; as the rabbi puts it to this community: "You do not live in America. No such place exists. Your clay is the clay of some Litvak shtetl, your air the air of the steppes."[12] Kushner's plot focuses on the plight of two couples, one that appears to be straight, the other gay. No sooner have these identities been established, however, than they begin to break down, as systems of identifications prove to be as vulnerable as immune systems. As Kushner explained in an interview:

> It is all neatly set up, but then it doesn't work out because of all sorts of internal stresses. The Mormon who is married is also gay, and one of the gay characters has AIDS and the other one can't deal with it. So within that seemingly homogeneous unit there is enormous conflict and potential for eruption.[13]

Cohn acts as the Satanic catalyst of the piece, forcing crises of identity and identification in many of the men who surround him. In part these crises are forced by Roy's insistence on his personal brand of social Darwinism, the primacy of the individual in the struggle for an existence. Demanding loyalty to himself, he nonetheless paradoxically preaches a gospel of self-sufficiency. He counsels Joe, the Mormon husband and a potential "Roy-toy," in the tones of the Great Tempter: "Love; that's a trap. Responsibility; that's a trap too. Like a father to a son I tell you this: Life is full of horror; nobody escapes, nobody; save yourself." Roy advises Joe against identifying with any other person or group; the Cohnian self must be created ex nihilo: "Don't be afraid; people are so afraid; don't be afraid to live in the raw wind, naked, alone" (1:58).

For his characterization of Cohn's sense of his own sexuality Kushner seems to have taken his cue from an unpublished fragment of a 1978 interview Cohn gave to Ken Auletta for *Esquire.* When asked about the rumors of his homosexuality, Cohn responded: "Anybody who knows anything about me or who knows the way I function in active life, would have an awfully hard time reconciling that with any kind of homosexuality. Every facet of my personality, of my aggressiveness, my toughness and everything along those lines is just totally, I suppose, incompatible with anything like that."[14] In Kushner's play Roy's parallel denial of his homosexuality takes place after his doctor has informed him that he has AIDS. Roy forces the physician to admit that he considers Roy a homosexual then gives the doctor a lesson in gender definitions:

> Your problem, Henry, is that you are hung up on words, on labels, that you believe they mean what they seem to mean. AIDS. Homosexual. Gay. Lesbian. You think these are names that tell you who someone sleeps with, but they don't tell you that. . . . Like all labels they tell you one thing and one thing only: where does an individual so identified fit in the food chain, in the pecking order? Not ideology, or sexual taste, but something much simpler: clout. Not who I fuck or who fucks me, but who will pick up the phone when I call, who owes me favors. This is what a label refers to. Now to someone who does not understand this, homosexual is what I am because I have sex with men. But really this is wrong. Homosexuals are not men who sleep with other men. Homosexuals are men who in fifteen years of trying cannot get a pissant antidiscrimination bill through City Council. Homosexuals are men who know nobody and who nobody knows. Who have zero clout. Does this sound like me, Henry? (1:45)

Cohn's sophistry embodies the intellectual, moral, and spiritual stagnation from which most of Kushner's characters and the nation itself are seen to suffer in *Angels in America.* Incapable of reconciling "homosexuality" and "clout," Roy chooses to remain in fundamental contradiction with himself. As he explains to his doctor: "Roy Cohn is not a homosexual. Roy Cohn is a heterosexual man, Henry, who fucks around with guys. . . . AIDS is what homosexuals have. I have liver cancer" (1:46). In refusing to allow corporeal information to shake his hegemonic power over what words mean, Cohn is this play's Angel of Death. It is his collapse at the end of part I that harbingers the messageless annunciation of a new angel that concludes the first half of *Angels in America*. While Roy insists to the ghost of Ethel Rosenberg that he is immortal ("I have *forced* my way into history. I ain't never gonna die"), Ethel, in her role as the play's prophet of liminality, responds that a new world order is about to be established: "History is about to crack wide open. Millennium approaches" (1:112).

The title of part 2 of Kushner's epic, *Perestroika*, acknowledges one of the many extraordinary challenges to the Cohnian worldview provided by the social and political changes of the mid-1980s at home and abroad. Indeed, Cohn's series of deathbed scenes serves as a metaphor for the collapse of the Manichaean paradigms upon which he built his life and career. But Roy refuses to go gentle into that good millennium. Indeed, the message the Angel has arrived to deliver is finally revealed and, ironically, echoes Roy's own constant telephonic injunction to "Hold." In Kushner's comic take on the interpretation of AIDS as divine instruction, he provides his angel with a negative message, a new gospel of stasis. All creation is to stop moving. God, it seems, has been missing from the heavens since 1906; because the angels know God loves movement, especially human movement, they hope that, by putting an end to human travel, thought, and imagination, they might force His reappearance. The message is refused by its human prophet, however, and with it the ethos of Roy Cohn. Roy begins *Millennium Approaches* with a bark into the phone—"Hold"—and he ends his human journey, some six and a half years later in *Perestroika,* with the same word.

Like Kushner's Angel, Roy's horror in the face of movement and change, his desire to keep everyone and everything on hold, evokes the image of Walter Benjamin's "angel of history":

A Klee painting named "Angelus Novus" shows an angel looking as though he is about to move away from something he is fixedly contemplating. His eyes are staring, his mouth wide open, his wings are spread. This is how one pictures the angel of history. His face is turned towards the past. Where we perceive a chain of events, he sees one single catastrophe which keeps piling wreckage upon wreckage and hurls it in front of his feet. The angel would like to stay, awaken the dead, and make whole what has been smashed. But a storm is blowing from

Paradise; it has got caught in his wings with such violence that the angel can no longer close them. This storm irresistibly propels him into the future to which his back is turned, while the pile of debris before him grows skyward. This storm is what we call progress.[15]

Not even Roy Cohn can resist the storm of progress; the world refuses to hold, and, at his hospital bedside, it begins its movement toward a new community based on a solidarity across both new and old lines of group identification as a queer assortment of mourners gathers to say Kaddish. Belize, a black ex–drag queen and Roy's former nurse, has come at least in part out of a sense of gay solidarity: "A queen can forgive her vanquished foe" (2:124). Louis, an out gay Jewish liberal who views Cohn as "the polestar of human evil" (2:95), has come to steal his supply of AZT for his former lover, a tacit acknowledgment of the lessons in power that Cohn might have to teach the gay community; he stays to confront, for the first time, the reality of death—a reality that caused him to abandon his lover and which is as horrible in an enemy as it is in a friend. Even Ethel Rosenberg is there; in her previous scene with Roy she confessed to hoping he would die a more terrible death than hers, but she went on to sing him a Yiddish lullaby. As she returns to say Kaddish over his dead body, we are invited to speculate that she does so as a Jewish mother. Louis and Ethel have not forgotten all that divides them from Roy Cohn, however; they end the prayer with their own contribution—"You sonofabitch" (2:126).

When Roy returns to earth for a final interview with his Mormon protégé, Kushner teases us with the possibility that Roy has been transformed by his final illness. After kissing the young man softly on the mouth, he offers a prophecy of his own: "You'll find, my friend, that what you love will take you places you never dreamed you'd go" (2:127). Yet in Roy's final appearance in the play, at a location in the next world characterized by *"volcanic, pulsating red light"* and *"a basso-profundo roar, like a thousand Bessemer furnaces,"* we learn that Roy has not changed; indeed, he has engaged a new client. He will defend God in a cosmic Family Court against angelic charges of abandonment—the apotheosis of his career as a lawyer for the rich and famous: "I'm an absolute fucking demon with Family Law. Just tell me who the judge is, and what kind of jewelry does he like" (2:138).

In Kushner's epilogue those left on earth crystallize into the new society they have struggled toward throughout the play. Male, female; straight, gay; black, white; agnostic, Mormon, Jew—they have survived the breakdown of families and relationships; the collapse of the Soviet Union, the ozone layer, and the immune system; the opportunistic diseases associated with AIDS; the messages of angels; and the mania of Roy Cohn. Roy was right; what they have loved has taken them places they never dreamed they'd go. But, unlike Roy, they look forward; they have come to accept not only that movement is essential to life but also that it is good. Like the character whose Benjaminian lines conclude the play proper, they share the belief that "Nothing's lost forever. In this world, there is a kind of painful progress. Longing for what we've left behind, and dreaming ahead" (2:144).

The new community of the epilogue is not, of course, based on the conventional union of happy couples; the play is ruthless in its assertion that two plus two is not a stable enough equation to base a life on, much less a progressive political vision. Neither has this community bought into the individualistic ethos of Cohn; the politics of one plus one does not add up fast enough, if it ever adds up at all. Instead, Kushner leaves us with the image of four individuals who, despite their very real differences, have chosen, based on their collective experience, to think about themselves as a community working for change. It is Prior, the AIDS patient who has rejected his role as prophet of stagnation, who offers the play's valedictory blessing—both on those gathered onstage, beneath the Angel of Bethesda Fountain in Central Park, and on those gathered offstage, in the audience: "You are fabulous creatures, each and every one" (2:148). His campy and powerful benediction suggests a third term that might mediate between the two Roy Cohn could not hold together—a quintessentially 1950s term recycled for 1990s resistance. What do you call a homosexual with clout? Just what Roy always feared. Queer.

NOTES

1. Larry Kramer, *The Normal Heart* (New York: New American Library, 1985), 114.

2. Martin Greif, *The Gay Book of Days: An Evocatively Illustrated Who's Who of Who Is, Was, May Have Been, Probably Was, and Almost Certainly Seems to Have Been Gay during the Past 5,000 Years* (New York: Carol Publishing Group, 1982).

3. Leigh W. Rutledge, *The Gay Book of Lists* (Boston: Alyson Publications, 1987), 46.

4. Nicholas von Hoffman, *Citizen Cohn* (New York: Doubleday, 1988).

5. Robert Sherrill, "King Cohn," *Nation*, 21 May 1988, 720.

6. Reported by Eve Kosofsky Sedgwick, *Epistemology of the Closet* (Berkeley: University of California Press, 1990), 243.

7. Alvin Krebs, "Roy Cohn, Aide to McCarthy and Fiery Lawyer, Dies at 59," *New York Times*, 3 August 1986.

8. Sedgwick, *Epistemology*, 243.

9. Jessica Hagedorn, "Ron Vawter," *BOMB* (Fall 1992): 46.

10. Program of the Royal National Theatre of Great Britain for *Angels in America: A Gay Fantasia on National Themes. Part One: Millennium Approaches* (British premiere at the Cottesloe Theatre, January 1992).

11. Arthur Lubrow, "Tony Kushner's Paradise Lost," *New Yorker*, 30 November 1992, 60.

12. Tony Kushner, *Angels in America: A Gay Fantasia on National Themes. Part One: Millennium Approaches* (New York: Theatre Communications Group, 1993), 10, 11. Subsequent references to the play will appear in the body of my text, as will references to the second part of Kushner's play, *Perestroika* (New York: Theatre Communications Group, 1994).

13. Hilary de Vries, "A Playwright Spreads His Wings," *Los Angeles Times*, 25 October 1992.

14. Reported by Sidney Zion, *The Autobiography of Roy Cohn* (Secaucus: Lyle Stuart, 1988), 240.

15. Walter Benjamin, "Theses on the Philosophy of History," in *Illuminations*, ed. Hannah Arendt, trans. Harry Zohn (New York: Schocken, 1968), 257–58. For another artistic appropriation of this passage, see Laurie Anderson's piece "The Dream Before" on her album *Strange Angels* (Warner Brothers Records, 1989).

The Vehicle of Democracy: Fantasies toward a (Queer) Nation

Ron Scapp

We the People of the United States, in Order to form a
more perfect Union, establish Justice, insure domestic
Tranquility, provide for the common defence, promote
the general Welfare, and secure the Blessings of Liberty to
ourselves and our Posterity, do ordain and establish this
Constitution for the United States of America.
                      —Preamble to the Constitution

"We the People" tell the Government what to do, it
doesn't tell us. "We the People" are the driver—the Government is the car. And we decide where it should go,
and by what route, and how fast. Almost all the world's
constitutions are documents in which governments tell
the people what their privileges are. Our Constitution is a
document in which "We the People" tell the Government what it is allowed to do. "We the People" are free.
                      —Ronald Reagan, Farewell Address

The white cracker who wrote the national anthem
knew what he was doing. He set the word "free" to a
note so high nobody can reach it. That was deliberate.
Nothing on earth sounds less like freedom to me.
      You come with me to room 1013 over at the
hospital, I'll show you America. Terminal, crazy
and mean.
      —Belize to Louis (*Angels in America: Perestroika*)

Servicing the Car: Maintaining the Vehicle of Democracy

One need not agree with Ronald Reagan in order to see that the
metaphor he employs in his farewell address is helpful in understanding the
way in which many Americans, including those on the Left, describe the

function and role of the U.S. government and Constitution. The comparison of driver to car, though simple, expresses people's belief that, if we only had a great "driver-representative," our car would be the best vehicle ever driven, capable of chauffeuring millions to the promised, that is, *future* destination of life, liberty, and prosperity.

Despite the blatant moving violation of Ronald Reagan's presidency, the Iran-Contra scandal, many Americans continue to view him as such a driver and have been willing to bestow this appellation upon others since him, like Speaker of the House Newt Gingrich, who appears to prefer driving without a map and only a contract. As the millennium approaches, it is perhaps a good time to reconsider the status of "We the People" and to ask some questions about the cost of maintaining this vehicle of ours.

In act 3, scene 2, of *Millennium Approaches,* Louis asks, "Why has democracy succeeded in America?" Immediately qualifying himself, he says, "Of course by succeeded I mean comparatively, not literally, *not in the present,* but what makes for the prospect of some sort of radical democracy spreading outward and growing up?" (1:89; emph. added). By the end of *Millennium Approaches* we are offered a complicated hint; though somewhat different from the Enlightenment-influenced "rights of man" discourse embraced by the authors of the Declaration of Independence and the Constitution, it is a hint that nevertheless maintains the narrative of democracy's future promise.

Prior Walter's ecstasy experienced upon the arrival of the Angel appears to suggest an alternative (AIDS produced?) fantasy about "what makes for the prospect" of American democracy. But his too is a fantasy that has been approaching ever since the construction of the political subject articulated within the Constitution became part of the very vehicle of democracy itself—namely, the promise of the future for every citizen, our prosperity. Kushner's breakdown (deconstruction?) of a rational narrative of progress by announcing "The Great Work begins:/The Messenger has arrived" (1:119) at the end of *Millennium Approaches* may powerfully and rightly demand that we reconsider the Reagan-Gingrich vehicular fantasy of democratic movement and progress, but it too reasserts and maintains *the future* as the promise of democracy. In so doing, *Angels in America* maintains the vehicle, that is, the fantasy of democracy: the future.

Angels in America, however, offers a "queer" vehicle toward progress—that is, the blessing of an Angel who is the Continental Principality of America: More Life! The blessing announces a queer vehicle because it is not simply gesturing toward an extension of the life of America as it has been historically constituted but, instead, offers a different future, a queer (a queer's) hope for the future. The bright rays of hope emanating from the blessing of the Angel can cast America in a different light. The hope is that the AIDS-produced vision of the Angel can cause America to change.

The Cause of America, the Future of the Cause

Thomas Paine boldly proclaimed that "the cause of America is in a great measure the cause of all mankind."[1] This bit of "common sense" universalized the struggle to construct a new state: all of mankind has a natural right to rise above the "wickedness" of government and to thrive within the "moral" strictures of society.[2] Paine's critique of England's exploitation of the Colonies reminds us that "the State" is a social invention and that the "cause of America" was the cause of all those willing to transgress and negate the boundaries of (the king's) state in favor of establishing one of their own.

At the close of *Perestroika* we find Prior, Louis, Belize, and Hannah at the Bethesda Fountain in Central Park all engaged in a discussion of global politics, taking us from the Berlin Wall to the former Czechoslovakia and Yugoslavia, from contemporary New York City to ancient Jerusalem, including the West Bank and the Gaza Strip. Here too we are reminded of the fantasies of nations, the tentativeness and violence of boundaries. This moment of recognition of the turmoil of and struggle for the future is complicated because it is a moment of hope and prediction, of death, overcoming and contradiction. Prior tells us:

> This disease will be the end of many of us, but not nearly all, and the dead will be commemorated and will struggle on with the living, and we are not going away. We won't die secret deaths anymore. The world only spins forward. We will be citizens. The time has come. (2:148)

The cause of those dying of AIDS becomes the cause of America, of humanity. This moment evokes a universal act of transgression, of trespassing the boundaries of some prior state of exclusion and denial (and political wickedness). This is one of the play's more Hegelian moments (*Aufheben*), for it compels us to face the negation of the state of things along with the preservation of the very "spirit" of the state of things themselves, while the world continues to spin only forward, toward the future, toward a state that has yet to come.

The dialectics of geopolitics infuses everyone with new blood and sends all of humanity "spreading outward," working on the (democratic) future. But before we get taken with (taken by?) the fantasy of such a project, the fantasy of acknowledging all citizens, we must return to some prior moment, the moment of political subjectivity itself—namely, the moment of being a member of the state.

The return to the hope of the state, of some future in which "we *will be* citizens," does not suggest that *Angels in America* is guilty of simply fantasizing a better state (a better vehicle), although one might read it that way, but, rather, that it *is* a fantasy about and beyond the present state (of things). *Angels in America* is an attempt to extend the political imagination of Americans through fantasy, that is to say, to broaden the fantasy of democracy through a "gay fantasia on national themes." The point here is to situate this fantasy, the play, as part of the history of the "cause of America," the history of the fantasy of America.

In short, we are confronted by a question: if our "democratic" Constitution was framed by a power elite who already dominated the courts, businesses, and churches, to what degree does "our" Constitution function as a vehicle of deception rather than as a vehicle of future possibility? Does the Constitution express a democratic experiment or provide a veil for the wickedness, the disease, of the state? Did the fanciful new Americans get cheated when they were awakened from their democratic reverie and realized that King George was now to be called President George?

When Washington Calls

It may be too difficult to imagine Roy Cohn as part of the historical consortium of drivers who have steered the vehicle of democracy this way and that, yet he clearly had the ear of some of those who have driven America (crazy?), if for only a moment. In a powerful and disturbing scene Roy tells Joe of his greatest feat, his moment at or near the steering wheel of democracy.

> *Roy:* . . . You know what my greatest accomplishment was, Joe, in my life, what I am able to look back on and be proudest of? And I have helped make Presidents and unmake them and mayors and more goddam judges than anyone in NYC ever— AND several million dollars, tax-free—and what do you think means the most to me?
> You ever hear of Ethel Rosenberg? Huh, Joe, huh?

Joe: Well, yeah, I guess I. . . . Yes.

Roy: Yes. Yes. You have heard of Ethel Rosenberg. Yes. Maybe you even read about her in the history books.

    If it wasn't for me, Joe, Ethel Rosenberg would be alive today, writing some personal-advice column for *Ms.* magazine. She isn't. Because during the trial, Joe, I was on the phone every day, talking with the judge . . .

                                     (1:107–8)

Although the complex relationships existing among corporate America (i.e., unfettered capitalism), the State, and "We the People" have made it difficult to identify exactly who has been steering at any given moment, Roy Cohn makes it clear that the vehicle of democracy cannot be driven by just anyone: certain things have to happen.

    In this regard Roy Cohn is following in the footsteps of other Americans who also felt passionately about the future of America. Alexander Hamilton's open distrust toward democracy, for example, strongly influenced the Constitutional Convention. Hamilton argued that

> all communities divide themselves into the few and the many. The first are the rich and well-born, the other the mass of the people. The voice of the people has been said to be the voice of God; and however generally this maxim has been quoted and believed, it is not true in fact. The people are turbulent and changing; they seldom judge or determine right. Give therefore the first class a distinct permanent share in the government. . . . Can a democratic assembly who annually revolve in the mass of the people be supposed steadily to pursue the public good? Nothing but a permanent body can check the imprudence of democracy.[3]

We can see from this that those who had been steering from afar, namely Parliament, had a profound influence upon at least some of the new leaders of our nation. True, the Constitutional Convention did not heed Hamilton's warning entirely; it did very carefully, however, make certain that some "safeguards" were to be put into place to secure the future of the new state. The convention, for example, did not provide for popular—that is, democratic—elections, except in the case of the House of Representatives and even there made sure that many people would be excluded by virtue of property qualifications established by the individual state legislatures. And, of course, women, Native Americans, and slaves could not vote under any circumstances.[4]

There were also those, like James Madison, who realized the importance of including the "popular" voice but in such a way as ultimately to render it silent. A quick look at the position he argues in Federalist Paper #10 shows that he recommends the virtues of a representative government solely in order to defuse factional struggles stemming from discontent over the "various and unequal distribution of property."[5] Madison reasoned that, if it were possible to establish the principle that one needed a majority, it would be possible to silence any one or even groups of rebellious states. As Madison put it, with an extensive republic "it will be more difficult for all who feel it to discover their own strength, and to act in union with each other"; he further suggests that the "influence of factious leaders may kindle a flame within their particular states, but will be unable to spread a general conflagration through the other states."[6]

Given the various economic interests expressed by the political statements of the Constitution itself, Ronald Reagan's vehicle for freedom becomes, in the words of historian Howard Zinn, "not simply the work of wise men trying to establish a decent and orderly society, but the work of certain groups trying to maintain their privileges, while giving just enough rights and liberties to enough people to ensure popular support."[7] Zinn's assessment of the work produced by the powerful men framing the future of America echoes the observations of social critics such as C. Wright Mills in *Power Elite* and before him Ferdinand Lundberg in *America's 60 Families* who offered us disconcerting information regarding the nature of the real work of the rich and powerful in America, challenging the fantasy of a better future for all who worked. This is perhaps why Roy's strong admonition to Joe, for even hesitating at the chance to go to work in Washington and to be part of the team who steers, expresses the (democratic) fantasy of the many who long to be in the driver's seat.

> *Roy: WASHINGTON!* When Washington called me I was younger
> than you, you think I said "Aw fuck no I can't go I got two
> fingers up my asshole and a little moral nosebleed to boot!"
> When Washington calls you my pretty young punk friend you
> go or you can fuck yourself sideways 'cause the train has pulled
> out of the station, and you are *out,* nowhere, out in the cold.
> Fuck you, Mary Jane, get outta here. (1:106)

The Roy Cohn of *Angels in America* should not be understood as merely a greedy immigrant variant of some puritan ideal of participation in our democracy. On the contrary, Roy Cohn *is* the democratic fantasy at work. We all work for a better tomorrow; some, however, like Roy Cohn, insist on profiting from the promise of tomorrow, from the hard work of others today.[8]

More Life, Liberty, and the Pursuit of Happiness in Time

In the Hall of the Continental Principalities the angel Europa attempts to persuade Prior that he should accept the text offered to him: "This is the Tome of Immobility, of respite, of cessation./Drink of its bitter water once, Prophet, and never thirst again." Prior's response is short and clear: "I can't./I still want. . . . My blessing. Even sick. I want to be alive." Prior gets his blessing, but the gesture is made in silence and only after he demands his life, "so much not enough, so inadequate" (2:136) though it might be. But he returns to live more life. In the epilogue of *Perestroika* Prior addresses the audience from his favorite place in New York City, his favorite place in the universe, the Bethesda Fountain. He tells us: "It's January 1990. I've been living with AIDS for five years. That's six whole months longer than I lived with Louis" (2:146).

The mood of this final scene is animated and upbeat. Louis, Belize, and Hannah are debating the events "of the time,"[9] the progress of human history, politics. Belize notes that "the world is faster than the mind," and Louis excitedly claims: "That's what politics is. The world moving ahead. And only in politics does the miraculous occur." Belize counters, "But that's a theory" (2:146). Perhaps it is *the* theory, the fantasy, of the play itself and the fantasy of America.

It has been suggested in this essay that the fantasy of democracy throughout America's history is the actual vehicle of democracy, more so than anything else. In other words, democracy has been a fantasy from the start and has been maintained (so far) because it is yet another expression of the belief in a metaphysics of unity, the representation of the one (or at least the very few) and the many.[10] The specific American expression of unity, "We the People," has been future bound since it was articulated. It has been embraced by (the) many for it is the very way "We the People" have been constituted. Though the desire for unity is not unique to America, it has found its own expression in America, through the future of America, the future of democracy.

Walt Whitman, commenting in *Democratic Vistas* on the fantasy of America, that is, its future, observed that

America, filling the present with great deeds and problems, cheer-
fully accepting the past, including feudalism (as, indeed, the present
is but the legitimate birth of the past, including feudalism), counts,
as I reckon, for her justification and success (for who, as yet dare
claim success?) almost entirely on *the future.* . . . For our New World
*I consider far less important for what it has done, or what it is, than for
results to come.*[11]

America, then, has misappropriated Nietzsche's edict to become what one
is; instead, America fantasizes about *what it someday will be.*

But there have been those queer few who have resisted or attempted to
resist the lure of participating in the national fantasy of the future and have
spoken powerfully of the past and present state of democracy. In a speech
made on 3 April 1964 in Cleveland, Ohio, Malcolm X insisted:

> I am one who doesn't believe in deluding myself. I'm not going to sit
> at your table and watch you eat, with nothing on my plate, and call
> myself a diner. Sitting at the table doesn't make you a diner, unless you
> eat some of what's on that plate. Being here in America doesn't make
> you an American. Being born here in America doesn't make you an
> American. Why, if birth made you American, you wouldn't need any
> legislation, you wouldn't need any amendments to the Constitution,
> you wouldn't be faced with civil-rights filibustering in Washington
> D.C., *right now.*[12]

The lived time of democracy is now. The fantasy of democracy, however,
is predicated on its future possibility. Thus, the existential tension (contradiction) is the fact that, in order to be an American now, you need to
believe in the fantasy of America someday. But, as Malcolm X reminds us,
not everyone is part of the future, and not everyone is willing or able to fan-
tasize.

In his speech Malcolm X negates the temporality of the future possibility of America. The fantasy, therefore, does not exist, and as a result he is
no American. He exhorts:

> No, I am not an American. I am one of the 22 million black people
> who are the victims of Americanism. One of the 22 million black peo-
> ple who are the victims of democracy, nothing but disguised hypocrisy.
> So, I'm not standing here speaking to you as an American, or a patriot,
> or a flag-saluter, or a flag-waver—no, not I. I'm speaking as a victim of
> the American system. And I see America through the eyes of the vic-
> tim. I don't see any American dream; I see an American nightmare.[13]

For many others the fantasy of the future has been and remains a nightmare.

Of course, *Angels in America* is not merely a repetition of the fantasy narrative that has been identified throughout this commentary as the vehicle of American democracy. Yet it is a narrative that appeals to the promise of better days to come and the necessity of such a promise. After all, we are led not simply to a new beginning but to a future. Prior tells us that we are all "fabulous creatures"; he blesses us with *"More Life"* and concludes with the statement, "The Great Work Begins" (2:148). In a moment of emotional solidarity we start again, at the end of the play, toward the future. We find ourselves gathered with the actors onstage, finally represented, a unified, singularly hopeful crowd of "fabulous citizens." But we also find ourselves being dispersed, projected somewhere down the line of temporal possibility—we begin again to write and rewrite the narrative of what has yet to come. "To this extent," Jacques Derrida notes,

> the effectivity or actuality of the democratic promise, like that of the communist promise, will always keep within it, and it must do so, this absolutely undetermined messianic hope at its heart, this eschatological relation to the to-come of an event *and* of a singularity, . . . that is, to the event that cannot be awaited *as such,* or recognized in advance therefore, to the event as the foreigner itself, to her or to him for whom one must leave an empty place, always, in memory of the hope.[14]

To this extent, then, Kushner has presented us with the full complexity of the temporality of democracy while embracing the hope of democracy. The last scene of the play is a hope-filled moment echoing Whitman's excitement over a democratic body electrified by the future.

Prior may reject the wholeness of the "Tome of Immobility," the unity and singularity of "respite" and "cessation," namely the death, offered to him *now* by the Continental Principalities, but he does not reject, nor can he, the unity offered to him and his friends through the fantasy of democracy. Nor should he. (Nor can any of us who still have political fantasies.) But, if courage is as important to social change as is hope, then, paradoxically, all of us must dare to embrace a different kind of unity and singularity that challenges the narrative of homogeneity, the narrative that attempts to make us all the same in the future. "We" must embrace those aspects of unity and singularity of purpose that enable us to challenge the disempowering fantasies of "We the People" with some different future possibilities. As Giorgio Agamben notes:

Whatever singularity, which wants to appropriate belonging itself, its own being-in-language, and thus rejects all identity and every condition of belonging, is the principal enemy of the State. Wherever these singularities peacefully demonstrate their being in common there will be a Tiananmen, and sooner or later, the tanks will appear.[15]

A fantasy of some future solidarity presumes neither the negation of singularity nor our naive participation in a totalizing myth of hope. Instead, it must be a courageous expression of convergence, here and now, of desire, of love. This is why *Angels in America* is not a straightforward fantasy but a queer expression of a nation that can still be in the future something different than it is at the present: something that genuinely and lovingly offers more life. For those of us, however, who see the tanks, democracy must move back from the future and be the vehicle *now* that it will supposedly someday become.

NOTES

President Reagan's "Farewell Address," delivered 11 January 1989. Transcript printed in *New York Times,* 12 January 1989, B8.

Tony Kushner, *Angels in America: A Gay Fantasia on National Themes. Part 2: Perestroika* (New York: Theatre Communications Group, 1994), 96. Hereafter all references to *Angels in America* will be made parenthetically in the text denoting *Part 1: Millennium Approaches* (1993) and *Part 2: Perestroika* (1994) as 1 and 2, respectively, followed by the page number(s).

1. Thomas Paine, *Common Sense, The Rights of Man and Other Essential Writings of Thomas Paine* (New York: Meridian, 1984), 23.

2. Ibid., 24.

3. Quoted in Howard Zinn, *A People's History of the United States* (New York: Harper and Row, 1980), 95.

4. It was only the Fifteenth Amendment, passed on 3 February 1870, that guaranteed that the "right of citizens of the United States to vote shall be not denied or abridged by the United States or by any State on account of race, color, or previous condition of servitude." Women had to wait until the passage of the Nineteenth Amendment (18 August 1920) before they could vote.

5. Quoted in Zinn, *People's History of the United States,* 96.

6. Quoted in ibid.

7. Ibid., 97.

8. At a time when many, especially the current leadership, of the Republican Party are attacking "big government"—that is to say, government as symbolized by Washington, D.C.—it would be a too facile criticism simply to suggest that gov-

ernment is evil. Many postmodernists have been accused of going too far in their criticisms of liberalism and, as a result, having contributed to the cynical political mood. That many individuals have worked hard to establish a meaningful structure for governing our democracy must be acknowledged; however, such recognition ought not to make us susceptible to the numerous myths that have worked to negate and erase the very real and even heroic efforts of those not legitimized in our history to date. That there are and have been many good people in and out of government working for the past, present, and future of the United States should not persuade us to ignore or forget those who work in the name of a better tomorrow solely to maintain the privileges they enjoy today.

9. Jacques Derrida, once again, punctuates a political inquiry in his complicated way. In *Specters of Marx* (New York: Routledge, 1994) Derrida has us thinking about the time of Marx within the context of time and temporality. He does so by having us consider the time of Marx, the specters of Marx, in relation to Hamlet's claim that "the time is out of joint." Thus, the very issue, "events of the time," gets complicated when one considers, following Derrida, that "time is either *le temps* itself, the temporality of time, or else what temporality makes possible . . . , or else, consequently, the *monde,* the world as it turns, our world today, our today, currentness itself, current affairs: there where it's going okay (whither) and there where it's not going so well, where it is rotting or withering, there where it's working . . . or not working well, there where it's going okay without running as it should nowadays. . . . Time is *le temps,* but also *l'histoire,* and it is *le monde,* time, history, world" (18–19). Hannah, Louis, Belize, and Prior are at/in such a time.

10. See Brian Seitz, *The Trace of Political Representation* (New York: State University of New York Press, 1995). Seitz offers an important analysis of the issue of the one and the many as it concerns the discussion of representation generally (see esp. 17–28).

11. Walt Whitman, *Walt Whitman: The Viking Portable Library,* selected by Mark Van Doren (New York: Viking, 1945), 389–90; emphasis added.

12. Malcolm X, *Malcolm X Speaks,* ed. George Breitman (New York: Grove Press, 1965), 26; emphasis added.

13. Ibid.

14. Derrida, *Specters of Marx,* 65.

15. Giorgio Agamben, *The Coming Community,* trans. Michael Hardt (Minneapolis: University of Minnesota Press, 1993), 87.

"I I I I": Identities in *Angels*

When Girls Collide: Considering Race in *Angels in America*

Framji Minwalla

One evening an actor asked me to write a play for
an all black cast. But what exactly is a black? First of
all, what's his color?
> —Jean Genet, "Preface to *The Blacks*"

Black folk say they believe Simpson is innocent,
and then the white gatekeepers of a media culture
cajolingly explain what black folk really mean when
they say it, offering the explanation from the highest of motives: because the alternative is a population that, by their lights, is not merely counter-nor-
mative, but crazy. Black folk may mean anything at
all; just not what they say they mean.
> —Henry Louis Gates Jr., "Thirteen Ways
> of Looking at a Black Man"

I am trapped in a world of white people. That's my
problem.
> —Belize, *Perestroika*

Fifty years ago Antonio Gramsci elegantly wrote in his *Prison Journals,*

The starting-point of critical elaboration is the consciousness of what
one really is, and is "knowing thyself" as a product of the historical
process to date, which has deposited in you an infinity of traces, without leaving an inventory; therefore it is imperative at the outset to
compile such an inventory.[1]

The interactive histories of race, gender, and class make up many of the
socially determined "traces" that need to be ferreted out and made available
for inspection; we ignore such "critical elaboration" at the risk of hopelessly
recreating the divisive thinking of the past. There have been many acutely
visible examples, in recent memory, of the way glib discussions of race have

led directly to easy racism: the spectacle of the O. J. Simpson trial and verdict, the Rodney King beating and subsequent riots in Los Angeles, the Anita Hill–Clarence Thomas hearings, the Willie Horton advertising campaign. Just this short list suggests that racial tensions in this country tend to conglomerate around black/white issues and have escalated rather than eased in recent years.

While we no longer gaze at the *representation* of yellowness, brownness, redness, blackness—though rarely whiteness—without considering a history of spiraled associations gathering around, or rippling off, racial and ethnic difference, we must start analyzing these categories within their social and demographic contexts. By separating, as we often do, race from class, gender, and local community, we deracinate the very foundations of identity, removing the analysis and judgment of an individual's behavior from the specific understanding provided by cultural memories and heritages.

In this essay I intend to racialize Tony Kushner's *Angels in America*. While the play is not explicitly about race, an anxiety about ethnicity, cultural heritage, and otherness completely saturates its imaginative space. From Rabbi Chemelwitz's opening speech about the impossibility of assimilation to Prior's sentimentally hopeful final lines proposing a new kind of global citizenship in the twenty-first century, Kushner seeds his "Gay Fantasia on National Themes" with direct and oblique allusions to attitudes about race in this country. While analyses of race in *Angels* might focus on the black characters in the play—Belize and Mr. Lies—Kushner's representation cuts much deeper. Race, here, takes under its umbrella such diverse identities as the Jewishness of Roy Cohn and the WASPiness of Prior Walter. While we might not ordinarily think of these characters as racially defined, Kushner makes it impossible for us not to look at them this way. By locating a black man at the ethical center of his fictive universe, and then playing his other characters off him, Kushner makes identity, especially racial and gendered identity, one of the central facts of his drama. Belize occupies that space against which we gauge the ideology, morality, actions—perhaps even the very humanity—of Kushner's other inventions.

Belize connects. Roy and Prior, Prior and Louis, Louis and Roy, Prior and Joe, all either use him as an intermediary or are brought together, intentionally or not, through him. He plays foil to Louis's political angst, confidant to Prior's emotional breakdown, bitch-queen Nurse Ratched to Roy. He is the rational, articulate fulcrum around whom other characters revolve.

Angels, however, is not about Belize. He is neither the focus of the work nor necessary to the plot. Scenes in which he appears seem like digressions—blips during which the forward movement of the drama stops. Belize becomes that character with whom others debate, on whom they test and sharpen their ideas and/or feelings (Louis, Prior), or against whom they measure their social status (Roy, Joe). We know almost nothing about his past or his present, and, when we do discover he has a lover in Harlem, it only confirms all that we don't, and will not, know. We catch marginal glimpses of how he thinks but only through his responses to other characters. He appears not to inhabit his opinions but, rather, to speak for and from the collapsed perspective of a black, leftist, ex–ex–drag queen whose chief concern is not himself but, rather, the physical and psychological welfare of other people.

Belize is a cipher, an enigma, a blankness. His name, even, is not his own—"Belize," as Kushner tells us in his list of character descriptions, is a drag role that stuck. Kushner renders him no personal history, no particular or idiosyncratic psychology. His sexuality, skin color, and ideological bent, however, represent—without the queering distinctions of individual difference—all those communities (gay, black, drag queen) whose identities converge with his. In this mainly white gay world Kushner has fashioned Belize as a complex signifier: the subversive bogeyman that conservatives might fabulate to scare their children. Yet he wants us to consider this possibly most transgressive of invented personae as also the most moral and stable character in the play. By locating Belize in this way, Kushner shifts blackness and effeminacy from the margins to the center, polishing the heterosexistly tarnished surfaces of these identity categories.

Of course, none of this suggests that *Angels* is a bad or flawed play or that it fails because Belize, instead of being "real" enough, serves as the rhetorical mouthpiece for Kushner's opinions. It is, in fact, Belize's very position as a largely iconic representation that gives the play thematic shape. Demonstrating how Kushner uses categories defined by race and gender to move beyond a politics of identity to a politics of citizenship is, perhaps, a more fruitful approach to his work.

One way to get at this is to consider the relationship the play presents between Jewishness and Blackness, specifically to look at how Kushner racializes Jewishness but not Blackness. Manning Marable writes:

> Blackness, in purely racial terms, only means belonging to a group of people who have in common a certain skin color and other physical features. . . . But today . . . Blackness, or African-American identity . . . is also the traditions, rituals, values, and belief systems of African-

American people . . . a cultural and ethnic awareness we have collec-
tively constructed for ourselves over hundreds of years. . . . When
African-Americans think about Blackness, we usually are referring to
both definitions simultaneously—racial identity, a category the Europeans created and deliberately imposed on us for the purpose of domi-
nation, and Black cultural identity, which we constantly reinvent . . .
for ourselves.[2]

Substitute *Jewishness* for *Blackness*, *Jews* for *African-Americans,* and these
words easily could be spoken by Rabbi Chemelwitz at the start of *Millennium Approaches*. Clearly, Kushner knows intimately more about Jews and
Jewish history, culture, and politics than he does about African Americans.
While on the surface the play is more evidently about Jews than it is about
blacks, Jewishness here could be seen as a mirror for all meanings reflected
off race.

The first speech in *Millennium* frames Jewish identity as a racial category. The Rabbi delivers, in a thick Yiddish accent, a eulogy for Sarah Ironson (Louis's grandmother): "I did not know this woman. . . . She preferred
silence. So I do not know her and yet I know her. She was . . . not a person but a *whole kind* of person."[3] This "whole kind" of person—one
embodying a distinct history and heritage, one who shares with the Rabbi a
cultural narrative etched in an immigrant past—becomes Kushner's
emblematic progenitor, Jewish Mother Earth, so to speak. As the Rabbi tells
us, she gave birth to an entire tribe, but the progression of names from her
children to her grandchildren marks the tribe's gradual Americanization:
Morris, Abraham, and Esther become Lesley, Angela, and Eric.

But Sarah Ironson, who crossed an ocean and brought with her "to
America the villages of Russia and Lithuania . . . so that you would not
grow up *here,* in this strange place, in the melting pot where nothing
melted" (1:10), is dead. The ethos she inhabited, the principles she
espoused, the very idea of community and culture within which she
ordered her life, exist only as nostalgic memory, as an imagined past. Kushner comments on the desire, in fact the absolute need, to replicate and sustain a distinct culture—to resist the corrupting hybridization that inevitably
turns an immigrant into a citizen—by placing it in the context of a funeral.
But identity categories are always unfixable, and hybridization, as Marable
suggests, is the inevitable result when communities inhabit the same geographical space. Inherited identities get subsumed by a communal identity
(used as a shield and a weapon against oppression) and by the values and rituals prevalent in the dominant culture.

Louis, Sarah's grandson, has become an American as much as Sarah attempted to remain Russian. But, while Louis is clearly a participant in, and is conditioned by, twentieth-century American culture, the history transmitted to him by his grandmother's generation remains imbedded in his cells; his angle of being is, on some fundamental level, tempered by the history of Jewish immigrants in America. He defines his self racially as an African American or Asian American might. And he does this by fashioning Prior, Joe Pitt, and Belize as "other," just as they shape and claim their own social and psychological selves as other than Louis.

The very concept of race and racial identity, of self and otherness, is further complicated by the way Kushner and his characters construct definitions of gayness. This is clearest in the way he situates Roy and Belize as cultural opposites. When Roy, delirious, asks Belize if they know each other, Belize identifies himself with brutal tenderness, "Your negation."[4] Roy is obviously powerful (in the moneyed, social sense), while Belize is powerless; Roy has merged completely with the club that runs America, while Belize remains plainly outside. Roy passes for a straight man; Belize is effeminate. But Roy, like Belize, is emblematic: he represents white America at its worst. And, also like Belize, he's homosexual.

Roy epitomizes bigoted, closeted, white America, the America that holds the voices of difference at (or preferably outside) its borders, that invests power in the inheritors of a predominantly Christian culture. He has delivered himself wholeheartedly to this cause, erasing his cultural heritage in favor of assimilation because he knows that assimilation brings authority. As he explains to his doctor:

> Labels . . . tell you one thing and one thing only: where does an individual so identified fit in the food chain, in the pecking order? . . . Not who I fuck or who fucks me, but who will pick up the phone when I call. . . . Homosexuals are not men who sleep with other men. Homosexuals are men who in fifteen years of trying cannot get a pissant antidiscrimination bill through City Council. Homosexuals are men who know nobody and who nobody knows. (1:45)

Roy could not be more right about where racial and sexual minorities—blacks, women, homosexuals—fit into America's power hierarchy. And on this scale Belize, a combination of all three (he is an ex–ex–drag queen, after all), weighs in right at the bottom. Obviously, the crucial contradiction Kushner wants to expose is Roy's belligerent blindspot about his own sexuality. He makes Roy into a victim of the social forces that hang homosexuality in the closet, just as he does Joe Pitt. The difference, obviously, is that Roy's homosexuality is an open secret, one that no one mentions because he has "clout," the kind that destroys lives. While Roy's sexuality and Jewishness both were distasteful to those in power, they dared not cross him because he "knew" things. Now outed by AIDS, and disbarred over a legal technicality, he's been disenfranchised. His nemesis, the ghost of Ethel Rosenberg, triumphantly recounts to Roy on his deathbed a comment made by a member of the committee that voted to take away from Roy the vocation he prized most: "Finally. I've hated that little faggot for thirty-six years" (2:113).

Kushner writes Roy with a full understanding of Foucault's knowledge/power axis, and he uses this to superb effect, making Roy simultaneously subversive (he flaunts his homosexuality without admitting its presence) and reactionary (he's a homophobe and a racist). And herein lies the rub—how do we assimilate Roy into our experience of the play? It's too simplistic to understand him as Louis does: "the polestar of human evil, . . . the worst human being who ever lived, [he isn't] *human* even" (2:95). Kushner deliberately goes to great length to make sure we don't make Roy just the villain we love to hate. Even though he has absolutely no redeeming qualities, we're forced to look at him through Belize's and Ethel's eyes. Both characters claim him as one of their own: Belize convinces Louis to pray over the dead body (he is, after all, part of the "family," one of the many felled by the plague), and Ethel leads Louis through the Kaddish (in death, if not in life, identifying Roy as a Jew).

AIDS reduces Roy to a terrified, sniveling animal furiously screaming for succor, till the last flexing his flabby muscles. But Belize and Ethel manage to lend him a modicum of humanity, casting him as an almost tragic figure. They restore to him his racial and sexual identity, and in this moment Roy becomes less than an abstraction, more an individual, defined so because he can be, and has been, acknowledged by larger communities. More important, he is accepted at the convergence of both identities he so categorically denied while alive.

It is Belize who clears the path for Roy's redemption. As he says when convincing Louis to recite the Kaddish: "He was a terrible person. He died a hard death. So maybe. . . . A queen can forgive her vanquished foe. It isn't easy, it doesn't count if it's easy, it's the hardest thing. Forgiveness. Which is where love and justice finally meet. Peace, at least" (2:124). These lines, so different from one of their earliest encounters in which Roy goads Belize, "Move your nigger cunt spade faggot lackey ass out of my room," and Belize spits back, "Shit-for-brains filthy-mouthed selfish motherfucking cowardly cock-sucking cloven-hoofed pig . . . Kike" (2:61), are a measure of how far Kushner has brought them. The sequence of scenes charting their developing relationship progresses from uncompromised disgust toward mutual respect.

Roy is a racist, yes, but not one easily dismissed. When he insults, he does so with dangerously seductive wit and intelligence. Lashing out, putting the squeeze on, hitting where it hurts, are all methods he uses to test his adversaries. His first encounter with Belize is a perfect example:

> I can get anyone to do anything I want. For instance: Let's be friends. *(Sings)* "We shall overcome . . ."
>
> Jews and coloreds, historical liberal coalition, right? My people being the first to sell retail to your people, your people being the first people my people could afford to hire to sweep out the store Saturday mornings, and then we all held hands and rode the bus to Selma. Not me of course, I don't ride buses, I take cabs. (2:27)

Instead of affirming the formation of alliances among marginalized communities, Roy deliberately pries them apart. His description of the "historical liberal coalition" is nothing less than slavery with wages. And the kicker—joining civil rights activists to protest discrimination—suggests the ultimate self-vindication. He wants a response to this, he wants company and conversation, and Belize dutifully replies but not nearly in the way Roy expects: "Mr. Cohn. I'd rather suck the pus out of an abscess. I'd rather drink a subway toilet. I'd rather chew off my tongue and spit it in your leathery face. So thanks for the offer of conversation, but I'd rather not" (2:28). Belize flouts Roy's authority because he knows Roy is dying and because he also knows he can control how comfortably Roy dies.

Roy, who always thought he needed no one, discovers on his deathbed that his physical and psychological well-being depends on two gay men, Belize and Joe. Roy considers Joe's confession of his homosexuality as the ultimate betrayal, and this is, in part, what finally dismantles him: "Every goddam thing I ever wanted they have taken from me. Mocked and reviled." Kushner's aim here is to strip Roy of all assumptions he has ever made about how the world ought to work. Here Belize arrives at his closest identification with Roy—"Join the club"—even offering his real name: "Norman Arriaga. Belize to my friends, but you can call me Norman Arriaga" (2:89).

The final redemption of Roy is one of the few brilliant scenes in contemporary American drama. It is thematically essential for Kushner in that it leads directly to Prior's sentimental envoi at the end of *Perestroika*. But, while Prior's prophecy impresses as a soft, fuzzy anticlimax, Belize's forgiving acceptance of Roy is as cold and hard as Antarctica. And, while Prior's easy lines "You are fabulous creatures, each and every one./And I bless you: *More Life.*/The Great Work Begins" deliver their glibly inclusive appeal to the audience (2:148), Belize, Louis, and Ethel's Kaddish is both symbolic and specific. Symbolic, in that the Kaddish is a performed ritual honoring the dead indirectly by exalting Yahweh; specific here, in that it's spoken to redeem a particular individual. In this moment these three come together— the executed communist, the black drag queen, and the guilty Jew—to mourn, forgive, attain resolution, relieve themselves of a moral burden, and to confront and embrace their other, thereby inventing a more complex yet exact sense of self and a more expansively conceived idea of community.

But Kushner never allows Belize to attain the kind of individuality that even Roy does as he's dying. In the crucial sequence of scenes between Belize and Louis as they debate politics and race in America, we consistently see and hear a particular position, rather than a particular character. Here Louis bumblingly argues as a liberal essentialist even while claiming to deplore this kind of thinking. Belize, throughout and with witty incision, deflates Louis's rhetoric.

The key to understanding the contradictions in Louis's politics is to see how he ignores (or takes for granted) his privileged position as an assimilated white man. Louis can exclaim adamantly, "Fuck assimilation" (1:90), because he doesn't appreciate his own complicity in the disenfranchisement of individuals who are racially other. Of course, his political posturing is entirely conditioned by the guilt and shame he feels at having abandoned Prior to the ravages of AIDS. And Kushner brings this home by visibly placing Prior on the opposite side of the stage—in a hospital bed, his arm hooked to an IV drip—throughout this scene. Louis, here, uses political rhetoric to hide his emotional ambivalence, only managing to betray his overwhelmed inability to grasp how convoluted his logic is.

He begins by claiming "ultimately what defines us isn't race, but politics" (1:90), thereby robbing race of its social meaning. But, as Stuart Hall reminds us,

> The moment the signifier "black" is torn from its historical, cultural and political embedding and lodged in a biologically constituted racial category, we valorize, by inversion, the very ground of the racism we are trying to deconstruct.[5]

This is exactly what Louis does. By refusing the dialogic engagement of race and politics, he falls into the same trap most liberals do: he paints the forest but loses the trees. Race, for Louis, becomes nothing more than skin color, and skin color, like other biologically inherited traits, can always be seen as a surmountable obstacle. As Benjamin DeMott put it in a finely written piece in the *New York Times:*

> Media images . . . remote from urban fact, have been teaching mass audiences everywhere that race differences belong to the past, that inequalities of power and status and means have disappeared, that at work and play blacks are as likely as whites to be found at the top as at the bottom, and that the agency responsible for the creation of near-universal black-white sameness—the only agency capable of producing progress—is that of friendship between the races. . . . Pop versions of history . . . are therefore at liberty either to delete the experience of separateness altogether or to transform slavery and the civil rights movement into periods of happy-black-white collaboration.[6]

Conditioned to see race in these terms, it's no wonder that speech fails Louis in the story he tells Belize:

> In London . . . I met this black guy from Jamaica who talked with a lilt . . . and [said] how the English never let him forget for a minute that he wasn't blue-eyed and pink and I said yeah, me too, these people are anti-Semites and he said yeah but the British Jews have the clothing business all sewed up and blacks there can't get a foothold. And it was an incredibly awkward moment of just. . . . I mean here we were, in this bar that was gay but it was a *pub* . . . just so British, so *old,* and I felt, well, there's no way out of this because both of us are, right now, too much immersed in this history, hope is dissolved in the sheer age of this place, where race is what counts and there's no real hope of change. (1:91)

Louis so obviously misses the delicate nuances of his position. It's not just that racial destiny is important for the British; race manifests itself in the political and economic life of this society so completely that to construct binary oppositions becomes not just impossible but irrelevant. Louis doesn't recognize that these historical valences—as present in Britain as they are in the United States—tangle and knot the lines of oppression in ways that always end up serving and furthering the cause of those oppressing, in his case the "monolith of . . . White Straight Male America" (1:90). To state, as he does, that gay men have "to adopt the same attitude towards drag as black women have to take toward black women blues singers" is to categorize indiscriminately watermelon and chicken soup without considering the intricate differences that make fruit different from broth (1:94).

When Louis says "race," he means "black" and not "Jew." Jewishness for him is an ethnic heritage he clings to because it provides all those cultural stabilizers—community, identity, belonging, history—that make him different from white people. He wants to be just as oppressed as Belize or the Jamaican because the alternative means speaking from, and being part of, the dominant culture, the one that oppresses. But he does this by staking faith in a leftist politics, subsuming his ethnicity in ideology. That's why he can insist that race isn't an overriding concern for Americans even while speaking from his racially defined identity.

Louis expects the fact of the Jamaican's gayness to overcome their racial difference, and is flummoxed when race becomes a barrier he cannot break through. He expects the same camaraderie when speaking with Belize and is equally flabbergasted when Belize keeps punching holes in his analysis. And the distinction Louis makes between Britain and the United States falls apart even as we hear him voice it simply because of Belize's black presence in the scene.

Kushner parallels Louis's story with Belize's pulp romance anecdote about a miscegenist relationship between a slave and the slave owner's daughter:

> "Real love isn't ambivalent." I'd swear that's a line from my favorite bestselling paperback novel, *In Love with the Night Mysterious*. . . . It's about this white woman . . . and her name is Margaret, and she's in love with her Daddy's number-one slave, and his name is Thaddeus. . . . And there's a lot of hot stuff going down when Margaret and Thaddeus can catch a spare torrid ten under the cotton-picking moon, and then of course the Yankees come, and they set the slaves free, and the slaves string up old Daddy, and so on. Historical fiction. Somewhere in there I recall Margaret and Thaddeus find the time to discuss the nature of love; her face is reflecting the flames of the burning plantation—you know, the way white people do—and his black face is dark in the night and she says to him, "Thaddeus, real love isn't ever ambivalent." (*Little pause. Emily [the nurse] enters and turns off [Prior's] IV drip.*) Thaddeus looks at her; he's contemplating her thesis; and he isn't sure he agrees. (1:96–97)

Margaret and Louis both encounter the same obstacle: they assume they know how the people they're with think, only to be brought up extremely short when they find out they're speaking not just a different dialect but another language altogether. Louis, at least, is horrified to find he inhabits a vernacular that simply doesn't describe the world in which the Jamaican lives. But he tries to sidestep this by distinguishing between the histories of England and America. The story Belize tells, then, becomes a brief lesson in alternative history, albeit a fictional history streaked with irony.

In Love with the Night Mysterious is obviously written by someone white. And Belize's acidic retelling is brilliant: it allows Kushner to bring together almost all the ideas about race he's packed into his plays. Thaddeus and Margaret represent a perverse white fantasy of erotic danger and desire. The image of the hunky black man sexually defiling the innocence of the fragile, white woman is a trope that extends to the most subliminal fears many Southern whites had, and still have, about interracial coupling.

The story is ambiguous; it's not clear whether Thaddeus doesn't agree with Margaret's thesis about "real love" because the weight of history makes him betray her or her, him. It's probable, though, that she will turn away from him in the aftermath of the Civil War, that the forces unleashed by the freeing of the slaves will inevitably send her scampering to the safety of her white husband and white world, while Thaddeus continues to live under the shadow of poverty and imminent persecution. Margaret clings to the vain hope that their unwavering love will bridge the racial divide, but her plea is ludicrous because we no longer believe in those chivalric codes prescribing love's endurance through all adversity. But the trope of forbidden sex is powerful here and recurs in *Perestroika* when Roy, high on morphine, mistaking Belize for the devil, invites him into his bed. "You wrap your arms around me now. Squeeze the bloody life from me. . . . Dark strong arms, take me like that. Deep and sincere but not too rough, just open me up to the end of me" (2:76). For Roy AIDS, gay sex, death, and blackness all intermingle, becoming, for his subconscious self, the representation of all that is other.

While it's crucial not to equate prescriptively either Prior with Thaddeus or Louis with Margaret, the two situations parallel each other in some not-at-all-obvious ways. Margaret will abandon Thaddeus just as Louis has abandoned Prior, not because she doesn't love him but because she, like Louis, is caught in the exigencies of fact: Thaddeus is black; Prior has AIDS. Belize's critique of Louis's unthinking platitude undermines Louis's argument completely. And it's clear Louis gets the point: the first question he asks after Belize finishes is, "How bad is he?" (1:97), referring, of course, to Prior's deteriorating condition visible on the other side of the stage. Kushner examines AIDS here as if it were a racial category itself. Roy's explicit and Louis's repressed reaction to it suggests that, like black skin, AIDS is an unerasable biological stigma (more obviously visible in Prior's case because his skin is spotted with sarcomas). AIDS provokes a different kind of prejudice, brilliantly articulated by Roy when he forces his doctor to diagnose him officially as suffering from liver cancer. Worst of all, AIDS produces discrimination not only from straight or closeted people but from the out and proud queer community itself. Louis places Prior in a separate category because he is dying. As Roy discovers: "The worst thing about being sick in America . . . is you are booted out of the parade. Americans have no use for sick" (2:62). It almost could be said that the afflicted and infirm are categorized as inferior just as certain races are and that queer discrimination against persons with AIDS (PWAs) is akin to black discrimination against black queers.

This is the stigma Kushner tries to take apart in his play. He upends easy assumptions about the virus: AIDS makes Prior a prophet, Roy a human being; AIDS teaches Louis and Ethel to forgive and accept. And AIDS reveals the two most "regular" characters in the play, Louis and Joe, to be conflicted charlatans wallowing in their own hypocrisies. What Kushner knows so well is that most gay, white men in America, especially those who will see his play, are just like these two.

One of the most obvious facts about HIV infection is that it doesn't discriminate. The disease includes in its ever-growing roster the rich, the poor, black, white, brown, red, yellow, men, women, children, straights, and queers. The community constructed by the virus is the best global representation of the Rainbow Coalition. AIDS is the melting pot in which ethnicity, gender, class, sexuality, all *have* melted. But this fatal infection also produces its own other—a striving for life, for going forward, for moving outside and beyond the disease.

This, finally, is Kushner's larger frame for *Angels,* the struggle between Prior the prophet who demands to live and the Angels who appointed him, who want him to die. The Angel of America's charge to Prior—contained in the text she/he gives him, *The Book of the Anti-Migratory Epistle*—is to preach a gospel of death.

> Forsake the Open Road:
> Neither Mix Nor Intermarry: Let Deep Roots Grow:
> If you do not MINGLE you will Cease to Progress:
> Seek Not to Fathom the World and its Delicate Particle Logic:
> You cannot Understand, You can only Destroy,
> You do not Advance, You only Trample.
> . . . .
> Vessel of the BOOK now: Oh Exemplum Paralyticum:
> On you in you in your blood we write have written:

STASIS!
The END.

(2:52, 54)

By making Prior into a symbol for all humanity, and then commanding him to give up, the Angels hope to end a world that has become a misery since the defection of their God. Belize's reaction to all this (as Prior replays the scene for him) is as always exactly right: "This is . . . worse than nuts, it's . . . well, don't migrate, don't mingle, that's . . . malevolent" (2:55). At stake here is the very idea of change, of movement from one condition to another, of the creation of history itself. And, while the Angels only see an inexorable devolution of the world toward apocalypse, Prior, Belize, Hannah, Harper, even Louis, hold to the hopeful possibility of improvement in the human condition. Migration, intermarriage, mingling, these contain the catalysts for change, for a potentially better future.

Belize's vision of Heaven—more a vision of the heaven he'd like to see reproduced on earth—might suggest Kushner's ideal community of the future. This heaven very much like San Francisco (but not the San Francisco right after the 1906 earthquake, where the Angels live) is a

Big city, overgrown with weeds, but flowering weeds. On every corner a wrecking crew and something new and crooked going up catty-corner to that. . . .

Piles of trash, but lapidary like rubies and obsidian, and diamond-colored cowspit streamers in the wind. . . .

And everyone in Balenciaga gowns with red corsages, and big dance palaces full of music and lights and racial impurity and gender confusion. . . .

Race, taste and history finally overcome. (2:77–78)

Roy, to whom Belize addresses this speech, mistakenly thinks it a description of Hell. His worldview converges with that of the Angels—resistant to any change in the social order, adamantly sustaining a power structure that even he has been ejected from. Both Roy and the Angels see migration as a metaphor for corruption, contamination, and decay rather than a trope signifying progress and hope. Kushner's appropriately chosen title for the second half of *Angels, Perestroika,* suggests which side of the contest he prefers: reconstruction and renovation. As Una Chaudhuri puts it, "the task of . . . *Perestroika* . . . is to remake a world of meaning that has been systematically unmade. . . . The challenge [America] faces is not . . . to find a new structure, but rather to demonstrate how life can—*must*—proceed without the consolation of fixed orders, 'beautiful theories.'"[7]

The struggle here between cessation and constant motion, between staying put and moving on, between death and "more life," is the struggle Prior embodies. It is in fact his body we see deconstructing even as he rejects the prophecy handed to him, favoring a vision that will lead not to the Angels' idea of paradise but to Belize's. Prior, not Louis, continues the journey Sarah Ironson began, and he continues it by moving past the contradiction that afflicted her immigrant generation, the contradiction inherent in the attempt to plant old roots in new soil. Prior's journey, though, has no foreseeable end. While this forever wandering has its cost, it also has a kind of solution. As Mr. Lies, the imaginary travel agent, tells Harper: "It's the price of rootlessness. Motion sickness. The only cure: to keep moving" (1:18).

Movement and rootedness are both essential facts of the human condition; we betray in countless ways this biological and psychological need to effect and to deny closure. It is appropriate, then, that Kushner's play avoids neat conclusions even while offering us an ending. While nothing appears resolved in the final scenes—Belize and Louis continue to argue; Roy, in Heaven, attempts to represent God in His/Her lawsuit against the Angels; Joe sits alone in Brooklyn, as always on the brink of choosing what next to do; Harper flies to San Francisco (whether real or imagined we don't know), chasing "the moon across America" (2:144)—Prior's final lines offer us an end to what has gone before *and* a way forward. He opens a passage to a new kind of citizenship in the world, one that embraces both the legal and spiritual notion of the word but one that also knows no national, racial, sexual, or economic boundaries. With this Kushner attempts to upset the homogeneity of an America that is only home for white men. But is this inclusive, expansive, pluralistic paradise dreamed of by Belize, seen by Harper, constructed by Prior, possible? Perhaps this, Kushner's central question, is best answered by Oscar Wilde:

> A map of the world that does not include Utopia is not worth even glancing at, for it leaves out the one country at which Humanity is always landing. And when Humanity lands there, it looks out, and, seeing a better country, sets sail. Progress is the realization of Utopias.[8]

NOTES

Special thanks to Alisa Solomon and Evan Zelermyer.

Jean Genet, *The Blacks: A Clown Show*, trans. Bernard Frechtman (New York: Grove Press, 1960), 3.

Henry Louis Gates Jr., "Thirteen Ways of Looking at a Black Man," *New Yorker*, 23 October 1995, 58.

1. Antonio Gramsci, *Selections from the Prison Notebooks*, ed. and trans. Quintin Hoare and Geoffrey Nowell Smith (New York: International Publishers, 1971).

2. Manning Marable, "Race, Identity, and Political Culture," in *Black Popular Culture*, ed. Gina Dent (Seattle: Bay Press, 1992), 295–96.

3. Tony Kushner, *Angels in America: A Gay Fantasia on National Themes. Part One: Millennium Approaches* (New York: Theatre Communications Group, 1994), 10; emph. added. All further citations will be noted in the text.

4. Tony Kushner, *Angels in America: A Gay Fantasia on National Themes. Part Two: Perestroika* (New York: Theatre Communications Group, 1993), 78. All further citations will be noted in the text.

5. Stuart Hall, "What Is This 'Black' in Black Popular Culture?" in *Black Popular Culture*, ed. Gina Dent (Seattle: Bay Press, 1992), 29–30.

6. Benjamin DeMott, "Sure, We're All Just One Big Happy Family," *New York Times*, 7 September 1996, sec. 2.

7. Una Chaudhuri, *Staging Place: The Geography of Modern Drama* (Ann Arbor: University of Michigan Press, 1995), 258–59. Chaudhuri gives a fascinating reading of Kushner's play, linking it to a larger "geopathology" of postcolonial migrations in contemporary drama.

8. Oscar Wilde, "The Soul of Man under Socialism," *De Profundis and Other Writings* (London: Penguin, 1954), 34.

Wrestling with *Angels:*
A Jewish Fantasia

Alisa Solomon

Joe Pitt's first homosexual act in *Angels in America* is to inhale. When Louis takes him home in the second scene of *Perestroika,* he seduces Joe by teaching him that "Smelling. Is desiring." Louis sniffs "Little molecules of Joe . . . Up my nose" and instructs Joe to do the same. "The nose," Louis proclaims, "is really a sexual organ."[1]

This scene daringly displays queer, polymorphous pleasure. Contrasting with both Louis's abject, aborted quickie in Central Park (1:52–58) and Joe's cold postcoitus curtness with Harper (2:106–7), this exchange offers the play's most erotic, most satisfying depiction of sex. The satisfaction is emotionally complicated, of course, by the audience's knowledge that for both partners the encounter is, in essence, adulterous: what makes this sex illicit is not that it is homo but that it has repercussions for Harper and for Prior. Throughout the play personal betrayals such as these get tangled up with issues of national and cosmic conscience.

Kushner (the son of a conductor, after all) chose well when he labeled *Angels in America* a "Gay Fantasia": in musical works that bear this name the composer's imagination takes precedence over conventional styles and forms, often allowing for a number of themes to develop contrapuntally. Indeed, Kushner's dramatic structure is itself pleasurably polymorphous. Constantly introducing new layers of irony, Kushner places each scene, no matter how domestic, within a complex psycho-sexual-political landscape. And, in turn, each scene shades in and textures more of that landscape.

But Kushner might just as well have subtitled *Angels* a "Jewish Fantasia"—at least in a more narrow use of the term, which describes compositions that develop preexisting themes (often drawn from opera) in an improvisatory style. *Angels* is saturated with familiar Jewish imagery and ideas. Obviously, the play features some central Jewish characters; it even opens with a rabbi. But the Jewish suffusion runs deeper. Subliminal associations between Jewishness and sexuality seep out of it like sweat. Its notions of angels, heaven, and a life hereafter are, like Judaism's, sardonic and spectacular. *Angels* shakes its fists at God with Old Testament fury; the divine shows itself in frenzied Kabbalistic figures. Crashing angels and flaming alephs notwithstanding, the play's emphasis in the end, like Judaism's, is on human ethical conduct on earth. And the play's attitude toward history and progress is downright Bundist.

Kushner riffs rhapsodically on these Jewish themes. He invokes them to establish a worldview, and then to queer it, in order to turn his fantasia thoroughly gay.

When Louis takes Joe home, the first thing he does is identify his neighborhood as the place where "Jews lived when they first arrived. And now, a hundred years later, the place to which their more seriously fucked-up grandchildren repair." Affecting a Yiddish accent, he adds, "This is progress?" (2:15). Having asserted his Jewishness once again—as Louis does repeatedly throughout *Angels*—he is ready to take Joe to bed. So he pursues the seduction by declaring his nose—his now unmistakably Jewish nose—a sexual organ. Louis is hardly the first to do so. Sander Gilman notes in *The Jew's Body* that, as anti-Semitism was secularized in eighteenth- and nineteenth-century Europe into a scientific discourse of difference, the Jewish man's nose, linked to his sexuality, was one feature (along with the voice and the feet) that was used to racialize and pathologize him. In popular cartoons and anatomical treatises alike, the male Jew's deformed nose, Gilman writes, "represented the hidden sign of his sexual difference, his circumcised penis."[2] By extension the grotesque Jewish nose connoted a depraved sexuality, at once menacing and effeminate. In celebrating homosexuality—also regarded as depraved, menacing, and effeminate—Kushner claims the nose as sexual organ in an affirming, salutary way. Joe's first queer act is to take a deep breath, that is, to make his nose Jewish.

In the only other major mention of the nose in *Angels,* Roy Cohn calls forth this image just as directly. About midway through *Perestroika* Joe receives Roy Cohn's blessing as Louis—it is a split scene—sits on a park bench waiting to seek Prior's blessing. Joe kneels in front of Roy in this sexually charged, oedipal exchange, and Roy banters about the blessing stolen by "what's-his-name in the Bible" from his father: "what was the guy's name?" (Isaac, Joe reminds him). "Yeah. The sacrifice. That jerk." Tellingly, these tales from the Torah prompt Roy's memory of his mother (soon to be figured through Ethel as an archetypal Yiddishe momma). "See this scar on my nose?" asks Roy. "When I was three months old, there was a bony spur, she made them operate, shave it off. They said I was too young for the surgery, I'd outgrow it but she insisted. I figure she wanted to toughen me up. And it worked" (2:82–83).

This symbolic circumcision simultaneously marks Roy's Jewishness and his refusal to participate in stereotypical Jewish victimhood. Claiming his place in the Zionized transformation of Jewish American moral identity that Paul Breines traces in his book, *Tough Jews*,[3] Roy contrasts with Louis who, in the lines immediately following, clings for moral legitimacy to his histrionic suffering. Justifying his flight from Prior, Louis casts himself as the wounded party and chastises Prior for usurping his role, his birthright: "You never trusted me," he says. "you never gave me a chance to find my footing, not really, you were so quick to attack and . . . I think, maybe just too much of a victim, finally" (2:84).

Certainly, the tough Jew and the victim are not the only roles a Jew can occupy, but they emerge out of a salient cultural tradition that Kushner critiques and queers. Cohn could be an exemplar of the villain described by Edward Coleman in *The Jew in English Drama*, with his "flapping hands, singsong English and Yiddish epithets";[4] Louis follows a long line of what Ellen Schiff, in her book *From Stereotype to Metaphor: The Jew in Contemporary Drama*, calls the "stunned seeker in a world from which all the accustomed values have vanished" in the form of the typical Jewish son—"neurotic, compulsive, plagued with an insatiable libido," and, of course, perpetually racked with guilt.[5]

Kushner juxtaposes these images not only against one another; at the same time, they act as, and are juxtaposed against, two common images of male gayness: the macho man and the sissy boy. Roy the tough Jew/tough queer (a "heterosexual . . . who fucks around with guys" [1:46]) gives his blessing to the Marlboro Man (as Prior designates Joe when he and Belize go to spy on him [2:91]). Meanwhile, Louis, the self-dramatizing Jew/self-victimizing queer (at least in the Central Park scene: "Keep going / Infect me / I don't care" [1:57]), is denied a blessing from Prior, the expiring drag queen who is not just a typical homosexual, as he tells Hannah, in one of the play's funniest and most resonant lines, but *stereo*typical (2:99). Without denuding Jewish tropes of their own meaning, Kushner employs them to reveal and comment on gay tropes. In doing so, Kushner prepares the way for Prior's great work to begin: the stereotypical gay man will become the metaphorical Jew, learning to grapple with life in what Sarah Ironson calls "Azoi toot a Yid" (2:138)—the Jewish way. What's more, making these comparisons, Kushner rebukes and reverses the contemporary right wing's use of anti-Semitic iconography to demonize lesbians and gay men.

The Paradigms of Prejudice

It is hardly a surprise that *Angels* was reviled by right-wing critics. But, more than spewing about the play's leftist vision, its celebration of queer life, or even its display of gay sex, reviews in publications like the *National Review, Washington Times,* and especially, of course, *Commentary* took particular offense at its radical Jewishness. This play, warned Richard Grenier in the *Washington Times,* summing up the nasty nexus of *Angels,* "is not for White Bread America. It's for people who eat bagels and lox, dress in drag, and hate Ronald Reagan. It was funded by (who else?) the National Endowment for the Arts."[6]

Thus, Grenier offers *Angels* as a sitting duck for potshots by the cultural warriors, invoking the specter of a powerful cultural elite controlled by liberal Jews and homos. For Grenier and his cronies *Jewish* and *queer* are rhetorical synonyms for power and moral corruption, always worth keeping on hand in case there is demagogic duty to do; for Kushner *Jewish* and *queer* are mutually revelatory by analogy. Both are potentially exogenous stances from which one might recognize—and maybe even organize folks to hold back—the piling-up wreckage of history. (Roy Cohn and Joe Pitt make certain that Kushner's circumspect optimism does not boil down to goopy identity politics.)

The difference between these two queer-Jewish associations is dialectical: *Angels* was positing promising parallels between queers and Jews at a moment when the anti-gay movement was turning to the structure of anti-Semitism as a template for its organizing.[7] In a 1991 direct-mail appeal for Concerned Women of America, for example, the organization's leader, Beverly LaHaye, asks, "Why do homosexuals, who represent at the very most only 1–2 per cent of the nation's population, wield such enormous political clout far beyond their numbers?" And she answers, "They are aided in the implementation of their hidden agenda by powerful allies in government, education, entertainment, and the media."[8] And we know who *those* folks are.

Bigotry toward scapegoats often takes similar forms, painting the pariah group as inhuman sexual predators, especially dangerous to children (as African Americans, Chinese railroad workers, and so-called witches have been in this country). A misogynist fear of gender confusion is common to all bigotry, too: the men of outcast groups are depicted as effeminate, the women as masculinized. All these common paradigms of prejudice operate in homophobic campaigns. But in recent years the Right has borrowed specific structures and imagery from European anti-Semitism at its most virulent. A cartoon published by the Oregon Citizens Alliance during the campaign for that state's anti-gay Ballot Measure 9 showed a gay man manipulating the strings of government and the economy. It was an exact copy of a famous Nazi cartoon that simply replaced the stooped, hook-nosed puppeteer with a fresh-faced gym boy. Last year on his daily TV pro-gram the "700 Club" Pat Robertson warned that a gay cabal is "rising to the tops of newsrooms" at ABC, CBS, NBC, *USA Today,* Knight-Ridder, the *Washington Post,* and the *New York Times* in order to push "the homosexual agenda."[9] Richard Butler, the founder of Aryan Nation, recently explained what he regards as ubiquitous gay wealth: "Homosexuality is financed by the Jews."[10]

In the paradigms of prejudice both Jews and gays are perceived as highly educated, economically well-off, and disproportionately represented in the "cultural elite" and thus are assumed to be gaining such privilege through corruption and conspiracy. Both groups are considered beyond the pale of Christian redemption because of a primal flaw based both on iden-tity and behavior (indeed, the extent to which the behavior constitutes the identity remains in question for both groups). Both can be reviled on the basis of so-called scriptural proof. And both can pass undetected in the dom-inant culture, hatching their conspiracies right under Christian noses.

Classic anti-Semitism stirs panic by describing Jews as sexually rampant and promiscuous, and it projects these fears onto children, as the victims of this lust. The age-old blood libel accuses Jews of slaughtering and feeding off Christian children. Today it is gay men (and when anyone bothers to mention them, lesbians) who are the ones regarded as preying on Christian innocents. A 1990 fund-raising letter from Lou Sheldon for his Traditional Values Coalition put it most bluntly: "They want your children."[11]

In his book *Toward a Definition of Anti-Semitism* Gavin Langmuir talks about the tendency, in the mythic thinking that is involved in bigotry, to confuse the literal and the figurative.[12] Langmuir shows how Germany obsessed about Jewish blood in the nineteenth century. Extremists described a cult of ritual murder, while liberals used blood as a metaphor for capitalist exploitation—a modern, secular crucifixion. Both came to regard Jews' own blood as impure and infectious. Some mixed this sym-bolic literalism with the image of the feminized Jew and alleged that Jew-ish men menstruated.

Homophobia commits a similar symbolic literalism, especially because the characteristics classically attached to a demonized group—uncontrol-lable sexuality, gender transgression, and impure blood—seem so palpably present in gays. AIDS gives literalness, though hardly accuracy, to accusations that gays, like Jews of old, will infect society with their poisoned blood. The religious Right's letters and pamphlets drip with warnings about the threat gays pose to public health.

Certainly, plays that have dealt with AIDS (not to mention AIDS service providers, activists, and public health officials) have countered such appalling lies, presenting sympathetic gay characters with whom mainstream audiences can identify and tossing in a little means-of-infection info along the way. Many of these plays have had gay, Jewish characters; indeed, practically all of them have. What's more, these gay Jews—in William Hoffman's *As Is,* Larry Kramer's *The Normal Heart,* William Finn's *Falsettos*—are the healthy lovers of gentile partners with AIDS. (Harvey Fierstein's *Torch Song Trilogy* predates AIDS, but it too features a Jewish protagonist with gentile boyfriends, and a fraught scene over the Kaddish. Even the first major gay American play gestures toward the gay-Jewish connection; in *The Boys in the Band* the most self-loathing character of all, Harold, describes himself as a "32-year-old pock-marked Jew fairy.")[13] But only *Angels* fords the cultural flood of gay-hatred as Jew-hatred, directly confronting the symbolic literalism of anti-Semitism and homophobia.

Queering the Stage Jew

These other plays, though different from one another in many respects, share a strategy of well-tempered empathy: the man with AIDS is likable, attractive, successful, in the young prime of life. The audience easily regards his illness as unfair and lamentable, guided in their responses by the Jewish boyfriend who fusses over him, frets about his pain, and despairs of the impending loss. His Jewishness serves several functions: it marks the sick lover's identity as "purely" gay; that is, it highlights the gayness of the goy as his primary characteristic, uninflected by ethnicity. Thus, the empathy is driven by an implied analogy: reviling gays is like reviling Jews. Further, the boyfriend, doubly feminized by his homosexuality and especially by his Jewishness, ministers like a Jewish wife, enabling a straight audience to see the lovers as any ordinary couple facing a disease, as just like them.

Not *Angels.* First, Kushner offers a range of Jewish characters and a range of non-Jews, who are also significantly Mormon, African American, or, in Prior's case, a WASP with a heritage. No one is "just gay," so the Jewishness of Louis and of Roy is not a foil for the others' sexuality, nor does it subsume their own. Besides, neither Roy nor Louis functions as a comforting guide through the sick man's suffering. Roy, himself dying, as he likes to say, of "liver cancer" (1:46), may not be summed up so simply as the "polestar of human evil" that Louis labels him (2:95), but he certainly does not offer the audience a model for responding to AIDS. Neither, of course, does Louis; unlike the loyal boyfriends in all those other AIDS plays, Louis bolts. One of many complicating results of this flight for the play's action is that it shapes our sympathy toward Prior: he is not the pitiable nonentity that the tabloids still like to call an "AIDS victim"; rather, he is a victim of Louis's lousiness. That Roy is worse, that even God abandoned humankind when things got messy, hardly lets Louis off the hook.

For all the millennial predictions in *Angels* the Judgment Day that may be dawning is more Talmudic than Christian. (Only Harper seems to have read the Book of Revelations. Everyone else's vatic visions—even Prior's and Hannah's—are thoroughly Old Testament.) Secular as he is, Louis has absorbed a central Talmudic precept: "When a man appears before the Throne of Judgment, the first question he will be asked is not 'Have you believed in God?' or 'Have you prayed and observed the ritual?'—but 'Have you dealt honorably with your fellow man?' "[14] The answer is obvious. Prior states in a stinging rebuke: "There are thousands of gay men in New York City with AIDS and every one of them is being taken care of . . . by a friend or by . . . a lover who has stuck by them through things worse than my. . . . So far. Everyone got that, except me. I got you" (2:88). In failing as a gay man, Louis fails as a Jew.

This connection has set off some of the most virulent attacks on *Angels* by conservative Jewish critics, who seem to resent the obverse suggestion that a good gay could be a good Jew. In a bizarre essay in *Commentary* Edward Norden accuses Kushner—more than Joe, more than Louis, more than the Almighty Himself—of being the great deserter of his people. Positing that, among today's generation of male Jews "gay life has become positively fashionable" and that "the absolute number of Jewish homosexuals has gone through the roof,"[15] Norden condemns the gay Jewish male—and the gay Jewish male playwright—for walking out on his duty as husband and father and for abandoning the Jewish family as the subject of his drama. "Has the American Jewish family of the last generation, a family more and more often with the father vanished, become a nursery for homosexual sons?" he asks, disinterring a gay teleology that really ought to stay buried. And why, he adds, have gay Jewish playwrights like Kushner "shunned the family topic as if *it* were the real plague?" The Ironsons, Norden concludes, "are kept out of sight and mind . . . sparing Kushner's own family."[16] For Norden (even for queer critic Leo Bersani, who should know better)[17] Kushner *is* Louis.

Certainly, the multiple ironies that bounce off of Louis should prevent us from regarding his obsessive, rambling investigations as the unmediated Voice of the Playwright. Some of his ideas are appealing, others half-baked, self-serving, or simply bone-headed; always they are tested against his behavior, and thus he, if not they, are found wanting.

Louis is a Jewish American liberal, and Kushner criticizes him for his failings of conduct and conscience as soundly as he condemns Roy's conservatism. Louis can talk a good game about equality and enfranchisement, but, as his long-winded gush on racism and democracy hilariously shows (1:89–100), his reference point is always himself. And, as his behavior shows, his principles remain abstract. As Belize puts it: "Louis and his Big Ideas. Big Ideas are all you love" (2:96). Prior diagnoses Louis's liberal predicament even better: "You cry, but you endanger nothing in yourself. It's like the idea of crying when you do it./Or the idea of love" (2:85).

An American theater audience—itself largely Jewish and liberal—should recognize him. What's more, in *Angels'* opening scene Kushner constructs the audience as part of Louis's family. Delivering Sarah Ironson's eulogy, Rabbi Chemelwitz addresses us in the second person, identifying us as the descendants of immigrant Jewish grandparents who cannot melt into America, despite the "goyische names" we give our children. Sarah's Great Voyage can no longer be made, the rabbi asserts in his emphatic, Yiddish syntax, admonishing: "But every day of your lives the miles that voyage between that place and this one you cross. Every day. You understand me? In you that journey is" (1:10–11).

But Louis is no simple, self-loathing Jewish stereotype. His gayness, perhaps, removes him from the lineage of sexual incompetents like Portnoy or Woody Allen. Certainly, he can be played as a shlemiel—whiny, sloppy, perpetually flustered—but he should not be. At the very least his sexual assurance with Joe declares him a hunk. When he is around his family, Prior notes, Louis becomes "butch," urging his relatives to call him Lou (1:19). For Prior that suggests that Louis is hiding his homosexuality; but Paul Breines might read it as an assertion of Tough Jew power in the face of pasty immigrant ancestors.

"Jews," the rabbi tells Louis when he seeks to confess, "believe in Guilt" (1:25), and that creed, at least, is one Louis can subscribe to. It is also, Kushner suggests, a liberal creed, one beneath which Louis denies his own power. Louis's family name underlines the strength he will not face up to. Louis Ironson is a man of steel. There is also a suggestion of the minerals surging healthfully in his blood. And he is full of irony: Louis may constantly assert his role as victim—when his argumentative powers fail with Belize, he falls back on the comforting rebuke: "You hate me because I'm a

Jew" (1:94), and he tells Joe, "if I failed to suffer the universe would become unbalanced" (2:33)—but, because we have seen Louis act contemptuously, his attempt to occupy the victim's place is not lovably comic. It may be funny, for being recognizable, but it is also off-putting; it reveals the place where Jewish American liberalism has gotten stuck. Through the course of the play Louis begins to budge. Though he may not be able to repeat his grandmother's Great Voyage, he makes a significant journey in *Angels:* in *Millennium Approaches* he leaves Prior; in *Perestroika* he finds a way back, taking a step, perhaps, beyond that sticking place by linking deed to principle, which is to say, by being Jewish and recognizing that in him that journey is.

Louis is the Jewish victim made victimizer, the limp wimp made lusty, the self-righteous do-gooder doing bad: Kushner calls forth self-conscious Jewish types precisely to undo them. Much as Brecht invokes, say, the image of the prostitute with a heart of gold in *Good Person of Setzuan* in order to unwrap it, Kushner lays these familiar Jewish images before us and invites us to see their contradictions and limitations.

Kushner skewers Roy Cohn in a more troubling way. Our first glimpse of Roy, furiously punching hold buttons and barking into the phone, places him in the tradition of what Ellen Schiff has called the "nefarious stage Jew,"[18] as surely as Shylock's entrance counting ducats establishes him as heir to a villainous line of usurers. In Jewish terms Roy's all-important clout contrasts with Louis's (and Jewish liberalism's) political ineffectiveness.

If we enter Rabbi Chemelwitz's embrace as a liberal Jewish audience, Roy is the villain we, like Louis, love to hate. Kushner makes that easy: Roy's rapaciousness is outrageous, at once appalling and hilarious. In his first appearance he tweaks that liberal audience. Telling one of the people on the other end of his phone to arrange some theater tickets for some clients, he sneers at "fucking tourists." Get them seats for anything at all, Roy instructs, "anything hard to get, I don't give a fuck what and neither will they" (1:12). The audience, smug in its deliberate choice of a serious play like *Angels,* is allowed to have a taste of the superiority that Roy constantly dines on. The joke is then topped by the insinuation of Roy's homosexuality: *La Cage aux Folles,* he tells Joe, is the "Best thing on Broadway. Maybe ever" (1:13).

But Roy's borscht-belt shtick is always accompanied by a sinister cynicism to remind us of the Republican relentlessness rumbling beneath the world of the play (and outside the walls of the theater). In the same scene Roy offers a vision of the universe that prefigures Kushner's image (via Walter Benjamin) of paradise: "I see the universe, Joe, as a kind of sandstorm in outer space with winds of mega-hurricane velocity, but instead of grains of sand it's shards and splinters of glass. . . . Ever have one of those days?" (1:13). Benjamin's (and Kushner's) angel of history has that kind of day all the time. The angel is caught in the "storm . . . blowing from Paradise . . . [that] irresistibly propels him into the future to which his back is turned, while the pile of debris before him grows skyward. This storm is what we call progress."[19] Here is where Louis might put on a Yiddish accent again and ask, "This is progress?" Roy merely ducks to avoid being sideswiped by debris in the storm.

Benjamin was not too sanguine about the ethic of progress, whether it came from the political Right or the Left. Kushner has his suspicions, too. Louis prattles about being a guy with a "neo-Hegelian positivist sense of constant historical progress towards happiness or perfection or something, who feels very powerful because he feels connected to these forces, moving uphill all the time" (1:25), at the very moment he consults the rabbi about abandoning a loved one in a time of need. In the split scene, as Joe's abandonment of Harper is foreshadowed, Joe echoes Louis from the other side of the political spectrum: "America has rediscovered itself. Its sacred position among nations. . . . The truth restored. Law restored. That's what President Reagan's done. . . . We become better. More good. I need to be a part of that, I need something big to lift me up" (1:26).

Roy, naturally, is not interested in progress at all but in power. Indeed, when his friend Martin extols the Reagan revolution to draw Joe to Washington, Roy is uncharacteristically noncommittal (1:63–64). What matters for him is having a toady in Justice—one to protect him from the anti-Semitism he assumes will seal his doom. Only in the face of disbarment does the Tough Jew imagine himself the Jewish victim: Roy suspects that those on the disbarment committee regard him as "some sort of filthy little Jewish troll" (1:67). But the jury never invokes Jewish epithets—only gay ones. Like Louis, in 1980s America Roy cannot retreat into Jewish abjecthood. These days, the target of anti-Semitism is queers. Reporting on the verdict, Ethel says, "One of the main guys on the Executive leaned over to his friend and said, 'Finally. I've hated that little faggot for thirty-six years'" (2:113).

The barking, the wheeler-dealering, the power-grabbing—Roy is a discomfiting caricature of the American Tough Jew who has climbed the ladder but still cannot pass at the country club. Certainly, Kushner exaggerates (in the *National Review* Richard Grenier brags about having known the real Roy Cohn and chastises Kushner for making him so "very Jewish").[20] As the iconic conservative closet case who sent the Rosenbergs to the electric chair and, as McCarthy's honcho henchman, picked off untold queers and Jews, Roy has to be extreme. Unlike Prior, both a typical and *stereo-*

typical homosexual, Roy is too excessive to be typical of anything. Liberal Louis still wants to claim a stake in what Kurt Dittmar called "the topos to which Jewish American literature essentially owes its victory in the period following the Second World War," namely, "the Jew as a morally sensitive outsider and exemplary victim in a world that had become inhuman."[21] "Fuck that," Roy might say. "Jews are insiders now. Who cares about inhuman?"

Roy can be out—and outrageous—as a Jew precisely because of the power he, and American Jews in general, have acquired. That same achievement deflects Louis's will to morally sensitive outsiderhood and exemplary victim status. The position will be passed to Prior (and echoed in Belize).

Roy's Yiddishisms are viciously comic. More than that, they humanize him even as they mock him. Roy's deathbed scene is a brilliant Brechtian mixture of pathos, slapstick, and moral disjunction. Even as Ethel pronounces her pleasure in his misery, Roy, delirious, sees her as his "Muddy" and makes her sing him a Yiddish lullaby. This is quintessential Broadway sentimentality: a yiddishe momma cooing that old favorite, "Tum-bal-alaike," to her expiring, prodigal *bocher*. Roy then springs up like a borscht-belt comic to deliver a joke that would get anyone booed off the stage at Grossinger's: "I fooled you Ethel . . . I just wanted to see if I could finally, finally make Ethel Rosenberg sing! I WIN!" (2:114–15). Shamelessly mawkish, the scene invites us to feel sorry for Roy then jolts us out of the schmaltz, allowing us to regard our own will to embrace Roy. Ethel becomes Ethel again and Roy her executioner.

Only the recitation of the Kaddish over Roy's body a few scenes later surpasses the complexity of Roy's death scene. This time the emotion is more raw.

All the troubled issues of *Angels* are economically recapitulated in this brilliant little scene, as if Kushner is gathering them together one last time before transforming them with the new variations to come: forgiveness, retribution, expiation, conservative savagery, unjust policies around AIDS, the meaning of being gay, the burden of being Jewish. And it is hysterical. "My New Deal Pinko Parents in Schenectady would never forgive me, they're already so disappointed," says Louis, summing up a generation of American Jewish history and culture. "'He's a fag. He's an office temp. And *now look*, he's saying Kaddish for Roy Cohn'" (2:124). The ironies are even thicker. In saying Kaddish for Roy Cohn, Louis secures the AZT: he finally does something to help Prior—but something, it turns out, that Prior does not want.

It hardly matters that Louis, "an intensely secular Jew" (2:125), does not know the prayer—nor even that it is written not in Hebrew but in Aramaic. Ethel is there to guide him.

My Yiddishe Commie

Ethel Rosenberg's presence in *Angels* is delicate, complex, and wonderfully impertinent. If Roy and Louis (however critically) inhabit two regions on the cultural and political map of Jewish-American experience, Ethel occupies a third, more discomfiting spot—indeed, one that questions some of the core principles of capitalist America itself. Ethel hovers outside the popular imagery within and against which Roy and Louis are defined, and this difference is marked, first of all, by her gender. (The ghost of Julius would hardly have done.)

The iconography inscribing tough Roy and wandering Lou and their sexual, circumcised noses is relentlessly masculine. Kushner has Ethel try on one role in the repertoire of Jewish archetypes available to middle-aged women: the Yiddishe momma. That Roy goads her into the performance, and then comically bursts the illusion, only emphasizes the artificiality and inapplicability of such cultural clichés for an unresolved figure like Ethel. Roy knocks her from this position when he tells Joe that winning the death penalty for the Rosenbergs was the greatest achievement of his career (justifying his illegal ex parte pleadings with "that timid Yid nebbish on the bench"). Roy mocks how "that sweet unprepossessing woman, two kids, boo-hoo-hoo, reminded us all of our little Jewish mamas" (1:108).

During the Rosenberg case this sweet, innocent image of Ethel, duped by idealism and a zealous husband, competed with charges that Ethel was the hardcore Commie who had dragged poor Julius along: portrayals of Ethel alternated between Yiddishe momma and castrating shrew. Kushner, not taking up the question of Ethel's guilt in the "atom spy" case, relieves her of both stereotypes. She can comment like a momma on her first entrance, that Roy used to be "Zaftig, mit hips" (1:111). At the same time, she not only cannot forgive him; she hopes to "see you die more terrible than I did. And you are, 'cause you're dying in shit, Roy, defeated. And you could kill me, but you couldn't ever defeat me" (2:114).

Whether the Rosenbergs were completely framed is not the issue for *Angels* (though the illegality of the proceedings is a fact Kushner makes sure to mention). What matters is Ethel's power to recall, in strong, testy terms, a Jewish-American politics that looked beyond Roy's rabid individualism and Louis's vapid liberalism. Ethel secures the structural link between Rabbi

Chemelwitz, who opens *Millennium Approaches* by delivering a eulogy for "a whole kind of person" (1:10), and the Oldest Living Bolshevik (played by the same actor), who opens *Perestroika,* delivering a eulogy for theory. The rabbi addresses the audience as the children of Jewish immigrants; the Bolshevik addresses us as comrades. Ethel, of course, is both.

Kushner doesn't argue for or even lay out Ethel's communist ideals. She is, indeed, a specter. She haunts, and taunts, her arch-conservative executioner. More figuratively, she shadows American Jewish liberalism, a ghost lingering in a politics without spirit.

Ethel also taps into a reservoir of cultural association between Jewish political radicalism and the erotic, a literary trope in Jewish American work that portrays, as David Biale suggests in *Eros and the Jews,* "immigrant, working-class, and left-wing Jews as positive erotic symbols [that] subvert both the male and female stereotypes of much of mass culture."[22] In E. L. Doctorow's fictional reconstruction of the Rosenberg case, *The Book of Daniel,* Biale argues, the couple offers "Jewish refutations of America's erotic and political hypocrisy."[23] Doctorow (who gives the Rosenbergs the suggestively sacrificial name Isaacson) emphasizes their healthy sexuality: "They used to make the house rock. They really went at it, they balled all the time."[24]

The prime example of what Biale calls the "wedding of Jewish political radicalism to sexual liberation" is Emma Goldman, a free-love anarchist, he writes, whose "utopian philosophy demonstrates that American Jews have a tradition of erotic revolution."[25] In fact, the first words out of Louis's mouth in *Angels* are "My grandmother actually saw Emma Goldman speak" (1:19).

Ethel's body may lie "a-moulderin' in the grave," as Roy sings about that other executed "traitor," abolitionist John Brown (2:112), but her "truth is marching on." It is Prior who picks up the banner.

Azoi Toot a Yid

In 1949 Leslie Fiedler rocked the literary world by asserting:

> in this apocalyptic period of atomization and uprooting, of a catholic terror and a universal alienation, the image of the Jew tends to become the image of everyone; and we are perhaps approaching the day when the Jew will come to seem the central symbol, the essential myth of the whole Western world.[26]

In *Angels* Kushner audaciously declares a new apocalyptic period, when the gay man with AIDS will become the essential myth of the whole Western world. Kushner assigns Prior this metaphorical role, and he does so by making him, in iconic terms, Jewish.

Having recalled and critically examined three Jewish American cultural and political traditions in Roy, Louis, and dead Ethel, Kushner suggests that American Jews, having achieved a level of comfort and even clout in the United States, have abandoned their commitment to erotic and political liberation. If the millennium is approaching, the religious tradition of Judaism is being supplanted by the worldwide reign of Christianity; perestroika, meanwhile, presages the worldwide reign of free-market capitalism, supplanting a secular vision of redemption (however failed) associated with leftist Jews. Now, Kushner ventures, it is queers, conflated with Jews in the cultural unconscious, who bear the responsibility.

Kushner is not so crass as to equate AIDS with the Holocaust (indeed, the Holocaust sits within the play's theme of God's abandonment with such implicit power that Kushner need not name it when the Angels and Prior catalogue the history of human horror). Still, in Prior's first scene he is associated with Louis's grandmother. We know what would have happened to her had she not made the Great Journey to America. Prior rolls up his sleeve to reveal the blue mark on his arm that condemns him to death (1:21). Near the play's end, denouncing God's disappearance, he counsels the Angels to "take Him to court. He walked out on us. He ought to pay" (2:136)—a theology that bears not a trace of Christianity.

The rabbi says that "such Great Voyages" as Sarah's "in this world do not any more exist" (1:10). But the primary action of *Angels* is Prior's Great Voyage, both in this world and beyond. Being *stereo*typical, he, like Sarah Ironson, is a "whole kind of person." Like Jacob, Prior wrestles with the Angel and seeks the blessing of more life. And, like Jacob, the struggle leaves him limping—Prior walks with a cane at the end of *Perestroika*. Most important, Prior takes on a new, collective identity by holding out against the Angel. Through the wrestling Jacob became Israel, the one who will strive and struggle with God—or, in Harold Bloom's evocative phrase, "God-clutcher."[27] Similarly, Prior becomes the "central symbol" Fiedler describes, acquiring the authority to stand in the place of Rabbi Chemelwitz and the Oldest Living Bolshevik and offer the audience the possibility of a new vision.

If the Rabbi and the Bolshevik constructed the audience as Jewish and communist, in *his* direct address Prior queers us. "You are fabulous creatures" is not a sop to a crowd that needs to be congratulated for sitting through a seven-hour epic drama (though it can, alas, be played that way) (2:148). Rather, Prior's closing lines, as reproving and hortatory as the Rabbi's and the Bolshevik's, include us in order to challenge us. Queers "will be citizens," he declares, without giving up their queerness, just as Jews in France demanded citizenship without assimilation.

Louis tells the story of Bethesda in Jerusalem, and Hannah promises to take Prior to bathe in the restorative fountain that will spring up where her foot touches down. That Louis is quick to point out (perhaps in contradiction to Hannah's view) that they do not *literally* mean Jerusalem—"I mean we don't want this to have sort of Zionist implications. . . . But on the other hand we *do* recognize the right of the state of Israel to exist"—yanks the play out of the sentimental closure that some directors might yearn to give it (2:148). The myth is comforting. But Louis and Belize's emerging debate over the rights of Palestinians (besides being funny and recapitulating Kushner's critique of the trajectory of Jewish American politics) reminds us that mythic stories offer, at best, imagery to inspire the search for redemption. Progress, that dubious but necessary goal, is made in the messy work of politics on earth. That is the "Great Work" Prior challenges us to engage. It "Begins" when we leave the theater.

NOTES

1. Tony Kushner, *Angels in America: A Gay Fantasia on National Themes. Part Two: Perestroika* (New York: Theatre Communications Group, 1994), 17. All subsequent quotations from *Angels,* including from *Part One: Millennium Approaches* (New York: Theatre Communications Group, 1993), will be included in parentheses in the text.

2. Sander Gilman, *The Jew's Body* (New York and London: Routledge, 1991), 189.

3. Paul Breines, *Tough Jews* (New York: Basic Books, 1990).

4. Edward Coleman, *The Jew in English Drama: An Annotated Bibliography* (1943; reprint, with Edgar Rosenberg, "The Jew in Western Drama: An Essay and a Checklist," and Flola L. Shepard, "Addenda to the Jew in English Drama," New York: New York Public Library and Ktav, 1968), xvii.

5. Ellen Schiff, *From Stereotype to Metaphor: The Jew in Contemporary Drama* (Albany: State University of New York Press, 1982), 150, 151.

6. Richard Grenier, "With Roy, Ethel, and 'Angels,'" *Washington Times,* 18 April 1993, B3.

7. This argument was first developed in a piece in the *Village Voice,* "The

Eternal Queer: In the Symbolic Landscape of Homophobia, We Are the Jews," 27 April 1993, 29, 34.

8. Beverly LaHaye, letter to "Concerned Friend," February 1991, mass mailing by Concerned Women of America.

9. Pat Robertson on the "700 Club," 30 May 1995, quoted by Frank Rich, "The Gloved Ones," *New York Times*, 18 June 1995, sec. 4, p. 15, col. 3.

10. Quoted by Phillip Weiss, "Off the Grid," *New York Times Magazine*, 8 January 1995, 38.

11. Reverend Louis P. Sheldon letter, 1990, mass mailing by the Traditional Values Coalition.

12. Gavin I. Langmuir, *Toward a Definition of Antisemitism* (Berkeley and Los Angeles: University of California Press, 1990). See also Langmuir, *History, Religion and Antisemitism* (Berkeley and Los Angeles: University of California Press, 1990).

13. Mart Crowley, *The Boys in the Band* (New York: Samuel French, 1968), 48.

14. Talmud: *Shabbath,* 31a, quoted in *Leo Rosten's Treasury of Jewish Quotations* (New York: McGraw-Hill, 1972), 279.

15. Edward Norden, "From Schnitzler to Kushner," *Commentary* (January 1995): 56.

16. Ibid., 57.

17. Leo Bersani, *Homos* (Cambridge: Harvard University Press, 1995), 69. Bersani, quoting the rambling speech to Belize on American democracy and racism (1:92), ascribes Louis Ironson's point of view to Kushner himself: "For Kushner, to be gay in the 1980s was to be a metaphor not only for Reagan's America but for the entire history of America, a country in which there are 'no gods . . . no ghosts and spirits . . . no angels . . . no spiritual past, no racial past, there's only the political.'"

18. Schiff, *From Stereotype to Metaphor*, 8.

19. Walter Benjamin, "Theses on the Philosophy of History," *Illuminations,* ed. Hannah Arendt, trans. Harry Zohn (New York: Schocken Books, 1969), 258.

20. Richard Grenier, "The Homosexual Millennium: Is It Here?" *National Review,* 7 June 1993, 55.

21. Kurt Dittmar, "Die jüdische 'Renaissance' in der Literatur der USA nach 1945," quoted (and trans.) by Breines in *Tough Jews,* 171.

22. David Biale, *Eros and the Jews: From Biblical Israel to Contemporary America* (New York: Basic Books, 1992), 222.

23. Ibid., 220.

24. E. L. Doctorow, *The Book of Daniel,* quoted in ibid., 220.

25. Ibid., 220.

26. Leslie Fiedler, "What Can We Do about Fagin?: The Jew-Villain in Western Tradition," *Commentary* (May 1949): 418.

27. Harold Bloom, *The Book of J* (New York: Vintage Books, 1990), 218.

Prior to the Normans:
The Anglo-Saxons in
Angels in America

Allen J. Frantzen

Rich in references to migratory voyages and the Chosen People, *Angels in America* advances a broad argument about history and progress. David Savran has shown the importance of Mormon "spiritual geography" to the play's "conceptualization of America as the site of a blessed past and a millennial future." Savran demonstrates that Mormonism was among the evangelical, communitarian sects formed in reaction to the individualism fostered by Jacksonian democracy and the ideology of Manifest Destiny.[1] My purpose in this essay is to examine a key element in the racial basis of Manifest Destiny, the ideology of Anglo-Saxonism, and its operations in the play.[2] *Anglo-Saxonism* is Reginald Horsman's term for the use of early English or Anglo-Saxon culture to serve political aims in later periods; its premise is that the English are a Chosen People and a superior race.[3] Anglo-Saxonism enters *Angels in America* through the lineage of Prior Walter, who is a token of the WASP culture against which the oppressed peoples of the play, Jews and blacks in particular, strive. Prior Walter traces his medieval origins to the Norman Conquest (A.D. 1066), but Anglo-Saxon history, and its use of the myth of the Chosen People, reach back well before the Venerable Bede's *Ecclesiastical History of the English People,* completed in 731. Bede's *History* is among the first Anglo-Saxonizing texts in English history; no work exerted greater influence on subsequent understandings of who the English were or how, as Christians, they came to be closely associated with the angelic.[4] Bede's portrayal of the English matches some features of the ideology of Manifest Destiny, which claimed for the Chosen People "a preeminent social worth, a distinctively lofty mission, and consequently unique rights in the application of moral principles."[5] Numerous nineteenth-century accounts used the racial purity of the Anglo-Saxons to justify westward expansion and empire building. Anglo-Saxon culture was thought to have been inherently democratic and the Anglo-Saxons egalitarian, self-governing, and free; the descendants of a people who so perfectly embodied the principles of American democracy had, it appeared, natural rights over lesser peoples and their lands.

The *Angli,* the Angels, and the English

In order to connect the Anglo-Saxon past to the play's themes of nationalism and political change, it is necessary to know how the Anglo-Saxons came to be seen as preeminently worthy. Bede's chief source for early British history was Gildas, from whom Bede derived the motif of the Chosen People.[6] Following the withdrawal of the Romans, the native British were briefly beset by Irish and Pictish assailants but soon enjoyed "an abundance of corn in the island as had never before been known." Thereupon both clergy and laity "cast off Christ's easy yoke and thrust their necks under the burden of drunkenness, hatred, quarrelling, strife, and envy and other similar crimes." Devastated by a plague, the British were again attacked by their enemies and requested assistance from the Angles, Saxons, and Jutes,[7] allies (they are thought to have arrived ca. A.D. 450) who turned on their hosts and conquered them. "To other unspeakable crimes, which Gildas their own historian describes in doleful words, was added this crime, that they never preached the faith to the Saxons or Angles who inhabited Britain with them," Bede writes. The Anglo-Saxons become the new Chosen People, but it is Gregory the Great (d. 604) who appoints "much worthier heralds of the truth to bring this people to the faith."[8]

Having shown that the British were unworthy of God's special protection, Bede turns to Rome both to indict the British for neglecting God's word and to establish the origins of English Christianity at the heart of God's kingdom on earth. He relates an anecdote that took place sometime before Gregory became pope in 590, when Gregory stopped at a marketplace where merchants were displaying their wares. "As well as other merchandise he saw some boys put up for sale, with fair complexions, handsome faces, and lovely hair," Bede writes. Gregory asked where the boys were from and learned that they were from Britain, where all the inhabitants were fair in appearance and also heathen. "Alas that the author of darkness should have men so bright of face in his grip," Gregory replied, "and that minds devoid of inward grace should bear so graceful an outward form." The boys were of the race of the *Angli.* "Good," he said, "they have the face of angels, and such men should be fellow-heirs of the angels in heaven." He learned that the people of the kingdom were the *Deiri.* "*Deiri,*" he replied, "*De ira!* good! snatched from the wrath of Christ and called to his mercy. And what is the name of the king of the land?" The king was *Ælle,* and this prompted Gregory's third pun. "Alleluia!" he said, "the praise of God the Creator must be sung in those parts."[9] The story aptly illustrates, as Bede has it, why Gregory "showed such earnest solicitude for the salvation of our race."[10] Eager to convert the Angli, Gregory went to the pope to volunteer for the mission himself. The pope was willing to grant his request, but the citizens of Rome would not allow him to leave. When Gregory became pope he sent preachers to the English with his encouragement and prayers.[11]

The boys whom Gregory saw were the untaught descendants of Anglo-Saxon invaders, who, 150 years after the Anglo-Saxon invasion (ca. A.D. 450) were still pagan. The translator to whom Gregory spoke knew that the boys had come from Anglia and called them *Angli,* a term that had specific cultural and geographic meaning for Bede. In his description of the settlements of Germanic tribes Bede explains that the Angli came "from the country of the Angles, that is, the land between the kingdoms of the Jutes and the Saxons, which is called *Angulus.*" He adds that "*Angulus* is said to have remained deserted from that day to this."[12] The term *Angli* seems to have had two geographical meanings for Bede. First, according to Bertram Colgrave and R. A. B. Mynors, Bede uses all occurrences of *Angli* and its derivatives in the *History* to mean "English."[13] Bede also uses *Anglian* in a more specific sense to distinguish specific regions where the continental tribes settled; in this second sense *Anglian* also refers to Anglia, Mercia, and Northumbria.[14] Born near the monastery of Monkwearmouth-Jarrow, Bede himself was both Northumbrian and Anglian.[15]

Seen in Bede's perspective, this anecdote shows a complete break between the lapsed early Christian communities of the British, who proved unworthy of God's protection, and the Anglo-Saxons, whose descendants were to be converted by Gregory's missionaries. Gregory's comparison of the Anglian boys to angels both elevated Bede's ancestry and his Northumbrian origins and resignified the word *Anglian* in a Christian context.[16] It is a story of linguistic conversion with immense consequences for the future of Christianity in England.

Bede's account of the incident in the marketplace affirms a natural affinity between Gregory and the Anglo-Saxons that transcends racial differences. It might seem curious that Gregory should find the boys attractive; his admiration suggests that he prefers their unfamiliar appearance (light complected and light haired) to that of his own people. The discrepancy can only be explained by acknowledging that the anecdote originates with an English author whose views Gregory is made to share and is merely a pretext for verbal play that valorizes their race, their nation, and their king.

Being young, innocent, and beautiful, the boys themselves represent a benign and neglected heathendom. As perfectly blank slates, they are promising images of a new beginning, not only a Chosen People but also angelic heralds of the new Christian age.

This angelic identity, superimposed on children who are slaves, is disquieting. The anecdote emphasizes the spiritual concerns both of Gregory, who wishes to convert these heathens, and of Bede, who, writing some 140 years after the episode, wishes to sustain the missionary zeal of the pope he so admired. But Bede achieves these aims only by suppressing two important considerations that trouble his image of the Chosen People. First, neither Gregory nor Bede remarks on the boys' status as slaves; for both, the boys' material condition is merely a figure for their spiritual condition. Bede ignores the depressing commercial reality of the boys' circumstances, which were bound up with the long-established institution of slavery in Anglo-Saxon England, and does not explain how the boys, although members of the dominant race, came to be slaves.[17] Second, Bede also ignores the sexual subtext of the episode. Young boys and some enslaved men were possibly made sexual slaves, as women often were.[18] It fell to John Bale, a Renaissance historian and polemicist writing in the 1540s, to accuse Gregory of wanting to buy the boys for sex.[19]

For all its piety the episode reflects earthly, political concerns of both men. Bede shows us Gregory's concern with establishing a new branch of the church, a Church of England, to correspond to the churches that Rome had already fostered so successfully elsewhere in Western Europe.[20] Bede's own concern is to bolster the success of that church, both in his own native region—Bede dedicated the work to the Northumbrian king Ceolwulf—and more widely. The reference to angels promotes practical concerns and symbolically assists not only the work of conversion but also the political work of affiliating the Anglo-Saxon church with Rome. With the people of Anglia now ready to be changed into "fellow-heirs of the angels in heaven," as Gregory wished,[21] a new age was approaching—the history of Bede's own beginnings. But the boys were not its heralds, any more than they were angels. The other messengers, "much worthier heralds"—worthier than the British, that is—who would bring "this people to the faith," were the missionaries Gregory sent to them long after the boys had been forgotten.[22] That the boys could be compared to angels was not testimony to their proximity to the divine, a role Bede reserved for real angels, but to the angel-like state of their descendants, who would be newly baptized, newly converted, and newly saved.

The Anglo-Saxons in *Angels in America*

The mystique of the Anglo-Saxons as a Chosen People operates through the
WASP stereotype that Kushner exploits in *Angels in America*. Kushner
locates Prior Walter's origins in the mid-eleventh-century, but the Anglo-
Saxon characteristics represented by Prior Walter are prior to the Normans,
whose conquest of England constitutes a particularly troubled originary
moment for the chief Anglo-Saxon of the play. The Anglo-Saxon subtext
of *Angels* emerges in both parts of the drama, *Millennium Approaches* and *Perestroika,* through the association of Prior Walter with the Angel. Prior's
WASP heritage provides a background to which the experiences of other
races and creeds are contrasted, especially those of blacks and Jews. An early
scene in each of the three acts of *Millennium Approaches* reveals something
about Prior's Anglo-Saxon identity (in *Millennium,* act 1, sc. 4; act 2, sc. 3;
and act 3, sc. 1). In the first of the scenes about his lineage Prior jokes with
Louis, his Jewish lover, after a funeral service for Louis's grandmother. Prior
comments on the difficulties that their relatives present for gay men:
"Bloodlines," he says, "Jewish curses are the worst. I personally would dis-
solve if anyone ever looked me in the eye and said 'Feh.' Fortunately,
WASPs don't say 'Feh'" (1:20).[23] A few moments later he reveals his first
AIDS lesions to Louis, who is horrified both by the lesions and by Prior's
mordant jocularity about them. This scene establishes Prior's AIDS status
and his WASP identity and introduces the largest of the cultural themes of
Angels in America: the resistance that biological descent and inherited tradition, embodied here in the body of the WASP, pose to political change.
Bloodlines are curses because they carry the past into the present, creating
resistance to the possibilities of change that the present raises. WASP blood
resists change because WASPs, as they are presented in this play, exist in a
culture of stasis, while other races and creeds, denied that stability and permanence and driven by persecution and need from place to place, have
developed migratory and transitional cultures open to, and indeed dependent on, change.

Having inherited a distinguished past, Prior faces an uncharacteristically
grim future (for a WASP) because he carries a fatal new element in his
bloodline, AIDS. The virus paradoxically reverses the deadening flow of
WASP tradition and prepares for a new social order whose values the
WASP himself will eventually espouse. The virus he bears is both literal
(HIV) and figurative; it is eventually identified as "the virus of time," the
"disease" of change and progress. The Angel who appears to Prior at the
end of *Millennium Approaches,* and who punctuates the play with intimations

of her arrival, claims to herald a new age. When Prior receives his first intimation of the angelic, a feather drops into his room, and an angelic voice
("an incredibly beautiful voice," the text specifies) commands: "Look up! .
. . Prepare the way!" (1:34–35). But the side of the angels is not what we
expect it to be. The angel is not pointing to a new age but, instead, is calling for a return to a previous one. The tradition and stasis that constitute
Prior's Anglo-Saxon heritage draw her; she believes that Prior will be a
worthy prophet precisely because he is a worthy WASP.

Prior is the only White Anglo-Saxon Protestant in the play, according
to Kushner, who happened on Prior's name when looking "for one of those
WASP names that nobody gets called anymore."[24] Discussing Walter Benjamin with a friend so interested in the philosopher that she sometimes
"thought she was Walter Benjamin reincarnated," Kushner referred to the
real Benjamin as the "prior" Walter.[25] The significance of Prior's name
unfolds in a subsequent dialogue between Louis and Emily, a nurse, after
Prior has been hospitalized. "Weird name. Prior Walter," says Emily. "Like,
'The Walter before this one.'" Louis replies: "Lots of Walters before this
one. Prior is an old old family name in an old old family. The Walters go
back to the Mayflower and beyond back to the Norman Conquest. He says
there's a Prior Walter stitched into the Bayeux tapestry" (1:51). As the oldest medieval record mentioned in *Angels in America,* the tapestry would
seem designed to surround Prior's origins with an aura of great antiquity.

The appearance of Prior Walter's name on the tapestry validates Louis's
claim that the Walter name is indeed an "old old" one. But it seriously complicates Kushner's announced aim of portraying Walter as a WASP. The
Bayeux Tapestry, an embroidery that measures 231 feet by 20 inches, is a
record of the political and military events surrounding the Norman Conquest of Anglo-Saxon England in 1066; it has long been regarded as a lucid
statement of Norman claims to the English throne.[26] The conquest has been
seen by most historians, medieval and modern, as the end of a distinctly
Anglo-Saxon culture; generations of Anglo-Saxonizing historians and writers regarded the arrival of the Normans as the pollution of the pure stock of
the race. Christopher Hill has shown that many historians believed that a
"Norman Yoke" had subjugated the Anglo-Saxons and made them subjects
to a foreign crown.[27]

As a record of the Conquest, the Bayeux Tapestry is, therefore, a curiously inappropriate icon of Prior's proud Anglo-Saxon ancestry; however
ancient, it testifies to the subjugation of the Anglo-Saxons, and it marks the
point at which the government and official vernacular language of England
were no longer English. As I will later suggest, Kushner, notoriously ironic

throughout *Angels in America*,[28] might have chosen the tapestry to register precisely this compromised aspect of Prior's lineage. But one's view of that lineage would seem to depend on the uses to which it is put in *Angels in America,* in which it seems intended to represent the Anglo-Saxons as a monolithic, triumphant culture that has reached a symbolic end point in Prior's blood.

Emily (played by the actress who plays the Angel) is somewhat baffled by Louis's high regard for Prior's ancient name and for the tapestry itself. Louis believes that the queen, "La Reine Mathilde," embroidered the tapestry while William was away fighting the English. In the long tradition of French historians and politicians who used the tapestry to arouse public sentiment to support nationalistic causes, including the Napoleonic Wars against the English,[29] Louis pictures Mathilda waiting at home, "stitching for years," waiting for William to return. "And if he had returned mutilated, ugly, full of infection and horror, she would still have loved him," Louis says (1:51–52). He is thinking penitently of Prior, who is also "full of infection and horror," whom Louis will soon abandon for Joe, the married Mormon lawyer with whom Louis has an affair. Louis's view of when and where the tapestry was made is popular but wrong. The tapestry was made in England, under the patronage of William's half-brother Odo, bishop of Bayeux and vice-regent of England, within a generation of 1066, not during the conquest itself, and then taken to the Bayeux Cathedral.[30]

Kushner's mistaken ideas of when, where, and by whom the Bayeux Tapestry was made have significant implications for his definition of *WASP*. Kushner invokes the conquest as if its chief force were to certify the antiquity and authenticity of Prior's Anglo-Saxon credentials and heritage, a point of origin for *English* identity, although, as I have shown, it traditionally represented the very betrayal of the racial purity that *Anglo-Saxon* came to represent. Louis's assertion that the name of a "Prior Walter" is stitched into the tapestry is also without foundation, for only a few characters are named there, none of them Anglo-Saxons.[31] If Prior Walter were an Anglo-Saxon, it is highly unlikely that he would be commemorated in the tapestry, although it is possible he could have been an English retainer of Harold (who was defeated by William). The name Prior Walter, however, is singularly inappropriate for an Anglo-Saxon; it strongly suggests an ecclesiastical, monastic context, as if *Prior Walter* were "Walter, prior of" some abbey, instead of the secular and heroic ethos usually called to mind by *Anglo-Saxon.* Apart from the tapestry there is no evidence either for or against an argument about Prior's origins. Although it is possible that his ancestors were Anglo-Saxon, it is more likely that they were Normans who, after the conquest, settled in England and established the line from which the Walters descended. The original Prior Walter might even have been a Norman who took part in the conquest of the English. If so, in a line of thirty-one men of the same name (or, by an alternate count, if bastard sons are included, thirty-three [1:86]) Prior Walter claims Anglo-Norman rather than Anglo-Saxon ancestry. His long genealogy, to which Louis proudly points, is hybrid at its origins.

We learn more about Prior's ancestry at the start of the third act, when two prior Priors appear to him in a dream (1:85–89). The first to appear, the "fifth of the name," is the thirteenth-century squire who is known as "Prior 1." He tells of the plague that wiped out whole villages, the "spotty monster" that killed him (1:86). They are joined by "Prior 2," who preceded the current Prior by some seventeen others and also died of the plague, "Black Jack," in London. Priors 1 and 2 are not merely ancient ancestors, however; they are the forerunners of the angel whose arrival spectacularly concludes the play. To *"Distant, Glorious Music"* (1:88) they recite the language later used by the angel; as her messengers, they are "sent to declare her fabulous incipience." "[The angels] chose us," Prior 2 declares, "because of the mortal affinities. In a family as long-descended as the Walters there are bound to be a few carried off by plague." Neither Prior 1 nor Prior 2 understands why Prior is unmarried and has no wife, although the second Prior understands that the plague infecting Prior is "the lamentable consequence of venery" (1:87). Only later, when they see him dancing with Louis, does Prior 1 understand: "Hah. Now I see why he's got no children. He's a sodomite" (1:114). Prior Walter is, therefore, the end of his line. After him the WASP hegemony of the Walters, apparently unbroken from the mid-eleventh century to the present, will cease to exist.

The vague and portentous sense of these genealogical relations is clarified in the next scene (1:89–96), in which Louis engages in a long, confused, and painfully naive monologue about race and identity politics in America, much to the disgust of his friend Belize, a black nurse and ex–drag queen.[32] Louis describes a difference between American and European peoples that encapsulates the tension between Anglo-Saxons and other races. "Ultimately what defines us [in America] isn't race, but politics," he says. "Not like any European country where there's an insurmountable fact of a kind of racial, or ethnic, monopoly, or monolith, like all Dutchmen, I mean Dutch people, are well, Dutch, and the Jews of Europe were never Europeans, just a small problem" (1:90). Significantly, Kushner chooses England as site for a scene in which, according to Louis, "the racial destiny," not "the political destiny," matters. In a gay bar in London, as a Jew, Louis found himself looked down upon by a Jamaican man who still spoke with a "lilt," even though his family had been in England for more than a century. At first this man, who complained that he was still treated as an outsider, struck Louis as a fellow traveler: "I said yeah, me too, these people are anti-Semites." But then the man criticized British Jews for keeping blacks out of the clothing business, and Louis realized how pervasive racial stereotypes could be (1:91). In America, Louis believes, there is no racial monopoly; in America "the monolith is missing" (1:90), and "reaching out for a spiritual past in a country where no indigenous spirits exist" is futile. The native peoples have been killed off: "now, . . . there are no angels in America, no spiritual past, no racial past, there's only the political, and the decoys and the ploys to maneuver around the inescapable battle of politics, the shifting downwards and outwards of political power to the people" (1:92). Wiped clean of its indigenous spirits, the nation as Louis sees it would seem to be a blank slate not unlike England before the Anglo-Saxons, ready for migratory peoples (including Jews and Mormons) who bring their past with them as they seek to build a new future. Belize holds Louis's liberal interpretation of American government and culture in utter contempt; Kushner insures that the naïveté of the Jew's liberalism will be exposed and contained by Belize's furious reply that in America race is more important than anything else.

Louis's speech reveals the meaning of *Anglo-Saxon* that is encapsulated in Prior's WASP identity. Although his Anglo-Norman genealogy contradicts Louis's point about the monolith of racial purity that the WASP supposedly represents, Prior is singled out as the recipient of the Angel's visit because he is made to represent the cultural monolith of WASP America, fixed and unchanging, embodying what Louis calls "an insurmountable fact of a kind of racial, or ethnic, monopoly, or monolith." WASP heritage stands conveniently juxtaposed both to Louis's vision and to Louis's own heritage of many small groups, "many small problems" (1:90). Although Kushner might have wished to represent the Anglo-Saxons only as a hybrid people, and hence introduced evidence that points to the eleventh-century intermingling of Norman blood, it seems evident to me that the racial dynamics of the play require that the Anglo-Saxons represent the "monolith" about which Louis speaks. Only then can other races and groups be set up in opposition to them.

Indeed, even in motion the Anglo-Saxons of *Angels in America* are oppressors. One of the most harrowing moments in *Millennium Approaches* is Prior's account of his ancestor, a ship's captain, who sent whale oil to Europe and brought back immigrants, "Irish mostly, packed in tight, so many dollars per head." The last ship he captained sank off Nova Scotia in a storm; the crew loaded seventy women and children onto an open boat but found that it was overcrowded and began throwing passengers overboard: "They walked up and down the longboat, eyes to the waterline, and when the boat rode low in the water they'd grab the nearest passenger and throw them into the sea." The boat arrived in Halifax carrying nine people. Crewmen are the captain's agents; the captain is at the bottom of the sea, but his "implacable, unsmiling men, irresistibly strong, seize . . . maybe the person next to you, maybe you" (1:41–42). The agents of the Anglo-Saxon arbitrarily decide the fates of the Irish in their care. The episode is a stark political allegory, a nationally rendered reminder of the rights of one group to survive at the expense of another, a deft miniature that reveals the power of the conquerors over the conquered, the interrelation of commerce and the immigration patterns of impoverished nations, and, most of all, "unique rights in the application of moral principles."[33]

The force of the association of stasis with Anglo-Saxon heritage—the grand design of *Angels in America*—emerges fully in *Perestroika,* when the Angel of America articulates her ambitions for the WASP and discloses the assumed affiliations between the Anglo-Saxons and the angels. The Angel attempts to persuade Prior to take up her prophecy. "I I I I/Am the Bird of America," she proclaims, saying that she has come to expose the fallacy of change and progress (2:44), "the Virus of TIME" that God released in man, enabling humans to explore and migrate. Angels do not migrate; instead, they stand firm (2:49). God himself found time irresistible and began to prefer human time to life in heaven. The Angel says:

> Paradise itself Shivers and Splits
> Each day when You awake, as though WE are only
>   the Dream of YOU.
> PROGRESS! MOVEMENT!
> Shaking HIM.
>
> (2:50)

A few moments later she shouts, "*YOU HAVE DRIVEN HIM AWAY!* YOU MUST STOP MOVING!" (2:52). God became so bored with the angels that he abandoned them on the day of the 1906 San Francisco earthquake. And who could blame him? In one of the three scenes that Kushner gives performers the permission to cut, if only in part (2:9–10), the angels are shown sitting around heaven listening to a malfunctioning 1940s radio over which they hear the broadcast of the meltdown of the Chernobyl reactor. Their real concern, however, is the radio's malfunctioning vacuum tube. They are a picture of feckless paralysis, obviously unable to respond to the changes forced on them by human or heavenly time. "More nightmare than utopia, marooned in history," Savran writes, "Heaven commemorates disaster, despair, and stasis."[34] The purpose of the Angel's visitation is to recruit Prior as the angels' prophet on earth. Angels, we see, are not messengers from the divine or heralds of change, although that is how we conventionally think of them, and also how Kushner and the play's publicity represent them. Angels are, instead, associated with stasis and with the power of ancient spirits to resist change. Opposed to the flow of power "downward and outward," as Louis puts it, of "power to the people," the angels want God to return to his place so that they can return to theirs.

The Angel's visit is not intended to save Prior from his disease but, rather, to use his disease against him, to try to persuade this "long descended" man (like the Angel in this) to stop the phenomenon of human progress, to get him to turn back the clock. The angel says that she has written "The END" in his blood (2:54). This could mean that the AIDS virus is supposed to ensure his desire to stop time—stop the progress of the disease—and prompt him to proclaim her message, although what is written in his blood could also be his homosexuality, which writes "The END" in a different sense, since it means that he is the last of his line. Later in the scene in which the Angel commands Prior to stand still, symbolically appealing to his Anglo-Saxon love of stability and tradition, Belize dismisses the vision as Prior recounts it: "This is just you, Prior, afraid of the future, afraid of time. Longing to go backwards so bad you made this angel up, a cosmic reactionary" (2:55). Prior and Belize were once lovers; Belize knows him well. Like Prior, three other figures—the Angel, Mrs. Ella Chapter (a friend of Joe's mother Hannah in Salt Lake City), and the nurse (all played by the actress who plays the Angel)—are fearful of movement. Emily does not want Louis to leave the hospital room (1:52). Before Hannah moves to New York to help Joe cope with his schizophrenic wife, Harper, Ella reminds her that Salt Lake City is "the right home of saints" and "the godliest place on earth" and then cautions, "Every step . . . away from here is . . . fraught with peril" (1:83). But Ella's is not a view that the play endorses. Hannah leaves anyway. All the Chosen People do.

Like her, Prior rejects the advice to stay put. He ignores the Angel's command precisely because "The END" is written in his blood; he interprets these words as the angel's wish that he die: "You want me dead" (2:53). No longer the Prior who joked fatalistically about his lesions outside the funeral home in act 1 of *Millennium,* he refuses to die. Because he has contracted "the virus of time," the WASP, who has the most to lose, turns from the past to the future. All the "good" characters in the play are already on the move, already evolving, even Joe's drug-maddened wife, just as all the valorized nations and races in the play have migrated. The prominence of migration and the movement away from racial purity are basic elements of Kushner's thesis about change, which is based on an idea of the Anglo-Saxons, the WASPS, as static, permanent, and fixed. Politics changes racial makeup and breaks down pure races and their racism. Kushner explains:

> Prior is the only character in the play with a Yankee WASP background; he can trace his lineage back for centuries, something most Americans can't reliably do. African-American family trees have to start after ancestors were brought over as slaves. Jews emigrated from a world nearly completely destroyed by European genocide. And most immigrant populations have been from poor and oppressed communities among which accurate genealogy was a luxury or an impossibility. . . . [A] certain sense of rootlessness is part of the American character.[35]

Had Kushner looked into Anglo-Saxon history prior to the Normans, he would have seen that "a certain sense of rootlessness" is also part of the Anglo-Saxon character. American rootlessness was inherited from the nation's Anglo-Saxon founders; Anglo-Saxons in America were hardly a people who wanted to stay put. It is because of their restlessness and their desire to move westward that Louis, as Kushner's surrogate,[36] can assert that there are no angels in America. Kushner's association of WASPs with stasis is his most interesting—and least accurate—reinterpretation of the historical record. Kushner seems to think that Anglo-Saxons—WASPs at least—are not a migratory people. But Bede tells us that after the migration of the Angles to Britain, the land of "Angulus" remained empty "from that day to this." Are there no angels in America? There are no angels in Angulus, either, because the entire population moved to Britain. Thus, the Angles took *their* ancient spirits with them, just as did blacks, Jews, and other migrant peoples.

Thus, Louis's view of history is easily discredited, and not only by Belize. The intermarrying of Anglo-Saxon and Norman families ended the pure monolith of "the English" that Prior Walter supposedly represents. What is true of Prior Walter and all WASPS was true for people in England even before the conquest. "Apartheid is hard enough to maintain," Susan Reynolds writes, "even when physical differences are obvious, political control is firm, and records of births, deaths, and marriages are kept. After a generation or two of post-Roman Britain not everyone, perhaps comparatively few people, can have been of pure native or invading descent. Who can have known who was descended from whom?" Reynolds draws the inescapable conclusion that "those whom we call Anglo-Saxons were not consistently distinguishable from everyone else."[37] After the conquest, of course, the Anglo-Saxons became less "Anglo-Saxon" than they had been earlier, but at no time were bloodlines in Anglo-Saxon England pure; like most bloodlines, they were even then more the consequence of politics than they were of race.

This severing of biological descent and culture is a denial of the power of race to unify a people. That is the good news of *Angels in America* for homosexuals, the new Chosen People of this epic (what epic does not have one?). Like Mormons, Jews, and other racial groups, gay people too are oppressed, without a homeland, and on the move. But, unlike those groups, gays are, first of all, a *political* people, not bound by nation or race. They have no common descent; there is no link between their sexual identity, which the play sees as their central affiliation, and either their biological or their cultural ancestry. So seen, gays are a perfect prophetic vehicle for Kushner's newly multicultural America. Prior succeeds in subverting the angels' design and persuading them to become his messenger; he has refused to become theirs. Their message is that the clock should be turned back to old values and stasis, staying put. His message is that change is good. Won over to humanity's view of time and place, the angels sue God, resorting to time-bound human processes (litigation) to redress grievances. The joke apparently is that the angels' heavenly wishes are inferior to the desires of humanity. The new angels of America know better than the Angel of America because Prior, their WASP spokesman, resoundingly refutes the Angel's call for stasis. God, however, will probably win; his lawyer is Roy Cohn, the demon in *Angels*. Discredited at this point, God is a disloyal lover who has abandoned his angels for (the men of?) San Francisco. The angels, in turn, are also discredited, for they have accepted Prior's suggestion that those who abandon their lovers should not be forgiven, just as Prior will not forgive or take back Louis (2:133, 136).

So Prior moves ahead, not in spite of AIDS but, rather, because of AIDS: the "virus of time" has jolted him out of torpor and self-pity and eventually transforms him into the play's strongest character, a position from which he waves an affectionate goodbye to the audience. Because he is a WASP the Angel singled him out, but because he is a PWA, a Person with AIDS, he rejects her. In *Angels in America* AIDS retains its deadly force (Cohn and others die of it) without killing the play's central character. Obviously weakened, but strong nonetheless, Prior survives. Having been visited by an angel, Prior all but becomes one. "You are fabulous creatures, each and every one," he says. "And I bless you: *More Life*. / The Great Work Begins" (2:148). He recapitulates the last lines of *Millennium Approaches,* in which the Angel declares: "Greetings, Prophet; / The Great Work begins: / The Messenger has arrived" (1:119). Another messenger has arrived at the end of *Perestroika,* and his name is Prior Walter. Prior's farewell to the audience, however moving, is a remarkable banality, a happy ending for the play's most stricken character.

Savran argues that the play, like *The Book of Mormon,* "demonstrates that there are angels in America, that America is in essence a utopian and theological construction, a nation with a divine mission."[38] It is possible to suggest that Bede and Kushner share a political purpose, which is to create the idea of a unified people. Bede does this with the term—the concept— *Angli,* which comes to mean "the English," a people elevated by their likeness to angels. Kushner is also out to unify a people, but more ambitiously and inclusively, and not a people to be compared to angels but, instead, a people to replace them. The threat that unifies the English is its heathen past; the threat that unifies Kushner's new angels is not AIDS, which only menaces a small percentage of them, but the old regimes of race that divide and weaken people and prevent change. Those forces are routed at the end of *Angels in America,* and the boards are clear for a new age.

In his admiring review of *Perestroika,* Frank Rich observed a similarity between the tone of this play and *The Wizard of Oz,* claiming that a fever dream in which Prior visits heaven was "as vivid as the one that propelled Judy Garland to Munchkinland."[39] There are many reasons to pursue this comparison, for both the film and the play expose as a fraud the master who supposedly controls the universe. God in *Perestroika* is a powerless power whose forces turn on him and who is reduced to seeking assistance for his defense from a notoriously corrupt lawyer. "You have nothing to plead," Roy tells him near the end, "but not to worry, darling, I will make something up" (2:139). God's imaginative capacities are exhausted; the new creator is closet queen. Kushner's Hollywood-derived, Oz-like, Broadwayesque version of heaven (and hell, for that matter: Roy Cohn making more deals) shows how irrelevant religious belief is to a vision of life at the millennium. Yet the play shares a spiritual aim with Bede's work as well as a political one. Kushner, too, makes use of the myth of a Chosen People who must be brought from captivity into freedom. For Bede these people are, first, the Anglo-Saxon invaders and then the *Angli,* their descendants. The Chosen People of *Angels in America,* it would seem, are homosexuals and their sympathizers. Bede's Chosen People are brought to the promised land of Christianity. The promised land of *Angels in America* is a multicultural, tolerant world in which biological descent counts for little (there are no successful marriages in the play) and cultural inheritance can impart defining characteristics to people without imposing barriers among them.

Although *Angels in America* seems to carry revolutionary ambitions, there is a quite traditional sense in which the play uses its WASP hero to conform to rather than to contradict the ideology of Manifest Destiny. "To be superior, to be a chosen people, meant to many New Englanders, and to some from other parts of the country, the necessity for restrained conduct befitting their high station," Horsman writes. Opponents of Manifest Destiny abhorred the violence and cant of its expansionist ideologues; "restraint," he observes, "could be a further proof of superiority," quoting Henry David Thoreau on the subject: "It is perfectly heathenish—a filibustering *toward* heaven by the great western route. No; they may go their way to their manifest destiny, which I trust is not mine."[40] There is no "filibustering toward heaven" in *Angels in America* but, rather, away from it. One leaves the play with the distinct impression that the new angels of America, however unruly and unconventional, follow the lead of the Anglo-Saxon whose proximity to the angelic, even if radically redefined, has opened up to them the promise of a new age.

NOTES

1. David Savran, "Ambivalence, Utopia, and a Queer Sort of Materialism: How *Angels in America* Reconstructs the Nation," *Theatre Journal* 47 (1995): 216–17. This essay is reprinted in the current volume.

2. The Anglo-Saxon evidence discussed in the first part of this essay appears in fuller form in "Gregory the Great, Bede's *History,* and John Bale," in *Anglo-Saxonism: The Idea of Anglo-Saxon England from the Anglo-Saxons to the Present Day,* ed. Allen J. Frantzen and John D. Niles (Gainesville: University Press of Florida, 1997). I thank Andrew Cole, Steven Kruger, John Niles, and Joyce Wexler for comments on drafts of this essay.

3. Reginald Horsman, *Race and Manifest Destiny: The Origins of American Racial Anglo-Saxonism* (Cambridge: Harvard University Press, 1981); the phrase *Manifest Destiny* was not coined until 1845 (see 219). On Anglo-Saxonism, see Allen J. Frantzen, *Desire for Origins: New Language, Old English, and Teaching the Tradition* (New Brunswick: Rutgers University Press, 1990), 15–18, 27–61, in which I comment on the phenomenon as a force in Anglo-Saxon studies from the Renaissance to the present.

4. Translated into Old English before the end of the ninth century, the *History* was continuously known in Latin editions throughout the Middle Ages; it was popular on both sides of the Reformation controversy in England in the sixteenth century. See Frantzen, *Desire for Origins,* 130–67.

5. Manifest Destiny had its roots in a theory of natural rights for a particular race that translated into nationalism and then imperialism. See Albert K. Weinberg, *Manifest Destiny* (1935; reprint, Chicago: Quadrangle, 1963), 8, 41.

6. Gildas's work *De Excidio Britonum* was written about 540. See *Gildas: The Ruin of Britain and Other Works,* ed. and trans. Michael Winterbottom (London: Phillimore, 1978); and Nicholas Howe, *Migration and Myth-Making in Anglo-Saxon England* (New Haven: Yale University Press, 1991), 33–49, for a discussion of Gildas and the pattern of prophetic history.

7. Bede, *Ecclesiastical History of the English People,* ed. and trans. Bertram Colgrave and R. A. B. Mynors (Oxford: Clarendon Press, 1969), 1:14, 48–49. See Sir Frank Stenton, *Anglo-Saxon England,* 3d ed. (Oxford: Oxford University Press, 1971), 1–18.

8. Bede, *Ecclesiastical History,* 1:22, 68–69.

9. Ibid., 2:1, 132–35. A version is found in the anonymous Whitby *Life* of Gregory, probably written between 704 and 714 but unknown to Bede when he finished the *Ecclesiastical History* in 731. See *The Earliest Life of Gregory the Great,* ed. and trans. Bertram Colgrave (Cambridge: Cambridge University Press, 1985), 49, 144–45.

10. Bede, *Ecclesiastical History,* 2:1, 132–33.

11. Ibid., 1:23–26, 68–79; 2:1, 132–33.

12. Ibid., 1:15, 50–51.

13. See entries for *Angli* in the glossary to Colgrave and Mynors, *Ecclesiastical History,* 596. The Anglo-Saxon evidence for use of the term is mixed, but the great preponderance of readings cited by the *Dictionary of Old English,* fasc. A., refer to *English* in the broad sense; the word also means "the Angles," and *Angeltheod* refers to "the northern English, the Angles." See *The Dictionary of Old English,* fasc. A, ed. Antonette diPaolo Healey, et al. (Toronto: Pontifical Institute of Mediaeval Studies, 1994).

14. Colgrave claims that, although the boys Gregory saw were called "Angli," "English," or "Anglian," they were, in Bede's mind, Northumbrians (*Earliest Life,* 144–45 n. 42).

15. See Bede, *Ecclesiastical History,* 5:24, 566–67.

16. According to Howe, the episode shows that each of the words on which Gregory puns "has an erroneous meaning in heathendom and a true meaning in Christendom" (*Migration and Myth-Making,* 119).

17. For general background, see David A. E. Pelteret, *Slavery in Early Medieval England: From the Reign of Alfred until the Twelfth Century* (Suffolk: Woodbridge, 1995); and Pelteret, "Slave Raiding and Slave Trading in Early England," *Anglo-Saxon England* 9 (1981): 99–114. The boys could have been captives or could have been sold because of their parents' debts, a practice dating from the early Anglo-Saxon period and decried by the eleventh-century homilist Wulfstan in his famous "Sermo Lupi ad Anglos," ed. and trans. Dorothy Whitelock, *English Historical Documents, I,* c. 500–1042 (London: Eyre Methuen, 1979), 929–34; see 930.

18. Ruth Mazo Karras comments on prostitution and female slaves in "Desire, Descendants, and Dominance: Slavery, the Exchange of Women, and Masculine Power," in *The Work of Work: Servitude, Slavery, and Labor in Medieval England* (Glasgow: Cruithne, 1994), 16–29.

19. I discuss Anglo-Saxon slavery and Bale's version of this episode in "Gregory the Great" (see n. 2); see also *Desire for Origins,* 47.

20. See Patrick Wormald, "Bede, the *Bretwaldas* and the Origins of the *Gens Anglorum,*" in *Ideal and Reality in Frankish and Anglo-Saxon Society: Studies Presented to J. M. Wallace-Hadrill,* ed. Patrick Wormald, et al. (Oxford: Blackwell, 1983), 124–25.

21. Bede, *Ecclesiastical History,* 2:1, 134–35.

22. Ibid., 1:22, 68–69.

23. Tony Kushner, *Angels in America: A Gay Fantasia on National Themes. Part One: Millennium Approaches* (New York: Theatre Communications Group, 1993); *Part Two: Perestroika* (New York: Theatre Communications Group, 1994). Further references are given in the text, cited by part number, 1 for *Millennium Approaches* and 2 for *Perestroika,* followed by page number.

24. Savran, "Ambivalence," 212 n. 14.

25. Ibid.

26. See Stenton, *Anglo-Saxon England,* 576–80.

27. Christopher Hill, "The Norman Yoke," *Puritanism and Revolution* (London: Sacker and Warburg, 1958), 19. For a recent appraisal of Hill's work and the place of the Conquest in the reception of Anglo-Saxon culture, see Clare A. Simmons, *Reversing the Conquest: History and Myth in 19th-Century British Literature* (New Brunswick: Rutgers University Press, 1990).

28. See Savran, "Ambivalence," 208–9, 222.

29. See David J. Bernstein, *The Mystery of the Bayeux Tapestry* (Chicago: University of Chicago Pres, 1986), 28–30, in which he reports that Hitler, like Napoleon, studied the tapestry when he contemplated an invasion of England.

30. Bernstein, *Mystery,* 14, 8.

31. Ibid., 30. Only four minor characters are named: "Turold," "Ælfgyva," "Wadard," and "Vital"; the rest are important figures (Harold, William, and others), most of them Norman and well-known from contemporary sources.

32. See Savran, "Ambivalence," 222–24, for an analysis of Kushner's treatment of identity politics and race in this scene.

33. Weinberg, *Manifest Destiny,* 8.

34. Savran, "Ambivalence," 213.

35. Tony Kushner, "The Secrets of 'Angels,'" *New York Times,* 27 March 1994, H5.

36. Several reviewers have commented on the identification of Louis with Kushner's own views. See, for example, John Simon, "Angelic Geometry," *New York,* 6 December 1993, 130. Savran sees Louis as "the most empathetic character in the play" ("Ambivalence," 223).

37. Susan Reynolds, "What Do We Mean by 'Anglo-Saxon' and 'Anglo-Saxons'?" *Journal of British Studies* 24 (1985): 402–3.

38. Savran, "Ambivalence," 222–23.

39. Frank Rich, "Following an Angel for a Healing Vision of Heaven on Earth," *New York Times,* 24 November 1993, B1, B4.

40. Horsman, *Race,* 256–57, 258.

Identity and Conversion
in *Angels in America*

Steven F. Kruger

The titles and subtitles of Tony Kushner's *Angels in America* emphasize
its status as political drama, announcing its exploration of "national themes"
at a particular moment in global and cosmic history—the moment of "perestroika" as "millennium approaches." At the same time, these titles and
subtitles call attention to the personal and psychological as crucial terms for
the play's political analysis. This is a "*gay fantasia* on national themes," an
intervention in American politics that comes from a specified identity position and that depends somehow upon fantasy. The "angels" of the play's
main title condense the political and personal in a particularly efficient manner: evoking at once Walter Benjamin's "angel of history"[1] and the guardian
angel who watches over a particular individual, Kushner's Angel is both
Prior Walter's fantasy creation and "the Continental Principality of America," one of seven "inconceivably powerful Celestial Apparatchik/Bureau-
crat-Angels" who preside over the continents and the ocean.[2] Like the
"angel of God" whose appearance to Joseph Smith is explained in *Perestroika*
("He had great need of understanding. Our Prophet. His desire made
prayer. His prayer made an angel. The angel was real. I believe that"
[2:103]), the Angel in Kushner's play is both evoked by individual desire and
somehow "real," speaking simultaneously to one person's needs ("For
behold an angel of the Lord came and stood before me [Joseph Smith]. It
was by night and he called me by name and he said the Lord had forgiven
me my sins") and to collective historical circumstances ("He revealed unto
me many things concerning the inhabitants of the earth which since have
been revealed in commandments and revelations").[3]

Constituting Identity

Written, as Kushner makes explicit, out of a "Left politics informed by liberation struggles . . . and by socialist and psychoanalytic theory" (2:154),

Angels in America is at least in part the product of gay identity politics, and central to its political argument is a consideration of sexual identity. The play explores Harper's troubled marriage to Joe, the ways in which this confines both her and him, and the ways in which Harper's fantasy life recapitulates but also enables a certain escape from the unsatisfactory heterosexual relation. The play depicts the closeted figures of Roy and Joe struggling to *dis*identify from gayness. And it displays complex, indeed contradictory, definitions of gayness as, for instance, both strength and weakness—in Roy's words: "Homosexuals are men who know nobody and who nobody knows. Who have zero clout" (1:45); in Prior's: "I can handle pressure, I am a gay man and I am used to pressure, to trouble, I am tough and strong" (1:117).

Closely wrapped up with the play's analysis of sexuality is a recognition of how AIDS—identified in the popular imagination with a gayness conceived of as always already diseased and weak—becomes not just a category of health or illness but also of identity. Roy's disavowal of gayness is simultaneously a disavowal of identity as a person with AIDS: "AIDS is what homosexuals have. I have liver cancer" (1:46). Prior, unlike Roy, claims despised identities, but his bitter assessment of the world's treatment of "faggots" and people with AIDS echoes Roy's: "We don't [count]; faggots; we're just a bad dream the real world is having" (2:42).

Race, ethnicity, and religion are similarly prominent, and similarly conflicted, categories of analysis in the play. Belize's and Louis's political positions are shown to differ particularly around the question of race, in ways clearly connected to their differing experiences of racial identity (1:89–96). Jewishness and Mormonism figure importantly in constituting a sense of identity for most of the play's characters—Louis and Roy, Hannah, Harper, and Joe. The marginality of each of these religious traditions is shown to contribute to the individual's sense of his or her place (or lack of place) in the structures of power. Even Roy, despite his self-confident assertions, feels Jewishness as an obstacle to maintaining political centrality: "The disbarment committee: genteel gentleman Brahmin lawyers, country-club men. I offend them, to these men . . . I'm what, Martin, some sort of filthy little Jewish troll?" (1:66–67). Prior Walter's identity as "scion of an ancient line" (1:115) is bodied forth onstage in the figures of the prior Priors who serve as the Angel's heralds; the stability of the Walter family seems a crucial factor in shaping Prior's emerging identity as (reluctant) prophet for the Angel's deeply conservative political project—"YOU MUST STOP MOVING!" (2:52)—a project that Belize suggests is Prior's own fantasy: "This is just you, Prior, afraid of the future, afraid of time. Longing to go backwards so bad you made this angel up, a cosmic reactionary" (2:55).[4]

While a gender analysis is less prominent in the play than the consideration of sexuality, AIDS, race, religion, and ethnicity,[5] it nonetheless remains important for the depiction of Harper, who, especially in her engagement with the fantasy figure of the Mormon Mother, recognizes something about her own silencing and disempowerment: "His mute wife. I'm waiting for her to speak. Bet her story's not so jolly" (2:70). And gender is important in the politics of some of the men's self-identifications—particularly those of Belize and Prior as ex– (or ex–ex–) drag queens; thus, though Belize himself suggests that "All this girl-talk shit is politically incorrect. . . . We should have dropped it back when we gave up drag" (1:61), he responds with anger to Louis's assessment of drag as "sexist" (1:94).

The play also importantly, if playfully, suggests that the very taking of political positions—Joe's being a Republican, for instance—may be an act of self-identification not unlike the claiming, or disclaiming, of a sexual identity, such as Joe's disavowal of gayness (see 1:29).

As this sketch of some of the play's identity concerns should suggest, *Angels in America* does not arise from or depict a politics that consists simply in embracing an identity position like gayness as the sufficient basis for a political movement. We might indeed see the play as in part a response to criticism, particularly from within feminism, of an identity politics that fails to recognize the multiple determinants of identity; in the words of Elizabeth Spelman, for instance:

> Dominant feminist theory locates a woman's true identity in a metaphysical space where gender is supposed to be able to roam free from race and class. . . . [T]hough doing this appears to be necessary for feminism, it has the effect of making certain women rather than others paradigmatic examples of "woman"—namely, those women who seem to have a gender identity untainted (I use the word advisedly) by racial or class identity, those women referred to in newspapers, magazines, and feminist journals simply as "women," without the qualifier "Black" or "Hispanic" or "Asian-American" or "poor."[6]

Kushner's interrogation of gayness similarly recognizes the nonunitary nature of such a category, its differential constitution in relation to other determinants of identity. The play presents us with gay men who are white and black, Jewish and Mormon, conservative and liberal, butch and femme, and certainly not easily unified or unifiable under a single political banner. Thus recognizing the differences within identity categories, the play furthermore emphasizes that any individual's identity is potentially contested and riven: sexuality, gender, and race do not come together without conflict and contradiction. Harper must negotiate between being a thoughtfully articulate woman and being a Mormon woman of whom silence is expected. Joe must navigate the rift between homoerotic desire and political and religious beliefs that insist on the repudiation of that desire. Roy, committed to Republican, McCarthyite political positions and to the political "clout" these bring him, denies as strongly as possible the potentially marginalizing force of his Jewishness and homosexuality. And so forth.

The complexity of identity in *Angels in America* also arises from Kushner's conception of it as social and relational: one is not oneself in isolation but only in contrast to, in solidarity and negotiation with a variety of other selves. This is obviously true among the main characters of the play, in which, for instance, Prior's state of health reveals or even determines much about how Louis thinks of himself or in which Joe's and Harper's decisions are crucially related to their sense of the other's identity. The others who shape the self may also be internalized figures from the past—an Ethel Rosenberg who returns punishingly to urge Roy on to death. They may be powerful historical presences like the Priors of Prior's heritage or like Louis's grandmother. And they may, most "bewilderingly" (1:30), be a complex mixture of the "real" and the fantastic, as when Prior and Harper, who have never met, somehow appear in each other's dreams/hallucinations to reveal crucial information about each other that each has not, at least consciously, realized (1:33–34, 2:68, 2:121–22). In such scenes even a character's fantasies and imaginations are conceived of as not solely his or hers. These gather their full meaning only in relation to, even interpenetration with, one another—just as, in Kushner's stagecraft, the "split scenes" suggest that discrete actions must, if we are to understand them fully, be read together: Harper and Joe's relationship defines Prior and Louis's, and vice versa, as both couples appear simultaneously onstage.

Identities so complexly defined entail certain *political* possibilities—cross-identifications like Harper's and Prior's and renegotiations of identity and difference that might make certain shifts in power relations possible, might, for instance, allow Joe to move from a simple disavowal of homosexuality to a reconsideration of it that also entails rethinking political and religious alignments. But the play also is careful not to depict identity simply as fluid and thus subject to easy, volitional change; nor does it attach a utopian political fantasy to the belief that identity might be renegotiated. Despite the presentation of identity as complex, as multiply determined, as relational, identity stubbornly remains identity, a marker of something unique to—given and intractable in—the person. Roy evokes "the immutable heart of what we are that bleeds through whatever we might become" (2:82), and, while Roy should by no means be taken as a reliable spokesman, the belief in such a "heart" is not his alone. A similar notion is at work when Harper reassures Prior that, despite his having AIDS, his "most inner part" is "free of disease" (1:34) or when Joe reassures Louis that, despite his having left Prior, he is "in [him]self a good, good man" (2:38) with "a good heart" (2:75). All of these assessments *may* be erroneous—they are each challenged elsewhere—but they nonetheless express a strong sense of the depth and stability of identity. The first speech of the play, Rabbi Isidor Chemelwitz's eulogy for Sarah Ironson, calls attention to a material heritage that is inescapable, "the clay of some Litvak shtetl" worked into her children's bones (1:10). The self may be always on a "voyage" and a "journey" (1:10–11), it may move somewhere new, but it also returns continually to a place of origin in a movement beyond the control of individual will, a function of constraints placed on the self by the history into which it is born.

If the self is not constituted by some simple, unconflicted claiming of identity, if, as well, it is not formed in isolation from others but, rather, responds to a whole variety of (political) pressures, it also is not so easily changed or reshaped. Indeed, having recognized, in Kushner's conception of identity, the potential for political change, we must also recognize that the *how* of that change is problematic. The "Great Question" with which *Perestroika* begins is "Are we doomed? . . . Will the Past release us? . . . Can we Change? In Time." Here, as stated by Prelapsarianov, the "World's Oldest Living Bolshevik," the question is explicitly political, and its "we" is the we of world history, not identity politics or personal psychology (2:13). But in Kushner's play, with its insistence on the merging of the political and the personal, the question does not only resonate with the grand narratives of international politics. Indeed, the same Great Question reappears later in *Perestroika,* transposed into the language of the individual: Harper asks her fantasy figure, the Mormon Mother, "How do people change?" (2:79). Whether raised by Harper with personal urgency or by Prelapsarianov as he searches for the next "Beautiful Theory" to "reorder the world" (2:14), this is perhaps the play's central political question.

Converting Identity?

Angels in America is in many ways a play about conversion. The experience of HIV illness is often conceived as involving a conversion of the self (we speak, e.g., of "seroconversion"), and Prior's discovery that he has AIDS is depicted in part as making him a new person: "I'm a lesionnaire" (1:21).

The Angel's visitation to Prior takes the form of a mission of conversion: given a new identity, Prior is, like Joseph Smith, to become Prophet of a new dispensation. Indeed, in the course of the play all its characters undergo startling shifts in identity. Hannah is not only physically transplanted to New York but becomes *"noticeably different—she looks like a New Yorker"* (2:145). Roy, who clings tenaciously to his professional status as a lawyer, is disbarred just before his death. Harper moves through a period of dysfunction to strike out on her own, choosing "the real San Francisco, on earth," with its "unspeakable beauty" (2:122), over her unsatisfying life with Joe, a fantasized Antarctica, and a "depressing" Heaven, "full of dead people and all" (2:122). Belize re-embraces a discarded drag identity (1:94) and, in *Perestroika*, works through his hatred for Roy Cohn toward some kind of "Forgiveness" (2:124). Louis and Joe each move out of "marriages" and into a new relationship with each other, a movement that, for both, entails a radical rethinking of the self. Louis is forced to consider whether he is capable of truly loving; when he decides that he is and tries to return to Prior, he finds that he "can't come back" (2:143), that the relation to Prior is now essentially changed. The couple that Prior and Louis once formed is replaced by the play's final argumentative, but communal, quartet of Prior, Louis, Belize, and Hannah. And Joe, the character whose fate is left least resolved at the end of *Perestroika,* is also perhaps the character who has undergone the most radical conversions. He admits his at first denied homosexuality. He moves from a heterosexual to a homosexual relationship, from a commitment to Reaganism and Mormonism to a willingness to "give up anything" for Louis (2:74), from "never [having] hit anyone before" to a violent attack on Louis (2:111–12). By the end of the play his relation to Harper has been precisely reversed. She is leaving him, having slapped him as he has just beaten Louis. He, not she, is now the one in need of psychological support that is not forthcoming, and, as she leaves, Harper transfers to Joe the Valium she herself once used in substitution for his missing support (2:143). As (a fantasized) Harper earlier suggests to Joe, "You're turning into me" (2:40).

It is not surprising, given the play's emphasis on such radical changes in self and self-conception, that it focuses so much attention on Mormonism and Judaism, both religions whose originary moment is a conversional one that involves a movement of dis- and relocation.[7] This is true in Mormonism not only in the revelation to Joseph Smith and the westward movement that this initiated but also in the opening visions of *The Book of Mormon,* in which Lehi is "commanded" to separate himself from the corrupt Jews of Jerusalem by "tak[ing] his family and depart[ing] into the wilderness" (1 Nephi 2:2). This founding moment of course echoes the founding of Judaism in God's command to Abraham: "Get thee out of thy country, and from thy kindred, and from thy father's house, unto a land that I will shew thee" (Genesis 12:1).[8] (The echo is intensified in the names of Abraham's and Lehi's wives—Sarai/Sarah and Sariah.) Mormonism is indeed explicitly recognized as a religion of conversion in *Angels in America;* in the play's only use of the word *convert* Prior responds to Hannah's unexpected solicitude toward him by saying, "Please, if you're trying to convert me this isn't a good time" (2:100).

But, while both Judaism and Mormonism originate in a radical movement away from a prior religious tradition, both also express a strong resistance to change. We remember, for instance, the words of the Rabbi that open the play and that make the Great Voyage of Jewish migration both an enormous dislocation and a refusal of "this strange place," a preservation of the "ancient, ancient culture and home" (1:10). Later Louis will recognize, comically, a circular movement enacted by Jewish immigrants and their descendants: "Alphabetland. This is where the Jews lived when they first arrived. And now, a hundred years later, the place to which their more seriously fucked-up grandchildren repair. . . . This is progress?" (2:15). Mormon social conservatism and traditionalism—"People ought to stay put" (1:82)—stands starkly against the radical break of its originary moment and founding mythos. Such ambivalence is already present in *The Book of Mormon*. Here the most radical conversions can occur; the black-skinned Lamanites can, with spiritual reform, turn white (see 3 Nephi 2:15–16). At the same time, however, the conception of Lamanite identity as essentially marred remains unchanged. The converting Lamanites *become* Nephites; the idea of a white Lamanite or of a morally upright black-skinned person is not admitted.[9]

An ambivalence similar to that present in both Judaism and Mormonism characterizes all the conversionary movements in *Angels in America*. The Angel's promise to undertake "a marvelous work and a wonder," to abolish "a great Lie," to correct "a great error" (1:62), turns out to be a call not for change but for its opposite, a project intended not to transform established identity categories or structures of power but, instead, to secure these with "Deep Roots": "Neither Mix Nor Intermarry . . . If you do not MINGLE you will Cease to Progress" (2:52). In the depiction of Prior it is an active question whether AIDS accomplishes a transformation of the self, with the play giving two contrasting answers: Prior's "I don't think there's any uninfected part of me. My heart is pumping polluted blood. I feel dirty" (1:34) posed against Harper's "deep inside you, there's a part of you, the

most inner part, entirely free of disease" (1:34), which Prior later echoes—
"my blood is clean, my brain is fine" (1:117). Louis changes position frequently in the play, but his movement is ultimately circular, a return to
where he began. With characters like Belize, Hannah, and Harper, one
wonders if apparent conversions might not be better understood as assertions of an identity "essential" to the self that has been temporarily suppressed. Belize, like Louis, moves in a circle, giving up drag only to re-
embrace it; his forgiving Roy Cohn alongside their agonistic relation echoes
his simultaneous antagonism and concern for Louis. Hannah is perhaps
poised, from her earliest moments in the play, to move away from her Mormon "demographic profile" (2:104): Sister Ella Chapter tells her, "you're
the only unfriendly Mormon I ever met" (1:82). Harper's identity as a "Jack
Mormon," her "always doing something wrong, like one step out of step"
(1:53), may similarly be seen as conditioning the change she ultimately
makes in her life. Roy, though "defeated" (2:114), moves one last time to
assert his power, using the pathos of his impending death to reaffirm
"clout": "I fooled you Ethel . . . I just wanted to see if I could finally, finally
make Ethel Rosenberg sing! I WIN!" (2:115). Indeed, the last words he
speaks while alive in the play exactly echo his first (cf. 1:11 and 2:115).

At the same time that the play displays each of its characters undergoing major changes, it thus also asks whether these in fact represent real
changes in the self or, rather, express or reaffirm a preexisting, stable identity. This double movement is especially evident in the treatment of the
changes that Joe undergoes. On the one hand, we may see Joe as radically
transformed in the course of the play. On the other, we might legitimately
ask whether his behavior, even as he comes out and becomes involved with
Louis, *really* changes. Isn't the concealment of his homosexuality from
Harper simply replaced by the concealment, from Louis, of his Mormonism, the meaning of his work as chief clerk in the Federal Court of
Appeals, and his connection to Roy Cohn? Just as much of *Millennium
Approaches* is devoted to Harper's uncovering of Joe's homosexuality, so *Perestroika* traces Louis's discovery of Joe's concealed religious and political
identities. Harper and Louis in essence "out" Joe's secrets, but Joe himself
continues to behave much as before, returning repeatedly to Roy and,
when his relationship with Louis fails, trying to return to Harper.

Skin and Bowels

The problem of identity and its possible conversion is worked out in *Angels
in America* particularly through a dialogue between external and internal self,

a thematics of skin and bowels. Skin recurs repeatedly in the play as necessary to the integrity of a self, both macro- and microcosmic. Thus, Harper,
in her opening speech, sees the "ozone layer" as "the crowning touch to the
creation of the world: guardian angels, hands linked, make a spherical net, a
blue-green nesting orb, a shell of safety for life itself" (1:16–17). "Safety
from what's outside" is central to her positive vision of the millennium, and
the flip side of that vision is the failure of protective covering: "the sky will
collapse" (1:18). Harper also makes clear that "people are like planets, you
need a thick skin" (1:17), and the decay of the ozone layer is matched at the
level of individuals by the loss of bodily integrity attendant upon AIDS, a
loss marked in the play (as in the popular imagination) particularly by the
skin lesions of Kaposi's sarcoma (1:21). Harper's "systems of defense giving
way" (1:17) reappear in Henry's description of the action of HIV, which
depends upon both a failure of the skin and damage to the internal "skin"
of immunity (see 1:42).

Susceptible to decay and invasion, the skin becomes a complex site—
protective, yes, but also the place at which the self is endangered and at
which one self may threaten another. Prior self-protectively insists that
Louis not touch him, but immediately after, having *"shit himself"* and bled,
he must warn Louis away: "Maybe you shouldn't touch it . . . me" (1:48).
His breached, fragile skin presents pain and danger both for himself and for
others. Elsewhere, the vulnerability of skin is recognized in ways not
directly connected to physical risk. Louis, feeling guilty for having abandoned Prior, warns Joe not to touch him: "your hand might fall off or
something." And, when Joe in fact touches Louis, he sees himself as violat-
ing a certain dangerous boundary: "I'm going to hell for doing this." As this
scene also demonstrates, however, skin and the crossing of its boundaries
provide the opportunity not only for wounding but for connection—here,
the sexual connection between Joe and Louis: "I . . . want . . . to touch you.
Can I please just touch you . . . um, here?" (1:116). Later Joe will also imagine the dissolution of a political boundary between himself and Louis:
"Freedom is where we bleed into one another. Right and Left. Freedom is
the far horizon where lines converge" (2:37). And the "ragged" skin that
Harper imagines precariously protecting the earth, in her most hopeful
vision, becomes a place of human interconnectedness:

> Souls were rising, from the earth far below, souls of the dead, of peo-
> ple who had perished, from famine, from war, from the plague, and
> they floated up, like skydivers in reverse, limbs all akimbo, wheeling
> and spinning. And the souls of these departed joined hands, clasped

ankles, and formed a web, a great net of souls, and the souls were three-atom oxygen molecules, of the stuff of ozone, and the outer rim absorbed them, and was repaired. (2:144)

Here Harper sees the merging of human efforts across the barrier of self, the paradoxical coming together of those who have lost bodily integrity, whose own protective skins have been stripped from them, to replenish the skin of the world.

Implied, of course, in the image of a skin that insures integrity but is vulnerable, that guarantees separate identity but allows interconnection, is a depth, the contents that the skin holds together and that are threatened by its potential collapse. The decay of the ozone layer helps make possible a more general "dissolving of the Great Design" (2:134), which the Angel comes to announce and which Prelapsarianov recognizes as "mad swirling planetary disorganization" (2:14; also see 2:45). A cosmic "searing of skin" and "boiling of blood" (2:52), external and internal destruction, occur simultaneously. And, for the individual, the attack on protective skin—most strikingly, the damage to the immune system in AIDS—leads to an emptying out of bodily contents: Roy says, "Now I look like a skeleton" (1:111).

Buried depth, and particularly a depth of internal organs, of heart and blood and bowels, is in the play as constitutive of humanness, of human institutions, and of the world as is the protective skin. Though the skin may be breached, life stubbornly holds on: "When they're more spirit than body, more sores than skin, when they're burned and in agony, when flies lay eggs in the corners of the eyes of their children, they live. Death usually has to *take* life away. I don't know if that's just the animal" (2:136). The human being is, at least in part, a "DISGUSTING SLURPING FEEDING ANIMAL" (1:104), and the life of that "animal" in the world, including its institutions, involves a messy corporeality. Thus, in Roy's view "the Law" is not "a dead and arbitrary collection of antiquated dictums" but, rather, "a pliable, breathing, sweating . . . *organ*" (1:66); "this is gastric juices churning, this is enzymes and acids, this is intestinal is what this is, bowel movement and blood-red meat—this stinks, this is *politics,* Joe, the game of being alive" (1:68).[10] Roy's perspective on the world is the opposite of Harper's, though it too makes the leap from macro- to microcosm; Roy looks at things from their bloody "heart" rather than their celestial skin: "Unafraid to look deep into the miasma at the heart of the world, what a pit, what a nightmare is there—*I* have looked, I have searched all my life for absolute bottom, and I found it, *believe* me: *Stygian*" (2:81).

Though the depths Roy describes mirror his own "brutal" and opportunistic misanthropy (2:81), the play also shows how such depths participate in loving human relations. If connections among people occur through the skin, true attachments depend upon a deeper, more intimate, mingling. Louis describes "smell" and "taste" as the "only two [senses] that go beyond the boundaries . . . of ourselves" and that thus allow an interpenetration of self and other: "Some part of you, where you meet the air, is airborne. . . . The nose tells the body—the heart, the mind, the fingers, the cock—what it wants, and then the tongue explores" (2:17–18). Desire is a matter of the whole body, its depths as well as its surfaces. As Harper suggests, "life" is "all a matter of the opposable thumb and forefinger; not of the hand but of the heart; we grab hold like nobody's business and then we don't seem to be able to let go" (2:122). Even when the heart's grasp fails, as Harper also recognizes, the rest of the body continues doggedly to desire: "When your heart breaks, you should die. / But there's still the rest of you. There's your breasts, and your genitals, and they're amazingly stupid, like babies or faithful dogs, they don't get it, they just want him" (2:20).

While transformation of the self, and of the world, is sometimes imaged in the play as operating on the skin's surface—"If anyone who was suffering, in the body or the spirit, walked through the waters of the fountain of Bethesda, they would be healed, washed clean of pain" (2:147)—equally crucial to the play's conception of conversion is a penetration of the self's depths. The heart that serves as "an anchor" for Harper must, the Mormon Mother insists, be left behind (2:71). The cosmic repairs that the Angel undertakes represent an attempt to transform the "battered heart, / Bleeding Life in the Universe of Wounds" (2:54), by paralyzing life's messy process, emptying out the self and the world. And the play several times brings internal and external change together. At the same moment that Roy advises Joe to live differently in the world by exposing himself, baring his skin ("don't be afraid to live in the raw wind, naked, alone" [1:58]), Louis self-destructively yearns to be penetrated ("fuck[ed]," "hurt," "ma[d]e [to] bleed," [1:54], even "infect[ed]" [1:57]). Roy himself will later ask Belize to "squeeze the bloody life from me" and to "open me up to the end of me" (2:76).

When Louis returns to Prior to "make up" with him (2:83), Prior insists that neither external nor internal change alone is sufficient to demonstrate Louis's conversion. He accuses Louis of presenting a surface that reflects no depth: "You cry, but you endanger nothing in yourself. It's like the idea of crying when you do it. / Or the idea of love" (2:85). But he is also suspicious of claims to internal change that fail to manifest themselves externally. When Louis tells him not to "waste energy beating up on me,

OK? I'm already taking care of that," Prior responds, "Don't see any bruises" (2:83), and, having exacted from Louis the confession that he is "really bruised inside" (2:88), Prior insists on external proof: "Come back to me when they're visible. I want to see black and blue, Louis, I want to see blood. Because I can't believe you even *have* blood in your veins till you show it to me" (2:89). Louis, having been beat up by Joe (2:111–12), "made . . . [to] bleed" (2:127), indeed returns to Prior with "visible scars" (2:141), which stand for a change in his way of being in the world. In the economy of the play it is not enough for Louis to leave Joe; he must also confront him, in the scene that leads to violence, with what he has discovered about Joe's decisions for the Court of Appeals, his relation to Roy Cohn, and his consequent entwinement in the history of McCarthyism. Louis's making external of his own internal change here operates through his "outing" of Joe's secrets, and, just as Louis's internality—the fact that he does "have blood in his veins"—is made literally visible, so the violent injustices of Joe's concealed political history are brought out in the violence he visits on Louis, a violence later explicitly approved by Roy: "Everybody could use a good beating" (2:127).

The play of surface and depth in *Angels in America* is particularly crucial in the depiction of Joe and his problematic conversions. At a moment when he is still fighting against his homoerotic feelings, Joe thinks of these as constituting something "deep within" that might be concealed or even expurgated: "I have fought, with everything I have, to kill it" (1:40). Joe's model of identity, the wished-for perfection of the "saints," is one in which internal and external selves correspond simply, unconflictedly, to each other: "Those who love God with an open heart unclouded by secrets and struggles are cheerful; God's easy simple love for them shows in how strong and happy they are" (1:54). (This is the flip side, or the positive image, of Roy's identification with "lower" life forms like HIV and "pubic lice," beings "too simple" to be killed, self-identical and transparent to themselves: "It [HIV] knows itself. It's harder to kill something if it knows what it is" [2:28].)

But, while Joe sometimes imagines that he has conquered his buried secret, made inside and outside concur, this is at the expense of both inside and outside. Joe sees his internal battle, his "secret struggles" (1:54), as leading not to a plenitude encompassing "heart" and worldly behavior, as with the "saints," but, rather, to an emptying out of the self, a "killing" of internal identity that leaves the external devoid of meaningful content: "For God's sake, there's nothing left, I'm a shell. There's nothing left to kill"

(1:40). Joe's disavowal of an unwanted depth, his attempt to hide and kill his secret self, in fact fails. The "heart" has a power that cannot simply be denied or suppressed: "I try to tighten my heart into a knot, a snarl, I try to learn to live dead, just numb, but then I see someone I want, and it's like a nail, like a hot spike right through my chest, and I know I'm losing" (1:77). Joe's disavowed depth makes itself known not just internally but externally; he develops a "bleeding ulcer" (1:106) that forces the messiness hidden inside to appear on the surface, with blood coming from his mouth (1:80).

One kind of attempt to convert the self, through the stifling of an unwanted internality, thus fails, and Joe moves toward a different sort of self-conversion—"I can't *be* this anymore. I need . . . a change" (1:73)—another attempt to make external and internal selves concur, but this time through a "coming out" that would bring the heart to the surface. For such a conversion to occur, however, Joe imagines that his skin, the "outside" that "never stood out" (1:53) and that has concealed his disavowed depth, cannot remain: "Very great. To shed your skin, every old skin, one by one and then walk away, unencumbered, into the morning" (1:72–73). But, just as the attempt to disavow his buried homosexuality involves a violence against the internal self, so Joe's coming out, his shedding the skin of his prior life, involves a violence against the self and its history: "I'm flayed. / No past now" (2:75). Here the skin represents the individual's connections and commitments in the world—"everything you owe anything to, justice, or love" (1:72)—and Joe's imagination of shedding his skin is an attempted disavowal of such commitments. In order to stay with Louis, Joe declares himself ready to shed his "fruity underwear," his "temple garment"—"Protection. A second skin. I can stop wearing it." When Louis objects—"How can you stop wearing it if it's a skin? Your past, your beliefs" (2:73)—Joe reiterates his willingness to shed not just this "second skin" but "anything. Whatever you want. I can give up anything. My skin" (2:74).

Though stripping off one's skin and strangling one's heart seem diametrically opposed models of conversion, each depends upon a radical denial of part of oneself—whether the depth of uncontrollable desire or a surface of connections and commitments, whether the repressed content of a secret self or the historical sediments of the self's past. Indeed, Joe's first fantasy of shedding his skin follows immediately upon his imagination of a certain emptying out of depth:

> It just flashed through my mind: The whole Hall of Justice, it's empty, it's deserted, it's gone out of business. Forever. The people that make it run have up and abandoned it. . . .

I felt that I was going to scream. Not because it was creepy, but because the emptiness felt so *fast*.

And . . . well, good. A . . . happy scream.

I just wondered what a thing it would be . . . if overnight everything you owe anything to, justice, or love, had really gone away. Free.

It would be . . . heartless terror. Yes. Terrible, and . . .

Very great. (1:72)

Just as the strangling of the heart leaves a self that is only a "shell," so the shedding of the skin depends upon an emptying out—a literalized heartlessness—that might leave the self "free" but also leaves it contentless, without past or history. Indeed, the impossibility or monstrousness of such a conversion is voiced not only by Louis but by Joe himself when he (homophobically) imagines, even as he claims "no past now," that his sexual relation with Louis has given him a new past—"Maybe . . . in what we've been doing, maybe I'm even infected" (2:75)—and a past that reinvests him with an internality felt (as with his buried homosexuality) to be out of his control. And, just as Joe's disavowed internality reasserted itself through his bleeding ulcer, so his disavowed political and religious connections, supposedly shed as a skin, return in the form of blood. When Joe visits Roy, from whom he never makes a definitive break, to reveal that he is "with a man" (2:86), Roy orders him to return to his prior life: "I want you home. With your wife." In order to reach Joe, Roy pulls the IV tube from his arm and ends up *"smearing [Joe's shirt] with blood."* Whereas Joe, despite his coming out, continues to imagine (not unlike Roy) that the greatest danger to himself comes from his homosexuality ("maybe I'm even infected"), the real danger is shown to be from his continued connection to Roy and his refusal, despite his conversion from closeted Mormon Republican to out gay man, to grapple with the meaning of that connection. Belize warns Joe to "get somewhere you can take off that shirt and throw it out, and don't touch the blood," an injunction that Joe cannot understand because Roy continues to conceal that he has AIDS, and because Joe himself continues blindly to dedicate himself to Roy (2:87). Though Joe claims that he has jettisoned his past, Roy's blood, and Joe's own political actions and commitments, continue to stain him; they are not so easily shed. One might indeed see Joe's skin as not sloughed off but, rather, pushed inward, replacing the secret of homosexuality with a heart that Roy can celebrate—"His strength is as the strength of ten because his heart is pure! *And* he's a Royboy, one hundred percent" (1:64)—but that must now be concealed from Louis. Indeed, though the image of the bloodied shirt continues to represent the past as surface, this is also seen as depth, and a depth susceptible to infection; in revealing to Louis the relationship between Joe and Roy, Belize says: "I don't know whether Mr. Cohn has penetrated more than his spiritual sphincter. All I'm saying is you better hope there's no GOP germ, Louis, 'cause if there is, you got it" (2:95).

In the depiction of Joe and the changes he undergoes, then, two seemingly opposed models for conversion—the strangling of the heart in the service of the skin and the shedding of the skin at the demand of the heart—come together, each shown to be inadequate, a killing of vitality, a denial of the past. Joe's strongest statement of the desire for conversion—"I pray for God to crush me, break me up into little pieces and start all over again" (1:49)—indeed denies both internal and external selves, both the depth of feeling that for Joe is identified with his homosexuality and the history of the self's relations in the world. Joe attempts first to deny feeling then to jettison the past, but he makes no real attempt to think how *both* surface and depth, skin and heart, constitute the self. In his last scene in the play, as he attempts to hold on to Harper, to return to a life he had seemingly left behind, he once again disavows a certain past—"I have done things, I'm ashamed"—but *which* past, whether his commitment to Roy or to Louis, remains unclear. He claims to "have changed," but, as he himself says, "I don't know how yet" (2:142). In some sense, for all his searching, Joe never finds a self of which *not* to be "ashamed"; for all his "changing," he never grapples with the self or its past history in such a way as to effect real change. Late in the play Harper can describe Joe much as he himself did before his "coming out": "sweet hollow center, but he's the nothing man" (2:122).

"To Make the Continuum of History Explode"

If Joe's changes in the play represent failed rather than successful attempts at conversion, they nonetheless point the way toward a conception of what it would mean truly to undergo conversion.[11] This would involve grappling with an internality, a depth, a passionate desire, in such a way as neither to deny its power nor to follow it without consideration for its effects on others. It would also mean shedding one's skin, changing one's way of being in the world, without merely throwing off the "past" and the "beliefs" imbedded in that skin (2:73).

Perhaps the play's most powerful image of a conversion that goes beyond what Joe is able to accomplish comes in the Mormon Mother's response to Harper's question, "How do people change?" (2:79). Her answer suggests that real change is difficult, painful, and violent and that its difficulty arises precisely because it does not follow the easier paths toward conversion that others in the play attempt to pursue. It does not reach for a simple obliteration of the self ("break me up into little pieces and start all over again" [1:49]) or an emptying out of a disturbing depth; nor does it operate through a sloughing off of "everything you owe anything to" (1:72) or an embracing of (angelic) "STASIS" (2:54). Addressing Harper's question, the Mormon Mother suggests that change "has something to do with God so it's not very nice":

> God splits the skin with a jagged thumbnail from throat to belly and then plunges a huge filthy hand in, he grabs hold of your bloody tubes and they slip to evade his grasp but he squeezes hard, he *insists,* he pulls and pulls till all your innards are yanked out and the pain! We can't even talk about that. And then he stuffs them back, dirty, tangled and torn. It's up to you to do the stitching.
> *Harper:* And then get up. And walk around.
> *Mormon Mother:* Just mangled guts pretending.
> *Harper:* That's how people change.
>
> (2:79)

Nothing here is simply cast off or emptied out. The skin is breached and remains to be stitched up; the bowels are "mangled" but remain themselves. A prior self is not left behind—commitments remain, desiring continues, the history of the self travels on with it—and yet change somehow occurs through a violent rearrangement over which one may have no control but also through patching one's own wounds, living with what is "dirty, tangled and torn," "pretending" to go on and thus in fact going on.

Harper herself moves into a new life and not by simply rejecting the past: "Nothing's lost forever. In this world, there's a kind of painful progress. Longing for what we've left behind, and dreaming ahead" (2:144). Torn open by Joe's lack of love, "heartbroken," she nonetheless "return[s] to the world" (2:121) and without denying her "devastating" experience or her pain:

> I feel like shit, but I've never felt more alive. I've finally found the secret of all that Mormon energy. Devastation. That's what makes people migrate, build things. Heartbroken people do it, people who have lost love. (2:122)

Here, of course, the play again connects one individual's movement to a broader social/political phenomenon, and, as in its treatment of individual conversion, it shows a real ambivalence about whether and how true historical change might occur. If Louis can claim that "both of us are, right now, too much immersed in this history . . . and there's no real hope of change" (1:91), just a few scenes later Ethel Rosenberg can announce that "history is about to crack wide open. Millennium approaches" (1:112). Again, as with individual conversion, there is deep skepticism about a project of historical transformation that would address either depth or surface alone. The Angel's project is ultimately shown to be bankrupt because it is an emptying out and arresting of the messiness that constitutes life itself. And, as Prelapsarianov warns at the beginning of *Perestroika,* the simple shedding of the past, without preparation of a new skin, without "the Theory . . . that will reorder the world," without the deep, transformative work—"the incredible bloody vegetable struggle up and through into Red Blooming" (2:14)—necessary to prepare the new, will lead to dissolution:

> If the snake sheds his skin before a new skin is ready, naked he will be in the world, prey to the forces of chaos. Without his skin he will be dismantled, lose coherence and die. Have you, my little serpents, a new skin? . . . Then we dare not, we *cannot,* we MUST NOT move ahead! (2:14–15)

Something like the Mormon Mother's prescription for change, something that would slit open the skin of the present, grapple with the world's messy violences, with the deep traumas of its history, without obliterating or denying these, seems to be called for. As the play draws to an end, Louis argues, contra Prelapsarianov, that "you can't wait around for a theory" (2:146), but Hannah corrects him, in a way that brings together his and Prelapsarianov's ideas about how to change the world: "You need an idea of the world to go out into the world. But it's the going into that makes the idea. You can't wait for a theory, but you have to have a theory" (2:147). The new skin cannot precede the world's new demands; it can only develop as those demands—messy, traumatic, life-threatening but also the conditions of any new life—are lived.

One must "mak[e] a leap into the unknown" but a leap informed by theory and by the past (2:146): casting off the skin cannot be a rejection of the history that formed it. Indeed, the "leap into the unknown" with which *Angels in America* ends evokes Walter Benjamin's "tiger's leap into the past" even as it is a movement into the future.[12] As Benjamin suggests, the revolutionary move is to discover in the past those moments that speak to the present, resonate with it, allow the vision of history as an uninterruptible "continuum" to be rent. In some sense this is the work of *Angels* itself. Asking how to move forward in a world whose present and past are both deeply traumatic, it insists that whatever "painful progress" (2:144) might be possible will be achieved not by moving beyond trauma but by grappling with a traumatic present and by recalling past traumas as a way of being released from these, just as the play itself grapples with the crises of its present moment (AIDS, environmental disaster, Reaganism) *and* reinvents the vexed, complex, and disturbing elements of the past (McCarthyism, the Mormon experiment, family histories) in order to facilitate a movement beyond these into an uncertain but promising future.

NOTES

1. See Walter Benjamin, "Theses on the Philosophy of History," in *Illuminations,* ed. Hannah Arendt, trans. Harry Cohn (1955; reprint, New York: Harcourt, Brace and World, 1968), 259. On Kushner's use of Benjamin, see Scott Tucker, "Our Queer World: A Storm Blowing from Paradise," *Humanist* 53 (November–December 1993): 32–35; and the essays by David Savran, Michael Cadden, Art Borreca, and Martin Harries in this volume.

2. Tony Kushner, *Angels in America: A Gay Fantasia on National Themes. Part One: Millennium Approaches* (New York: Theatre Communications Group, 1993), 3; *Angels in America: A Gay Fantasia on National Themes. Part Two: Perestroika* (New York: Theatre Communications Group, 1994), 3, 4. Future references will be given parenthetically in the text.

3. Joseph Smith, *The Essential Joseph Smith* (Salt Lake City: Signature Books, 1995), 28. Also see the more elaborate account in *The Book of Mormon: An Account Written by the Hand of Mormon upon Plates: Taken from the Plates of Nephi,* trans. Joseph Smith Jr. (1830; reprint, Salt Lake City: The Church of Jesus Christ of Latter-Day Saints, 1950), prefatory material: "Origin of the Book of Mormon." Future references to *The Book of Mormon* will be given parenthetically in the text.

4. See Allen J. Frantzen, in this volume, for a reading of the play's depiction of Prior's ethnic identity.

5. Class identity is less fully interrogated through the depiction of the play's characters than are other identity categories, though the play certainly shows itself aware of the centrality of class in U.S. politics during the Reagan era.

6. Elizabeth V. Spelman, *Inessential Woman: Problems of Exclusion in Feminist Thought* (Boston: Beacon Press, 1988), 186.

7. See Kushner's comments on the "interesting similarities between Mormonism and Judaism" (101), in David Savran, "Tony Kushner Considers the Long-

standing Problems of Virtue and Happiness: An Interview," *American Theatre* 11:8 (October 1994): 20–27, 100–104, esp. 101–3.

8. I quote from the King James Version, *The Holy Bible* (New York and Scarborough, Ont.: New American Library, 1974).

9. Also see 2 Nephi 5:21 and Alma 3:6 in *The Book of Mormon*. Joseph Smith's own views on race and slavery seem to have shifted; see Smith, *Essential Joseph Smith*, 85–90, a letter of 1836 speaking against abolitionism; and 213–25, a statement of 1844 against the abuse of federal power that calls the "goodly inhabitants of the slave states" to "petition . . . your legislators to abolish slavery by the year 1850, or now" (221).

10. Roy's language here brings the play's doctrinaire McCarthyite/Reaganite together with its Bolshevik, Prelapsarianov (cf. 2:14).

11. This section's title is taken from Benjamin, "Theses on the Philosophy of History," 263.

12. Ibid.

Apocalyptic Imaginations:
Kushner's Theater
of the Millennium

Angels in America: The Millennium and Postmodern Memory

Stanton B. Garner Jr.

The last few years have been marked by an inverted millenarianism in which premonitions of the future, cata-
strophic or redemptive, have been replaced by senses of
the end of this or that (the end of ideology, art, or social
class; the "crisis" of Leninism, social democracy, or the
welfare state, etc., etc.); taken together, all of these perhaps constitute what is increasingly called postmodernism.
The case for its existence depends on the hypothesis of
some radical break or *coupure,* generally traced back to the
end of the 1950s or the early 1960s.
> —Fredric Jameson, *Postmodernism;*
> *or The Cultural Logic of Late Capitalism*

As I surveyed that historical site and looked eastward at
the Atlantic beneath that dazzling moon, I was gripped by
the renewed realization that a dread disease had fastened
itself upon the lands sending forth our forefathers. . . .
And I mourned more deeply because the same sickness
was fastening itself upon my land, the new world so sin-
cerely dedicated to God three hundred and seventy-five
years ago.
> —Pat Robertson, standing near Cape Henry in
> Maryland, in *The Secret Kingdom*

History is about to crack wide open. Millennium
approaches.
> —Ethel Rosenberg, in Tony Kushner, *Angels in
> America: Millennium Approaches*

Postmodernism and the Apocalypse

I open the following reflections on postmodernism, the apocalypse,
and Tony Kushner's play *Angels in America* with these quotations because

they suggest a discursive, cultural, and ideological field within which we might situate both postmodernism as a movement (or set of movements) and *Angels* as a literary/theatrical phenomenon. As the twentieth century confronts its own "last days," millenarianism and apocalypticism have come to constitute a nexus where high culture and low, belief and behavior, meet and overlap. Millenarian and apocalyptic preoccupations are equally evident in the writings of Jacques Derrida and Bible prophecy seminars, in Jean Baudrillard's recent writings and the artifacts of what Paul Boyer calls "end-time" kitsch: paintings of the Beast from Revelations, Rapture bumper stickers, and wrist watches ("One Hour Nearer the Lord's Return").[1] Eschatological belief, of course, has a long heritage, stretching back through Christian apocalypticism into Jewish Messianism. That such beliefs have become more widespread as we approach the year 2000 is not surprising. Millenarianism (the belief in the inauguration of a divinely ruled Golden Age after a cataclysmic upheaval) has tended to intensify at the close of centuries and at larger epochal markers: according to some historians, widespread panic broke out in Europe at the end of the first millennium in the year 1000. But apocalypticism has not been restricted to the transitional moments of calendrical history; this "pattern of anxiety" (to borrow Frank Kermode's phrase)[2] has emerged during other times of crisis and social upheaval—the fourteenth-century plague, the English Civil War—and in connection with nationalist movements in the nineteenth and twentieth centuries.[3] In the words of Michael Barkun millenarian movements constitute "the artifacts of disaster."[4]

From the Puritan settlers, who brought to the New World their vision of a New Jerusalem, through the Mormons, who carried a similar vision in their settlements westward, millenarianism has been an intricate part of the American national myth. During the twentieth century, and particularly after World War II, a darker view of America's millenarian role has prevailed. As the Pat Robertson passage illustrates, the United States has been seen by recent prophecy commentators as a nation whose sinfulness makes it a subject for apocalyptic purging. This heightening of apocalyptic rhetoric formed part of the deeper millenarianism that characterized the Cold War imagination. East-West antagonisms were frequently interpreted in the context of biblical prophecy; as we know, Ronald Reagan and others in his administration were among those who read the U.S.-Soviet confrontation in terms of end-time scenarios. What fueled the postwar escalation in apocalyptic anxiety, of course, was the emergent nuclear threat and the suddenly achievable realities of annihilation. From "Armageddon" to "New World Order," from the Cuban Missile Crisis to Chernobyl, the rhetoric and events of the Cold War reflect an often obsessive awareness of the eschatological brink. Reinforced by economic crisis, ecological disaster, overpopulation, the AIDS epidemic, and the fall of European communism, this anxiety both enacts and exceeds the specifically Christian narrative of Last Days.

As one of the products of this contemporary field, postmodernism is deeply informed by the rhetoric and psychosocial preoccupations of Cold War millenarianism, with its utopian imaginings and its even stronger apprehension of catastrophe. In Linda Hutcheon's words, "The advent of the postmodern condition has been characterized by nothing if not by self-consciousness and by metadiscursive pondering on catastrophe and change."[5] Steven Best and Douglas Kellner attribute the sense of a break in history and the inauguration of a new era on the part of French postmodern theorists to the rupture produced by the events of 1968.[6] But Derrida's observation concerning deconstruction suggests that this sense of an imminent break derives, more broadly, from what he calls the "nuclear epoch": "the hypothesis of [the] total destructibility [of the archive] watches over deconstruction, it guides our footsteps. Literature," he writes, "belongs to this nuclear epoch, that of the crisis and of nuclear criticism, at least if we mean by this the historical and ahistorical horizons of an absolute self-destructibility without apocalypse [in the sense of disclosure], without revelation of its own truth, without absolute knowledge."[7]

At the same time, as Derrida's remarks suggest, the relationship of postmodernism to apocalypticism is profoundly ambivalent. Even as postmodern theorists and writers borrow the rhetoric of rupture and transformation, and even as their writings reflect a culture profoundly oriented in terms of the threat (and promise) of endings, most retain a skepticism concerning the master narrative of millenarianism, with its totalizing temporal structures and its sense of ultimacy. Rupture, destruction, and the violent emergence of the new are also, we should remind ourselves, tropes of modernism. Many of the twentieth century's most powerful millenarian visions can be found in the cultural products of World War I: Tzara's Dada manifestos, Picasso's *Guernica,* and the poetry of Yeats and Eliot (to say nothing of the Soviet Union of Lenin and Stalin and Hitler's messianic Third Reich). Postmodern apocalyptic theorists, by contrast, often engage what Jameson calls an "inverted millenarianism," problematizing the ideas of finitude and conclusion even as they advance them.[8]

Baudrillard, for instance, certainly the most apocalyptic of postmodern writers, with his pronouncements on the end of history and the collapse of the real, reflects this ambivalence toward ending and end-time frameworks. In his essay "The Anorexic Ruins" (published in a collection entitled *Look-*

ing Back on the End of the World) he tries to imagine postmodernity in terms of the traditional/modernist millenarian narrative:

> The pole of reckoning, dénouement, and apocalypse (in the good and the bad sense of the word), which we had been able to postpone until the infiniteness of the Day of Judgment, this pole has come infinitely closer, and one could join [Elias] Canetti in saying that we have already passed it unawares and now find ourselves in the situation of having overextended our own finalities, of having short-circuited our own perspectives, and of already being in the hereafter, that is, without horizon and without hope.[9]

Apocalypse, for Baudrillard, is the defining trope of the contemporary world, yet his is an apocalypse without finality or transformation, in which the epoch of history and the real is replaced by the epoch of simulation. History, Baudrillard writes in his most recent book *The Illusion of the End,* "is no longer able to transcend itself, to envisage its own finality, to dream of its own end."[10] In this belief he joins Peter Brückner and other Continental theorists of *Posthistoire,* who see the contemporary as a meaningless but ever continuing sequence of events, situated beyond the historical.[11]

"In concepts of time," Baudrillard writes, "the point at issue is the end of final calculations. . . . This concludes the attempt at imagining a rupture."[12] Baudrillard is the anti-apocalyptic witness to the apocalypse, or (better) an apocalyptic witness to the anti-apocalypse. In his simultaneous commitment to millenarian narrative and its impossibility, he embodies the ambivalence and self-subversion that characterizes postmodern eschatology. The very instability of the *post* in *postmodernism,* the movement's contradictory, undecidable self-positioning in terms of history and periodization, owes much to such ambivalent appropriation of apocalypse and its narratives of epoch and ultimacy.

Angels and Endings

Angels in America: A Gay Fantasia on National Themes is animated by the terms and imagery of millenarian discourse. Characters speak of the world "coming to an end" (1:28), "threshold of revelation" (1:33), "the grim Unfolding of these Latter Days" (2:134), and "Apocalypse Descending" (2:135).[13] Prior Walter, AIDS sufferer and prophet *malgré lui,* announces: "I believe I've seen the end of things" (2:56). Another of the play's characters, Harper Pitt, whose journey of self-discovery counterpoints that of her husband, Joe, speaks of personal and social disintegration in some of the play's

most direct apocalyptic terms: "Everywhere, things are collapsing, lies surfacing, systems of defense giving way" (1:17). And later: "The end of the
world is at hand. . . . Nothing like storm clouds over Manhattan to get you
in the mood for Judgment Day" (2:101). With an angel crashing through
the roof, flaming Hebrew letters, and a heaven that (covered with rubble) is
designed to resemble San Francisco after the earthquake, the play's mise-en-
scène intensifies this apocalyptic iconography.

Yet, even as it exploits the discourse of millenarianism, *Angels in America* is situated within the postmodern problematic of history and ending. On
the one hand, the play evokes the closure essential to apocalypticism, its
vision of cataclysm and its dual prospects of annihilation and utopian transformation. Harper articulates these eschatological scenarios:

> I feel . . . that something's going to give. It's 1985. Fifteen years till the
> third millennium. Maybe Christ will come again. Maybe seeds will be
> planted, maybe there'll be harvests then, maybe early figs to eat, maybe
> new life, maybe fresh blood, maybe companionship and love and pro-
> tection, safety from what's outside . . . or maybe . . . the troubles will
> come, and the end will come, and the sky will collapse and there will
> be terrible rains and showers of poison light. (1:18)

Like the apocalyptic allusions elsewhere in Kushner's play, Harper's imagery
reflects eschatological anxieties particular to this century's end: global
warming, nuclear war, and AIDS. Her concern with holes in the ozone
layer—"Over Antarctica. Skin burns, birds go blind, icebergs melt. The
world's coming to an end" (1:28)—embodies the nightmare of ecocatastro-
phe, while her obsession with "systems of defense giving way" conflates the
Cold War anxiety over atmospheric nuclear attack (Star Wars paranoia) with
the image of a body's immune system collapsing.

At the same time, the play is characterized by a subtle undermining of
the narrative of rupture and ultimacy and the biblical imagery that accompanies it. Kushner accomplishes this undermining, most directly, through a
parodic self-consciousness that tends to undercut the metaphysical. The
apocalyptic entrance of the Angel at the end of part 1, for instance, is staged
(Kushner specifies) as a specifically *theatrical* illusion, and the sound effects
anticipating this awe-inspiring moment are greeted by Prior's aside: "God
almighty . . . / *Very* Steven Spielberg" (1:118). But parody and other forms
of stylistic subversion are only one way by which Kushner calls eschatological closure into question. The sense of endings essential to the millenarian
scheme is also problematized through principles of supplementarity and
deferral, what we might think of as "false apocalypse." These principles

derive, in part, from the play's specific historical setting. Since the play's story takes place between 1985 and 1991, its scope includes both the intensified millenarianism of the Reagan Cold War and the breathtaking changes that occurred with the revolutions in Eastern Europe, the reforms of Gorbachev, and the fall of the Berlin Wall in 1989. When Harper speaks of "beautiful systems dying, old orders spiraling apart," she evokes a cultural response to these events that was itself deeply imbued with the idiom of apocalypse (consider, for instance, conservative heraldings of the fall of the Soviet Empire as the "end of history").[14] But the specter of 1989 serves to complicate the issue of apocalyptic closure, so strongly associated with the ends of centuries. If the fall of European communism represents an end to the ideological confrontation that stretches back to 1945 (and, further, to 1917), and if it signals the eclipse of an ideological movement that extends even beyond Marx and Engels, then there is indeed a sense in which 1989 stands as a terminal point, the end of an era. With the year 2000 still on the horizon, the presence of this rival end point leaves *Angels in America* caught between apocalypses, contemplating the end of a century that has, in a Baudrillardian sense, already outlived itself.

Within the play itself, of course, cataclysmic points of crisis, redemptive or otherwise, never come, and the play continues beyond its apparent points of closure. Despite Ethel Rosenberg's warning that History is about to "crack wide open," part 1 is followed by part 2, an extension of the narrative beyond its projected narrative culmination (Kushner has indicated that he may write an additional play on the stories of these characters, and more beyond this, in a repetition of this process of supplementation, of continuing beyond endings).[15] The urgency of apocalypse may frame *Angels in America,* but Kushner also establishes currents of indeterminacy and persistence that subvert this eschatological *grand récit.* "While time is running out I find myself drawn to anything that's suspended, that lacks an ending," Prior tells his lover Louis (1:42), and the play displays an anti-apocalyptic willingness to contemplate uncertain outcomes. It also explores the willingness to continue living beyond the undeniable certainties of death and the end-time narrative of AIDS; as Prior says in part 2, "We live past hope" (2:136). From this perspective the refusal of closure allows an opening into the play's peculiarly late-Shakespearean world of unexpected opportunities, temporary reprieves, and second chances.

History and Counterhistory

False apocalypse, postponed apocalypse, the apocalypse that (in Baudrillard's phrase) "we pass unawares"—indeterminacy and deferral complicate the millenarian meditation of *Angels in America*. At the same time, we must not over stress the play's parodic and narrative subversions of eschatological patterns. Tropes of ending are given substance and urgency by the reality of the AIDS epidemic, which Derrida calls "one of the most 'apocalyptic' [events facing humanity] in its most essential and 'interior' history."[16] Particularly in the gay community, AIDS has precipitated a crisis in which apocalyptic anxiety is inescapable. In his book *Apocalyptic Overtures: Sexual Politics and the Sense of an Ending* Richard Dellamora writes:

> AIDS has not destroyed the memory of gay existence, but it has made such destruction imaginable. Under the circumstances, gay writers have been pressed into service as angels of the millennium. Bearing messages to gays and others, they remind us that an archive does exist and that it is our responsibility to carry its words.[17]

Dellamora's formulation of the task of gay writers is useful, for it reminds us of what Kermode first underscored in his 1967 book *The Sense of an Ending:* that apocalypse is ultimately about narrative and about the writing of histories, both private and collective. By positing end-times, millenarian discourse seeks a shape in history, and in its attempts to contextualize the present it is as much about beginnings as it is about endings. For a gay writer apocalypse is a particularly charged narrative field, since in its stark moral polarities, its figurations of sinfulness and evil, and what Barkun calls its "paranoid style"[18] millenarianism has often formed the discursive pretext for the demonizing of otherness and the persecution of minority groups. Gays, of course, have formed a particular and recurrent target of apocalyptic discourse: sex between men has long been associated with end times, as Dellamora notes, and, along with their characterization of a sinful America as Sodom, many contemporary prophecy writers have argued that the Antichrist himself will be homosexual.[19] The AIDS epidemic, not surprisingly, has formed a major topic for recent chroniclers of end-time signals.[20]

Apocalyptic discourse, then, enables Tony Kushner to engage the question of history with a dual agenda: challenging totalizing forms of historical narrative while seeking to find spaces within these narratives for marginal and emergent lines of historical inheritance. The present's problematic relationship to its historical contexts, equally central to millenarianism, postmodernism, and an increasingly multicultural American landscape, is announced in the opening scene to each part of *Angels in America*. *Millennium Approaches* opens with a speech, delivered by an Orthodox rabbi, commemorating the immigrant journey to America, the "Great Voyages" that "do not any more exist" (1:10). Similarly, *Perestroika* opens with a speech delivered by Aleksii Antedilluvianovich Prelapsarianov, the World's Oldest

Living Bolshevik, in 1986 to the Soviet Reformers in the Kremlin Hall of
Deputies. Recalling the guiding vision of the Revolution and its
founders—"like standing atop the highest peak in the mighty Caucasus,
and viewing in one all-knowing glance the mountainous, granite order of
creation"—Prelapsarianov deplores the loss of such totalizing systems:
"What System of Thought have these Reformers to present to this mad
swirling planetary disorganization, to the Inevitable Welter of fact, event,
phenomenon, calamity?" (2:13–14).

Both prologues raise the question of the past, its powerful master narratives, and its role as a repository of identity and models of understanding
and action. Proceeding from these opening scenes, the two parts of *Angels*
demonstrate the persistence of history in an apparently discontinuous present. Rabbi Chemelwitz concludes, "Descendants of this immigrant woman
. . . she worked that earth into your bones, and you pass it to your children,
this ancient, ancient culture and home" (1:10). As Prior's name suggests,
history haunts *Angels in America,* from the thirteenth- and seventeenth-cen-
tury Prior Walters who died in earlier plagues to the Mormon pioneer wife
who steps out of her silence in the visitor center diorama and accompanies
Harper on her own wilderness journey. The play's opening scenes demonstrate Kushner's interest in a specifically gay counterhistory: "It is incum-
bent upon us," he has said, "to examine history and be aware of history, of
where we've come from and what has given us the freedom to talk the way
we do now."[21] But this counterhistory is by no means separatist; it intersects
with and emerges from the wider tapestry of American history, often
rereading the more public forms of this history and reconstructing its conti-
nuities and lineages. Harper's discussion of the Mormon explorations in *Perestroika,* itself an act of feminist revisionism, is followed by Louis teaching
Joe about the history of gay encounters in the dunes at Jones Beach:
"Exploration. Across an unmapped terrain. The body of the homosexual
human male. . . . Hardy pioneers. Like your ancestors" (2:72). Historical re-
narrations such as these establish what Frank Lentricchia has called, in
another context, a field of "histories within history . . . [which] thicken and
make heterogeneous historical textures that tradition and system would
homogenize."[22]

The character of Roy Cohn serves as a vehicle for Kushner's most
telling act of counterhistory. As a "Saint of the Right" (1:64), Cohn represents a point of continuity between the anticommunism of the 1950s and
the Republican ascendancy of the Reagan 1980s. The millenarian overtones
of this ascendancy are made clear in Martin's glorification of the Reagan
revolution:

It's really the end of Liberalism. The end of New Deal Socialism. The
end of ipso facto secular humanism. The dawning of a genuinely
American political personality. Modeled on Ronald Wilson Reagan.
(1:63)

For Cohn the Republican tradition is patriarchal at heart, and it perpetuates
itself through the relationship of fathers and sons; as he tells Joe: "I've had
many fathers, I owe my life to them, powerful, powerful men. Walter
Winchell, Edgar Hoover, Joe McCarthy most of all" (1:56). The word
fathers, of course, resonates deep within the American historical imagination, and the sense of male power as something handed down through a
cruel but loving struggle—"Sometimes a father's love has to be very, very
hard, unfair even, cold to make his son grow strong in a world like this"
(1:56)—is central to the masculinist tradition of American drama against
which Kushner writes.

At the same time, and through a remarkable play of double meanings,
Cohn's description of the father-son bond is coded in terms of the homosexual desire he seeks both to indulge and conceal. The language of love,
struggle, and transmission—"The son offers the father his life as a vessel for
carrying forth his father's dream" (1:56)—is animated by a subtext of sexual
encounter, its sadomasochism mirrored in the sexual encounter (Louis and
the Man in the Park) with which this scene is intercut. As embodied in
Cohn and his Royboys (and in Joe, the play's other gay Republican),
homosexual desire is disclosed as countercurrent to the conservative discourse of male inheritance. This current is at once a culmination of this discourse's fixation on male relationship and its subversion. On the eve of the
Republican millennium the official narrative of heterosexual male hegemony reveals the rival narrative—silenced, disowned, the site of surrepti-
tious sexuality—at its heart.

As Tony Kushner exploits and revises the discourse and figures of
apocalypse, in other words, he finds in this discourse, as did Baudrillard,
issues of history and postmodern memory. Unlike Baudrillard, however,
Kushner finds not the eclipse of history but, rather, the necessity (and the
opportunity) of reimagining its forms of legacy. Baudrillard's apocalypticism
represents (like Beckett's) a form of mourning—in this case for the space of
the real and for the tangibility of a history not lost to simulacra. Kushner, on
the other hand, takes the apocalyptic invitation to history as a way of opening the spaces within its master narratives, affirming the lines of historical
identity even as it radically reconfigures them. Both the utopianism and the
disaster imagination that Kushner appropriates from millenarianism are,

finally, not imaginable outside history. Kushner says this of Walter Benjamin, whose Angel of History looks over the rubble of history as it is blown into the future: "Benjamin's sense of utopianism is also so profoundly apocalyptic: a teleology, but not a guarantee, or a guarantee that Utopia will be as fraught and as infected with history."[23] Kushner's final verb here is not without its contemporary urgency.

Kushner returns to millenarian iconography in the closing moments of *Perestroika*. Harper recounts a dream as she sits in an airplane on her way to San Francisco. In this dream she flies above the depleted ozone layer, which has served throughout *Angels in America* as an image of systems collapsing. In her dream, though,

> Souls were rising, from the earth far below, souls of the dead, of people who had perished, from famine, from war, from the plague, and they floated up, like skydivers in reverse, limbs all akimbo, wheeling and spinning. And the souls of these departed joined hands, clasped ankles, and formed a web, a great net of souls, and the souls were three-atom oxygen molecules, of the stuff of ozone, and the outer rim absorbed them, and was repaired. (2:144)

The image draws directly upon millenarian iconography, specifically that of the Rapture, with its souls called from their graves, along with the living, on Judgment Day. But, while the Rapture is conventionally figured in terms of the Saved and the Damned, with the emphasis on punishment and retribution, Harper's vision of resurrection is universal in its inclusiveness, and its focus is on healing and repair. Beyond Harper's speech, in the epilogue to this two-part epic that keeps outlasting itself, Hannah Pitt evokes the millennium as she sits with Louis, Belize, and Prior (who has not died) under the statue of the angel Bethesda: "When the Millennium comes . . . the fountain of Bethesda will flow again. . . . We will all bathe ourselves clean" (2:147). The Berlin Wall has fallen; Perestroika is transforming the Soviet Union; "the whole world is changing! Overnight!" (2:145). The inauguration of a new age, with the attendant promise of rebirth, seems everywhere at the end of *Angels in America*.

In their recourse to millenarian imagery these closing scenes represent Kushner's final attempt to rewrite apocalypse, to borrow its urgency and its transformative imagination while challenging its exclusions and maintaining an awareness of its precarious fictionality. All will be included in the benediction of the millennium, even (perhaps) Roy. At the same time, the presence of a weakened Prior—and the proximity of death that has haunted this play from its opening moments—reminds us of the wishfulness of even these millenarian projections. In its utopian, as in its cataclysmic, forms this vision of endings and new beginnings remains a kind of dream, a way of imagining the future and seeking meaning for the present. Reality marks the limits of the miraculous. Millenarianism may offer narratives of the new, but its transformative scenarios remain shadowed by what has been lost and by the knowledge—intimate apocalypse, to be sure—of what will be.

NOTES

Fredric Jameson, *Postmodernism; or The Cultural Logic of Late Capitalism* (Durham, N.C.: Duke University Press, 1991), 1; Pat Robertson, *The Secret Kingdom* (New York: Bantam Books, 1982), 14; Tony Kushner, *Angels in America: A Gay Fantasia on National Themes. Part One: Millennium Approaches* (New York: Theatre Communications Group, 1993), 112. Subsequent references to *Millennium Approaches* will be indicated parenthetically in the text.

1. Paul Boyer, *When Time Shall Be No More: Prophecy Belief in Modern American Culture* (Cambridge, Mass.: Harvard University Press, 1992), 7–8.
2. Frank Kermode, *The Sense of an Ending: Studies in the Theory of Fiction* (New Haven, Conn.: Yale University Press, 1967), 96.
3. See, for example, Hillel Schwartz, *Century's End: A Cultural History of the Fin de Siècle from the 990s through the 1990s* (New York: Doubleday, 1990); and Dragan Klaic, *The Plot of the Future* (Ann Arbor: University of Michigan Press, 1991), 19–22. The classic study of medieval millenarianism is Norman Cohn, *The Pursuit of the Millennium: Revolutionary Millenarians and Mystical Anarchists of the Middle Ages*, rev. ed. (London: Temple Smith, 1970).
4. Michael Barkun, *Disaster and the Millennium* (New Haven, Conn.: Yale University Press, 1974), 55.
5. Linda Hutcheon, *The Poetics of Postmodernism: History, Theory, Fiction* (New York: Routledge, 1988), 75.
6. Steven Best and Douglas Kellner, *Postmodern Theory: Critical Interrogations* (New York: Guilford, 1991), 15.
7. Jacques Derrida, "No Apocalypse, Not Now (Full Speed Ahead, Seven Missiles, Seven Missives)," *diacritics* 14 (Summer 1984): 27. See also "Of an Apocalyptic Tone Recently Adopted in Philosophy," *Oxford Literary Review* 6 (1984): 3–37.
8. See also Lois Parkinson Zamora's study *Writing the Apocalypse: Historical Vision in Contemporary U.S. and Latin American Fiction* (Cambridge: Cambridge University Press, 1989). John Barth and Julio Cortázar, for example, use "the mythic vision and narrative structures of apocalypse to embody the postmodern skepticism about the very possibility of conclusion" (5).
9. Jean Baudrillard, "The Anorexic Ruins," in *Looking Back on the End of the World*, ed. Dietmar Kamper and Christophe Wulf, trans. David Antal (New York: Semiotext[e], 1989), 33.

10. Jean Baudrillard, *The Illusion of the End,* trans. Chris Turner (Stanford: Stanford University Press, 1994), 4. See also "The Year 2000 Has Already Happened," in *Body Invaders: Panic Sex in America,* ed. Arthur Kroker and Marilouise Kroker (Montreal: New World Perspectives, 1988), 35–44.

11 See Lutz Niethammer, *Posthistoire: Has History Come to an End?* trans. Patrick Camiller (London: Verso, 1992), 138.

12. Baudrillard, "Anorexic Ruins," 41–42.

13. The last two quotations are from Tony Kushner, *Angels in America: A Gay Fantasia on National Themes. Part Two: Perestroika* (New York: Theatre Communications Group, 1994). Subsequent references to *Perestroika* will be indicated parenthetically in the text.

14. See, for example, Francis Fukuyama, "The End of History?" *National Interest* 16 (Summer 1989): 3–18.

15. Tony Kushner, quoted in David Savran, "Tony Kushner Considers the Longstanding Problems of Virtue and Happiness," *American Theatre* 11 (October 1994): 104.

16. Jacques Derrida, "The Rhetoric of Drugs: An Interview," trans. Michael Israel, *differences* 5 (Spring 1993): 5.

17. Richard Dellamora, *Apocalyptic Overtures: Sexual Politics and the Sense of an Ending* (New Brunswick, N.J.: Rutgers University Press, 1994), 28.

18. Barkun, *Disaster and the Millennium,* 152.

19. Dellamora, *Apocalyptic Overtures,* 3; Boyer, *When Time Shall Be No More,* 234.

20. See, for example, Hal Lindsey, *Planet Earth—2000 A.D.* (Palos Verdes, CA: Western Front Ltd., 1994), 101–18 ("Is AIDS Just the Beginning?"). The recurrent metaphor of sinfulness as a disease, deployed in the Robertson epigraph, suggests why this association has proven so irresistible. AIDS, according to this equation, conflates both transgression and its punishment.

21. Tony Kushner, quoted in Savran, "Tony Kushner Considers," 25.

22. Frank Lentricchia, *Criticism and Social Change* (Chicago: University of Chicago Press, 1983), 70.

23. Kushner, quoted in Savran, "Tony Kushner Considers," 26.

Flying the Angel of History

Martin Harries

Damn braces; Bless relaxes.
—William Blake, *The Marriage of Heaven and Hell*

The first "angel" in *Angels in America,* after the title, is the Kaposi's sarcoma lesion that Prior shows Louis. As if to find solace and shelter in word games, puns, and allusions, Prior delivers a baroque diagnosis: "The wine-dark kiss of the angel of death."[1] Prior's overdetermined phrase captures the powerful mix of the erotic and the fatal that marks the angels of Kushner's work. As Prior's angel is the symptom of a bodily illness, Kushner's angels in America are the heralds of a damaged polis. With its allusion to the seas of Homer, Prior's phrase also encapsulates the epic aspirations of *Angels in America.* Another epic tradition is at work here as well: Prior, whose pun alludes to Homer, occupies a dramatic space indebted to Brecht. But Kushner revises the Brechtian tradition in crucial ways; central to this revision is his return to the supernatural. Understanding Kushner's staging of angels requires an investigation of his theatricalization of the thought of Walter Benjamin, in particular his reworking of Benjamin's angel of history. It is one of the epic projects of *Angels in America,* to use the stage technician's term, to "fly" that angel. That difficult flying, at once technical feat, theatrical spectacle, and critical strategy, illustrates the contemporary necessity of supernatural representation but also forces questions about the sacral character of closure in *Angels in America.*

A telling imperative appears among the lessons in Roland Barthes's elegant summary of Brechtian dramaturgy: "the theater must cease to be magical in order to become critical."[2] A stage direction in both parts of *Angels* best shows how Kushner upends this Brechtian imperative and tradition:

> The moments of magic—the appearance and disappearance of Mr. Lies and the ghosts, the Book hallucination, and the ending—are to be fully realized, as bits of wonderful *theatrical* illusion—which means it's OK if the wires show, and maybe it's good that they do, but the magic should at the same time be thoroughly amazing. (1:5)[3]

Without Brecht *Angels in America* would be unimaginable. It is, however, equally unimaginable that Brecht might have attempted something like Kushner's play. Brecht demanded that the theater confess the means of its production; in his theater of estrangement the spectator sees through the construction of "wonderful theatrical illusions" and is therefore invulnerable to any magic. Kushner, by contrast, remains uncertain: "maybe it's good" that "the wires show," maybe not. It would, however, be a mistake to see *Angels in America* as sheer demolition of the Brechtian tradition of demystification.

The shift from Brecht's disenchantment to Kushner's openly theatrical yet still "thoroughly amazing" magic marks a larger change. In a specific aesthetic sense *Angels in America* is postmodern. An aversion to supernatural spectacle characterizes "modern" drama: Brecht is, for once, representative of a larger modernist tradition in seeking to cease being magical. With a few very problematic exceptions—for instance, Lorca's Moon in *Blood Wedding* or Brecht's own "gods" in *The Good Person of Szechwan* or Sartre's flies—a taboo against magic ruled the modern stage from the slamming of the door at the end of *A Doll's House* to the 1960s.[4] One can think of Beckett's Godot: there are formal as well as philosophical reasons why Godot cannot arrive. ("The bastard! He doesn't exist!")[5] The impossibility of such an arrival puts into starker contrast the problem posed by the Angel that bursts through the ceiling at the end of *Millennium Approaches*. Why *can* that Angel arrive?

Angels in America occupies a peculiar and fascinating moment in the history of the representation of the supernatural onstage. The work captures, in intriguing and troubling ways, mutations in a larger world of social "magic." To understand this moment of the supernatural one can reverse Barthes's lesson: to become critical the theater must begin again to be magical. This change does not contradict but, instead, continues the work of Brecht's defamiliarization effect. *Angels in America* grapples with the dilemma that "disenchanted" icons of modernism—including the narrow example of the taboo against representation of the supernatural onstage—have themselves becomes magical. The disenchantment of the stage has by no means been coterminous with the supposed disenchantment of the social world, that larger late Enlightenment project to which modern, especially Brechtian, stagecraft was allied. Indeed, a paradox of the contemporary moment is that enchantment itself now proceeds with Brechtian gestures. Apparatuses of many kinds—theatrical, audiovisual, political—announce and celebrate the ways in which they are constructed. Consider the sudden ubiquity of the hand-held camera or the cult of the pollster and campaign

manager or, more generally, the rise of an "insider culture" in which everyone is left out in the cold.[6] Political and entertainment apparatuses advertise
their constructedness, paradoxically reenacting a classic maneuver of disenchantment: to show the "inner workings" of power should demystify it. But
this putative demystification has the opposite effect: "disenchantment" itself
becomes supernatural; the disavowal of magic becomes magical. The look
of the hand-held camera now forms part of a "style," laboriously achieved.
Once disenchanted apparatuses defamiliarized the real; now these same
apparatuses have become so familiar that they conceal what they should
estrange. In *Angels in America* estranging the real now includes the imperative to estrange a new sort of magic: that is, the theater must represent the
new social magic as magic in order to demystify it.

Stage history supplies an allegory of the matter of the "wires": technical problems with flying the angel delayed the Broadway openings of both
Millennium Approaches and *Perestroika*.[7] The wires, it seems, showed too
much. This technical problem illustrates the limits of demystification in
Angels. On the wandering path of *Angels* from San Francisco to London to
Los Angeles to Broadway the artifice behind the magic became less and less
palatable, as a sketch of the plays' stage history will show. Ellen McLaughlin recalls playing the angel in San Francisco: "I hung on a rope."[8] In London, writes Art Borreca, the director, Declan Donnellan, "made the
moments of magic utterly artificial, and therefore more completely magical."[9] The Los Angeles production never staged the arrival of the Angel at
the end of *Millennium Approaches* to the playwright's satisfaction: "Finally,"
Kushner remembered, "we got it so that if nobody breathed in the theater
and we got the lights off quickly, you wouldn't see her start spinning. But
she always sort of torqued a little bit to the left."[10] The Broadway angel,
then, appears to be the solution to this history of technical problems. This
state of technical perfection, however, raises questions about *Angels'* critical
attitude toward the supernatural. A note to *Perestroika* recommends:

> *Flying:* If you are mounting a production of the play, and you
> plan to have an airborne angel, which is a good thing, be
> warned: It's incredibly hard to make the flying work. Add a
> week to tech time.
>
> (2:9)

Angels in America, it seems, must enchant the audience before the work of
estrangement can begin. One can blame this progressively more elaborate
concession to convincing stage magic on a pandering to Broadway's

demands for the spectacular deus ex machina, whether it be the helicopter in *Miss Saigon* or the falling chandelier in *Phantom of the Opera*. This explanation, however, fails to account for an ambivalence about the supernatural within Kushner's plays themselves, an ambivalence that becomes especially remarkable in *Perestroika*.

I have so far implied that Kushner's project is consistent with a Brechtian one and that Kushner, like Brecht, seeks to estrange the audience from a postmodern moment in which Brechtian tools of demystification have themselves become mystified. This implication misses important differences between the two parts of *Angels*. Whereas *Millennium Approaches* quite rigorously subjects the play's various forms of the supernatural to questioning, ending with the spectacularly questionable shape of the angel's appearance, *Perestroika* finds closure in a kind of domesticated supernatural power. Prior rejects the mission the Angel gives to him, but a rescue of the supernatural—*Perestroika*'s blessing—accompanies that refusal. It may be that this rescued supernatural residue echoes Benjamin's revolutionary "weak messianic power, a power to which the past has a claim."[11] It may also be, however, that this power is more in conformity with the disturbing and symptomatic Angelmania of our fin de siècle: angels *are* everywhere in America, and this is not necessarily an encouraging sign.[12]

It is the project of *Angels,* one can say, to stage the reconciliation between theology and historical materialism that was Benjamin's final, doomed project in "Theses on the Philosophy of History." Is this reconciliation timely? It is possible that, just as Brecht's alienation effects have become tools of the very apparatuses from which they should distance the spectator, Benjamin's project, part politics and part theology, is not made for these times. To ask these questions in a concentrated way I will focus on Kushner's figures of the storm in *Millennium Approaches;* on the question of blessing in *Perestroika;* and on what becomes of the exposed wires and of the metatheatrical *Angels*.

Kushner stages Benjamin's angel.[13] He also brings Benjamin's Marxist revision of Jewish messianism to Broadway. The millennium is, one can say, the storm of storms, the storm after which there will be no more storms. Harper speaks of the coming millennium:

> It's 1985. Fifteen years till the third millennium. Maybe Christ will come again. Maybe seeds will be planted, maybe there'll be harvests then, maybe early figs to eat, maybe new life, maybe fresh blood, maybe companionship and love and protection, safety from what's outside, maybe the door will hold, or maybe . . . maybe the troubles

will come, and the end will come, and the sky will collapse and there will be terrible rains and showers of poison light. (1:18)

Much later Prior describes a different millennium, "Not the year two thousand, but the Capital M Millennium" (2:147). To Prior it is incidental that 2000 approaches. According to Benjamin's understanding, the millennium would be simultaneous with revolution as understood by Marx. There is no special magic in a date: the year 2000 or 2001 is no more "shot through" with "chips of Messianic time" than the present moment (T 263).

Benjamin's well-known passage resonates throughout *Angels,* and therefore I quote it in full:

A Klee painting named "Angelus Novus" shows an angel looking as though he is about to move away from something he is fixedly contemplating. His eyes are staring, his mouth is open, his wings are spread. The angel of history must appear in this way. He has turned his face toward the past. Where a chain of events appears before us, there *he* sees one single catastrophe, which incessantly piles ruin upon ruin and hurls it in front of his feet. The angel would like to stay, awaken the dead, and join together what has been smashed apart. But a storm blows out from Paradise, which has captured him in his wings and is so strong that the angel can no longer close them. This storm irresistibly propels him into the future, to which his back is turned, while the pile of debris before him grows skyward. That, which we call progress, is *this* storm. (T 257–58)[14]

We are not meant to celebrate Benjamin's angel any more than we are to worship Kushner's. Benjamin describes what the angel of history cannot do: he cannot stay, cannot awaken the dead, cannot join together what has been smashed. Desire to act—"The angel would like to stay"—coupled with the inability to act recalls the bureaucrat angels of *Perestroika.* (Indeed, if Benjamin's "Theses" ask for reverence at all, it is for the hunchback who guides the hands of the puppet that is "historical materialism" [T 253].) Many questions follow from the dialogue between the "Theses on the Philosophy of History" and *Angels in America,* and I turn to the end of *Millennium Approaches.* A spectrum of brilliant color concludes in *"spectacular royal purple"* then silence:

Prior *(An awestruck whisper):* God almighty . . .
 Very Steven Spielberg.
 (A sound, like a plummeting meteor, tears down from very, very far

above the earth, hurtling at an incredible velocity towards the bedroom;
. . . as the room reaches darkness, we hear a terrifying CRASH *as*
something immense strikes earth; the whole building shudders and a
part of the bedroom ceiling . . . crashes to the floor. And then in a
shower of unearthly white light, spreading great opalescent gray-silver
wings, the Angel descends into the room and floats above the bed.)
Angel:

>   Greetings, Prophet;
>   The Great Work begins:
>   The Messenger has arrived.

(1:118–19)

With a blackout *Millennium Approaches* ends. This angelic visitation is
not a resort to some sudden and unexpected deus ex machina. *Millennium
Approaches* is already full of storms and angels before this climactic moment;
the various facets of this storm are worth investigation. Indeed, even the
spectrum of colors echoes earlier moments in the play. The climactic purple recalls earlier dialogue in which Belize admonishes Louis:

>   Oh cheer up, Louis. Look at that heavy sky out there.
>   *Louis:* Purple.
>   *Belize: Purple?* Boy, what kind of homosexual are you, anyway?
>   That's not purple, Mary, that color up there is *(Very grand)*
>   *mauve.*

(1:100)

On the one hand, this is a perfect campy joke. On the other hand, this dialogue gets to the play's theological core. Louis's misrecognition of the color
of the sky is symptomatic of a play in which every character is to some
extent a false prophet. Louis may be wrong about the color at this moment,
but purple is also the last color in the spectacular sequence before the arrival
of the Angel. It is as if Louis is given a premature intimation of the Angel's
presence. Benjamin's notion that every generation possesses a "weak messianic power" haunts *Millennium Approaches* (T 254). With the problematic
exception of Belize each major character in *Millennium Approaches* has a sort
of partial and profane illumination.[15] Those Benjaminian "chips" of messianic power are evenly distributed: for each character a different millennium. But these remain chips only, fragments of a revelation that is by no
means the sum of these broken parts. For one character's ecological fantasy
the play delivers another's Reaganite second coming. The visitation at the

play's end, then, comes as the synthesis of its dialectical shuttling between those contrary versions of apocalypse. The rubble contemplated by the angel in *Millennium Approaches* includes, along with Prior's bedroom ceiling, the debris of faulty, incomplete angelologies, storm warnings, and ideologies. Indeed, what exactly the singling out of Prior as a true Prophet represents is a large question, one that *Perestroika* further complicates. Prior may be left in the ruins of his apartment—the ruins that, one might say, it is the work of *Perestroika* to rebuild or reassemble—but, unlike Louis, for instance, he can read the color of the sky, has heard the storm, and seen an angel. Kushner the playwright plays the role of the hidden hunchback, bringing together Louis, the dialectical materialist, and Prior, the angelologist.[16]

The audience first hears of a storm not from Prior but from the character who is in many ways his foil, Roy Cohn. (Prior is a reluctant "prophet," while Cohn, according to a Reaganite member of the Justice Department, "is a Saint of the Right" [1:64]; Prior and Cohn never share the stage.)[17] Cohn interrupts himself on the telephone to deliver this "philosophical" reflection to the rattled Joe Pitt:

> I see the universe, Joe, as a kind of sandstorm in outer space with winds
> of mega-hurricane velocity, but instead of grains of sand it's shards and
> splinters of glass. You ever feel that way? Ever have one of those days?
> (1:13)

Cohn alludes to this storm later, when he advises Joe: "don't be afraid to live in the raw wind, naked, alone" (1:58). Cohn's doctrine of rugged Republican individualism has an almost immediate echo in Harper Pitt's first monologue about the ozone layer:

> It's a kind of gift, from God, the crowning touch to the creation of the
> world: guardian angels, hands linked, make a spherical net, a blue-
> green nesting orb, a shell of safety for life itself. But everywhere, things
> are collapsing, lies surfacing, systems of defense giving way. (1:16–17)

Harper imagines the ozone layer as a strategic defense initiative, so to speak, against the brutality of Cohn's storm. Yet the play can participate in Harper's fantasy no more than it can in Cohn's. And so we encounter dialectics on Broadway: *Millennium Approaches* raises Cohn's brutal version of the storm and Harper's New Age–tinged cosmology in order to criticize them.

It is in this dialectical context that one should understand the central speech in which Louis—who indirectly describes himself as "a person who has this neo-Hegelian positivist sense of constant historical progress towards happiness or perfection or something" (1:25)—denies the existence of "angels in America":

> the spiritualists try to use that stuff, are you enlightened, are you cen-
> tered, channeled, whatever, this reaching out for a spiritual past in a
> country where no indigenous spirits exist—only the Indians, I mean
> Native American spirits and we killed them off so now, there are no
> gods here, no ghosts and spirits in America, there are no angels in
> America, no spiritual past, no racial past, there's only the political, and
> the decoys and the ploys to maneuver around the inescapable battle of
> politics, the shifting downwards and outwards of political power to the
> . . . people.

Belize interrupts:

> POWER to the people! AMEN! *(Looking at his watch)* OH MY GOODNESS!
> Will you look at the time, I gotta . . . (1:92)

Belize's look at his watch is at once the familiar strategy for avoiding the irritating and a register of the belatedness of the sort of analysis Louis offers. Louis's denial of the existence of angels in America at once contradicts the evidence of the play: the previous scene ends with Prior Walter's ancestors and namesakes preparing him for the climactic angelic visitation.[18] More-over, Belize's mocking of Louis's reversion to the slogan of the 1960s implies that the ideological analysis Louis offers is out of date. Yet hurriedly to claim that the play as a whole simply joins Belize in rejecting Louis's analysis of the function of the supernatural in America is to move too quickly. As I have argued, the play conjures supernaturally figured ideolog-ical positions in order to criticize them. (Again, the Brechtian precedent is crucial.) The play, however, cannot disavow the movement from macro-cosm to microcosm that is typical of these characters' constructions: Roy Cohn moves from universal storm to griping about a bad day; Harper offers one of the play's allegories for AIDS with her picture of the ozone layer and "systems of defense giving way"; Louis uses his "neo-Hegelian" philosophy of history to explain his abandonment of Prior. A similar movement between parts and totality marks the play itself, and the Angel is in many ways the culmination of this movement.

There are many links between Broadway's postmodernist, pre-Raphaelite Angel and Klee's more modest, bewildered new angel. Con-templating Klee's picture, Benjamin writes: "The angel of history must appear in this way." For Benjamin, as for Kushner, the crucial question is one of the accurate representation of history, of how this angel must be represented. And one may locate the spectator's problem in the always problematic genitive, in the "of" in Benjamin's phrase, the "angel of history." One must wonder how the angel belongs to history, whether it is the angel as product or as agent of history.

The spectator gets a clue from Prior's reaction to the spectacular preamble to the visitation—the parade of lights—when he wisecracks, "*Very Steven Spielberg.*"[19] Prior knows this spectacular purple light belongs to Hollywood. For a moment Prior is the disenchanted spectator who can identify the machinery behind the spectacle. Yet, immediately afterward, the Angel does arrive, and the arrival leaves Prior silent, caught in the same storm that drives the Angel through the ceiling. And *Millennium Approaches* is itself caught in this storm. The play historicizes the recent past and demands that the audience see that the way to perform this historical work accurately is to represent that historical moment as haunted, as supernatural. If, for Brecht, a schematic staging of the forces in conflict in society might have the force of political education, Kushner's project involves the recognition that many of the forces at work in Reagan's America had their basis in fantasy and that to represent these forces accurately demands supernatural representation. One can think (to bring together a constellation suggested by *Angels*) of the Star Wars initiative, the demonization of gay men with AIDS and the singling out of so-called "innocent victims," not to mention Nancy Reagan's consulting an astrologer while her husband laid plans for waging war on the Evil Empire.

The scene in the Mormon Visitor's Center Diorama Room, *Angels'* "Mousetrap," provides a crucial example for the investigation of *Angels'* supernatural and theatrical nexus. First, the scene treats technical difficulties in the staging of an epic inspired by an angel. In a line that has surely amused stagehands in several cities, Harper jokes, "They're having trouble with the machinery" (2:63). The scene offers an allegory of producing *Angels* for the stage: it is precisely in witnessing "trouble with the machinery," problems with the wires—in the lack of purely successful illusion—that the post-Brechtian audience realizes the steady demystification of the angels. But the epic Mormon scene Harper and Prior watch also stages fact: the superimposition of Joe and Louis's affair on the story of the westward migration functions as a double plot for *Angels* itself. The diorama is another of *Angels'* microcosms, a case study for the work's suggestion that the paranormal is at once a theatrical accident and, to use the phrase shared by Harper and Prior that resurfaces in the Visitor's Center, "Threshold . . . of revelation" (2:70–71). Harper cannot put the pieces of the disrupted representation together and complains that Louis has "got absolutely *nothing* to do with the story" (2:67); Prior sees that this problematic machinery has revealed to him what has become of Louis. Harper, however cynically, links what happens in the diorama to the supernatural apparatus of *Angels* as a whole: "I told you it wasn't working right, it's just . . . the magic of the theatre or something" (2:68). Harper knows that "the magic of the theatre" is a cliché, but she also knows that it is only a partial explanation for what they have seen. The shared hallucination echoes the central dramatic conceit of *Angels:* the audience sees and comes to believe in "the magic of the theatre," in angels in America. But the diorama scene also stresses the loss implicit in the staging of angels. As the scene recapitulates the abandonment of Harper by Joe and of Prior by Louis, *Angels* as a whole recapitulates what it announces: the loss of angels. The supernatural in *Angels* first works by negation: it offers a convincing image of what is not available to us, of the "spiritual" messenger we have lost or never had.

Kushner's supernatural project, however, works not only by negation of these phantasms. The project of his theater, to put it baldly, is to concoct a countermagic that not only disenchants but also has its own sacred force. This is crucial to understanding the ending of *Perestroika,* with Prior's blessing. Roy Cohn blesses Joe; Ethel Rosenberg and Louis say Kaddish for Cohn; Prior blesses the audience. Our wrestling with *Angels in America,* the ending suggests, should be like Jacob's wrestling with the angel: we emerge with the play's blessing. *Angels* offers a way out of the angelic, reactionary, Reaganite supernatural nexus, but it is through the supernatural performance of a blessing. A blunt question remains: does the audience deserve the blessing? Kushner told an interviewer that an earlier version of Prior's final speech used to include "very confrontational" material: "We won't die for you anymore, and fuck you if you can't accept it." This sort of speech, Kushner decided, "would only work if it could be understood in the context of an embracing gesture the play is making and that I want the play to make."[20] Evidently, Kushner decided that the two modes were incompatible: the blessing and the curse became irreconcilable.[21] Ethel Rosenberg's choice to end the Kaddish for Cohn with "You sonofabitch" presents a model for a mixed blessing Kushner's conclusion does not follow (2:126).

"Art is a negative knowledge of the actual world," writes Adorno.[22] *Angels in America* as it closes, forgoes the dialectical task of negating what it affirms. The play blesses where, perhaps, it should curse. It is worth looking, in this connection, at Harper's final vision:

> Souls were rising, from the earth far below, souls of the dead, of people who had perished, from famine, from war, from the plague, and they floated up, like skydivers in reverse, limbs all akimbo, wheeling and spinning. And the souls of these departed joined hands, clasped ankles, and formed a web, a great net of souls, and the souls were three-atom molecules, of the stuff of ozone, and the outer rim absorbed them, and was repaired. (2:144)

Harper remains absent among those who join Prior in Central Park at the play's end. *Perestroika* may not include Harper or Joe in the play's blessing. The ending implies that the long education of *Angels* has not included these two lapsed Mormons. And yet the play does not simply reject Harper's vision and its New Age occultism; its compensatory logic—the dead end up saving us—is not so different from what Prior promises: "the dead will be commemorated and will struggle on with the living, and we are not going away" (2:148). Are "we" the dead or the living? Prior echoes Benjamin:

> Only that historian will have the gift of fanning the spark of hope in the past who is firmly convinced that *even the dead* will not be safe from the enemy if he wins. And this enemy has not ceased to be victorious. (T 255)

Kushner's echo, however, reverses Benjamin. In the "Theses on the Philosophy of History" it is the living who keep the dead safe and not the other way around.

Kushner also directly echoes one of Harper's phrases—the "net of souls"—in the "Afterword" that forms part of the published text of *Perestroika*:

> Marx was right: The smallest divisible human unit is two people, not one; one is a fiction. From such nets of souls societies, the social world, human life springs. And also plays. (2:158)

The jump from Marx's two people to Kushner's nets of souls is a jump from a footnote in *Capital* to the rhetoric of New Age humanism.[23] Kushner reminds the audience that to stress repeatedly the value of the individual becomes especially dangerous in a time when material safety nets are everywhere giving way. But his phrase *nets of souls* recalls the "spiritual" domain *Angels* shows to be suspect. Nets of souls are also a fiction. As fiction, as metaphor, the notion does no harm; it may even have the political force of offering a fragment of a future that it is not only important but also necessary to grasp. Surely America needs models for community. But premature belief in the myth of nets of souls may also be dangerous. Material fact snaps the wires holding such nets together, and yet myth can survive such snapping, leaving the illusion that nothing has broken. The blessing can happen; one can "fly" an angel—but one can only stage blessing and angel. To forget the wires is to fall.[24]

NOTES

1. Tony Kushner, *Angels in America: A Gay Fantasia on National Themes. Part One: Millennium Approaches* (New York: Theatre Communications Group, 1993), 21. Further references appear in the text.

2. Roland Barthes, "The Brechtian Revolution," *Critical Essays,* trans. Richard Howard (Evanston, Ill.: Northwestern University Press, 1972), 38.

3. The stage direction also appears, with slight variations, in *Angels in America: A Gay Fantasia on National Themes. Part Two: Perestroika* (New York: Theatre Communications Group, 1994), 8. Further references appear in the text.

4. The work of Artaud offers the most important exception to this rule: his project in *The Theater and Its Double* is explicitly magical. Artaud's antipathy toward the mass of the dramatic work of his contemporaries, indeed, stems partly from his revulsion against the refusal to be magical that Barthes describes. It is worth noting here that, when Kushner adapted a play of Brecht's at the La Jolla Playhouse in 1994, he chose *The Good Person of Szechwan;* Brecht's ineffectual gods occupy a bough on the family tree of Kushner's more spectacular angels. As if to emphasize the allure of both Brechtian disenchantment and Artaudian magic that marks *Angels,* Kushner has also recently published a prose piece in many ways redolent of Artaud. See his essay "The Theater of Utopia," *Theater* 26, no. 1 (1995): 9–11.

5. Samuel Beckett, *Endgame* (New York: Grove, 1958), 55.

6. I owe this last sentence and the phrase in scare quotes to conversations with Shawn Rosenheim.

7. For the delay in opening *Millennium Approaches,* see Bruce Weber, "*Angels'* Angels," *New York Times Magazine,* 25 April 1993, 56; for *Perestroika,* see Weber, "Two Wings, a Prayer and Backstage Help," *New York Times,* 5 January 1994, c15, c16.

8. Weber, "Two Wings."

9. Art Borreca, review of *Millennium Approaches,* by Tony Kushner, as performed by the Royal National Theatre, London, *Theatre Journal* 45 (1993): 237.

10. Weber, "*Angels'* Angels," 52.

11. Walter Benjamin, "Theses on the Philosophy of History," in *Illuminations,* ed. Hannah Arendt, trans. Harry Zohn (New York: Schocken Books, 1969), 254; hereafter cited parenthetically as T.

12. Angels are rampant. For preliminary notes on this, see the rich and bizarre *Time* cover story by Nancy Gibbs, "Angels among Us," 27 December 1993, 56–65.

13. Benjamin's influence on Kushner is well documented. In an afterword to

Perestroika Kushner describes his friendship with Kimberly T. Flynn, which led to his reading of Benjamin, "whose importance for me rests primarily in his introduction into the 'scientific' disciplines of Marx and Freud a Kabbalist-inflected mysticism and a dark, apocalyptic spirituality" (2:154).

14. I have slightly modified the translation to bring out some of the vividness of Benjamin's descriptions of disaster. For the German text, see Benjamin's "Über den Begriff der Geschichte," in *Gesammelte Schriften,* 1:2, ed. Rolf Tiedemann and Hermann Schweppenhäuser (Frankfurt: Suhrkamp, 1980), 697–98. Scott Tucker anticipates many in suggesting a link between this passage and Kushner's play in his column "Our Queer World," *Humanist* 53:6 (November–December 1993): 35. Tucker also makes some provocative comments (34–35) about the dangers of "transcendental humanism" and observes a possible precedent for Kushner's finale in a fragment from Kafka's diary discussed by Robert Alter in *Necessary Angels: Tradition and Modernity in Kafka, Benjamin, and Scholem* (Cambridge: Harvard University Press, 1991), 116–17. Also see David Savran's essay "Ambivalence, Utopia, and a Queer Sort of Materialism: How *Angels in America* Constructs the Nation," *Theatre Journal* 47:2 (May 1995): 207–27; our arguments overlap in many places. Savran's essay is reprinted in the current volume.

15. Belize, too, has what turns out to be a quite accurate vision of heaven in *Perestroika* (2:77).

16. The only angel Louis contemplates is the stone statue of the Bethesda Fountain in Central Park. Indeed, Belize compares Louis to that angel, "too far off the earth to pick out the details" (2:96).

17. Frank Rich makes this last point in his review of *Millennium Approaches* in New York, "Embracing All Possibilities in Art and Life," *New York Times,* 5 May 1993, c15, c16.

18. There is an echo of Louis's claim—"there are no angels in America"—when Mr. Lies, the fantastic travel agent, tells Harper in the Arctic regions, "There are no Eskimo in Antarctica" (1:102). Soon enough Harper encounters one.

19. After *Schindler's List* this comment itself now seems oddly dated, part of the recent past that *Angels* narrates.

20. Don Shewey, "Tony Kushner's Sexy Ethics," *Village Voice,* 20 April 1993, 32–36. Scott Tucker also quotes this passage; his response to it and his analysis of the problem of "inclusiveness" are valuable ("Our Queer World," 34).

21. Another quirk of stage history: it is as if Stephen Spinella, who played Prior on Broadway, got to deliver the excised curse as Pandarus at the end of *Troilus and Cressida* in the New York Shakespeare Festival production in Central Park in the summer of 1995. Angry beyond Kushner's imagining, the curse came complete with antisuburban interpolation:

Brethren and sisters of the hold-door trade,
Some two months hence my will shall here be made.
It should be now, but that my fear is this,
Some galled goose of [Westchester] would hiss.
Till then I'll sweat and seek about for eases,
And at that time bequeath you my diseases.

(5.10.51–56).

A tale of two revisions, it may be: the revision of Shakespeare targets the audience for whom Kushner revised the ending of *Perestroika*.

22. Adorno, "Reconciliation under Duress," in Ernst Bloch, et al., *Aesthetics and Politics* (London: Verso, 1977), 160.

23. I am not certain that Kushner has this particular passage from *Capital* in mind: "In a certain sense, a man is in the same situation as a commodity. As he neither enters into the world in possession of a mirror, nor as a Fichtean philosopher who can say 'I am I,' a man first sees and recognizes himself in another man" (Karl Marx, *Capital,* intro. Ernest Mandel, trans. Ben Fowkes [New York: Vintage, 1977], 144n.).

24. Thanks to an audience who heard a version of this essay as a talk at Princeton in January 1994 and to Jay Dickson, Adrienne Donald, Diana Fuss, and Laurie Edelstein.

"The Delicate Ecology
of Your Delusions":
Insanity, Theatricality, and
the Thresholds of Revelation
in Kushner's *Angels in America*

Deborah R. Geis

In the new century I think we will all be insane.
   —Woman in the South Bronx, *Angels in America*

The Woman in the South Bronx, a minor character in *Angels in America, is*—like Prior Walter—an earthly prophet; she even tells Hannah Pitt that Nostradamus is "some guy I went out with once somewhere." Yet she is also marked clearly as an outcast, as one of the "insane" herself. And Hannah (who is trying to find out from her where Brooklyn is) responds, with characteristic frankness, "I am sorry you're psychotic but just make the effort" (1:105).

The Woman's homelessness also marks her as a product of the insanity known as Reaganomics; we do not know how she arrived in her current position, nor do we see her elsewhere in the play, but her presence echoes throughout—and, appropriately, she is played by the same actor as the Angel. Her prophecy of shared insanity for the coming century is rich with multiple implications, suggesting simultaneously a kind of social leveling (all will share her position); an apocalyptic vision (the supposed inevitability of judgment and revelation); and also, perhaps, a vision of universal plague (AIDS dementia).[1]

This brief scene is, I think, a fit starting point for my exploration of Kushner's complex sense of what "insanity" means, both in *Angels* and, implicitly, in the world in which the play takes place. His emphasis throughout the two parts of *Angels* on thresholds, on liminality, incorporates a vision not simply of insanity/prophecy and the politics thereof but also a (postmodern) metatheatrical sense of the possibility of performance to blur, cross, and explode boundaries and limits. Harper, whose apocalyptic visions seem to parallel those of the Woman, describes Judgment as a day when everyone will think they're crazy now, not just me, everyone will see things. Sick men will see angels, women who *have* houses will sell their houses, dimestore dummies will rear up on their wood-putty legs and roam the land, looking for brides.[2]

Like Prior, Harper is a reluctant prophet; she says that she sees "more than I want to see" (2:39). The "threshold of revelation" (1:33) is both the edge or brink of Revelation and the ability to balance through one's psychic, or sixth, sense in a liminal, extrasensory space that is outside of reality, or paranormal. Prophecy is a form of insanity and vice versa, as we see in the South Bronx Woman; to be insane or to be a prophet is to live on the periphery of society, to inhabit the in-between spaces, the Derridean *brisures*. In *Madness and Civilization* Michel Foucault repeatedly uses metaphors of thresholds and liminality to characterize society's efforts to separate reason and madness.[3] But the complicating trick in Harper's passage is that each of the supposedly apocalyptic things she mentions has already (more or less) occurred within the narrative of the play. This calls attention both to the sense that the future apocalypse is "now" and to the relationships between theatricality and insanity/revelation (the threshold of revelation is also, after all, a visual and spatial metaphor): it is within the world of the play that the everyday (women selling houses) and the extraordinary or fantastical (sick men talking to angels, dimestore dummies searching for brides) are collapsed and confused, for in the theater insanity is permissible or perhaps even required.

The first time that Harper appears in the play she is *"talking to herself, as she often does"*; Kushner's stage directions indicate that she addresses the audience directly as she says, "People who are lonely, people left alone, sit talking nonsense to the air, imagining . . . beautiful systems dying, old fixed orders spiraling apart" (1:16). Her words, again, merge images of theatricality and insanity: to speak monologically is a form of insane, or "deviant," discourse, but it is also an inherently *dramatic* act.[4]

Harper speaks repeatedly, especially in the early scenes of *Millennium Approaches,* about her fear of the holes in the ozone layer "over Antarctica" (1:28). The ozone, a "shell of safety for life itself" (1:16–17), provides the world with protection but is now in jeopardy, as "everywhere, things are collapsing, lies surfacing, systems of defense giving way" (1:17). Her image invokes the tears or holes in her own protective boundary between sanity and insanity as well as an image both worldly (i.e., of pollution) and spiritual (i.e., apocalyptic) of the approaching millennium. Although Harper is not schizophrenic in a clinical sense, her images of tears or holes reflect the schizophrenic confusion of surface and depth that Gilles Deleuze, Fredric Jameson, and others have characterized as part of the postmodern condition; Deleuze, writing about schizophrenic language in Lewis Carroll and Antonin Artaud, remarks: "The great problem, the first evidence of schizophrenia, is that the surface is punctured. Bodies no longer have a surface. The schizophrenic body appears as a kind of body-sieve."[5] Harper also begins, but never finishes, a story she is about to tell Joe: "And today out the window on Atlantic Avenue there was a schizophrenic traffic cop who was making these . . ."; Joe cuts her off by saying that she is not making sense and that he is trying to make a point. Harper responds, "So am I," and tries to tell him, "My point is the world seems just as . . ."—but she is not able to complete the thought (1:26). What kinds of signals *does* a schizophrenic traffic cop make? Does he perhaps direct imaginary traffic, traffic only he can see? The clash of worlds, between the everyday authority of the traffic cop and the one who lives in an altered or fragmented subworld of his own, is an apt reflection of Harper's own splintered consciousness.

Her flights of fantasy, partially pill induced, are part of her desire to "go traveling" (1:17), and the "guide" for these fantastic voyages is the imaginary Mr. Lies, the travel agent who acts as a sort of facilitator for Harper's explorations of hallucinatory, sometimes troubling or surprising worlds. The Antarctica to which Mr. Lies "takes" Harper is, at least initially, a source of comfort in its *lack* (though the Kingdom of Ice is also an image from Dante's Hell); he tells her:

> This is a retreat, a vacuum, its virtue is that it lacks everything; deepfreeze for feelings. You can be numb and safe here, that's what you came for. Respect the delicate ecology of your delusions. (1:102)

Mr. Lies's last sentence here reflects the precarious nature of the holes in the ozone layer, or the holes in Harper's own consciousness. Yet, true to his name (and like the schizophrenic traffic cop), Mr. Lies cannot fully control and direct her visions; he says that there are no Eskimos because "even hallucinations have laws" (1:102), but one (played by the actor who plays Joe) appears nevertheless. Ever mindful of his own role as manipulator of his characters' voyages, Kushner (according to John Lahr) mentioned at one point in his production notes on Harper that he particularly loved the way her character is "both very brave and amazingly inventive in her avoidance, she creates spectacular routes of escape and then unravels them because she knows they're untrue."[6]

The baby that Harper, in an earlier sequence, tells Joe that she envisions herself having, "born addicted to pills," poses a striking image: it would, she says, "hallucinate" rather than dream and would stare at its parents "with big mirror eyes and . . . not know who we are" (1:41). The image of the "mirror eyes" plays ironically upon the traditional trope of seeing oneself reflected in the eyes of one's child. In other words, the baby is little more than Harper and Joe's own reflections; it seems to be an object of longing, an object to nurture, but at the same time its identity is frozen in Harper's Kingdom of Ice, unable to surpass the boundaries of her own troubled identity. It is a part of her splintered self, created out of her imagination (and out of her frustrated union with Joe, the "Eskimo" who also keeps appearing in her hallucinations), rather than a source of transcendence.

Indeed, when Harper later imagines the baby "covered with thick white fur," she seems to envision herself being protected by the baby rather than the reverse: "And if it gets really cold, she'll have a pouch I can crawl into. Like a marsupial" (1:103). By the time we find Harper at the beginning of *Perestroika* (after Joe has left her), her Antarctic world itself seems no longer to be a retreat, a haven; she refers, instead, to the TV show she saw in which "female polar bears were being chased by men in snowsuits" who knocked them out with "hypodermic needles" and "shoved frozen polar bear sperm pencils up their cooters" (2:33–34). Harper's breakdown of sorts—from which she emerges gradually—reflects her earlier fear of the "men with knives" whom Joe recognizes as representing himself (1:79): in her Antarctica, her retreat into a sort of frozen womb, images of patriarchal/phallic violation nevertheless present themselves. It is striking that she tells Hannah, after being picked up by the police in Prospect Park, "I thought I was a beaver" (2:32)—an obvious pun on a colloquial term for female genitalia. Perhaps her attempt to chew down a tree is an effort, on some primal (or Freudian) level, to gnaw her way back into an identity, though she first must work through (via her hallucinated encounters with Joe in the Mormon diorama room and via her conversations with Prior) the pain she feels at the dissolution of her marriage.

At the end of *Perestroika* Harper gives Joe two of her Valium pills and says: "Get lost. Joe. Go exploring" (2:143), and she herself takes off, though this time presumably on a real trip rather than an imagined one—but still a voyage with no particular destination. Although David Savran has a point in calling Harper "pathologized," arguing that, "with her hallucinations and 'emotional problems' (1:27), she functions as a scapegoat for Joe, the displacement of his sexual problems,"[7] it is also worth pointing out that by the end of the play Harper has clearly grown beyond this role. It is only by being willing to test the boundaries of sanity, the borders between real and imagined worlds, Harper seems to tell Joe, that he will be able to acknowledge and discover his plural subjectivities. Harper dreams that her plane reaches the ozone layer and she sees "a great net" of souls of the dead forming a web that is absorbed into and repairs the great holes in the ozone (2:144). Her hallucinations of collapse have given way to visions of healing and repair—she may have reached a kind of peace—and yet it is clear that her "healing" must include her insanity or visionary abilities (the threshold of revelation), rather than reject such qualities or reabsorb them into so-called normalcy.

While Prior dwells, like Harper, on the borderland between prophecy/insanity and the so-called normal world—and he shares in the threshold of revelation, even meeting at times with Harper in mutual hallucinations[8]—his fear for his sanity is caught up more intensely in his bodied experience, as he worries constantly that he has lapsed into AIDS dementia. This seems to be the one possibility that worries Belize the most; he tells Prior: "Don't go crazy on me, girlfriend, I already got enough crazy queens for one lifetime. For two. I can't be bothering with dementia" (1:61). Yet even this moment is followed immediately by the Voice (of the Angel) that Prior and the audience, but not Belize, hear speaking. The thresholds between sanity/insanity and health/sickness are difficult ones to stand upon; just as the threshold of revelation tells Prior that Louis is seeing a Mormon (Joe), though, he responds to Louis's plea for reasonableness by saying: "*Reasonable? Limits?* Tell it to my *lungs,* stupid, tell it to my lesions, tell it to the cotton-woolly patches in my eyes" (2:85). The corporeal reality of his illness, according to Prior, forces a reinterrogation of limits and thresholds; just as the human body fighting AIDS has its defenses pushed to their limits, so, too, are the boundaries of the "rational" challenged and reconfigured. Like Harper, Prior experiences a radical sense of separation from himself, from his actions, as his subjectivity is fractured and splintered. Jan Zita Grover remarks in "AIDS, Keywords, and Cultural Work":

A significant number of people I've known with AIDS and HIV infection have talked about their very jarring sense of no longer feeling themselves as an integrated self, but instead as a container for the virus. I've sat with people who just stare at their arm and say, "I know what's going on in there, it looks just the same but there's this thing in there, this universe in me, that's eating me out from the inside"—this really jarring, disorienting sense that you are now merely an encasement—you are inhabited by a world, by a universe, the swarm.[9]

When the two "prior Priors" visit Prior in one of his hallucinations, they call him "Prophet. Seer. Revelator" (1:88). While Harper's visions are of a world—including her personal sphere—"spiraling apart," on the brink of chaos, apocalypse, revelation, Prior's hallucinations connect him to a past that is both individual (his ancestors) and synchronic or transhistorical (they, too, died of various forms of the "plague"). Harper's hallucinatory world draws upon the geographical and religious images that surround her, while Prior's madness is framed by postmodernist, queer/campy evocations of the recent pop cultural past (when he encounters the two Priors, he sings, "All I want is a room somewhere," from *My Fair Lady* [1:88], paralleling his later evocations of Steven Spielberg at the end of *Millennium Approaches* and his references throughout both parts to *A Streetcar Named Desire, The Wizard of Oz,* etc.). Foucault underscores the connection between the fears of death and madness and the use of absurdity as a distancing strategy:

> Fear in the face of the absolute limit of death turns inward in continuous irony; man disarms it in advance, making it an object of derision by giving it an everyday, tamed form, by constantly renewing it in the spectacle of life, by scattering it throughout the vices, the difficulties, the absurdities of all men. . . . [W]hen the madman laughs, he already laughs with the laugh of death; the lunatic, anticipating the macabre, has disarmed it.[10]

Yet these intertextual bits mingle increasingly through the play with the inexplicable, the truly fabulous, visionary world of angels and prophecy that begins to lay claim to Prior's senses. As a result, Prior struggles between the fear that such visions are the mark of AIDS dementia and the incredible attraction he feels toward the visions themselves (he tells Belize: "I want the voice; it's wonderful. It's all that's keeping me alive" [1:60]). And again, by letting the *audience* share in Prior's hallucinations, Kushner blurs the lines between the "insane" and the magical or revelatory (and the theatrical).

When Prior attempts to explain to Emily, the nurse, his fear that he is losing his mind, his language echoes the attack/defense imagery used by Henry (Roy's doctor) earlier in the play to explain the way AIDS devastates the human body. Prior says, "I feel like something terrifying is on its way, you know, like a missile from outer space, and it's plummeting down towards the earth, and I'm ground zero" (1:98). At the same time, his words reflect the feeling of imminence/immanence, of the threshold of revelation (in its multiple senses), that was evident in Harper's expressions of incipient insanity. The "combination of hyperclosure (the millennium)," Una Chaudhuri argues,

> and hyperdispersal (history has splintered into a hundred narratives, all equally impotent in the face of the scourges of the present: AIDS, homelessness, ecological catastrophe) leaves Prior suspended between two temporalities, both of which seem marked with death.[11]

The feeling or force that approaches Prior is at once physical and spiritual in its potential for personal and cosmic disruption; this is confirmed in the moments immediately following, when Emily assures Prior that there is nothing wrong with him, but then he (and the audience) hears her speak to him in Hebrew, and a flaming letter *Aleph* appears. As one of the many "miracles" in the play, the flaming *Aleph* (with its multiple connotations of God, of the "flaming" homosexual, of the Scarlet Letter, of *A* for AIDS, etc.) simultaneously confirms Prior's "madness" and suggests that he is indeed linked with prophecy, with magic, with revelation. As Judith Pastore points out, William F. Buckley suggested at one point (with utter seriousness) that people infected with HIV should have a scarlet *A* branded on their buttocks or forearms.[12] And Kushner, speaking of the flaming letter with William Harris in a *New York Times* interview, emphasizes that the Aleph is "the first letter of the Hebrew alphabet, the seed word, the God letter."[13] As the play goes on, though, Prior tries repeatedly to talk himself out of his own potential to summon forth visions; at one point he admonishes himself, "No more mad scene, hush, hush" (1:115), thus underscoring the histrionic nature of such visions, despite the seductiveness of that particular moment as he hallucinates a slow waltz with Louis. Yet the mad/prophetic (and highly theatrical) visions break persistently through, causing Prior to struggle to regain control over a series of unreadable narratives that threatens to consume him yet entices him so that he feels "wonderful and horrible all at once," as if—to re-invoke the battle metaphor— "there's a war inside" (2:23).

Prior has terrible visions, including one so terrible that he tears off the glasses ("Peep-stones" [2:47]) that the Angel gives him in *Perestroika*. Kushner tells William Harris:

> The Angel Moroni led Joseph Smith to the Hill Cumorah, the burial site of the plates on which the Book of Mormon was inscribed. Smith unearthed, along with the plates, "bronze bows" with stones set in them. These I take to have been Bible-era spectacles with rocks for lenses, the Urim and the Thummim. Before he became a prophet,

Smith was known in upstate New York for his ability to locate buried
treasure with the use of "peep-stones." These stones assisted him, as
they assist Prior in *Perestroika,* in the act of translating ancient writings.[14]

At the same time, Prior has been insisting repeatedly that his eyes are failing
him: like dementia, the failing eyesight is linked both with HIV infection
(CMV retinitis) and with the blindness/insight that is the traditional trope
of prophecy. He says: "I believe I've seen the end of things. And having
seen, I'm going blind, as prophets do. It makes a certain sense to me" (2:56).
The image echoes the Angel's depiction of "poor blind Children, abandoned on the Earth" (2:52) and even the description of Prelapsarianov, who
begins *Perestroika,* as *"unimaginably old and totally blind"* (2:13).[15] (And, of
course, when we see Prior at the end of the play he is wearing thick glasses.)
Like Harper, though, Prior sees more than he wants to see. His struggle against his visions is complicated by his belief that he is struggling against
AIDS dementia. Belize insists that what Prior is experiencing is not dementia but a desire to go backward in time, to reset the narrative of his life—a
desire so strong that, Belize tells him, "you made this angel up, a cosmic
reactionary." Prior's response here is to link what is happening to him with
the sense that all of those who are dying of AIDS (theoretically, all of those
who are going blind, experiencing dementia, etc.) are, like him, prophets:
"maybe we've caught the virus of prophecy" (2:55). For Prior fully to
accept this interpretation is to accede to a kind of romanticizing of AIDS; at
the same time, to resist it is to refuse the potential of the visionary or revelatory side, the cosmic/spiritual/"fabulous" side, which becomes increasingly important to his changing sense of his place in the world (and in
"other" worlds). What is crucial, then, is Prior's *struggle* with the Angel
(both in this scene and later when he asks for "more life" [2:135]): he has to
accept *both* the possibility of insanity/prophecy (the world of the Imagination) and the right to do so on his own terms, so that by the end of the play,
when he says that "the world only spins forward" (2:148), his narrative
vision reverses Belize's earlier description of Prior's longing for the back-
wardness of the "cosmic reactionary" angel. When, on his trip back to
Heaven to return the book that the Angel gave him, Prior sees the Rabbi
and Sarah Ironson (Louis's grandmother) playing cards, the Rabbi tells him
that the "pleasures of Paradise" lie in *"Indeterminacy"*: "It ain't all so much
mechanical as they think" (2:137). Acknowledging the potential for chance,
for incipient chaos or disruption, to be a source of pleasure rather than a
threatening force allows Prior, paradoxically, to regain some sense of control over his own life. John Clum notes in *Acting Gay* that, despite the "bat-

tles waged throughout *Angels in America* between order/stasis [what the angels want] and chaos/change," the "new" chaos—mourned by the World's Oldest Living Bolshevik for its lack of Theory—is what emerges in a form that "Kushner and his characters can both lament and celebrate."[16]

The uncontrollable realm of the Imaginary, the insane, is one that both Prior and Harper learn to accept, despite its perils; as Prior tells Harper when they meet in the Mormon diorama room, "Imagination is a dangerous thing"; Harper agrees that "it can blow up in your face. If it turns out to be true" (2:70). Earlier in *Millennium Approaches,* when the two encounter each other for the first time (in a mutual hallucination), Harper tells Prior:

> Imagination can't create anything new, can it? It only recycles bits and pieces from the world and reassembles them into visions. . . . So when we think we've escaped the unbearable ordinariness and, well, untruthfulness of our lives, it's really only the same old ordinariness and falseness rearranged into the appearance of novelty and truth. (1:32)

Una Chaudhuri points out that "a crucial insight of the 'threshold of revelation' is that imagination is constrained by history."[17] I would add that the previous passage is a postmodern interpretation of "imagination": it depicts a culture in which the new is actually a series of recyclings of the old. And yet the play itself calls into doubt Harper's assertion that these reassembled visions are merely old material "rearranged into the appearance of novelty and truth"—or, better yet, one might question in a postmodern universe what it means to valorize "novelty" and "truth" in the first place. If the moments of hallucination, the jumps onto the threshold of revelation, are (like dreams or like contemporary texts) composed of relics and detritus of the everyday reconfigured into visions, then Kushner's own theatrical text is created by similar means. Kushner, like Harper and Prior, is a *bricoleur* of the imagination; theatricality is not a means to escape the ordinary or everyday in the traditional sense but, rather, a way to re-encounter it and to transform it into something admittedly crazy, something fabulous.

NOTES

Tony Kushner, *Angels in America: A Gay Fantasia on National Themes. Part One: Millennium Approaches* (New York: Theatre Communications Group, 1993), 105. Future references will be noted in the text.

1. Michel Foucault's *Madness and Civilization: A History of Insanity in the Age of Reason* makes a salient observation about the connection between fears of madness and of the apocalypse:

> It is no longer the end of time and of the world which will show retrospectively that men were mad not to have been prepared for them; it is the tide of madness, its secret invasion, that shows the world is near its final catastrophe; it is man's insanity that invokes and makes necessary the world's end. (Trans. Richard Howard [New York: Random House, Vintage, 1965], 17)

The beast that the Bronx Woman addresses also echoes Foucault's description of apocalyptic visions of the "animal" inside humankind (see 21, 23).

2. Tony Kushner, *Angels in America: A Gay Fantasia on National Themes. Part Two: Perestroika* (New York: Theatre Communications Group, 1994), 101. Future references will be noted in the text.

3. Foucault's discussion relies on the following sort of vocabulary: "experience of division," "one side or the other," "uncomfortable region," "caesura," "scission," "void," "apart," "disjunct," "breach." He adds that this is "a realm, no doubt, where what is in question is the limits rather than the identity of a culture" (*Madness and Civilization,* ix).

4. See my discussion in Deborah R. Geis, *Postmodern Theatric(k)s: Monologue in Contemporary American Drama* (Ann Arbor: University of Michigan Press, 1993); see also Ken Frieden, *Genius and Monologue* (Ithaca, N.Y.: Cornell University Press, 1985), esp. 133.

5. Gilles Deleuze, "The Schizophrenic and Language: Surface and Depth in Lewis Carroll and Antonin Artaud," in *Textual Strategies: Perspectives in Post-Structuralist Criticism,* ed. and trans. Josué V. Harari (Ithaca, N.Y.: Cornell University Press, 1979), 286.

6. Quoted in John Lahr, "Earth Angels," *New Yorker,* 13 December 1993, 130.

7. David Savran, "Ambivalence, Utopia, and a Queer Sort of Materialism: How *Angels in America* Reconstructs the Nation," *Theatre Journal* 47 (May 1995): 215. This essay is reprinted in the current volume.

8. Una Chaudhuri comments that the "threshold of revelation" is a "suitable updating of Huxley's 'doors of perception'" (*Staging Place: The Geography of Modern Drama* [Ann Arbor: University of Michigan Press, 1995], 254).

9. Jan Zita Grover, "AIDS, Keywords, and Cultural Work," in *Cultural Studies,* ed. Lawrence Grossberg, Cary Nelson, and Paula Treichler (New York and London: Routledge, 1992), 239.

10. Foucault, *Madness and Civilization,* 16.

11. Chaudhuri, *Staging Place,* 255.

12. Judith Laurence Pastore, "What Are the Responsibilities of Representing AIDS?" in *Confronting AIDS through Literature,* ed. Pastore (Urbana and Chicago: University of Illinois Press, 1993), 17. Pastore is quoting William F. Buckley, "Identify All the Carriers," *New York Times,* 18 March 1986, A27.

13. Tony Kushner (as told to William Harris), "The Secrets of 'Angels,'" *New York Times,* 27 March 1994, H5.

14. Ibid.

15. See also Savran, "Ambivalence, Utopia, and a Queer Sort of Materialism," 209.

16. John M. Clum, *Acting Gay: Male Homosexuality in Modern Drama,* rev. ed. (New York: Columbia University Press, 1994), 314–15.

17. Chaudhuri, *Staging Place,* 255.

Theater of the Fabulous:
Angels in Performance Contexts

Design for *Angels in America:* Envisioning the Millennium

Arnold Aronson

There are two essential questions to be answered in considering the scenography of *Angels in America*. One is a fundamental scenographic question for any play: where are we? (and how do we, as an audience, know where we are?). The other is a practical one: how can the sheer magnitude of the play be dealt with? *Angels in America* unfolds through two parts, eight acts, and an epilogue, consisting of some sixty scenes, a significant number of which are "split"—presenting two locales simultaneously. Some, such as the Brooklyn apartment of Joe and Harper, Prior's bedroom, or the hospital room of Roy Cohn, are recurring, but many are seen only once, resulting in a dizzying array of settings through which the spectators must be led on their theatrical journey. The practical question is a daunting one because the visual landscape must have a unity that provides an overall structure for the production while at the same time providing enough specificity to allow the audience to locate itself within the ever-changing geography of the play. Yet, from a practical point of view, the sixty scene changes must not be allowed to become time-consuming or disruptive to the emotional and narrative progression of the play; they must flow with the ineluctable logic and fluidity of a dream.

The solution to the practical problems will ultimately be determined by the approach to the more philosophical question of location. If we begin with "where," the answer is, on the surface, relatively simple: we are in America. More precisely, we are in various specified locations in New York City in the latter half of the 1980s as well as in apparently hallucinatory images and fantasies of various characters. It is from these simple observations that the visual environment—the world—of *Angels* must be drawn.

How does one present the idea of "America"? Is there an obvious imagistic or emblematic representation? Is there a single icon, perhaps, that will provide the audience with a sense of time, place, tone, and point of view? The British production, for example, directed by Declan Donnellan

213

and designed by Nick Ormerod at the Royal National Theatre in London, attempted to do so by transforming the stage into a "stars and stripes" background against which the play unfolded quite simply. But it is much easier to convey the concept of a foreign nation to an audience than to confront spectators with their own culture and heritage. For a British audience (indeed, for any non-American audience) the mere sight of the emblem of the United States is sufficient to evoke a vast array of associations; the simple environment suggested that all the characters and their actions were enmeshed in America, whatever that might mean for each individual spectator. Tony Kushner, himself, plays with that sort of iconography when he calls for a "great red flag" behind Prelapsarianov at the start of *Perestroika*. But in the United States the subtleties, contradictions, and even violently opposing concepts of America make such simple emblematic scenography problematic, if not impossible.

In fact, at least part of the play's theme is wrapped up in the epic struggle to come to terms with what America means as the millennium approaches. Just as Prior wrestles with the Angel, so must the scenographer contend with the landscape of the play. At the start of part 1 the Rabbi, talking to the mourners of Sarah Ironson (though addressing the audience in the theater) states: "You do not live in America. No such place exists."[1] America is a fantasy, a chimera, made up of the individual perceptions, expectations, and projections of hundreds of millions of individuals whose true roots are elsewhere. How remarkable to be told in the first moments of the play that the very location identified in the title is nonexistent—a state of mind. It is, perhaps, not unlike Alfred Jarry's siting of *Ubu Roi* in Poland— "that is to say," as Jarry explained in his address to the audience at the first performance, "nowhere."[2] Jarry's Poland was "nowhere" because it was a country that, historically, existed more often as a concept of nationhood in the souls of its people than as a political entity. America, on the other hand, has been a political entity for over two centuries, yet it consists of such a commingling of disparate peoples that its identity as a nation has always been a subject of debate, never more so than now. Kushner's dramatis personae contains a veritable catalogue of individuals who fly in the face of the Reaganite image of America. It is not that Kushner's image has more truth than any other; it simply emphasizes the difficulty of arriving at a unified coherent image. There is no landscape that easily will provide the world of Kushner's vision.

In the production at the Mark Taper Forum in Los Angeles, director Oskar Eustis and set designer John Conklin nonetheless sought a unifying image that would evoke Americana without overly specifying or imposing a narrow view. The back wall of Conklin's set was the facade of a house that combined elements of a New England meetinghouse with Jeffersonian classicism. The meetinghouse was evoked largely by a geometrically square floor of natural wood planks set on gray boulders suggestive of a Maine or California coast. The image suggested simplicity, sturdiness, and a connection with the continent itself—all elements of American mythology. The facade was a pastiche of windows, doors, and cornices based on the designs of Thomas Jefferson, the towering intellect of the American Revolution. The total effect, though obviously a theatricalized amalgamation, was of distinctly American architecture. It created, according to Conklin, a "civilized public space."[3] The choice was inspired: the American home, as developed over the last three centuries, has been considered the country's most original contribution to architecture. Jefferson's classicism, of course, was based on European Renaissance models, which, in turn, were drawn from ancient Roman and Greek sources. So the visual imagery echoed the Eurocentric foundation of America that is depicted in the play. Here was a visual iconography that evoked the idea of America without being overly symbolic or trite.

But Conklin took the concept of the house-as-metaphor one step further by creating a large jagged split down the center of the facade to create, as he noted, "an ideal that was cracked."[4] The Angel flew in through this crack in the wall, rather than through the ceiling, which did not exist in this production.

The Broadway production, directed by George C. Wolfe and designed by Robin Wagner, opted for neutrality rather than visual metaphor. Unity was achieved by the proscenium arch itself and ever-changing configurations of black velour flats in chrome frames. Perhaps the production's very presence in New York City, the center of the American theater world, the place where Kushner developed as a playwright, a center of gay culture and consciousness, and a place where much of the audience would know firsthand the sites referred to in the text, mitigated the need for some other visual element as a unifying image.

Interestingly, the Los Angeles production never sought to suggest New York City as a locale nor to use images of the city in an iconographic way. It would not be unreasonable for a designer to use the visual iconography of New York City as a unifying framework, but, other than, perhaps, Bethesda Fountain in Central Park, Kushner sets none of the play in a recognizable locale. (There are many specific locations, such as the Mormon Visitor's Center, but they are not instantly recognizable landmarks as is, say, the Empire State Building, which was the locale for the conclusion of *Perestroika*

Stephen Spinella and Ellen McLaughlin in the 1992 Mark Taper
Forum production of *Angels in America,* directed by Oskar Eustis and
Tony Taccone. *(Photo by Jay Thompson, courtesy Mark Taper Forum.)*

in an early draft of the script.) The play ranges through unremarkable apartments, offices, and streetscapes that carry no particular resonance except what is bestowed upon them by their occupants. And that is as it should be. New York City is vital to the play because it is the historical point of entry to America for immigrants on their journey to a new land, and it is still the destination for those from within the country who seek refuge from their own bleak landscape; it is a place for those who do not fit elsewhere. It is a city of the displaced, the outsiders, the adventurers, the seekers and searchers. In its diversity and lack of apparent cohesion, in its gaudy excess as well as decay, it seems to defy the standard images of America. It is the place of the "other," and thus it serves as America's other. But, as the home for everyone and a repository of history, it embodies all that is America and makes it the quintessential emblem of America at the millennium. This is an "everytown," which is to say "our town."

If *Angels in America* has a precedent in American theater history, it is surely Thornton Wilder's *Our Town,* and a comparison of the two is instructive. Wilder combined aspects of Italian futurism, German expressionism, other European vanguard movements, and the ideas of Gertrude Stein with American sensibilities, especially emotional realism, to create not only innovative forms of drama but also a new way of physical presentation. Though Wilder did not invent the bare stage or emblematic scenery, he popularized them as a means of economic staging while inviting a wider audience imagination—a kind of radio for the eyes. Wilder's play is both a reading of the geography of America in the first third of the American century as well as a teleological explication of human existence. At the end of act 1 of Wilder's play, Rebecca Gibbs remarks on a letter her friend had received that was addressed to "Jane Crofut; The Crofut Farm; Grover's Corners; Sutton County; New Hampshire; United States of America . . . Continent of North America; Western Hemisphere; the Earth; the Solar System; the Universe; the Mind of God."[5] Just as Wilder provides a few scenic items "for those who think they have to have scenery,"[6] he also provides this simple explanation of the microcosm within the macrocosm for those who might need an explanation. Tony Kushner's version of "our town" is not as idyllic as Wilder's world, and God, we are told, has been missing since the San Francisco earthquake of 1906, but the play unfolds, nonetheless, in Heaven as well as on earth and in the minds of the characters, who—given the Judeo-Christian matrix of the play—were created in God's image. And, if anyone doubts the connection to *Our Town,* it is made at the very end of the play, in the epilogue, as several of the characters sit around Bethesda Fountain. Prior, like a latter-day stage manager, approaches the audience and says:

Ellen McLaughlin in the Mark Taper Forum production of *Angels in America*. (Copyright © 1992 Craig Schwartz.)

They'll be at it for hours. It's not that what they're saying isn't important, it's just . . .

This is my favorite place in New York City. No, in the whole universe. The parts of it I have seen.

On a day like today. A sunny winter's day, warm and cold at once. The sky's a little hazy, so the sunlight has a physical presence, a character. In autumn, those trees across the lake are yellow, and the sun strikes those most brilliantly. Against the blue of the sky, that sad fall blue, those trees are more light than vegetation. They are Yankee trees, New England transplants. They're barren now. It's January 1990. I've been living with AIDS for five years.[7]

Just as Wilder realized that the best setting for his play was the bare signifying stage, so Kushner places his play on an essentially empty stage with minimal emblematic elements to guide us. A reading of the stage directions reveals almost no description. The first time we see the Pitt apartment in Brooklyn the stage directions read only: "*Harper at home, alone. She is listening to the radio and talking to herself, as she often does. She speaks to the audience*" (1:16). No description of ground plan, furniture, light, atmosphere, bric-a-brac; no adjectives. Somewhat like the captured soldier's recitation of name, rank, and serial number, Kushner gives us only place, character, and basic action. In the case of Joe and Harper Pitt we discover all we need to know about them through dialogue, action, response to other characters, and, in the case of Harper, her hallucinations and fantasies. The style of furniture, the color of the walls, the decorations, and the relative tidiness of the apartment—the sort of information often vital to our understanding of characters in O'Neill, Odets, Williams, Miller, or even Shepard or Mamet—is irrelevant here and would be distracting and limiting even if it were practical to provide such complete and illusionistic settings. Kushner's landscape, like Wilder's, is the stage, which takes us directly from the individual characters to the "mind of God" with only a bench, a chair, a bed, or "*an impressive desk, bare except for a very elaborate phone system*" (1:11). It is worth noting, though, that Wilder provides one of the most evocative elements possible in his settings: sound. His scenes are enhanced by specific aural effects that, to paraphrase *Hamlet,* allow us to see with the mind's ear. Kushner rarely indicates sound.

But there are, nonetheless, clues about the look of this landscape to be found in his text. When settings *are* described or when characters talk of locales, they tend to describe barren and bleak sites. Most obvious is Harper's recurring hallucination of Antarctica, though a confused Antarctica with Eskimos. Mr. Lies describes it as "a retreat, a vacuum, its virtue is that it lacks everything; deep-freeze for feelings" (1:102). Harper is a person at odds with the given landscape of New York City. As an agoraphobic, she remains in her apartment envisioning her own private Antarctica. When she does venture outside she rarely remains in perceived reality; she interacts with the inanimate diorama of Mormon history, and even in Prospect Park she fights the surroundings to maintain her vision of Antarctica:

> For a moment, the magical antarctic light begins to dim, replaced by the glare of sodium park lights; the sea sounds and wind are drowned out by the sound of traffic as heard from the middle of a city park at night; Harper looks about, and as she does, Antarctica is restored a bit, though the city lights and sounds do not retreat entirely. (2:19)

The arrival of Hannah Pitt occurs in the South Bronx, and it is one of the few scenes with any sort of physical description of location: "*An abandoned lot in the South Bronx. A homeless Woman is standing near an oil drum in which a fire is burning. Snowfall. Trash around*" (1:103). It is a scene of desolation and urban blight—a vision of Hell. This vision is echoed in part 2, when Belize describes Heaven to Roy Cohn:

> Big city, overgrown with weeds, but flowering weeds. On every corner a wrecking crew and something new and crooked going up catty-corner to that. Windows missing in every edifice like broken teeth, fierce gusts of gritty wind, and a gray high sky full of ravens. . . . Piles of trash, but lapidary like rubies and obsidian, and diamond-colored cowspit streamers in the wind. (2:77)

This diction elevates aspects of *Angels* to the poetic, but it would be a mistake to use these tonal clues as a guide for literal scenography. The magic of the scene with Harper in the park is created through sound and light and is made possible by the essentially neutral canvas of the stage. As appropriate as any overriding image may be metaphorically, it becomes an inflexible and immutable landscape that, when realized onstage, can never fulfill the grand canvas of the text. The stage has the remarkable power to transform any object that is placed upon it; these objects acquire, said Russian folklorist Petr Bogatyrev, "special features, qualities and attributes that they do not have in real life."[8] The moment anything specific is placed on the stage, be it a bed, a living room, or a trash heap, its details begin to acquire special significance that starts a process, however subconscious, of interpretation on the part of the spectator. This is a play in which light, sound, and suggestion become crucial.

Ultimately, any production is faced with the overwhelming question of practicality. How are transitions made from one scene to the next? The answer will be informed in part by the way in which the director and designer interpret the structure of the play. Is the structure seen in terms of a Shakespearean or possibly Brechtian model? Is it perhaps seen as an example of the episodic structure of medieval or Expressionist drama? Or is it conceived of as cinematic—that is, a series of cross-fades, jump cuts, and montage among related but disparate scenes? Since the 1930s many critics have seen the inevitable influence of movies upon the theater and have designated almost any play that moves through multiple scenes as cinematic. Though *Angels* clearly has affinities to all these forms and undoubtedly draws from them—consciously or not—I would suggest that the play's organization and scenic movement derive from something else. Its structure is inevitably informed by contemporary sensibilities and perceptions of the world, and film is no longer the defining mode of perception. Neither, needless to say, is a medieval or Renaissance or early-twentieth-century perspective. Unless Kushner were to say that his play was based upon one of these theatrical forms, to attempt to solve the scenographic problems posed by the play by utilizing historical models will result in a clash of sensibilities.

Ours is a paradoxical world of isolation and interconnection. Certainly, the audiences of Tony Kushner's generation are comfortable with rapidly shifting barrages of images and sounds presented in overlapping, incongruent, dissociated juxtaposition. The world of computers, VCRs, and fax machines allows unfathomable amounts of information and imagery—virtually all knowledge and culture—to be accessible almost on demand. Significantly, it is no longer necessary to go to the concert hall, the museum, the movie house, or even the library in order to consume these products of culture. They can be brought into the private realm, freed from the temporal constraints of exhibition or performance. They can be fragmented, deconstructed, juxtaposed. All this has contributed to our transformation into a society of isolated individuals, both producing and consuming all this information in the privacy of homes or offices away from the life of cities. Television has produced the anomaly of audiences of one hundred million or more, each at his or her own private screen. This is the generation that has produced the neologism *cyberspace* to define a location, occupied by millions, that does not exist. We are, to quote Michel Foucault, in

the epoch of space. We are in the epoch of simultaneity: we are in the epoch of juxtaposition, the epoch of the near and far, of side-by-side, of the dispersed. We are at a moment, I believe, when our experience of the world is less that of a long life developing through time than that of a network that connects points and intersects with its own skein. One could perhaps say that certain ideological conflicts animating present-day polemics oppose the pious descendants of time and the determined inhabitants of space.[9]

It would be absurd to suggest that *Angels in America* is some sort of cyber-tech futuristic play or a theatrical analogue to the Internet. Far from it. Spiritually, the play and its characters are closer to the sociopolitical dramas of the 1930s than to the avant-garde, and it remains a piece of theater abiding by relatively well-established conventions of theatrical presentation. But it is in its *structure* and *spatial sensibility* that it reflects most definitely the dominant forces of our time. The philosopher Henri Lefebvre, in his major work *The Production of Space,* points out that "every society . . . produces a space, its own space. The city of the ancient world cannot be understood [merely] as a collection of people and things in space. . . . Each society offers up its own peculiar space, as it were, as an 'object' for analysis and overall theoretical explication."[10]

Our space is, as Foucault suggests, nonlinear, nongeometric, disjointed, juxtapositional; one moves not from one contiguous space to another but across disparate spatial and temporal boundaries. Ours is the space of hypertext. In the age of computers and fiber-optic technology it seems unexceptional to be able to connect any two or more points regardless of their seeming disparity; in cyberspace the laws of geometry do not prevail. With the click of a button, words, symbols, and images can be connected in an almost infinite string of associations. In hypertext, just as in dreams and imagination, key words or images can transport us from one locale to another, from one world to another. This is the driving logic of *Angels in America*. It is a way of thinking, seeing, and conceptualizing the world that has surreptitiously entered the consciousness of contemporary culture and utterly transformed the society.

A pervasive computer culture is a recent phenomenon. But before hypertext was a familiar concept Foucault described what he called "heterotopias." "We do not live inside a void that could be colored with diverse shades of light," he wrote, "we live inside a set of relations that delineates sites which are irreducible to one another and absolutely not superimposable on one another. . . . The heterotopia is capable of juxtaposing in a single real place several spaces, several sites that are in themselves incompatible."[11] While Foucault was using the *heterotopia* to analyze such varied societal institutions as churches, vacation villages, fairgrounds, and brothels, the term works superbly as a description of theater. The stage, after all, is a single real space that can hold a multitude of places.

This heterotopic/hypertextual idea is not a recent phenomenon in theater. The simultaneous stage of the Middle Ages, the split scenes and vision scenes of melodrama, the flashback (credited to playwright Elmer Rice), and Sergei Eisenstein's idea of montage all predate in practice what Foucault described in theory. As a result, *Angels* can seem part of an old theatrical tradition, but Kushner pushes it further. Act 3, scene 5, of *Perestroika,* for instance, begins on the Brooklyn Heights Promenade with Harper talking to the Mormon Mother seen earlier as part of the diorama of the Mormon Visitor's Center. But the characters from the previous two scenes remain onstage. This means that Joe and Louis are at Jones Beach, while Roy Cohn and Belize are in Cohn's hospital room. During this scene Prior becomes visible in his bedroom; Louis leaves Joe and is suddenly at a pay phone in Manhattan calling Prior. This layering of scenes and transpositions of characters resemble "windows" on a computer screen: multiple locations, some hidden behind others, but any one available to foreground at any moment and in any sequence. Kushner has interwoven seven characters (one a hallucination) and five locations and has collapsed time. Another slightly different example of this hypertextual space can be found in the interconnection of Harper's Valium-induced hallucination with Prior's dream in part 1, one of the wonderful conceits of this play. In this scene not only are the conventions of theatrical fantasy transcended, but mental space is bridged as well. The scene almost suggests the reconciliation between conceptual space and social space discussed by Lefebvre. The scene is an initially comic reconciliation, with echoes of the narrative and structural logic of Buster Keaton films. But, again, there is a more contemporary resonance in this strange dislocation.

But the practical considerations still haunt the designer. There is, after all, no button to click that will take the viewer from screen to screen, leaping through cyberspace in milliseconds. The stage is still bound by the laws of physics, Euclidean geometry, linear time, and the limitations of human actors. And, even if it were possible somehow to recreate the speed and spatiality of hypertext, to do so would subvert the spirit of the play, which is based on fundamental human relationships. Kushner is fairly clear about the type of production he desires in his note on staging, and it sounds very much like the *Our Town* school of theater:

> The play benefits from a pared-down style of presentation, with minimal scenery and scene shifts done rapidly (no blackouts!), employing the cast as well as stagehands—which makes an actor-driven event, as

this must be. The moments of magic . . . are to be fully realized, as bits of wonderful *theatrical* illusion—which means it's OK if the wires show. (1:5)

One reads Kushner's injunction with vigorous agreement, but it is not as easy to achieve as it may seem. There are a limited number of ways to accomplish Kushner's goal, and all of them have certain drawbacks. If one were to make a list of the minimum set pieces required to produce the play (as some scholars have done for Shakespeare), the list would be fairly short—an amazingly iconographic collection of elements: a bed, a park bench, a hospital bed, a chair, a desk. Other than the unique scenes such as the diorama in the Mormon Visitor's Center, very little else is needed. Does Prior's bed need to be different from Louis's? Does his hospital bed need to be different from Cohn's? Does one park bench need to be different from another? If there is a willingness to use emblematic furniture and stick to the bare minimum, it could be possible to set at least the recurrent scenes more or less permanently on the stage so that scene shifts might be achieved largely through lighting changes and actor movement. This, indeed, was the original intent of Conklin and Eustis at the Taper: to place essential scenic pieces against the cracked facade of the background. During the development process more specific scenery was added, and the final product was, as so many theater pieces are, a compromise among several visions. The more elements that need to move on and off the stage, the more one is dependent on actors or stage hands to do the moving. In a play with so many changes this parade of furniture-toting figures ultimately adds not simply an encumbrance or distraction but also another level of text—a secondary play about furniture moving that exists in the interstices of the primary text.

The Broadway production had the resources—and perhaps the temptation—to employ technology for fluidity. The relatively small stage of the Walter Kerr Theatre was fitted with an elaborate winch system that allowed wagons (movable stage platforms) to glide on and off the stage with seeming ease as other units flew in or out. This is a different kind of magic, though. It is the slickness and trickery of Broadway musicals that "wows" an audience with scenery that is as choreographed as the dancers. Nevertheless, there is no question that, once the decision had been made to depict each room, park, hospital room, and office with individualized scenic units, then Wagner's solution to the problem of scene shifts was the most efficient one possible. Action or dialogue could start as one wagon rolled on while another rolled off; scenes could overlap, intersect, and recombine. The proscenium stage, however, imposes a limitation on movement: wagons can roll on from stage right or stage left, and there is only so much variety possible. A certain repetitive monotony was inevitable with such a scheme. *Village Voice* critic Michael Feingold may have summed it up best when he noted that the set, "too elaborate for the pared-down version Kushner's notes request, yet too sparing of its effects to drown the play in glitz . . . gets the many scenes on and off with a flat, neat efficiency."[12]

Since the play's New York staging, productions of *Angels* have proliferated. The approaches to design have used some variant or combination of the approaches described here: unifying, metaphorical environment or neutral space; multiple scene changes or some sort of simultaneous setting. Most have sought some way visually to encapsulate the idea of America. Interestingly, discussions with several individuals who had seen more than one production suggested that the most emotionally powerful ones were those that, because of necessity or choice, were utterly simple and even had a "rough theater" quality to them. Notable were the production by graduate acting students at New York University and a reading of *Millennium Approaches* at the Taper as a prelude to the theater's first production of *Perestroika*. Some of the response, of course, may have to do with audience expectations and production context. We neither want nor expect production values in a reading; we come to focus on the text. But it does suggest that Kushner is right in asking for a pared-down production, and perhaps the play, somewhat like Marc Blitzstein's opera *The Cradle Will Rock,* benefits from a dramatic equivalent of a concert performance. It also suggests that the play's depth and power is such that, like most good theater, it not only tolerates but demands scenographic exploration and experimentation. There is no one correct way to design *Angels*.

NOTES

1. Tony Kushner, *Angels in America: A Gay Fantasia on National Themes. Part One: Millennium Approaches* (New York: Theatre Communications Group, 1993), 10. All subsequent references to part 1 will be indicated in parentheses in the text.

2. Alfred Jarry, "Preliminary Address at the First Performance of *Ubu Roi,* December 10, 1896," in *Selected Works of Alfred Jarry,* ed. Roger Shattuck and Simon Watson Taylor (New York: Grove Press, 1980), 78.

3. John Conklin, personal interview, 2 January 1996.

4. Ibid.

5. Thornton Wilder, *Our Town,* act 1, in *Three Plays* (New York: Avon Books, 1976), 28.

6. Ibid., 6.

7. Tony Kushner, *Angels in America: A Gay Fantasia on National Themes. Part Two: Perestroika* (New York: Theatre Communications Group, 1994), 146. All subsequent references to part 2 will be indicated in parentheses in the text.

8. Quoted in Keir Elam, *The Semiotics of Theatre and Drama* (New York and London: Methuen, 1980, 1983), 7.

9. Michel Foucault, "Of Other Spaces," *diacritics* 16 (1986): 22.

10. Henri Lefebvre, *The Production of Space,* trans. Donald Nicholson-Smith (Oxford, U.K., and Cambridge, Mass.: Blackwell Publishers, 1991), 31.

11. Foucault, "Of Other Spaces," 25.

12. Michael Feingold, "Building the Monolith," review of *Angels in America* by Tony Kushner, *Village Voice,* 18 May 1993, 218–19.

On Filming *Angels*

Robert Altman

An interview with Deborah R. Geis
and Steven F. Kruger

Editors' Note: Subsequent to this interview we learned that Robert Altman will not be directing the film version of *Angels* and has agreed to pass the project on to another filmmaker, P. J. Hogan. He has, however, graciously consented to the publication of this dialogue, which we have included for its insights into the cinematic potential of Kushner's play as well as its interest to scholars of Altman's work.

Deborah Geis: We wanted to begin by asking you what attracted you to Tony Kushner's play, if there are any particular angles on it, any aspects of the play, that you were particularly drawn to.

Robert Altman: Well, when I first saw it, I saw it in Los Angeles, a company out here, before it [went to Broadway]. . . . I don't know how many years ago it was, it seems forever. [The Mark Taper Forum production opened in November 1992.] When it first opened out here, I saw them both together in a marathon. The second piece [*Perestroika*] has been changed quite a bit since then. And I just was moved by it, I thought it was terrific, I liked the cinematic [quality]—it was written almost like a film. And I just loved the language and what it had to say.

DG: Going back to *Brewster McCloud,* I think of the imagery in your films of angels or of flying at least. Kushner's "theater of the fabulous" mixes cosmic visions and voices and fantasy, and yet I don't think of you as a fantasy kind of director. We were wondering if you had any thoughts about how you would convey on film what is very much a *theatrical* vision. It's interesting that you mentioned that the play was cinematic; how would you convey the fantastic side of the play?

RA: I think that in the film in general, the scenes should be fairly nitty-gritty and realistic. In the theater it was set forward—actually, [e.g.], they were sitting at a cafe talking—for many of those scenes, there were only two people onstage. I think in the film there would be, you know, eighty people and you'd find the group that's doing the talking or sitting on the steps of the building in Washington or wherever it was, you'd find them amongst a whole tableau of life. And there'd be a lot of action, so that when the Angel comes, the Angel brings the fantasy to it. I think the Angel has to be the biggest problem in presenting it on the screen.

Steven Kruger: We were actually talking about that yesterday and imagining how you might do the Angel.

RA: My Angel, I think, will be a hermaphrodite. I mean it will have breasts and probably a little penis tucked away like David, and I think it will have feathers, down, instead of pubic hair, and I think it will be kind of beat-up and naked. I don't think the Angel should be wearing a white dress or anything. And I think the wind should be [blowing], there should be feathers broken off, and you know, that Angel's in a war.

SK: So, a kind of decrepit angel.

RA: Well, a little beat-up. And on a losing mission. But that's the concept. The rest of the danger in the film is that the scenes are written like film scenes, so he's written it like a movie and put it on a stage, and you take it and put it back into a movie, it may just be a movie. That would be too bad.

DG: I'm thinking of the staging you did years ago at University of Michigan of *A Rake's Progress*—do you remember the giant scaffold that you used on the stage for that?

RA: Yes.

DG: I thought of that when you were talking about having all the people there at one time, and I think Kushner really does have that sense of multiple staging, the split staging. It's interesting, though, that in your previous adaptations of stage plays, often the challenge seems to be opening out the script; I'm thinking of *Streamers* or *Jimmy Dean* or *Fool for Love*.

RA: For *Streamers* or *Jimmy Dean* or *Secret Honor* there was never a screenplay written. We took the Samuel French copy of the play, and it was in my hip pocket, and it was done, and the *Caine Mutiny Court Martial*—those were all done exactly from the stage text. The only one I did a screenplay on, so to speak, was *Beyond Therapy.* The easiest one to talk about is *Streamers,* because all I did there was just put a fourth wall in.

DG: Are you working with Kushner on this project?

RA: Oh, I'm working with him all the time, of course.

DG: Kushner also has written a play that's very much aware of its own status as theater; he says that he wants the wires to show for the Angel, and so forth. I wonder what you do with that impulse, and here I'm thinking of something like *Buffalo Bill and the Indians* or *The Player,* where there's very much an awareness of acting or performance as fraud on some level.

RA: I think that, taking the play literally, the Angel exists in the mind of Prior, as do all of those characters [e.g., the prior Priors], and Ethel Rosenberg exists in Roy Cohn's mind. It's not going to be anything that's going to be done with a lot of—anything I do, I think you should see the tricks, and I think they should be simple and I think they should be fairly mechanical. You can do anything today on film and video in terms of special effects, anything can be achieved, and so consequently it becomes boring. It doesn't become interesting, it's as though it's [just] more of that. So I think you have to show the device, and I think it has to be an effort. I think you have to show the effort.

DG: An angel crashing through the ceiling is spectacular onstage, but filmgoers tend to be much more inured, I think.

RA: Well, unless it's done kind of in an unspectacular way. But, when you try to go compete with Kevin Costner and Arnold Schwarzenegger and most of that shit that we have out there, it's foolish; it's a lost cause.

SK: Have you thought through other sorts of technical transformations you're going to need to do in moving from the play to the film? We were thinking, for instance, of the length of the play.

RA: We don't know how we're, where we're, going to do it yet. If it's two theatrical films, they'll probably be close to three hours apiece and nobody wants to do that, everybody's scared to death of that. We're talking about doing it on cable, actually, and running it at its full length, because I think if you truncate it in any way and you just get down to the bare bones of "oh, this is what the story is," it's nothing. The verbiage and the poetry, the talk, is what makes it what it is, and its weight—it needs the weight. So, that's why it's been so difficult to get it, and it's going to continue to be difficult to get it, made. I don't know that we'll ever achieve this, you know.

DG: We were going to ask you what stage this was in right now.

RA: Well, we're sitting there with a piece of material that you know something about in a world that's interested in—we're sitting there with a pair of gloves in a world that sells shoes.

DG: We were also curious about where you would like to film it, what sorts of locations, because it seems very much a New York play but also one that incorporates the West.

RA: Tony wants to shoot it in New York, of course. That's his thought—in the winter, which again adds millions of dollars to it. I think probably, practically, I would shoot it in Montreal. Most of it. You could do a lot of stuff with the scenes in New York, but I think Montreal would be the most economical place to shoot it. But I think that [the location] actually doesn't make a lot of difference.

SK: In the same way that you've thought about how the angel will be presented, have you thought about the fantastic locales and how you would do those—the heaven, the Antarctica scenes?

RA: They would be very, very simple. One idea that we've had would be to do them on television—where, for instance, she's [Harper's] sitting there watching television and Mr. Lies appears and all that. I don't know how that's going to end up. Prior's relatives could come right out of a *Highlanders* film and turn right off the television set and talk to him. I don't know. These are thoughts we've had.

SK: In terms of the way you would present the fantasy material, would the Mormon diorama work in a similar way to Harper's fantasies, or would that be done differently?

RA: I don't even know. I think that those kind of things will solve themselves. It's all a matter of degree, and that'll dictate itself.

DG: The few other feature films that have been made on the subject of AIDS—*Philadelphia* and some of the others—have sometimes been criticized for treating homosexuality problematically and for diminishing the real agony of the AIDS crisis. I'm wondering, since Kushner's take on that is very different, what do you do in your film with AIDS to make it have an immediate kind of bodily impact? How important do you think AIDS is to the play?

RA: That's what it's about, it's about the pestilence. And I don't know what it is—I think it's best told through the combination of Roy Cohn and Prior, the two of them . . . [taking] two shots at it, and AIDS is a part of it.

SK: We were thinking of the ways in which the play is careful to set itself at a particular historical moment, in 1986, and we wondered if you had thoughts about how crucial that would be in the film.

RA: I think it's what the play is about. I mean, the play is set in a political time, and, if it were set in today, it would be a different play. Scary as it was at the time, then, it's scarier times right now, and I think it has to be dealt with in terms of the Reagan period. Because that's really what it's about.

DG: We're also wondering about your thoughts on Roy Cohn, either the real Roy Cohn or Kushner's version of him, because he does seem to be the real historical character at the center of the play, and as you said he's also a crucial part of the AIDS text.

RA: He and Ethel Rosenberg are the two historical characters, and I think we should see more of Ethel. I don't think we have to know who she is, but I think she should be a specter throughout this thing as it builds. The Roy Cohn character I think is very . . . written; it's just written.

DG: So, you would actually have Ethel there as a presence throughout.

RA: I might see her on a bus or walking down the street or at a table—anywhere Roy can see her.

DG: Oh, that's fascinating, because I think she very much is there in that sense for him.

RA: Because Roy's the only one that sees her. I mean, she's in his mind. Everybody else has forgotten her.

DG: In some ways Roy Cohn is the scene stealer in the play, at least in the New York production, the way that he was done, he was so over-the-top, such a caricature, that he sort of stole the attention from everyone else in the play. How do you envision your actor playing Roy Cohn?

RA: Oh, I don't know. That's something that's going to develop as we do it. It's going to depend on the actor, and the actor is going to make a lot of those decisions.

SK: One of the interesting things that happens with Roy Cohn and Ethel Rosenberg and also Louis is a focusing of the play on Jewishness as a question, and, of course, there's the Mormon material and the material about race with Belize and Louis. How crucial is the theme of race, ethnicity, and religion in your view of the play, and how might you go about treating that?

RA: Again, it's written. It's something we face that's a very, very, very big part of our lives and motivates every single thing that happens in our culture. We sweep it under the rug all the time, and we lie about it, but it's most definitely there, and it has to be. . . . Tony deals with it, that's all. But it isn't getting any better, you know.

DG: Do you see your project on *Angels* as having any connection to other projects that you have planned on down the line? I know you're just coming off of *Kansas City* right now; do you see this project as part of something else that you would like to work on, a different trend in your filmmaking?

RA: In all my thirty, forty, films, whatever, I've been involved in, one just follows the other, and if there's a connection there I don't know about it, but I'm sure there is.

DG: Or other people will find it.

RA: Somebody will tell me what it was. After the fact. But [it's like] the way the farmer trains the mule: you get a brickbat and hit him on the head real hard. It's whatever gets my attention.

Notes on *Angels in America* as American Epic Theater

Janelle Reinelt

Many have the feeling that democracy is of such a
nature that it could disappear from one hour to the
next.
> —Bertolt Brecht, "Letter to an Adult American"

I.

Bert Brecht never really made it in America. We all know that. James Lyons
finishes his portrait of Brecht in America by concluding, "Brecht was probably too far ahead of his time and too uncompromising in promoting his
kind of theater in his own way to have succeeded in an alien environment
like America."[1] Even suggesting that Brecht's day in the United States came
in the 1960s and 1970s doesn't quite wash. Surveying the situation with
fresh eyes for a special issue of *Theater,* Peter Ferran commented that "the
main force in this American avant-garde theater turned out to be Artaud,
not Brecht."[2] In light of all the bad publicity surrounding Brecht's treatment
of his women collaborators, combined with a new attack on his politics—
mostly from John Fuegi's hatchet-job biography *Brecht and Company*—there
may be many who will wonder why I want to drag Brecht into a discussion
of *Angels in America.*

Of course, he's already there, already present. Kushner himself evokes
Brecht and all his contradictions in his own musings in the published text of
Perestroika.[3] And then there are the names, scattered all through Kushner's
acknowledgments, of the members of the Eureka Theatre Company: Oskar
Eustis, Tony Taccone, Sigrid Wurschmidt. For ten years or so, in the mid-
1970s to the mid-1980s, they were part of an epic theater in San Francisco
that held the promise of a genuinely American appropriation and transformation of Brechtian dramaturgy. Kushner had his work produced there; in
fact, the first production of *Millennium* and the first reading of what was to
become *Perestroika* took place at the Eureka. There were other short-lived
but vibrant experiments—the Brecht Company in Ann Arbor and Epic

West in Berkeley come at once to mind. But Kushner was associated through the Eureka with a group of artists who, while not Brechtians themselves, particularly, were making a certain kind of politically engaged, left-wing theater on epic principles.[4]

These "epic principles" are summarized by familiar terms from the Brechtian lexicon: the historicization of the incidents, social gestus as mise-en-scène, and the odd *Verfremdungseffekt*. These parts of the epic critique still seem valid and necessary (even after the end of the Cold War has supposedly made socialism obsolete), although they might go by slightly different descriptions now that class society is passé and scientism has been shown to have its limits. Historicizing the incidents might become "A Gay Fantasia on National Themes," for instance. Social gestus means diverse and contradictory identity constructions within a cast not headed by a single hero-protagonist: certainly not Prior Walter nor even Roy Cohn but, rather, the group of characters, as they bump and collide throughout the play, ringing the changes on race, gender, age, religion, and, of course, sexuality. And *Verfremdungseffekt*? Lots to choose from there—cross-dressing, metatheatrical directions from Kushner that the magic has to be amazing but it's "OK if the wires show,"[5] or the scene at the Diorama Room of the Mormon Visitor's Center where, as Harper says, "They're having trouble with the machinery" (2:63).

Finally, I couldn't get Brecht out of my mind while I was watching the play—on either coast. In the East I faulted the production for not being Brechtian enough; in the West I praised the production because it finally achieved American epic style. It was actually *Caucasian Chalk Circle* I kept thinking about and *Good Person of Setzuan,* too. And how in recent decades, Brecht was criticized for his impossible "closed" dramaturgy and utopian play making. Suddenly Brecht seemed like a specter, like Ethel Rosenberg or Roy Cohn in the play: a specific historical presence conjured up, but as a dramatic fiction, to haunt the play through both limitation and aspiration.

II.

Louis makes most of the political arguments in the script. He puts the discourse of democracy in play, although Roy Cohn also speaks a powerful political discourse. If considered abstractly, as a kind of "red thread" through the playtext, this democratic discourse emerges as a series of questions: how to reconcile difference, how to establish justice, how to effect social change, how to effect personal change, how to progress? This dimension of the social, of the body politic, is represented on the bodies of characters struggling for personal solutions to the contradictions of American life. They become sites for the traffic of history and the ideology of democracy: Mormon history, Red-baiting history, Jewish history, "family values history," sin and guilt through history, traditions of prophecy and transcendence. Incidents in the lives of the characters are typical of many contemporary Americans, and every character, from Hannah to Belize, Joe to Harper, represents one of these types. The social gestus of the playtexts seems to be disconnecting from identity, a kind of cutting loose from moorings, a not-very-Marxist letting go of fiercely held convictions or practices, or the refusal of great regressive temptations (most forcefully materialized in the person of the Angel) as the various characters "travel," or put themselves in motion away from the contexts and subject positions that have held them in place. By the end of *Perestroika,* and just barely, one sees the outline for a different society. And that is all there can really be—a glimmer. Otherwise, any firmer answer, any true solution, seems prescriptive and preachy, trite or sentimental, and ultimately false. Of course, *Angels* comes perilously close to that trap all through its text. In this regard, however, *Angels* is more closely related to *Good Person of Setzuan* than to the more sentimental parable, *Caucasian Chalk Circle.* Brecht posits a world in which Shui Ta is necessary and subjectivity is hopelessly split, throwing the dilemma back to the audience to "fix." In *Chalk Circle* Azdak, the mythical judge who made justice possible but then disappeared, and may never have been real in the first place (it's a "story"), offers more of a prescription: the land should be planted for the good of all, private property notwithstanding. No prescriptions end *Angels in America.* The last scene leaves Louis and Belize fighting about politics, their differences unresolved; it leaves Harper suspended on a "*jumbo-jet, airborne*" (2:144). Prior Walter remains alive, perhaps because of the AZT Belize commandeered from Roy Cohn, but has not been cured. The final gesture is toward a possibility of healing and progress, but the details have to be worked out in human space/time within the American national context. Not an easy task.

Epic theater needs to construct the experience of ideological contradiction as the mode of subjectivity it projects for spectators rather than the ideological totalization implied in *supporter, judgment, empathy,* or even *detachment.* This is an epic play *if* the spectators engage the problems and understand the constraints operating on the nation and on themselves as social subjects. It is an epic play *if* some sense of what might be done next is suggested but not spelled out. It is an epic play *if* it does not let spectators off the hook by allowing too much psychological investment in particular characters or too much good feeling of resolution at the end.

III.

The subjunctive mode is always an essential part of epic theater. First, the provisional positing of a different way of organizing social life—what if the world were not like this? Second, the conditional—*if* the spectators and the actors and the play form a Brechtian triangle of speculation and critique, aesthetic pleasure, and political engagement, *then* the "epic" happens. Thus, even if Tony Kushner has written a perfectly crafted, totally brilliant epic playscript, whether or not it will result in an epic production is always an open question—that's always the gamble of political theater.

George C. Wolfe and Mark Wing-Davey, directors of the 1993 New York production and the 1994 San Francisco production, respectively, have different strengths as directors. Wolfe understands polish and theatrics and how to make a play succeed on Broadway. Wing-Davey has had success in New York, too, but he is a drier, starker, anti-illusionist and antisentimental director. His success with Caryl Churchill's *Mad Forest,* in New York and also in Berkeley, already marks him as an epic director. Then there are the audiences themselves. Seeing *Angels in America* toward the end of its successful New York run in April 1994, I was surrounded by comfortable upper-middle-class people who could easily afford the expensive tickets. Lots of gay couples, but lots of straight ones also, mixed with the crowd. Not too many people looked like students. It was a festive crowd, riding the crest of having one of the hottest tickets on Broadway. They reacted as if they were at an Alan Ayckbourn comedy—jolly, even boisterous, lots of laughter, and not much tension. In San Francisco some months later a quieter, more diverse crowd laughed while listening more intently. Class, age, race, and sexuality seemed more widely represented, and the mood of reception had clearly shifted.

Searching for these differences through reviews of the different productions, I find traces of production values and audience expectations that document both the latent epic qualities and the Broadway qualities of this play in performance. Clive Barnes finds "curious" what I find fundamental: "Curiously, when I first saw the play last year at Britain's National Theater—a far harsher, more political reading of a virtually identical text—its impact seemed greater."[6]

The reviews of the New York production praise Wolfe's directing for its technical acumen, the performances of Ron Leibman and Stephen Spinella for their richness and virtuosity, and the author for his inventiveness, literary capabilities, and theatrical savvy. Yet the comments that provide the traces I'm seeking are those that describe precisely what is valued by the reviewers. One of the most positive comments on the play is also the most damning from the point of view of the seeker after an American epic theater: "This heretofore almost unknown playwright is such a delightful, luscious, funny writer that, for all the political rage and the scathing unsanitized horror, the hours zip by with the breezy enjoyment of a great page-turner or a popcorn movie."[7] It is not the popular culture comparisons to popcorn movies that chill—after all, old Bert Brecht himself wanted a popular theater in that sense, theater to be like boxing not opera—it is the notion that a good night out in the theater dishes up politics and genuinely horrible insights in order to accommodate them to the culinary tastes of an audience for whom these things must be rendered palatable. Complaining about opera in the context of his discussion of the culinary, Brecht writes: "Values evolve which are based on the fodder principle. And this leads to a general habit of judging works of art by their suitability for the apparatus without ever judging the apparatus by its suitability for the work."[8] Thus poised between Barnes's suspicion that the British production, with its harsher politics, made a greater impact on its audience and Winer's assessment of the New York success based on its culinary pleasures, a trace of epic dramaturgy and its absence marks out a space of possibility. The shape of an American epic emerges.

It is too simple to say that the San Francisco production of *Angels in America* realized the promise of a great American epic dramaturgy. I do not even really believe that is the case. But both my own experience in the theater at the American Conservatory Theater (ACT) production and the San Francisco reviews do support the view that the play has epic capabilities that are sometimes reached in performance.

The San Francisco reception is clouded by the relationship between the play and the playwright and the San Francisco theater community. Almost every review begins with some claim on the play because of its San Francisco genesis. Perhaps because I also shared a commitment to the Eureka Theatre and identify closely with the Bay Area, my own view of the play is less than completely objective, but I prefer to stress that an emphasis on location, or rather on "the politics of location," may lead not only to local squabbles but also to a cultural and political investment in the production that activates spectatorial engagement. Headlines such as "'Angels' comes home to The City," "'Angels' Is Born Again," "Tony Kushner's epic returns home," all make a sentimental connection between the play and the city but also foreground it as something important to San Franciscans, something to be seen, responded to, and assessed from a position of relationship rather than distance. One could also argue that the play actually received extra critical scrutiny from the beginning, when director Mark Wing-Davey did not cast enough local actors to suit some portions of the San Francisco theater community. Comparisons to the Eureka production of *Millennium* and the memory of earlier performances also dot the journalism concerned with the play.

Most significant for the issues under discussion here are the aspects of the Wing-Davey production that mark it as deliberately epic. He provided abrupt and rapid transitions between scenes. In the New York production Wolfe staged the "split screen" scenes in *Millennium* as simultaneous but discretely separate scenes in stable space. Wing-Davey reframed these scenes as interconnected and uncontainable (actors "violated" one another's stage space to produce this effect of overflowing boundaries), staging the dissolution and blending of identities. As for the emotion/sentiment questions, Wing-Davey perhaps answered New York's Winer: "What I'm working toward is a sense of the fun but also the mess of the play—the circumstances, the disease, the visceral nature of the play. It should not be sanitized. It will not be polished in the sense that you can see your own reflection. . . . But maybe you can."[9] There is lots of blood on the stage; I wondered why I hadn't noticed that in New York.

The set design for the ACT production emerged as a key marker of the epic nature of the production because it was very controversial. Made up of industrial materials, large, almost oversized metal ramps and bridges, exposed light instruments, and aluminum rigging for the angel, Kate Edmunds's set either pleased people or raised their critical eyebrows. "'Angels': Wires and Pulleys" ran the headlines.[10] Steven Winn wrote that "the results range from striking scenic coups . . . to distracting clutter"; Robert Hurwitt found the set "harshly anti-illusionist"; while Judith Green claimed that the "production goes out of its way to give visual offense."[11]

I found the set exactly the appropriate sort of Brechtian backdrop for a play intended to be about "national themes." New York reviewers often made reference to the domestic situation of the play or to its conventional depiction of three households. This kind of talk does not apply so easily to the San Francisco version, because the materials and scope of the set— industrial, urban, explicitly theatrical—continually place the domestic scenes within the context of the social, economic, and political structures of our nation at century's end. The detritus is real, and it is part and parcel of the emotional fallout facing the play's characters in their personal lives. In fact, the setting enhances or completes the play in this regard, strengthening the epic qualities and mitigating the tendency for the playscript to slip into bourgeois individualism but isolating personal, realistic spaces. In looking at

From left to right: Garret Dillahunt (Prior), Julia Gibson (Harper), and
Ben Shenkman (Louis) in the 1994 American Conservatory Theater
production of *Angels in America,* directed by Mark Wing-Davey.
(Photo by Ken Friedman, courtesy ACT)

Caspar Neher's drawings for Brecht's productions, the central tenet of epic
staging is apparent: let the set contextualize or frame the action in such a
way that it comments on the social world of the play. Let the props and the
costumes also aspire to a functional realism that documents how people live
and work in such a milieu.

The placement of the bedroom and hospital scenes on a kind of
bridge/ramp that flew in undercut sentimentalism but raised the ire of one
reviewer.[12] The many mechanized and working appliances in Harper's
kitchen emphasized the mechanical, enforced domesticity of her life. Roy
Cohn's plastic telephone and high-tech desk set functioned as both a toy
and the key to his power in a telecom age. It followed him to his hospital
bed as a portable switchboard. The Marines Memorial Theatre, where the
plays were performed because ACT's regular venue, the Geary Theatre, had
been damaged in the 1989 earthquake, became the focus of criticism for
being too small for the set. The claustrophobia and clutter, however,
seemed evocative of our current cultural life, with its bombardment of
commodities, information, and garbage. Kate Edmunds's set for the San

Steven Culp (Joe), *left,* and Peter Zapp (Roy Cohn) in the 1994 American Conservatory Theater production of *Angels in America.* *(Photo by Ken Friedman, courtesy ACT)*

Francisco production of *Angels* was uncomfortable because it took these aesthetics as a starting point. She also, however, enabled the "fantasia on national themes" to evoke the nation and its contemporary structures.

This comparison of the New York and San Francisco productions merely establishes the different potentialities of the play in production under various circumstances for various audiences. Others will want to compare Los Angeles, London, or Chicago performances. That is, perhaps, exactly the point: that it is possible but not inevitable to see *Angels in America* as an American epic play and that it is also desirable and preferable to see it in this light.

IV.

Howard Brenton, the contemporary British writer, remarked, "I sorted my mind out about Bert Brecht, the greatest playwright of our century, yes, the greatest, the best we have, alas."[13] He was trying to "sort out" both an homage to Brecht and a sense of failure that Brecht wasn't good enough and to say that it is a shame we don't have more and even better writers. I am persuaded of a similar attitude toward Tony Kushner in the context of this specific decade and nation. Hungrily seeking a left-wing voice in the American theater with the scope and ambition to work on a truly epic canvas, I am attracted to Kushner's themes, goals, theatrical accomplishments. Wanting the theater to become a site of national discourse about the future, I also wish for these plays to overreach themselves.

Like that of Bertolt Brecht, Kushner's work is based on the Enlightenment project of reason and progress; like Walter Benjamin's, it rests on a messianic desire. Because we are seemingly stuck in time, a leap or jump or break seems essential. While for Brecht socialism figured as a horizon of concrete possibility, for Kushner, in an age in which the grand narrative of Marxism is bankrupt, the leap catapults him into identity politics and a relative detachment from economic and social structural change. Backing off of Marx, however, produces a kind of liberal pluralism or benign tolerance, a promise but no program.

David Savran, in his brilliant analysis of *Angels in America,* has criticized the play for mobilizing a consensual politics that masquerades as dissensual in order to make an appeal to a possible utopian nation that rests on Enlightenment principles of rationalism, communitarianism, and progress.[14] Seeing this epistemology as part rational, part messianic, Savran also thinks it explains the play's great popular success: "*Angels* reassures an 'audience that knows it has lost control over events' not by enabling it to 'regain . . . control' but by letting it know 'that history is nevertheless controlled by an underlying order and that it has a purpose that is nearing fulfillment.'"[15] Thus, the play promises too much and too little, finally signifying American liberal ideology as usual.

While I am generally persuaded by Savran's analysis, I wish to place the dilemmas of which he speaks within slightly different terms. Rather than focusing on the reiteration of liberal themes, I regret Kushner's drift away from socialist themes. The replacement of class analysis by other identity categories, while useful and strategic in terms of contemporary exigencies, leaves the play with no other foundation for social change than the individual subject, dependent on an atomized agency. Since this subjectivity is contradictory and collapsed, the only horizon of hope must be transcendent.

One key moment will illustrate how the playscript becomes entrapped in the ideology of individualism. It occurs when Belize takes the AZT from Roy Cohn. In this scene the black man (who is, of course, tokenized and sentimentalized insofar as he is the great caretaker of the play, a fact many critics have realized) takes away the privileged man's private stash of medicine in order to share the wealth:

Belize: If you live fifty more years you won't swallow all these
pills. *(Pause)* I want some.
Roy: That's illegal.
Belize: Ten bottles.
Roy: I'm gonna report you.
Belize: There's a nursing shortage. I'm in a union. I'm real
scared. I have friends who need them. Bad.

(2:60)

After a fierce argument Belize leaves with three bottles. Later, after Cohn's
death, Belize gives a full bag to Prior.

What I am going to say next may seem completely unfair: that scene,
those events, aren't good enough for an American epic play. But it is precisely the evocation of personal friends who need the medicine that
undercuts a social critique by keeping the discourse personal. Nowhere in
the play is there any indication of the community organizing, political agi-
tation, liberal church and other networks involved in fighting AIDS. Prior
and Louis and Joe are all left with their private consciousnesses to sort
their doubts and fears out *on their own.* The play needs some gesture to the
power of social and political organizing; that is, we need to see the social
environment, ranges, background, mode of production. In this scene all
the ingredients are there—Belize evokes his union to counter Roy's
threat to his job. Why couldn't he also mention a network or organization
in connection with the friends needing AZT? I do not presume to rewrite
this scene; I do want to underscore the structural absence in the play of
alternatives to bourgeois individualism.

On the other hand, perhaps any overt gesture to this kind of political solution would seem too programmatic, too Marxist, too *Caucasian
Chalk Circle.* We do not, after all, live in a time when a rationalist epistemology convinces (even if a nostalgia for the unified subject still
lingers). In the absence of programmatics, however, the kind of liberal
pluralism tinged with despair that marks America at the end of the century goes unchallenged, in fact is reinscribed. The millennial hope of the
last scene of the play must be founded on the transcendental *if* there is
no basis for social change within the representation. The imperative to
signal beyond its own terms marks *Angels in America.* But the play leaves
us waiting at the fountain to discover an immanent means of making
things better, of healing, of constructing democracy. The best we have,
alas. For now.

NOTES

1. James K. Lyons, *Bertolt Brecht in America* (Princeton, N.J.: Princeton University Press, 1980), 347.

2. Peter W. Ferran, "New Measures for Brecht in America," *Theater* 25:2 (1994): 9.

3. Tony Kushner, *Angels in America: A Gay Fantasia on National Themes. Part Two: Perestroika* (New York: Theatre Communications Group, 1994), 153. All further citations will be included in parentheses in the text.

4. Sigrid Wurschmidt, a brilliant actress whose life was tragically cut short by breast cancer, was the inspiration for the Angel. Kushner first met her in the Eureka's production of Kushner's play *A Bright Room Called Day*. For a profile of the company up to 1985, see my essay "New Beginnings/Second Wind: The Eureka Theatre," *Theater* 16:3 (Summer–Fall 1985): 17–21.

5. Tony Kushner, *Angels in America: A Gay Fantasia on National Themes. Part One: Millennium Approaches* (New York: Theatre Communications Group, 1993), 5. All further citations will be included in parentheses in the text.

6. Clive Barnes, "Angelically Gay about Our Decay," *New York Post,* 5 May 1993. (Also in *New York Theatre Critics' Reviews* 14:11 [1993]: 211.)

7. Linda Winer, "Pulitzer-Winning 'Angels' Emerges from the Wings," *New York Newsday,* 5 May 1993. (Also in *New York Theatre Critics' Reviews* 14:11 [1993]: 209.)

8. Bertolt Brecht, *Brecht On Theatre,* ed. and trans. John Willett (New York: Hill and Wang, 1964), 34.

9. Michael Fox, "Director Wing-Davey Does It His Way," *San Francisco Chronicle,* 5 September 1994, Datebook 33.

10. Laura Evenson, "'Angels' They Have Hoisted on High," *San Francisco Chronicle,* 10 October 1994, E1, 2.

11. Stephen Winn, "'Angels' Is Born Again," *San Francisco Chronicle,* 14 October 1994, C1, 5, 18; Robert Hurwitt, "Return of the Millennium," *San Francisco Examiner,* 13 October 1994, C1, 12; Judith Green, "A Chorus of Angels," *San Jose Mercury News,* 21 October 1994, 41, 42.

12. Green, "Chorus of Angels."

13. Howard Brenton, "The Best We Have Alas: Bertolt Brecht," *Hot Irons* (London: Nick Herne Books, 1995), 64.

14. David Savran, "Ambivalence, Utopia, and a Queer Sort of Materialism: How *Angels in America* Reconstructs the Nation," *Theatre Journal* 47 (May 1995): 221ff. This essay is reprinted in the current volume.

15. Here Savran is glossing Barry Brummett, *Contemporary Apocalyptic Rhetoric* (New York: Praeger, 1991), 37–38.

"Dramaturging" the Dialectic: Brecht, Benjamin, and Declan Donnellan's Production of *Angels in America*

Art Borreca

I told you it wasn't working right, it's just . . . the
magic of the theatre or something.
                              —Harper, *Perestroika*

The significance of Brechtian epic theater for Tony Kushner, not only
as a playwright but also as a sociohistorical thinker who thinks *in* and *through*
his drama, is abundantly evident in *Angels in America*. Although the play
owes a great deal to other theatrical traditions and genres—for example, the
poetic realism of O'Neill and Williams; the avant-garde "theater of images";
the Theatre of the Ridiculous; the realistic AIDS play—a Brechtian spirit
resides at the center of the work.[1] This spirit is evident in such classic
Brechtian techniques as episodic structure, emblematic and "ideologized"
characters, and theatrical montage, and in the use of these techniques to
"estrange" or "defamiliarize" sociohistorical conditions in a particular place
and time (in this case, late-twentieth-century America).[2] The play's epic
techniques and effect, especially as manifested in its conception of epic stage
space, poses special challenges to staging. Declan Donnellan's production of
the play at London's Royal National Theatre (1992–93) met those challenges superbly, bringing to the play the distinctive qualities on which he
has built his reputation as a director of Shakespeare and other seventeenth-
century dramatists: a highly refined theatricality; a choreographic respect for
stage movement; crystalline renderings of the text.[3] Donnellan's production
of *Angels* demonstrated that the English synthesis of the "Shakespearean"
and the "Brechtian," which can be traced to play writing and production in
the 1960s, is still a theatrically vital one.[4]

What follows is a variation on a dramaturg's protocol for the epic staging of *Angels in America:* an essay that explores how the play might be staged
according to its Brechtian dynamic.[5] This essay will proceed from theory to
practice. First, it will identify the Brechtian aspects of *Angels;* then it will

examine the play's social and theatrical dialectics, exploring how these are crucial to a stage interpretation of the play. Finally, the essay will explore the ramifications of those dialectics for scene design and staging, using Donnellan's production as a central point of reference and placing special emphasis on the use of theatrical space.

Brecht and Stylistic Montage

The special demands *Angels* makes on production are not matters of epic technique but, in a very particular sense, of *style*. The distinction is a fine but important one. Brecht developed the techniques of "epic montage"—the juxtaposition of contrasting stage imagery, action, and language from scene to scene and within individual scenes—in order to focus the spectator on the socioeconomic forces underlying the dramatic action. And yet neither those techniques nor the montage they effect make *Angels,* or any play for that matter, "epic" in the Brechtian sense. As Pia Kleber has written, "The only constant component Brecht and his disciples share is a dialectical way of thinking"; to this one might add a dialectical method of dramatizing such thinking.[6]

What gives *Angels in America* a special place in the Brechtian tradition is that it elaborates the dialectical principles of epic montage onto the level of theatrical style. Although other playwrights (most notably Caryl Churchill) have experimented with stylistic montage, Kushner's play is distinguished by a Promethean synthesis of realistic and nonrealistic styles and by the effort to construct an epistemologically stable mode of sociohistorical perception through that synthesis. The play counterposes psychologically realistic speech against the self-consciously stylized (and stylistically self-referential) language of camp; the Aristotelian structure of individual scenes (every scene builds through rising suspense to a climactic reversal) against the non-Aristotelian (i.e., epic) structure of the drama as a whole; that structure's estrangement of the action against moments of sensuous theatricalism; the psychologically and socially realistic development of characters against their quasisurrealistic, hallucinatory experiences. In performance these traditionally opposed styles function dialectically, fusing the play's aesthetic action (its experiment with stylistic montage as a mode of sociohistorical perception) with its dramatic action (the representation of the narratives of Prior, Louis, Joe, Harper, etc.), and placing the spectator's sense of his or her sociosexual identity, as well as his or her idea of "America," in relation to that being dramatized onstage. Although the play's nonrealistic elements have less in common with Brecht than with the philosophical avant-garde of, say, Richard Foreman, the play deploys them as part of what might be termed its "epic architectonics" and their exploration of the dialectic between the ideal and reality of America.

In those "epic architectonics" each style correlates to a major component of the work's sociohistorical vision, while each stylistic element correlates to an aspect of that component. For example, Roy's realistic language, with its power-driven rhythm and its obscenities, dramatizes one part of American realpolitik: politics as a form of making and selling the self. But at times Roy also speaks with a camp inflection, suggesting a self-consciousness that could, were it not sufficiently repressed, undermine the political self he has created. Moving between these two styles of speech, the character of Roy, as well as the spectator's (epic) view of that character, arises from a dialectic between the styles of social realism and gay camp theater. Each style adds to and takes away from the other, much as Roy himself negotiates the contradiction between his sexual and political identities. *Angels in America* thus engages the spectator not only in the dialectic between those identities but also in that between the styles by which the character is represented: not only in a drama in which Roy figures significantly but also in the dramatic procedure by which contradictory styles of representation combine, break apart, and recombine.

Benjamin and Anti-Brechtian Spectacle

In its stylistic dialectics *Angels in America* makes special use of the overall epic structure of its plot lines—*their* montage—and the anti-Brechtian spectacle of particular scenes. The play asks, can a nation built on the ideal of social equality and the myths of the New World and the frontier, as well as the realities of socioeconomic and cultural expansionism and repression, go on excluding homosexuals—and by extension anyone who does not fit a demographic profile favored by the existing hegemony—from the full rights of citizenship? Dramatizing this question, the play makes a "frontier" of theatrical space, "filling" it with diverse styles and synthesizing them in a vision of dialectical theater. At the outer reaches of that frontier is the theatrical spectacle of Prior's and Harper's hallucinations or visions, which intimate (or theatricalize the intimation of) divine revelation, provoking the spectator to wonder if such revelation will redeem America from a polarizing hegemony enforced by the political clout of white heterosexual men, replacing it with a more inclusive society. In its most spectacular moments, such as the appearance of the Angel at the end of *Millennium Approaches,* a production can stimulate the spectator to anticipate apocalyptic destruction followed by redemption. Such anticipation is shaped on the one hand by the spectator's (dumb) awe at the spectacle but on the other by the sense that it is only part of the show, an element in a theatrical representation. Like Prior, who is both awed by the Angel and secure enough to offer a camp response—"God almighty . . . / *Very* Steven Spielberg"—the spectator can "frame" the Angel as a product of theater, questioning not only its divinity but also its magnificence as spectacle.[7] Prior's awe at the Angel is tempered by his skepticism as a late-twentieth-century gay man who lies in bed, struck unjustly by AIDS; the spectator's awe at the Angel consists of amazement at its theatrical construction out of flesh and blood, makeup, costuming, stage mechanics, and heavy-duty (we hope!) wire. But, just as the Angel calls on Prior to be a prophet in part 2, so the play calls upon the spectator to imagine the *possibility* of the divine—and of a spectacle that intimates that possibility—within the work's dramatization of "America."

By employing spectacle in this way, *Angels in America* owes a debt to an intellectual and spiritual compatriot of Brecht's, Walter Benjamin. Kushner has stated that the play was inspired in part by the visionary historical materialism of Benjamin's "Theses on the Philosophy of History," especially by his reference to Paul Klee's 1920 painting *Angelus Novus*.[8] Imagining that the painting depicts the "angel of history," with the wreckage of the past piling at his feet and "a storm . . . blowing from Paradise . . . [propelling] him into the future," Benjamin calls on the materialist to reject the rationalist view of sociohistorical progress and enlightenment:

> [Materialist] thinking involves not only the flow of thoughts, but their arrest as well. Where thinking suddenly stops in a configuration pregnant with tension, it gives that configuration a shock, by which it crystallizes into a monad. . . . In this structure [the materialist] recognizes the sign of a Messianic cessation of happening . . . a revolutionary chance in the fight for the oppressed past.[9]

In other words: at a critical historical moment in which the wreckage of the past converges with the inevitable flight into the future, rational analysis can give way to a totalizing vision of the past as it has traditionally been interpreted and of a future that will redeem all of the past's oppressions. Benjamin goes on to write that the materialist's messianic vision "[blasts] a specific era out of the homogeneous course of history—blasting a specific life out of the era or a specific work of art out of the lifework"; through visionary materialism "[the era] is preserved in [the lifework] and at the same time canceled . . . and in the era the entire course of history."[10]

Just such an apocalyptic vision resonates throughout *Angels;* Benjamin could be describing Prior Walter's role in Kushner's play. Through his dreams and visions Prior is "blasted" out of his era, compelled into the role of prophet, just as he has been blasted out of the course of his life by AIDS. The blasting of Prior is basic to the play's blasting of an era—mid-1980s Reaganite America—out of "homogeneous" history. Dramatizing a historical moment in which absolutist conservatism and pluralist liberalism clashed over AIDS policy, Kushner's play "preserves" these forces in Prior's historical experience; yet the forces almost "cancel" themselves in Prior's prophecy. And, while the play "preserves" the forces by dramatizing their clash, it also yearns to "cancel" the legacy of the mid-1980s through the epic provocation of the spectator.

Furthermore, Prior's crisis is but one of several that typify the critical moment of the mid-1980s; all of the major characters are compounded of dialectically opposed impulses that manifest the dynamics of that moment in a "Benjaminian" way. Louis, for one, rationalizes his treatment of Prior by describing himself as a "neo-Hegelian positivist" whose "sense of constant historical progress towards happiness or perfection or something . . . can't . . . incorporate sickness into his sense of how things are supposed to go" (1:25). Louis is the dialectical opposite to Prior as prophet: a liberal-rationalist who subscribes to the myth of a progressive, enlightened America but whose interpretation of those ideals is as misplaced as his abandonment of Prior is cowardly. Harper's abandonment by Joe sets her on a journey of discovery with respect to the wreckage not only of her own life but also that of society; Joe's conservatism denies his sexual impulses and any awareness that the contradiction between those impulses and his belief system is socially constructed and therefore changeable. If Louis is Prior's rationalist opposite, Cohn is his historical and ideological nemesis, whose life incarnates the era's repression and oppression of homosexuality. Whereas AIDS brings Prior to "thresholds of revelation" (1:33), it exacerbates the contradictions of Cohn's identity—so he ends in Hell, doing a deal with God.

Angels in America, however, is by no means a purely Benjaminian play; paradoxically, the work adapts Benjamin's visionary materialism to a historiography founded on faith in enlightened historical progress. Although the Angel signifies "a Messianic cessation of happening"—indeed, she bears a divine call to antimigration—her Messianism is false, expressed as it is by an Angel abandoned by God to a world similarly abandoned. The Angel does not offer a chance to remake the past; she only seeks relief from its ruin and despair. Prior rejects her demands, asking the Continental Principalities to "Bless me anyway . . . I want more life" (2:135) and affirming the possibilities of personal and social progress that the phrase *more life* implies. Prior embraces life in the face of death, in the chain of historical events, and in the face of the destructive past, despite its painful and pain-inducing contradictions. Moreover, Prior does this not in the hope of redemption but with a kind of postmodern heroism, the bravery to muddle through but somehow to live—and to feel alive—in doing so. The choice is echoed by Belize's faith in forgiveness and Harper's insight that "nothing's lost forever. In this world, there is a kind of painful progress" (2:144). Kushner's vision is thus more teleological than apocalyptic: the drama is built around, and terminates in, Prior's and Harper's anagnorises, which are dramatized in a virtually Aristotelian manner, despite the play's epic form.

This modification of Benjamin's apocalyptic dialectics is mirrored in the play's stylistic montage. Alternating between various plot lines, the play dramatizes the intersection of each character's personal crisis with the sociopolitical Zeitgeist of the Reagan years, dramatizing an epic space in which none of the character's situations can be seen independently of the others. The play repeatedly disrupts this "defamiliarization" of the individual plot lines with dreams and "divine" spectacles, not only in the montage of plot lines and styles but also within the plot lines themselves. Viewed on its own dramatic terms, for example, Prior and Louis's story is, at base, classically structured and realistic; yet it is also repeatedly interrupted by Prior's visions, all of which are theatricalized in a nonrealistic manner. When the plot returns, as it does repeatedly, to its realistic portrayal of Prior's life, Prior returns to the realities of his disease. A similar pattern is at work in the story of Harper and Joe, which is punctuated by Harper's hallucinations, and in that of Roy and Joe, which gives way to visitations from Ethel Rosenberg.

These nonrealistic (and otherwise extraordinary) disruptions are signs of the play's stylistic montage at work. While the play juxtaposes realistic plot lines in order to dramatize a social picture of the mid-1980s, it counterposes that picture and its realism against the nonrealistic dream and hallucination scenes. These scenes describe a key structural arc through the two parts of the play. Although their overt function is to set painful psychological and social realities against the revelatory potential of dreams, they also form an ironically linear progress toward such revelation as can *in reality*—in the world of the play's epic social realism—be possessed. In Kushner's stylistic dialectics the Louis/Joe story contrasts stylistically with the dream meetings of Prior and Harper but serves a comparable dramatic function, becoming, in part 2, a nonhallucinatory but extraordinary source of disruption in all of the characters' lives, while the Prior/Harper scenes unfold in sync with the play's realistic narratives, "privileging" the attainment of "more life." Along the way the play's split scenes, which combine aspects of

Brechtian scene-to-scene and intrascene montage, contribute to the play's epic social picture but, more important, dramatize the sense that the simultaneously lived, collective life of society overrides personal experience, time, and space. The play's dialectical method thus turns realism and nonrealism to uses contrary to their origins, dramatizing a teleology that unmasks as false the possibility of redemption outside history.

While on the surface the play's dream scenes do not resemble the nonlinear disruptions in Brecht's plays, in terms of their epic function they can be compared to Brechtian songs. Although the scenes, unlike Brecht's songs, do not comment explicitly on the dramatic action nor address the audience directly, they break up the realistic narratives and dramatize what America and the characters are repressing, socially and emotionally, within those narratives. In the first dream scene between Harper and Prior, for example, Harper approaches a "threshold of revelation" about Joe's homosexuality. While suggesting the power of the unconscious in shaping individual and social consciousness, the scene "comments" ironically on a society that would rather keep homosexuals in the closet and does so from a nonrealistic realm that the spectator might not expect to provide such comment.

Another stylistic element that functions in the manner of Brechtian songs is Prior, Louis, and Belize's use of camp. This is not the place to enter the debate over the functions of camp in gay subculture but, rather, to broach the function of camp within Kushner's stylistic dialectics.[11] All of the play's styles, realistic and nonrealistic, are suffused with camp: it is woven into the fabric of Prior's and Belize's and, to a lesser extent, Louis's language and action, and the play's stylistic montage itself could be seen as an act of theatrical camp on the playwright's part.[12] Throughout the play camp emerges as a theatricalized mode of social interaction (or a self-referential form of social performance), which subverts the larger culture's expectations with respect to sociosexual identity yet also reinforces—and herein there is room for debate—hegemonic gender stereotypes. The mode's self-consciousness with respect to those stereotypes manifests itself overtly when Prior and Belize remark, in the midst of a camp interaction, "All this girl-talk shit is politically incorrect, you know" (1:61); and when Louis criticizes Belize's return to the stage as a drag queen. More important, at times "camp turns" recede with the characters' emerging awareness of those turns as *acts,* in both senses of that term, against painful social and psychological realities. For example, when Belize first visits Prior in the hospital, their camp turns move among various levels of playful theatricality, from Belize treating Prior's illness as an insult to his appearance ("You look like shit, why yes indeed you do, comme la merde!" [1:59]) to both characters imitating Katharine Hepburn ("Men are beasts" [1:61]). In only two moments—when Prior expresses his anger toward Louis and when Belize, just before he exits, says, "Why'd they have to pick on you?"—camp gives way to painful awareness, but the characters quickly resume their camp dialogue: Belize, for example, adds the exit line, "And eat more, girlfriend, you really do look like shit" (1:62). Rather than denying reality, this line confronts the pain of the moment with humor, embracing life as compounded of both pain and humor and reaffirming Prior and Belize's shared identity as gay men. The silence that precedes the line adumbrates Prior's epilogue speech and its invisible, gentle "embrace" of the audience, in which all humor, camp and otherwise, terminates, having served a special function in the play's stylistic dialectics and the triumph of "more life" over either despair or hope of redemption.

Staging the Dialectic

In Kushner's stylistic dialectics one dialectic in particular is pivotal to staging: that between the epic structuring of the play's plot lines and styles on the one hand and its scenes of anti-Brechtian spectacle on the other. Declan Donnellan's production was distinguished partly by the way it dramatized that dialectic, through an interplay between epic space and singular spectacle, between the sociohistorical "estrangement" of the spectator and the intimation of possible redemption. If Brecht and Benjamin were critical points of departure for Kushner's dialectics, a major point of departure for Donnellan's production was the conventions of epic staging that have evolved in Britain since the 1960s: the use of a bare or empty playing space and of only those set pieces and props essential to the action; highly fluid physical staging; the theatrical "writing" of the action and its social significance with those set pieces and props and that staging, as well as with performances that "foreground" the characters' social relations.[13] Donnellan deployed these conventions economically, with respect for the text and a dynamic sense of stage space, and he used them not only to evoke epic estrangement but also to create moments of spectacle that were at once sensuous, highly emotionalized, and theatrically self-conscious.

This is not to say that the production was influenced in any conscious or unconscious way either by Brecht or by Benjamin nor that Donnellan's production presented the only way to represent Kushner's dialectics, but it is to say that it married *Angels in America* as a Brechtian/Benjaminian work and a British epic staging with Donnellan's particular directorial sensibility.

And it did so in a theatrical vision of mid-1980s America as a place in which the slow erosion of democratic ideals ran up against a yearning to revitalize those ideals. This marriage and this vision provide a unique basis for exploring the essential relations between Kushner's dialectics and the use of epic theatrical space.

Scenography as an Element of Performance

In a fine analysis of Brechtian staging Michael Evenden explains that Brecht's stage was "a composite stage" consisting of three parts: center stage, the place of dramatic time and space and of fictionalized action; downstage, a space impinging upon audience time and space, from which characters and narrators typically address the audience directly; and upstage, the place of the cyclorama and slide screen, a "realm of obscured realities, of the invisible causes of the dramatic situation"—which Evenden calls "the obscured plane."[14] Donnellan's production worked a variation on just such a composite stage, which holds a great deal in common, conceptually and imaginatively, with Kushner's dialectics.

Donnellan's *Angels* was staged in the Cottesloe, the smallest of the Royal National Theatre's three theaters, a black box with a slightly raised, modified thrust stage at one end. For *Millennium Approaches* Donnellan and his designer/collaborator, Nick Ormerod, kept the stage empty and black, adding to it only one element: a Jasper Johns–like American flag, painted on the rear wall. This image, a self-aware *re*presentation of Johns's representation—and thus a postmodernist representation of a traditional symbol of America—established the Cottesloe stage as a variation on Brecht's composite stage, calling attention to "obscured realities" behind the action. Yet, unlike the Brechtian "obscured plane," whose slides usually implicate realities outside the theater in the stage action, Ormerod's flag signified a more highly obscured social context: that of America *as an idea* partly situated in symbols (and in symbols of symbols). Implicit in this signification of America was a subversive impulse to represent America in contradiction to tradition, but counterposed against this impulse was the image's explicit, historically determined reference to an ideal, unified nation.

All dramatic events, from the dramatic scenes to the scene changes, unfolded beneath the flag and were "actor driven," as Kushner calls for them to be: actors and stagehands moved set pieces with precision in and out of the space, making those changes an integral part of the performance; the last moment of each scene cued the scene changes and their musical accompaniment, a recorded score by Paddy Cunneen that worked pained variations on American jazz.[15] The black box, the flag, and the fluid staging suggested a realm in which ideas of and about America (the idea of the play, the ideas debated in the play, the ideas provoked in the audience) were being *thought through*. Seen underneath and against the flag, the drama unfolded as if it were theatrically articulating its own idea of the American nation, its ideals, and its success or failure in achieving them. The spectator viewed that emerging idea—as well as the conflicting ideologies of Louis, Belize, Roy, and others—*against* the unchanging possibility of defining America.

Donnellan and Ormerod's scenography showed that, while *Millennium* benefits from an empty stage space, this space has to be sharply and ideographically defined by spare design elements and a conception of how these function in the scene-to-scene montage as well as of how that montage unfolds in and through theatrical space and time. The stage world needs to be stabilized—for example, by the metaphorical situating of the space as a "consciousness of America"—yet the dramatic action must be able to resituate place and time within the stage space from scene to scene. While that world's fixed elements can suggest the larger dialectic to which the play contributes (e.g., the idea *of* defining America), the scene-to-scene montage can suggest the dynamics of that dialectic while realizing the montage's own dialectical elements. In this connection one might bear in mind Brecht's distinction between the *Bühnenbildner* (set designer) and the *Bühnenbauer* (scenographer), whose object is, as one critic has put it, "to create or build a scene as an integral component of the play's dramaturgy and which therefore [can] be considered an act of performance."[16]

In terms of the composite stage the action of *Angels in America* seems as if it should gravitate mostly toward the fictionalized realm of center stage, yet, whereas Brecht's plays tend to delineate a "fictionalized" space in relation to "audience space" and the world outside the theater, *Angels in America* thrives on an epic space that implies a separation between stage and audience while intimating a social consciousness that is emerging between them. In Donnellan's production the flag signified the consciousness within which the play unfolds, while a fictionalized stage action arose out of that consciousness. Fictionalized space incorporated both center stage and downstage: at one extreme, it pressed toward the audience and, at another, receded toward the flag. All invocations of the world outside the theater arose from the play's references to AIDS and American politics, while the play only addressed the audience directly at the end of *Perestroika;* its stylistic montage situated the spectator socially and ideologically—as disinterested witness, absorbed "participant," and so on—in relation to the action.

The precise dynamic of this "estranged" stage/spectator relationship depends entirely on how spatial realms are delineated for the play's stylistic montage; how scenographic elements signify the realms and the relations between them; how they are made to interpenetrate one another scenographically and performatively; and, fundamentally, the type of theater in which those realms are signified. As both an epic work and one that calls for a particular level of theatrical "magic," *Angels in America* is well served by either a proscenium stage or a stage that is clearly defined, as Donnellan's was, at one end of a large black box, while theaters-in-the-round, although they lend themselves to fluid staging, do not possess an obscured plane and require the director and the designer to work out how the spectator's view of the audience will function in the epic dynamics of the action. But even a stage that lends itself readily to epic scenography and staging demands that its spatial realms be precisely delineated. At one extreme one can imagine a production in which slides of mid-1980s America—Reagan, AIDS victims, gay rights marches—are projected upstage, while center stage is used primarily for dream scenes, downstage for realistic scenes, and upstage for magical appearances. Such a production might suggest a sharp dialectic between the play as a multifarious social fiction and the world outside the theater, yet it might also deflect too much attention from the montage of the drama and overschematize the concepts of "fictional" and "real" worlds. While *Angels in America* refers to undeniable social realities, its epic dialectics are more richly conceived in terms of a theatricalized "mind of the nation." The play needs an epic stage delineated in terms of fictionalized social reality and the possibility of totalizing thought and, as such, is best served by a sharply defined, uncluttered upstage and a solidly but flexibly conceived center stage/downstage.

Through Split-Scenes to Spectacle and Back

The scenographic approach to *Angels in America* needs to address how scene-to-scene montage effects a change in stage space over time. For example, in *Millennium Approaches* how does the nonrealistic disruption of realistic action, and the decomposition of realistic scenes into split scenes and spectacle, transfigure the space? How does *Perestroika* either follow or subvert the spatial patterns of *Millennium*? The latter question is key to conceptualizing stage space for the two parts of the drama. Kushner explains that differences between *Millennium* and *Perestroika* "should be reflected in their designs": "*Perestroika* proceeds forward from the wreckage made by the Angel's traumatic entry at the end of *Millennium*. A membrane has broken; there is disarray and debris" (2:8). The key phrase here is "proceeds forward." If space is transfigured by the wreckage at the end of *Millennium,* then the crucial question for *Perestroika* becomes: what is the nature of that transfiguration, and how does the use of stage space in *Perestroika* dramatize the play's teleology?

Dramatic patterns within the play's stylistic montage can help address these questions. On one level the montage of part 1 manifests itself theatrically in the play's split scenes; on another level it becomes evident in the play's dream scenes. (The Harper/Prior dream scene, e.g., can be seen as a species of split scene that superimposes the characters' simultaneous, unconscious visions upon one another.) The realistic plot lines of *Millennium Approaches* become intertwined dramatically through more and more emotionally charged split scenes. In terms of traditional psychological realism these come to a climax in act 2, scene 9, in which Prior and Louis's and Harper and Joe's relationships simultaneously fall apart. After this climax the split scenes remain highly charged in their emotional realism (e.g., Belize confronts Prior at the cafe; Louis and Joe begin their relationship in the park), yet they also interweave ideological argument with psycho-emotional conflict, creating a social context for the play's major *realistic* climax: Joe's refusal of Roy's offer of a job in Washington. At the same time, the drama proceeds toward greater and greater nonrealism and spectacle, which comes to dominate Harper's and Prior's stories and, more important, the split scenes after act 2, scene 9. For example, in act 3, scene 2, Prior has visions at the clinic while Belize and Louis argue at the cafe. Snow appears "outside" the cafe, "becoming" the snow of "Antarctica" in the next scene and of the South Bronx in the scene after that. In the ensuing, and last, three scenes of the play Ethel Rosenberg appears to Roy in his apartment (after Joe leaves, having turned down the Washington job); the historical Priors, and then a vision of Louis, appear to Prior in his bedroom; and the Angel descends upon Prior.

In the first half of *Millennium Approaches* stylistic montage manifests itself theatrically in the split scenes, which spatially juxtapose characters and their actions in order to suggest their social interrelatedness, and in the dream scenes, which disrupt the development of realistically driven stage action. In these ways the first half of the play "cracks open" its realistic narratives in two directions: toward an image of larger society and toward the possibility of nonrational vision. Once the realistic plots reach their first emotional climax, the split scenes themselves begin to crack open to the visionary dimensions of the play, and the proportion of nonrealism to realism shifts noticeably. The teleology of the realistic narratives, as well as of the play's styles, accelerates toward the possibility of, in Benjamin's terms, a visionary "monad."

Several principles of staging can be derived from these dramatic patterns. In the first half of the play split scenes need to adhere to whatever conventions of realistic space are established in the staging of individual scenes. The "bleeding" of spaces into one another can be deployed to suggest that the realistic dimension of the play is coming under the sway of forces intimated in the dream scenes. (Kushner cues this in act 2, scene 9, which integrates the Prior/Louis and Harper/Joe dialogues in a manner distinct from the previous split scenes.) During all of the realistically based split scenes in Donnellan's production—for example, the juxtaposition of Harper asking Joe, "Are you a homo?" (1:37), with Louis asking Prior, "What if I walked out on this?" (1:40)—the performers observed clearly defined "domestic" spaces marked out by spare furniture center stage or downstage. By contrast, in dream scenes the whole stage was transformed by some theatrical device: for example, Mr. Lies shimmied onto stage, bringing a shift in lighting with him; or paper snow filled the stage, taking Harper and the spectator to Antarctica. The physical stagings of the individual scenes within a split scene did not cross into each other's space until act 2, scene 9. Whereas the staging of previous split scenes had divided stage space more or less symmetrically, counterposing one narrative against another, act 2, scene 9 signaled a breakdown of such delineations and initiated a series of spatial transformations in which the play's visionary elements penetrated its realistic ones.

In the final scene the Angel crashed through the back wall—through the flag. Realistic space had been cracking open to visionary space; Prior's visions, Antarctica, and Ethel Rosenberg (who emerged from the back wall, in bright light beneath the flag) had either filled the stage or seemed to anticipate its transfiguration: the reunification of spatial—and socially fragmented—realms. The dialectics of the play's realistic narratives, and of its realism and nonrealism, had progressed toward a theatrical synthesis pervaded by an antidialectical spirit. So the Angel broke through the one fixed element of the epic stage: the upstage flag that suggested America as an idea in the process of being conceived and implemented. Wreckage filled the stage, yet, like all other moments of spectacle, the Angel's arrival was a clearly *theatrical* event, which seemed to transform a stage space conceived for the purpose of provoking social awareness into a space in which theatricalist spectacle prefigured redemption. The falseness of the spectacle—and the false hope of redemption—was made apparent in Prior's camp response, his pointing up of the vision *as constructed by theater.*

The Teleology of Stage Space

Despite Kushner's insistence that the plays be distinct in design, there are clear patterns to the teleology of stage space suggested by the text of *Perestroika*. Although the play starts from a point at which "a membrane has broken," the action must progress to "more life"; although history has appeared to crack open, it *goes on,* if in greater proximity to the possibility of apocalypse. *Perestroika* proceeds from the principle, developed in *Millennium Approaches,* of dramatic and spatial realms interpenetrating one another. From the start realistically based scenes are haunted by ghostly figures: Harper appears to Joe while he is in bed with Louis; Joe and Louis appear in the diorama; Ethel is a regular visitor in Roy's hospital room. In terms of their theatrical function these hauntings paradoxically resemble the realism of *Millennium:* they are the *assumed* reality of the play. Yet to dramatize this reality a staging cannot start exactly where *Millennium* left off, treating stage space as if it were a newly redeemed, unified realm of spectacle. The staging needs to reestablish realistic as against visionary realms such that, in the hauntings, the latter appears to penetrate the former and such that, in Prior's visions and journey to Heaven, the dialectic of the "real" and the "visionary" gives way to a total transformation of the stage.

There are two keys to unlocking the spatial patterns of *Perestroika:* first, Harper's gradual return to the realm of the real and, second, the epilogue. These are easily overlooked because it is tempting to focus primarily on Prior's progression toward Heaven and back. That progression can be staged according to the basic principles of *Millennium*—that is, in terms of realism giving way to nonrealism and spectacle. In contrast, Harper's journey calls for a gradual "re-delineation" of stage space in epic terms, a movement from a stage wholly transformed by theatricality (in Antarctica/Prospect Park) to Harper's reentry into realistically apportioned realms (apartment, diorama room, Brooklyn Heights Promenade) to her seizing of a tiny, personal space (the airplane window) from which she envisions something no stage world can contain. In both dramatic and spatial terms this progression unfolds in counterpoint to Prior's.

The epilogue, in which Prior directly addresses the audience, is the only scene in the play to evoke the Brechtian downstage. In this scene the spectacle of the Benjaminian shock is gone; the entire stage is used to suggest Central Park and the Bethesda Fountain. It is crucial that this fountain *appear* to be a replica that refers to the world outside the theater, for in this scene the play's teleological consciousness is broken in a manner opposite to that which has been previously disrupted by theatricalist spectacle. It is cracked open to link the stage world to the world of the audience, to join Prior and the spectator in the desire for "more life." In this moment the play refuses Benjamin's visionary leap beyond historical dialectics, choosing, instead, the uncertainty of the historical future that is in the process of being shaped by those dialectics. The moment is the culmination of the play's teleological vision of history and society: it implicitly calls for the spectator to make his or her own choice for more life while remaining aware of the contradictory sociohistorical forces that the play has dramatized. The moment affirms this choice as one by which the destructive course of history might be altered, the impasse between ideal and reality transcended, and society redeemed—all *from within*.

NOTES

Tony Kushner, *Angels in America: A Gay Fantasia on National Themes. Part Two: Perestroika* (New York: Theatre Communications Group, 1994), 68. All further citations of this play refer to this edition and appear parenthetically in the text.

1. Kushner acknowledges his debt to the Brechtian tradition. See David Savran, "Tony Kushner Considers the Longstanding Problems of Virtue and Happiness," interview with Tony Kushner, *American Theatre* 11 (October 1994): 23–26.

2. The literature on Brecht's concepts and techniques is vast. Three exceptional discussions are: Eric Bentley, "Stagecraft of Bertolt Brecht," *The Brecht Commentaries* (New York: Grove, 1987), 56–71; Peter Brooker, "Key Words in Brecht's Theory and Practice of Theatre," *The Cambridge Companion to Brecht,* ed. Peter Thomson and Glendyr Sacks (Cambridge: Cambridge University Press, 1994),185–200; and Michael Evenden, "Beyond *Verfremdung:* Notes toward a Brechtian 'Theatreturgy,'" in *Before His Eyes: Essays in Honor of Stanley Kauffmann,* ed. Bert Cardullo (Lanham, Md.: University Press of America, 1986), 129–47.

3. With the touring company Cheek by Jowl. Cf. Robert Hewison, "Puritan Talent," interview with Declan Donnellan, *Sunday Times* (London), 21 November 1993, sec. 9, 18–19.

4. Cf. Art Borreca, "Brecht-Fetishism and the British History Play after 1956," in *Brecht Unbound,* ed. James Lyon and Hans-Peter Breuer (Newark: University of Delaware Press, 1995), 189–208.

5. For a description of a "compleat" protocol—of which the current essay can only be considered a beginning—see Leon Katz, "The Compleat Dramaturg," *What Is Dramaturgy?* ed. Bert Cardullo (New York: Peter Lang, 1995), 13–16.

6. Pia Kleber, introduction, in *Re-Interpreting Brecht: His Influence on Contemporary Drama and Film,* ed. Pia Kleber and Colin Visser (Cambridge University Press, 1990), 12. Brecht himself came to prefer the term *dialectical theatre* to *epic theatre*. See Brooker, "Key Words," 190–91.

7. Tony Kushner, *Angels in America: A Gay Fantasia on National Themes. Part One: Millennium Approaches* (New York: Theatre Communications Group, 1993), 118. All further citations of this play refer to this edition and appear parenthetically in the text.

8. Savran interview, "Tony Kushner," 25–26. "Theses on the Philosophy of History" can be found in Walter Benjamin, *Illuminations,* ed. Hannah Arendt, trans. Harry Zohn (New York: Schocken, 1969), 253–64; see esp. 257–58.

9. Ibid., 262–63.

10. Ibid, 263.

11. For such discussion, see Jonathan Dollimore, *Sexual Dissidence: Augustine to Wilde, Freud to Foucault* (Oxford: Oxford University Press, 1991).

12. Cf. Savran interview, "Tony Kushner," 21–22, 24–26.

13. See Borreca, "Brecht-Fetishism."

14. Evenden, "Beyond *Verfremdung,*" 138–40, esp. 139.

15. My comments on Donnellan's production are derived from my own viewing of *Part One: Millennium Approaches* in July 1992 and from reviews of *Part Two: Perestroika,* which I regrettably did not see. (The bulk of my comments are directed at part 1.) Useful reviews of *Millennium* include Michael Billington, "Nation Built on Guilt," *Guardian,* 25 January 1992, 21; and Carl Miller, "Dreams of Zion," *New Statesman,* 31 January 1992, 31–33. For *Perestroika,* see Andy Lavender, "Cottage Industry," *New Statesman,* 26 November 1993, 35–36; and Barbara Norden, "Angels in the Age of AIDS," *Times Literary Supplement,* 3 December 1993, 35–36. Also see Vincent Canby's "Two 'Angels,' Two Journeys in London and New York," *New York Times,* 30 January 1994, sec. 2, 5, 22.

16. Christopher Baugh, "Brecht and Stage Design: The *Bühnenbildner* and the *Bühnenbauer,*" *Cambridge Companion to Brecht,* ed. Thomson and Sacks, 239.

Representing Sex
on the British Stage:
The Importance of
Angels in America

Nicholas de Jongh

It may seem aimlessly perverse to draw a point of connection between the British premiere of Tony Kushner's *Angels in America* at the National Theatre's Cottesloe auditorium in 1992 and the uproar from vigilant church leaders and members of the public that led to the censoring by the British theater's official censor, the Lord Chamberlain, of an unusual heterosexual seduction scene in a Hungarian play, Ernest Vadja's *Fata Morgana,* seen in London during the summer and autumn of 1924. And it is not, of course, my intention to suggest that either part of Kushner's play deals in great or sensational detail with the mimetic representation of sexual activity.

I shall argue that the impact and significance of *Angels in America,* as performed in the London of the early 1990s, can only be fully appreciated by understanding how far Kushner's epic represents an acute departure from those modes of theater writing in which British dramatists have dealt with crises and problems in which any sort of sexual desire is implicated. And since, from 1737 until 1968, the texts of plays performed in public theaters had to be approved in advance by a senior member of the Royal Household—the Lord Chamberlain was responsible by act of Parliament for the licensing and, where necessary, censoring of both words and action onstage—sexual candor was outlawed.[1]

The row over *Fata Morgana,* therefore, typified the prevalent anxiety of twentieth-century Lords Chamberlain about the depiction and discussion of erotic activity onstage, particularly where such behavior departed from received ideas about conventional sexuality. And until 1957, when the Chamberlain announced that he would permit the subject of homosexuality to be mentioned upon the English stage, Lords Chamberlain regarded homosexuality—the discussion, description, and depiction of it—with particularizing abhorrence and anxiety. In keeping the drama under strict surveillance, they ensured that no new play contained views, language, or incidents that would offend the feelings and views of the inhabitants of an upper-middle-class drawing room.

More important, they all subscribed to a traditional English belief, which reached its zenith in the nineteenth century, that the theater was endowed with a seductive potency, a capacity to provoke insurrectionary behavior. Audiences could, the theory went, all too easily be incited to depart from the straight and narrow of heterosexual relations within marriage, let alone be diverted to homosexuality. In 1965, when John Osborne's play *A Patriot for Me* was refused a license to be performed onstage, one of the Lord Chamberlain's censors observed that the drag ball scene might encourage homosexual practices because the men in drag were made up to look like attractive women.[2] Even in 1995, some twenty-seven years after the repeal of the Lord Chamberlain's statutory duty to license and censor plays for public performance according to his own notions of propriety, the British theater's treatment of sexuality still bears damaging signs of being influenced by that long tradition of censorship.

Yet, despite the enthusiastic responses of national newspaper and magazine critics to the London productions of the two parts of *Angels in America,* none of us captured the sense of Kushner's simple, epoch-making breach with Britain's theatrical past. That breach had to do with the fact that English dramatists in the twentieth century, contending with the Lord Chamberlain's ban upon homosexuality, reacted by dealing with the question of unorthodox sexual behavior as a problem in isolation from the society imposing that orthodoxy or any exploration of that society's traditions and mores.

The extent of Kushner's departure from the old English theatrical tradition of silence and reticence where sex threatens to rear its head is betrayed by the response of the conservative *Daily Telegraph*'s theater critic. Under the subheading "Charles Spencer is appalled and exhilarated by a play that confronts AIDS," the reviewer begins by referring to *Angels in America*'s program note and its warning about "scenes and language that may be considered unsuitable for young people." He suggests that "many middle-aged and old people" were likely to be similarly affronted. He exudes alarm and dismay.

> In the second interval . . . several hardened theatre critics were looking distinctly green about the gills. . . . Its author spares his audiences nothing. The language would make a swearing squaddie blush, while the depiction of the messy misery of full-blown AIDS and of a brutal homosexual encounter in New York's Central Park are almost unbear-

able to watch, even though the latter scene is mimed, with the two actors standing several yards apart.[3]

In all due fairness to Spencer it must be said that, despite the critic's reservations about *Millennium Approaches,* he admires "Kushner's highly individual talent" and "the drama's theatrical power." But there is no missing the sense in which he feels the play moves into terrain from which he would wish to be spared. The language is too candid. His colleagues, laughably described as "hardened," are supposed to be "green-gilled" in shock. The suffering of an incontinent man in the midst of an AIDS-related illness is too messy. And an act of botched though consensual buggery is only made bearable by the fact that it is mimed, with the actors standing decently apart and avoiding any simulated action. That he characterizes this incident as "brutal" appears to have more to do with the fact of buggery than the fact that Louis asks to be screwed without a condom, in a gesture that is shocking because it proclaims his suicidal depression (1:57).

This rather lurid response, from an intelligent critic who is not yet forty, deserves consideration, for it represents the view of a distinct section of theatergoers. Our English stages may be purged of censorship, but the old tradition, which insists that our theater should avoid the authenticity of a news bulletin, still survives. And the nature of that tradition becomes vivid when you consider the *Fata Morgana* affair.

In the high summer and autumn of 1924 the London Council for Public Morality, whose president was the bishop of London, the Westminster Catholic Federation, and assorted members of the public expressed their anxiety and concern at what was happening on the stage of the Ambassadors Theatre, where Vadja's *Fata Morgana* was being presented. The Lord Chamberlain had passed the play as suitable for public performance. "The dubious part is artistically done," he wrote, referring to an incident in which "a sexually experienced married woman" seduced an eighteen-year-old male, "and I do not consider I should be justified in withholding a licence."[4]

The cause for the moralists' concern was, the Public Morality Council wrote, a brief scene in which the married woman "Madam Fay," sitting on a chair on the right of the stage and dressed in a kimono, "very skilfully manoeuvres her dress to display both legs (in flesh coloured tights) above the knees." There was, apparently, no missing the fact that "her attitude was one of inviting ravishment." The Lord Chamberlain, Lord Cromer, an aristocratic theater lover of views that could be regarded as conservative in the 1920s, responded by successfully demanding that the management impose "certain [unspecified] modifications of dress and business." But this change

did not stop a succession of female letter writers—perhaps inspired by the
very active Council and Federation—from complaining about the scene to
the Lord Chamberlain. On 16 February 1925 a woman named Mrs. Munro
Faure wrote for the second time, saying, "A clean play has no chance in face
of the competition offered by aliens [a reference to Vadja] whose only
object seems to be filth and more filth." And, even though an enraged Lord
Cromer warned that his instructions about the behavior in relation to the
revelation of naked female thigh and the actress's deportment must be
observed, there were further complaints, from officials of the Middlesex
County Council, when the play went out on tour. The Chief Constables of
Glasgow and of Portsmouth were required by the Lord Chamberlain to
send detectives to performances in these towns and to report on how the
seduction scene was performed.

A Detective Inspector and a Detective Sergeant in Glasgow reported to
the Chief Constable on incidents in this scene, as a result of which changes
were made. The dutiful detectives returned and reported how the actress
(Jeanne de Cassalis) playing the role of the femme fatale

> sat on the sofa and called on George to kiss her hand. This he did after
> which Matilda [the character's original name had been changed] then
> lay back in an inviting attitude but did not bare her legs and George
> remained standing in front of her for a moment before going away. I
> do not think it would appeal to everyone as an incident without sug-
> gesting a certain degree of impropriety.

I make much of this fracas because it helps illuminate a lost world of
theater whose ghosts still bear down upon us today and which Kushner's
Angels in America helps to exorcise. In dramatizing an average incident of
sexual seduction, Vadja offended against the 1920s theater code, which outlawed the sight of any bare female flesh except for bare face, hands, arms,
and lower legs. But, more important, *Fata Morgana* could be described in
some sense as a queer, subversive drama. It dealt with what was then
regarded as perverse and unnatural—an older woman, who would be
regarded as defying the dictates of her gender by taking the supposedly male
and active sexual role in an encounter with a very young man, who was
depicted as both susceptible and virgin. The scene reverses the traditional
process of heterosexual seduction and endows the woman with active sexual desire and will. She would have been thought to be challenging those
attributes of naturalness, conventionality, and decorum that the British theater believed it had to promote. The angry reaction to all this typifies the

twentieth-century censoring process, with its refusal to contend with the sexual or to adopt a tone governed by candor.

As a result of this defining and proscribing activity, the questions arising from forms of sexuality reckoned a threat to conformity returned and recurred in English theater as a motor force. English drama, from the sixteenth century onward, often sought to articulate dissident and nonconformist views. Jacobean and Caroline censors were primarily concerned with the drama's political content and excised material critical of English royalty, influential members of the ruling classes, and friendly foreign powers. Profanity was similarly forbidden. In the nineteenth century the Lord Chamberlain's Examiners of Plays, urged on by Queen Victoria herself, were increasingly concerned with themes, scenes, actions, and words that challenged or criticized idealized norms of upper-middle-class social and sexual behavior and the relations between the sexes.[5] In the modern English drama the unmentionable, unrepresentable theatrical subject of homosexuality came to be considered only as a discrete problem, to be treated in isolation from any social, political, and religious contexts or from other forms of institutionalized intolerance. The typifying twentieth-century play in England about homosexuality saw no further than the sensational fact of illicit gay relations. John Osborne's *A Patriot for Me* is the exception confirming the rule and, in any case, deals with a premodern society: the Austro-Hungarian, with its own social and military codes that bear down upon the soldier whose Jewishness, humble origins, and suppressed gay desires help make him a suitable candidate for blackmail. Larry Kramer's play *The Normal Heart,* which reached London in the 1980s, works as impassioned polemic, though its historical sense is deformed by hysteria. To compare the sufferings of people with AIDS and those sent to be gassed in the Nazis' concentration camps is to indulge in the crude sweep of exaggeration and a failure to distinguish between a state-instituted program of extermination and a country's relative indifference to the fate of homosexuals succumbing to a sexually transmitted virus. Another American play, Martin Sherman's *Bent,* which was premiered in London, does illuminate a vital portion of suppressed gay history, though through compelling theatrical narrative rather than in Kushner's epic mode.

The characteristic twentieth-century English play about homosexuality lacked Kushner's analytic rigor. It would not have dreamed of relating sexual repression to any other form of social coercion or intolerance that governments might promulgate. And in unwavering fashion from J. R. Ackerley's *Prisoners of War* in 1925 to Charles Dyer's *Staircase* in 1966 homosexuality was just a tragic problem depicted melodramatically in a drawing room void.

Kushner puts an end to all that. The importance of *Angels in America* depends, then, upon the way Kushner breaches such narrow parameters and subsumes his gay-related themes within an all embracing historic and religious frame of reference, an overarching political pattern. He regards the play's gay deceivers—the Mormon Joseph Porter Pitt, who hides his queer desires under the cover of marriage, and Roy Cohn—and its stricken sufferer from AIDS, Prior Walter, as far more than the clichéd victims of prejudice in the midst of an epidemic. One or two of the critics attending that astonishing first night in London in January 1992 detected some trace of the playwright's ambitious scheme. "What Kushner seems to be saying," Michael Billington, the *Guardian's* theater critic wrote cautiously, "is that guilt is part of America's Judaic and Puritan inheritance, and that it has been exacerbated by society's failure to live up to its Utopian dreams."[6] Benedict Nightingale of the *Times* discerned a sense "of moral chaos predictably (this being 1985) attributed to the temper of the times."[7] My own reaction, traveling on parallel lines of argument, was to see the play as "a state of the nation report, relating the AIDS epidemic and those caught in its horrible throes to America's political and social condition," with "rounds of furtive sexual politics . . . conducted in the midst of a debate about America itself—accused of lacking an indigenous, spiritual past."[8] These responses—and my own and that of the *Times* had to be written in the space of a couple of hours after the premiere—give some idea of the large impression that the production, and indeed the play, made upon us.

I fear, however, that the general critical response on the part of the English theater critics to the premiere of *Perestroika* showed no signs of advance beyond this initial assessment. In particular, none of us paid sufficient attention to the ways in which these plays, and their gay characters, are haunted by religion. The Angel who comes clamorously to earth spreading fear and dread, the camp scenes in a heaven reduced to almost worldly proportions, the dead who rise up to haunt Prior's dreams, all suggest Kushner's fascination with the imposing paraphernalia of religions that would sooner pretend that homosexuality and homosexuals have no place or function in the real world.

None of us realized what Kushner was, by implication, suggesting about the inhumane and destructive animus of organized religion in America, of how it anathematizes the sexual outsider in general and the gay man in particular. The playwright recognizes the force and sway of religious orthodoxy as it influences or coerces the offender against heterosexual norms. Western religion, whether Puritan, Mormon, or Jewish, by its traditions and living affirmations, by its legitimizing of sexual pleasure only within marriage, justifies the stigmatization of gay behavior, of those who nominate themselves homosexual and may suffer the unique ravages of AIDS. How, then, does the homosexual in a time of epidemic and in a country where religious dogma keeps hold flourish or even survive? Will those who control the codes of morality ever allow the homosexual to be welcomed within their religious frames?

England offers the dustiest of answers to such questions. The bishop of London, the third most senior cleric in the church of England, has recently given a dire warning in a *Guardian* newspaper interview that "the moral capital is running out and there is a danger of barbarism."[9] By this he meant, he said, that there was "a lack of care for the weak, the mentally handicapped and 'the stranger in our midst.'" That last reference might have been an echo from *Angels in America*. But, as it turns out, this is not at all the case. Quite the reverse. The Church of England's moral capital, even if replenished, is not to include homosexuals in its embrace. "The Christian tradition is clear: either celibacy or life-long relationships, which are interpreted as between a man and a woman. We are not empowered—now suddenly because this issue had come up very recently. These are the rules." The bishop—who may emerge early in the twenty-first century to become the next archbishop of Canterbury—"could not accept the blessing of homosexual unions in church, nor clergy in homosexual relationships." All he could offer from the depths of his religious heart was a commitment not to "harry" those priests who had "long-term [gay] companions." And the bishop speaks for a ruling religious constituency far beyond England. The gay man and the lesbian remain the stranger in the religious midst—and it is just that sense of apartness that characterizes Kushner's gay characters.

In his comment on the religious slanting of *Millennium Approaches,* the *Financial Times* reviewer wrote, "The message is that none of them (Mormonism, Judaism, Protestantism, and Catholicism) know how to cope with homosexual passion."[10] That judgment fails to acknowledge the negative sense in which clerics do deal with any sort of homosexuality. The religious leaders cope by anathematizing sexual outsiders and induce a sense of guilty inadequacy by so doing. "Catholics believe in forgiveness. Jews believe in Guilt," says the Rabbi astutely to Louis (1:25). And it is a residue of sexual guilt, and of prevaricating self-deception, that variously possesses Joe, Roy Cohn, and Louis. Cohn has so far and so guiltily accepted the pejorative interpretation of what it means to be homosexual that he, the maestro of the convincing lie, has made a bonfire of the definitions. Cohn's outrageous, constructionist interpretation of himself as a heterosexual depends upon his fascination with worldly power—that attribute by which the male sex has defined its value and ascendancy. "Homosexuals are men who in fifteen years of trying cannot get a pissant antidiscrimination bill through City Council. Homosexuals are men who know nobody and who nobody knows" (1:45). A man is defined not by what he does in bed but by how much power he accumulates out of it.

As if recoiling from such definitions and proscriptions, *Angels in America* puts its faith in humanism—and does so despite its millennial longing for universal harmony and gay peace or its fascination with the alluring paraphernalia of religion and its emblematic apparatus. And Kushner discerns important links between the quality of a country's religious and political beliefs. It is here that the angels of the title assume importance. They are both negatively and positively defined by Kushner in the play's most argumentative scene. "There are no gods here, no ghosts and spirits in America," Louis, Prior's double-dealing boyfriend, tells Belize, the drag queen nurse. "There are no angels in America, no spiritual past, no racial past, there's only the political" (1:92). In *Perestroika* Joe's mother, Hannah, more simply observes, "An angel is just a belief, with wings and arms that can carry you" (2:105).

I interpret these angels, then, not as they appear in their camp, Victorian manifestation but as ideas whose force and fury have been the making of the America on which Kushner sets his targets. The Jew (Cohn), the descendant of a Puritan founding father (Prior), and the Mormon (Joe) are incorporated within the grand design to remind us that America does indeed have a past, despite Louis's disavowal. And the past of this country has allowed or welcomed devout religious outsiders to such an extent that it might almost be described as a country of exiles. The rabbi who buries Louis's grandmother in the first scene has come as a refugee from a Russia that persecuted Jews, and he can only speak English with difficulty. Prior has origins that go back to England. But Louis implies—and he is always the most seriously eloquent of Kushner's characters—that those long dead religious immigrants who found a place and a life in a strange country have themselves been betrayers. Having found a welcome in America, they will welcome into their midst only those who conform to the set and limit of their religious standards. Like the bishop of London, they will not allow gay men and lesbians to come in from the religious cold.

Kushner sees these supposed moralists, relishing the iron hand of their religious authority, as a match for the American body politic, which has no sense of true spirituality, no sense of community, nor any developed feeling of tolerance. For these modern people there is only the credo of selfhood, of lip service to human rights. They mouth their smug, religious platitudes about freedom and seek to deny gay men the freedom to live their sexual lives in defiance of prescriptive interpretations of the Bible. "What AIDS shows us," says Louis, "is the limits of tolerance, that it's not enough to be tolerated, because when the shit hits the fan you find out how much tolerance is worth. Nothing. And underneath all the tolerance is intense, passionate hatred" (1:90). That hatred, that fear of the different and the afflicted, is directly inspired by the organized religions. And the secular state, basking in the implicit approval of the churches, has with impunity and confidence fought to exclude homosexual men and women from the ranks of the accepted and acceptable.

Power, Louis submits, is what matters in this American world in which, he insists, no real angels of compassion exist and the battle of politics is all that matters. It is an analysis with which Kushner's version of Cohn, and surely the original, living, scheming Roy Cohn, would enthusiastically agree. The Cohn of *Angels in America*—and the author takes care in an introductory disclaimer to emphasize that "this Roy is a work of dramatic fiction" (1:5)—labors to achieve the consummation that Kushner devoutly fears as the worst of nightmares: "the end of New Deal Socialism. The end of ipso facto secular humanism. The dawning of a genuinely American political personality"; "Affirmative action? Take it to court. . . . we'll get our way on just about everything: abortion, defense, Central America, family values, a live investment climate" (1:63).

That the nightmare has failed to materialize does not invalidate Kushner's foreboding. In his description of this "American political personality," the impact of the religious Right, the so-called moral majority, is apparent. It is such religious groupings that hanker for a new program that would make America a more uncomfortable and inhospitable place for sexual outsiders like Louis, Prior, and Joe. Kushner suggests in his notes to *Perestroika*, a play in which Louis manifests an already dated belief in Gorbachev as "the greatest political thinker since Lenin" (2:145), that this play involves a process of letting go of the past, of embracing change and losing with grace. Kushner's aspiration to show such a process of renunciation and an eagerness to change is not fully reflected in his thematic and dramatic organization. But the final image of Prior, still robustly alive and brimming with an optimism that defies the odds, suggests a kind of willful, transcendent optimism: "We are not going away. We won't die secret deaths. . . . We will be citizens" (2:148). It is the *cri de coeur* of those who refuse the exile status that

Kushner's politicians and religionists demand. It is a cry of defiance. We have heard such rousing sounds before. At least, though, in *Angels in America* the old world of politics and religion, which put homosexuals in the cold, is explored with a vigor that no English playwright has mustered. If sexuality and AIDS pose daunting problems in *Angels in America*—and of course they do—then Kushner leaves us in no lurking doubt that the problem has to do with a rotten inheritance and traditions ripe for discarding.

NOTES

1. See G. E. Bentley, *The Jacobean and Caroline Stage,* 7 vols. (Oxford: Clarendon Press, 1941–68), for an account of censorship by Jacobean and Caroline censors. Margot Heinemann, *Puritanism and Theatre: Thomas Middleton and Opposition Drama under the Early Stuarts* (Cambridge and New York: Cambridge University Press, 1980), provides a valuable antidote to the notion that all Puritans were opposed to theater performances. Richard Findlater, *Banned! A Review of Theatrical Censorship in Britain* (London: MacGibbon and Kee, 1967), provides a brief history of stage censorship in Britain and an informative though unsystematic account of the Lord Chamberlain's censoring activities in the twentieth century. John Johnston, *The Lord Chamberlain's Blue Pencil* (London: Hodder and Stoughton, 1990), is the highly partisan work of a former senior official in the Lord Chamberlain's office who dealt with censorship matters. Some of the information is most revealing, but there are elementary factual errors, and Sir John misleads in suggesting that the Lord Chamberlain enjoyed a fair degree of support from the theatrical profession.

2. The battle over *A Patriot for Me* is described in my book *Not in Front of the Audience: Homosexuality on Stage* (London and New York: Routledge, 1992).

3. *Daily Telegraph,* 27 January 1992.

4. All the details and quotations relating to Ernest Vadja's *Fata Morgana* are taken from the relevant file in the British Library's collection of documents relating to the Lord Chamberlain's licensing of plays from 1901–68. These files may be read by anyone with a British Library ticket.

5. Heinemann, *Puritanism and Theatre,* 39. And see John Russell Stephens, *The Censorship of English Drama, 1824–1901* (Cambridge and New York: Cambridge University Press, 1980), for a useful account of the Lord Chamberlain's censorship in the Victorian period.

6. *Guardian,* 26 January 1992.

7. *London Times,* 25 January 1992.

8. *Evening Standard,* 25 January 1992.

9. The new bishop of London, Richard Chartres, in an interview (*Guardian,* 25 January 1996).

10. *Financial Times,* 28 January 1992.

"Free[ing] the Erotic Angels": Performing Liberation in the 1970s and 1990s

Gregory W. Bredbeck

Liberation Theory and Performance

Sometime in the late 1970s or early 1980s gay and lesbian people stopped saying "gay liberation" and started saying "gay and lesbian civil rights." The part of me that believes conspiracies account for most of life would like to find proof of a clandestine meeting of people who initiated this change, but really it is not like this; it is the effect of a process so slow and unconscious, so much the complex aggregate of the inexorable increments of history, as to be practically indiscernible. It relates, certainly, to the hard-won advances of other populations working for civil rights.[1] It relates, just as certainly, to the discrete geographical (primarily urban) and demographical (primarily young) origins of gay liberation[2] and its inability to speak forcefully as an enduring and totalizing theory as the times, places, and politics of praxis progressed; and so much are "we," as "gay and lesbian people," the product of this same flow that seeing change within it is tantamount to acknowledging the potentially transitory aspects of what enables "our" very ability to think of "we" as an "us": history can empower, but it can also frighten, and hence it is common to read *gay lib* and *gay and lesbian civil rights* as synonyms rather than marks of ideological change.

Of all the many things that Tony Kushner's *Angels in America* is, one that has not been much commented on is its function as a profound rumination on the historicity of gay liberation theory. Kushner himself points to this idea in his afterword to the published edition of *Perestroika*. Discussing the deep influence of his friend Kimberly T. Flynn on his development as a playwright, Kushner states,

> Kimberly and I share Louisiana childhoods . . . we share different but equally complicated, powerful religious traditions and a deep ambivalence towards those traditions; Left politics *informed by liberation struggles (she as a feminist, I as a gay man)* and by socialist and psychoanalytic the-

271

ory; and a belief in the effectiveness of activism and the possibility of progress.[3]

Because the word *liberation* circulates as a general noun in many political circles, it is easy to forget that, when linked with the word *gay,* it also refers to a specific canon of tracts and series of actions in the wake of the Stonewall Riots.[4] I would like to trace how Liberation Theory—and I will capitalize it in order to foreground that I am speaking of an identifiable historical political movement—informs *Angels in America.* American theater has a discernible tradition of what I will call Liberation performance, and placing *Angels in America* within this history helps both to explicate aspects of its dramaturgy and to allow its dramaturgy to reveal that thing both empowering and frightening: the historicity of identity politics and, indeed, of identity itself.

One place to start a history of Liberation performance—though an admittedly arbitrary one—is on Sunday, 6 October 1969, when on Lower Sproul Plaza at the University of California, Berkeley, a student group called Gay Liberation Theatre performed a play as a part of the campus's first (and, I think, only) "Disorientation Week." The play is structured around Gale, a student, and his coming-out process. One of the loosely connected scenes features Gale promoting a Gay Lib meeting to Lendon and Richard—two men who are homosexual but not, at this point in history, gay. They are reticent:

> *Lendon:* Well, we're not really into this gay militant thing. We
> feel that by working within our community and by affiliating
> ourselves with existent revolutionary groups we can really be of
> more help to the movement.
>
> *Richard:* Of course our friends know, but . . .
> *Lendon:* I mean, we're not flagrant about it—we go to no great
> pains to conceal it, but we don't feel we have to parade around
> on street corners or anything.[5]

At which point a nameless straight friend enters and, when informed of the efforts of the Gay Lib group, responds:

> All that just to suck cocks. Really, I don't see what that has to do with
> the revolution. People are starving. You should be fighting the pigs
> with us, fighting real oppression.

Confronting both the homosexual Right and the heterosexual Left, Gale delivers his version of enlightenment, his version of Gay Lib:

The same society that has bent your minds and fucked you over has conditioned us to stifle our sexuality. Your sexuality is at the root of your being, the core of your identity. If Ladybird had been a better lay, we might not be fucking Vietnam. Sexual repression is basic, sexual revolution is essential. We work with you. You work with us. (103)

This brief scene is polemical and propagandistic, and it is also a perfect performance of Liberation Theory. Gay Lib exists for Gale not as the assertion of a specific identity or identification but as a sort of master trope of revolution, a true marriage of theory and action—a true praxis—that will upheave the very conditions of identity—"the root of your being." It is an intervention not into the ethics of sexual etiquette but, rather, into the very power that motivates imperialism—"If Ladybird had been a better lay, we might not be fucking Vietnam."

The politics underpinning this performance can be mapped by another Berkeley performance, this one textual. In December 1969, almost six months to the day after the Stonewall Riots and two months after the Gay Liberation Theatre performance, Carl Wittman published a radical manifesto in the *Berkeley Tribe* titled "Refugees from Amerika: A Gay Perspective." The tract clearly foreshadows gay activist programs of visibility and intervention, for it mandates that "we" must "free ourselves: come out, everywhere; initiate self defense and political activity."[6] But, at the same time, it also rallies on behalf of a liberation of desire, demanding that we "free the homosexual in everyone" (21):

We are children of straight society. We still think straight; that is part of our oppression. . . .

We have lived in these [heterosexual] institutions all our lives. Naturally we mimic the roles. For too long we mimicked these roles to protect ourselves—a survival mechanism. Now we are becoming free enough to shed the roles which we've picked up from the institutions which have imprisoned us.

It specifies the goal of Gay Liberation: "our first job is to free ourselves, and that means clearing our heads of the garbage that's been poured into them." It is precisely this act of strategic opposition that *gay* is meant to enact: "We'll be gay until everyone has forgotten that it's an issue. Then we'll begin to be complete" (12).

The "Statement" published by the Chicago Third World Gay Revolution and Gay Liberation Front in the June 1971 edition of *Chicago Gay Pride* expresses a similarly bifurcated understanding. Like Wittman's tract, it begins with the assumption that the enactment of change within the system is of paramount importance and that the "long accepted subhuman status" of homosexuals must be changed.[7] At the same time, it also marks the futility of such efforts: "But individuals refusing to keep their places do not equally threaten a class structure (whether it be of economic class, sex, race, or whatever). It can easier afford to allow an individual from a lower stratum to try to enter upper strata than vice versa. This reinforces the preeminence of the ruling group and keeps the oppressed divided and competing" (255). Even as the tract mandates a change in status for homosexual individuals, it defines *change, status, homosexual,* and *individual* as terms that, in and of themselves, perpetuate the system. This sort of split consciousness culminates in an astonishing rhetorical barrage that is worth considering in its entirety:

> Gay is good if we declare it so. Gay can be a force for everyone's ultimate liberation if we recognize it as such. Though to us as individual gay people gay represents potential for love with equality and freedom, that's only the first level of gay is good. . . . A higher level of gay is good is as a tool to break down enforced heterosexuality, sex roles, the impoverished categories of straight, gay, and bisexual, male supremacy, programming of children, ownership of children, the nuclear family, monogamy, possessiveness, exclusiveness of "love," insecurity, jealousy, competition, privilege, individual isolation, ego-tripping, power-tripping, money-tripping, people as property, people as machines, rejection of the body, repression of emotions, anti-eroticism, authoritarian anti-human religion, conformity, regimentation, polarization of "masculine" and "feminine," categorization of male and female emotions, abilities, interests, clothing, etc., fragmentation of the self by these outlines, isolation and elitism of the arts, uniform standards of beauty, dependency on leaders, unquestioning submission to authority, power hierarchies, caste, racism, militarism, imperialism, national chauvinism, cultural chauvinism, domination, exploitation, division, inequality, and repression as the cultural and politico-economic norms, all manifestations of non-respect and non-love for what is human (not to mention animals and plants)—maybe even up to private property and the state. (258)

Gay is not a person, nor is it a thing; rather, "gay is the revolution" (259).

Gay's history as a term of radical opposition reveals some unsettling ideas about sex, power, and identity. Typically, sex and sexual relations are thought to be the effect of human identity. Because there are people, this idea goes, and because these people have particular patterns of desire, certain interpersonal relations of sex and power arise; in other words, sex is the cause, and power relations are the effect. The early texts of Gay Lib begin with the opposite assumption, arguing that, because there are particular patterns of power within capitalist cultures, certain patterns of desire emerge that then replicate, repeat, and proliferate these power dynamics in both social and interpersonal contexts; in other words, power relations are the cause, and sex is the effect. For Gay Liberation power and politics are not systems arising from a notion of "who I am"; rather, "who I am" is the effect of the oppression inherent in the capitalist systems of power and politics.

Equality for gay men and lesbians is an oxymoron within this mode of thinking, for the categories of sex and gender that must be presupposed to even imagine uttering the words *gay men and lesbians* are the very categories that create inequality in the first place. To *be* gay men and lesbians is to proliferate the conditions of oppression. As Charles Thorp, an early student leader in the gay liberation movement, stated in his address to the 1970 National Gay Liberation Front Student Conference, *gay* and *homosexual* "are opposites, and not just two words expressing similar objects, because only one talks about objects."[8] The binary of gay and straight is meaningless in the gay revolution, for the binary governing this ideology is entirely different and entirely utopian: one can be gay, or one can be straight in any of its manifestations—man or woman, homosexual or heterosexual, subject or object.[9]

It is worth seeing the statements of Gay Liberation in such detail, for their redaction into the dynamics of performance frequently results in only the voicing of recognizable tag lines that, while now seemingly slight, would have, in their own moments, invoked these entire fields of thought. Consider, for example, the closing chorus from the Gay Liberation Theatre's play:

Gay is good.
Our freedom is your freedom.
If it feels good, do it.
They've got the guns but we've got the numbers.
Free the erotic angels.
Gay is Beautiful.

(104)

This is not a collection of bumper stickers, although the history that has followed these lines and its efforts to commodify a system of lifestyle politics may make them sound as such. Even in such "sound-bite" forms the strategies of Gay Lib can be seen. Gay is modified by adjectives, but it is not quantified into a noun. It exists as a social impulse of action. The we that this gay forms is not something determinable as an identity but, rather, something cohered by a common and unsettling attitude toward power: "*We* want a revolution NOW" (104; emph. mine).[10]

Performing Liberation: A Short History in Two Moments

Ludlam's Angels: Around 1970

If Liberation performance seeks to "free the erotic angels" of America, nowhere does this impulse find a more fully developed dramaturgy than in the Ridiculous Theatre of Charles Ludlam.[11] *Bluebeard: A Melodrama in Three Acts* maps out most strikingly the ways in which Ludlam's work is propelled by the attitudes of Liberation Theory, which is not surprising, considering that it debuted in 1970 at Christopher's End, "a sleazy gay bar"[12] with an active back room on the waterfront of the West Village of New York City. The play is a campy reworking of H. G. Wells's *The Island of Dr. Moreau,* through the structure of Marlowe's *Doctor Faustus,* with bits of *The Bride of Frankenstein* tacked on. Yet, unlike Moreau, Faustus, or Frankenstein, who quest for supreme knowledge, Baron Khanazar von Bluebeard, an alchemist, quests for a supreme gender. In an exposition that directly imitates Marlowe's play Bluebeard presents his polymorphously perverse version of Faustus's complaint, saying:

> Give up your passions, Bluebeard, and become the thing you claim to be. Is to end desire desire's chiefest end? Does it afford no greater miracles? Have all my perversions and monstrosities, my fuckings and suckings, led me to this? This little death at the climax followed by slumber? Yet chastity ravishes me. And yet the cunt gapes like the jaws of hell, an unfathomable abyss; or the boy-ass used to buggery spread wide to swallow me up its bung; or the mouth sucking out my life! Aaagh! If only there were some new and gentle genital that would combine with me and, mutually interpenetrated, steer me through this storm in paradise! . . . They said I was mad at medical school. They said no third genital was possible. Yang and yin, male and female, and that's that.[13]

Following this speech, and further strengthening the parallel with *Doctor Faustus,* a good and bad angel enter and tempt him with conflicting advice in rough iambic pentameter: "Take half—one sex, that's all—for that is nature's way"; "Be thou on earth as God is in the sky, / Master and possessor of both sexes" (*CP* 119). Bluebeard responds with his own rhymed quatrain:

> Love must be reinvented, that's obvious.
> Sex to me no longer is mysterious
> And so I swear that while my beard is blue,
> I'll twist some human flesh into a genital new.
>
> (*CP* 119)

These angels are not, however, the angels of the medieval morality tradition. They are, rather, the "erotic angels" of Liberation Theory. Remove the campiness and egomania from this exposition, and it reads as a restatement of Liberation Theory. The heterosexually coded vagina, the homosexually coded anus, and the polymorphously coded mouth all exist as equally devalued options. Bluebeard desires to transcend them *all,* not to choose *between* them. Ludlam himself signals this desire as the definitive aspect of Bluebeard's motivation; as he says:

> Bluebeard is an intellectual who really doesn't like either of the existing sexes, so he's trying to make a new one. To me, the third genital means the synthesis of the sexes. I like that speech Aristophanes makes in Plato's *Symposium,* where he says people were once shaped like spheres, but that the gods got angry and split them into male and female, and now each person goes through life looking for his or her other half. (*RT* 24)

Bluebeard imagines a scientific breakthrough that will render the traditionally gendered body obsolete and change the dynamics of sex toward mutuality, the "interpenetration" of new genitalia rather than the penetration of an object by a subject; Ludlam speculates on an ur-form of existence not yet broken into the divisions of gender and sex—a sort of horizon concept that envisions *all* discrete divisions of being and the body as acts of godly punishment. Ludlam and Bluebeard merge in their ability to see the status quo of the body and identity not as foundations from which to examine a problem but as a part of the problem itself. And in this sense Ludlam and Bluebeard both merge with the utopic rhetoric of Liberation Theory and performance.

Bluebeard is not an isolated example in Ludlam's canon. Indeed, the

island of Baron Bluebeard seems to resurface again in *The Isle of Hermaphrodites, or the Murdered Minion* (1976), an eclectic "history" play about Henry
III and Catherine de Médicis draped over parts of Marlowe's *The Jew of
Malta*. The hermaphrodites that figure so prominently in the title seem to
bespeak a "third sex," a blending of genders to approximate a new one. So
too are there parallels between *Bluebeard* and *Eunuchs of the Forbidden City*
(1971), an aesthetically luxurious Chinese history play—castration being,
again, a rather extreme attempt at making the genitals something different
altogether. But, given the utopic transiency and impermanence of Liberation Theory, it is all too appropriate that the strongest corroboration of
Bluebeard's engagement of liberation theory can be found in a performance
that never happened.

Throughout his career, it can now be seen, Ludlam manifested an
intense imaginative link with Oscar Wilde, and his extant notes for a
planned but unproduced performance of *Salomé* provide one of the most
subtle examples of Ludlam's engagement of Liberation Theory. For Ludlam
the tragedy of *Salomé* is firmly rooted in the ways in which erotic love in
Western culture is used to express and construct differentials of power.

> Indeed we have all been rejected sexually by someone with a holier-
> than-thou attitude such as the one characteristic of John the Baptist
> a.k.a. Iokanaan in Oscar Wilde's erotic tragedy. Salomé's press agent
> might point out that everyone in the Bible is holy. But holiness these
> days is just a form of stick-in-the-mudishness anyway. Iokanaan
> rejected her, which led to his decapitation/castration, since the penis
> like the body has a head, and all penises seem equally intelligent.

Ludlam continues:

> Against a background of satiric religious discussion, Wilde set the
> tragedy of woman's sexuality, which in this aspect is synonymous with
> homosexuality: both risk the possibility of rejection by the male. The
> tragedy of one who aggresses toward the male. . . . If a man aggresses,
> expresses desire toward a woman, he pays homage to her and reenacts
> the ancient ritual of pursuit of the male for the female. . . . Woman
> waits. (*RT* 164–65)

The equation between homosexuality and femininity, which could initially
seem to reinscribe very bad stereotypes such as the "feminine faggot," is not
achieved through a belief that gender is a foundational and totalizing discourse but, rather, is activated by a recognition that the position of woman

as an "inferior" gender and homosexuality as an "abnormal" sexuality are both *always already* the *effects* of the production of social power, with both roles being rendered synonymous not through an interchange of gender and sexuality but through the third term of value, in this case the head/penis/man; as Ludlam phrases it, "The deadness of the head she kisses is as unrewarding as a limp cock" (*RT* 165). Excluded from the living, relevant, cultural head, the head of the king or the head of the turgid, reproductive penis, Salomé becomes Ludlam, and Ludlam becomes Salomé not through a transposition, coordination, or programmatization of sexuality and gender but, instead, through an exposition of each as the product and producer of the production of social power.[14]

The fragmentary nature of Ludlam's notes demands that much be read into them, but this interpolation is justified by a more direct comment on Wilde supplied in an essay entitled "Sexuality":

> The thing that created the biggest furor at Oscar Wilde's trial was that he had taken this boy who was a very low-class kid and bought him the uniform of Eton, dressed him in the best colors of this aristocratic school, and was walking around with him. That's what they were mostly angry about—that he was trying to pass off this ragamuffin as an aristocrat of birth.

Ludlam summarizes the importance of this episode in rhetoric that could easily circulate as one of the slogans of Gay Liberation Theory: "Gay has a revolutionary aspect in this creation of a spectacular upward mobility that is inexplicable to the outside world and is rather frightening" (*RT* 240). Ludlam's theatrical identity politics, then, do not try to situate a politics based on identity but, in the best traditions of Gay Liberation, attempt to expose identity as one of the commodities produced by social forces, one of the tangible sites that knot and tether together subject, subjectivity, and subjection. In this sense it is all the more appropriate that Ludlam should be attracted to Wilde, for— and this is a point seldom noted—Wilde's place within "gay history" was secured not because he *was* a sodomite but because he *denied* being a sodomite; his trials, without which he might never have reached such historical stature, rested precisely on his desire and need *not to be that thing*.[15]

Kushner's Angels: Around 1990

The Liberation Theory that colors Ludlam's performances also tints the two parts of *Angels in America*. In *Perestroika* it surfaces as the explanation of creation itself:

Angel:
REGINA VAGINA!
Hermaphroditically Equipped as well with a Bouquet of
Phalli . . .
I I I I am Your Released Female Essence Ascendant.

Prior (To Belize): The sexual politics of this are *very* confusing.
   God, for example is a man. Well, not a man, he's a flaming
   Hebrew letter, but a male flaming Hebrew letter.

Angel:
The Aleph Glyph. Deus Erectus! Pater Omnipotens!

Prior: Angelic orgasm makes protomatter, which fuels the
   Engine of Creation. They used to copulate *ceaselessly* before . . .
      Each Angel is an infinite aggregate myriad entity, they're
   basically incredibly powerful bureaucrats, they have no
   imagination, they can *do* anything but they can't invent,
   create, they're sort of fabulous and dull all at once:

Angel:
Made for His Pleasure, We can only ADORE:
Seeking something New . . .

Prior:
God split the World in Two . . .

Angel:
And made YOU:

Prior and Angel:
Human Beings:
Uni-Genitaled: Female. Male.

Angel:
In creating You, Our Father-Lover unleashed
Sleeping Creation's Potential for Change.
In YOU the Virus of TIME began!

                                             (2:48–49)

The copiously hermaphroditic disposition of the Angel recalls *Bluebeard's*
quest for a supreme gender. Moreover, the Angel's explanation of creation
is another retelling of Aristophanes's theory of sexuality from the *Sympo-
sium,* the same text Ludlam cites when explaining his play. Angels are not
just fabulous; they are also liberated, unfettered by the arbitrary divisions of
gendered meaning that motivate human existence.

In *Millennium Approaches* Liberation is mouthed by the Left ideologue and errant lover of Prior, Louis. In one of his characteristically long and pompous speeches Louis asks:

> Why has democracy succeeded in America? Of course by succeeded I mean comparatively, not literally, not in the present, but what makes for the prospect of some sort of radical democracy spreading outward and growing up? Why does the power that was once so carefully preserved at the top of the pyramid by the original framers of the Constitution seem drawn inexorably downward and outward in spite of the best effort of the Right to stop this? I mean it's the really hard thing about being Left in this country, the American Left can't help but trip over all these petrified little fetishes: freedom, that's the worst; . . . these people don't begin to know what, ontologically, freedom is or human rights, like they see these bourgeois property-based Rights-of-Man-type rights but that's not enfranchisement, not democracy, not what's implicit, what's potential within the idea, not the idea with blood in it.[16]

Like Liberation Theory, which defined *gay* as the opposite of homosexual, Louis here draws a binary distinction between two versions of democracy. One, the narrow and rejected one, implies an equality of rights within the system of governance; the other, a more "ontological" version, implies the dissolution of systematicity itself and the replacement of it with a sort of organic and indeterminant flow of human power. Louis ends with a sound-bite that would fit nicely in the Berkeley performance: "*Power* is the object, not being tolerated. Fuck assimilation" (1:90). Louis will not be trapped, he thinks, into "bourgeois property-based Rights-of-Man-type rights"; Louis, like the theorists of Gay Liberation, "want[s] a revolution NOW,"[17] "maybe even up to private property and the state."[18]

What is immediately striking about each of these imbeddings of Liberation Theory is the extent to which they are failures. The Angel coughs like "a cat hacking up a furball" (2:9) and can no longer fuck because God is gone. Prior, the selected prophet, rejects the liberationally drawn heaven she espouses in favor of "more life" (2:136), the temporal experience of the "uni-genitaled." Louis is at best a flawed revolutionary, having already abandoned his sick lover and taken up with a known Republican clerk of the court. His questionable views on race suggest that perhaps he has not fully thought through the ramifications of his theory (1:90–92), and, like the Angel, he too ends up being rejected by the prophet. Liberation Theory is not presented as the universal panacea that it appeared to be for Berkeley Liberation Theatre nor as the desirable and downright campy discourse it provided for Ludlam. It is, rather, an object of ambivalence.

Both moments of Liberation Theory in the plays are crucially inflected, the Angel's through the fact that she carries the potentiality of divine validation and Louis's through Kushner's afterword to the published texts. Acknowledging his debt to Oskar Eustis, Kushner states, "Oskar and I share a romantic-ambivalent love for American history and a belief in what the character Louis Ironson calls, 'the prospect of some sort of radical democracy spreading outward and growing up'" (2:156). It is this combination of beliefs that "created the optimistic heart of the plays" (2:157). Louis's belief in radical democracy is both owned and validated by the playwright. Moreover, the link between this democracy and American history is strengthened in the afterword, in which Kushner specifically labels his style of writing as a national trait:

> Given the bloody opulence of this country's great and terrible history, given its newness and its grand improbability, its artists are bound to be tempted towards large gestures and big embraces—a proclivity de Tocqueville deplored as a national artistic trait nearly two hundred years ago. (2:151–52)

Nationalism such as this, which ascribes an inherent potentiality to a people simply on the basis of affiliation with a geopolitical concept, hardly seems congruent with Liberation Theory. It was, after all, Liberation Theory that labeled gay people "refugees from Amerika"[19] and called on them to aid "the fight of the Cuban and other Third World peoples against the imperialism of the U.S. and its lackeys."[20] Yet, even as the afterword constructs this seemingly retrograde appeal to an ideal of national identity, it also espouses an anticapitalist ideology that would seem to be a pure reincarnation of Liberation Theory:

> We pay high prices for the maintenance of the myth of the Individual: we have no system of universal health care, we don't educate our children, we can't pass sane gun control laws, we elect presidents like Reagan, we hate and fear inevitable processes like aging and death, and on and on. . . .
>
> Anyone interested in exploring alternatives to Individualism and the political economy it serves, capitalism, has to be willing to ask hard questions about the ego, both as abstraction and as exemplified in oneself. (2:150, 152)

To be determinant Americans; *not to be* individualistically determined: these polarities of being and not being form the raw material of the ambivalence within the play. The play, like the afterword, voices the possibilities of true liberation in its most radical sense yet refuses to disavow entirely the system that is America; at the same time, it also refuses to let the idea that is America exist imperiously and unquestioned, in the absence of Liberation Theory.

"Contradictions," Kushner says in reference to Brecht, "do not point simply towards hypocrisy or bad faith. . . . They also locate the most difficult and exciting complexities" (2:153)—which is precisely the case in *Angels in America*. National identity in the plays is not simple nationalism; it is, rather, intimately linked with issues of immigration and ethnicity. Sarah Ironson, whose funeral opens *Millennium Approaches,* was, as Rabbi Chemelwitz phrases it, "not a person but a whole kind of person, the ones who crossed the ocean, who brought . . . to America the villages of Russia and Lithuania" (1:10); she is, as he specifies, "the last of the Mohicans, this one" (1:11), which links the idea of the immigrant with the idea of a preceding identity displaced by American politics. The "problem" of the human race according to the polymorphous logic of the "Liberation Theory" Angel is that human beings move, they break the world into "particle logic" (2:134), a logic of discrete, discernible, and separate things. When Louis's Liberation Theory lapses into an offensive and inchoate rant, it does so specifically when the questions of national identity and racial identity emerge.

In all of these examples the type of identifications that shatter the efficacy of Liberation Theory are also identifications associated with dominant nodes of thought in the struggles for civil rights: emigration and immigration, ethnic and religious identification, and, above all, *discernible* differences between people. These are the historical topics that set the stage for the emergence of the phrase *gay and lesbian civil rights* in the 1980s. This emergence is profoundly visible in the cause célèbre of gay theater that preceded *Angels,* Harvey Fierstein's Tony winner, *Torch Song Trilogy.* In the tour-de-force monologue that opens the play, Arnold, dressed as Virginia Hamm, ruminates on political history:

> See, I'm among the last of a dying breed. Once the E.R.A. and gay civil rights bills have been passed, me and mine will find ourselves swept under the carpets like the blacks done to Amos, Andy and Aunt Jemima. But that's alright too. With a voice and face like this I got nothing to worry about, I can always drive a cab. And that, chillun', is caused by power. Be it gay, black or flowered it always comes down to the survival of the majority.[21]

Speaking just a moment before the dominant adoption of civil rights theory, Arnold speaks from a point before it but also recognizes its inevitability. As in *Angels,* Arnold speaks of power, yet power, for Arnold, seems already to be the province of an inevitable civil rights surge that rides a momentum from the African-American movement, to the ERA movement, right into a program of gay civil rights. Arnold's resignation that this movement will result in an erasure of certain things is telling, for it points out the hidden histories that *Angels* refuses to leave obscured. Dressed as a drag queen, an icon of Stonewall rebellion, Arnold resigns himself to the erasure of his space and time. *Angels* and its afterword reopen this space and time, presenting the current moment of lesbigay/queer politics as a disparate economy of discernible political discourses whose cohesion and monocularity is achieved only through repression. They show, in other words, that Gay Liberation and gay and lesbian civil rights are, in actuality, different things—and, given the totalizing trajectory of mainstream gay and lesbian politics, this showing is no small feat.

Liberating History: Historicizing Liberation

So much of *Angels in America* is woven from the threads of contemporary life and from the yarns of fantasy that it is easy to forget that it also presents itself as a history play. Ethel Rosenberg returns to teach a new era—an era that might not remember Judy Garland's stellar performance of the same role and that probably did not get much access to history in normative high school "history" texts—the genocidal potential of the American government; prior Prior Walters appear to historicize the idea of plague. It is this attention to history that demands that the play situate itself in a tension between Gay Liberation and gay and lesbian civil rights. *Angels in America* is not *caught* in a fissure between these two discourses but, rather, *displays* this fissure as one of its objects of performance. Liberation Theory, in its simplest form, espoused the idea that differences are "bad," that they represent the produced false consciousness of capitalism. Civil rights theory, in its simplest form, claims differences to be "good," things to be valued rather than repudiated. There is an inherent antagonism between these two discourses, and that *Angels* opens them both to view exposes its own imbeddedness as a historical text.

Urvashi Vaid, one of the few major national gay and lesbian leaders to critique the assumption of *gay and lesbian civil rights,* notes:

> the Stonewall-era ideal of liberation and radical social change ceased to dominate the mainstream of gay and lesbian politics nearly twenty years ago, in the late 1970s. From that period on, the gay and lesbian political movement pursued social, legal, cultural, and political legitima-

tion—what I call mainstreaming—rather than social change. The dramatic but partial end-point of the legitimation strategy has become clear in the 1990s.[22]

The performances of liberation that I have traced specifically map the temporal margins of what Vaid calls "mainstreaming" and what I call gay and lesbian civil rights.[23] Writing from about 1960 up until his death from AIDS in 1983, Ludlam embodies the possibilities of representation just before mainstreaming; debuting in 1990, Kushner's performance of liberation exists exactly at the moment of its "partial end-point." I am drawn to this phrase *partial end-point,* for its incompleteness can aptly describe the status of *all* political discourses in *Angels in America.* Liberation Theory in this performance finds its partial end-point at the same point at which civil rights theory emerges; civil rights theory finds its partial end-point at the same point at which Liberation Theory emerges.

While I approve of Vaid's efforts to educate a new generation of lesbigay/queer leaders, I stress the ability to trace commonalities among Kushner, Ludlam, and Berkeley Liberation Theatre in order to complement and modify her historiography. The images of progression and displacement that attend Vaid's summary are betrayed by Kushner's plays, for the rhetoric that appears in the spaces opened by the partial end-point of the mainstreaming of the 1980s is, in point of fact, the discourse of the 1970s that Vaid suggests is already lost. Liberation Theory in these plays is not something that is lost but is something that emerges for viewing when the discourses of civil rights fail to establish themselves as the totalizing object of political and spectatorial interest. *Angels in America,* therefore, suggests that rather than being a progress of displacements history is an inchoate and incremental layering. Like the prior Priors who instruct Prior Walter, history appears as an eclectic mix of potentialities, complexly melded over time yet discernible, sometimes not visible yet never quite invisible. Ethel Rosenberg, herself a victim of American history, voices the historical poetics of the plays best when she says at the end of *Millennium Approaches* that "history is about to crack wide open" (1:112). This is not about the end of history but about its inability to hold a monolithic and unified aspect, its inability to conceal the cacophony of histories that will never appear, as Belize the black drag queen puts it, if "you" spend "the rest of your life trying to get through *Democracy in America*" (1:96). And not only is it the end of the history of America that obscures the *histories* of America but also of the history of gay and lesbian civil rights that obscures the *histories* of lesbigay/queer political struggles.

The best way to summarize the interplay of history and politics in

Angels in America is this: while the plays recognize that history establishes multiple discourses of political possibility, they also recognize that this same process renders hegemony—the ability of any *one* discourse to control artistic and/or political representation absolutely—as something that, at best, is only fleetingly held by any single discourse.[24] Both the hope (if things are bad) and the despair (if things are good) reside here in the same place—the place where, according to the Angel, human life exists, change is possible, and permanence is impossible. By historicizing Liberation and showing its theory to be a still present but nonhegemonic possibility, Kushner also liberates history from its illusory pose as a unified and determining trajectory.[25]

It is not too surprising that, when such historical teleology leaves, so, too, does God; for, one might assert, it is only a faith in a unified history that enables a faith in a unified God, some primum mobile that infuses experience with coherence and congruence. What does a people—American, Jewish, queer, or other—do in the absence of God, some now missing center that fucks angels and releases the spooj of hope? How, with no such God, does one free erotic angels? This is, in effect, the same question posed by Aleksii Antedilluvianovich Prelapsarianov to the Hall of Deputies in the Kremlin at the opening of *Perestroika*: "And what have you to offer now, children of this Theory? What have you to offer in its place?" But, unlike Prelapsarianov, who believes that change cannot happen without the "next Beautiful Theory" (2:14), *Angels* teaches differently. Sitting this time before a concrete angel constructed by humans, Louis, Belize, and Hannah deliver the play's own restatement of the Bolshevik's concern:

> *Louis:* Whatever comes, what you have to admire in
> Gorbachev, in the Russians is that they're making a leap into
> the unknown. You can't wait around for a theory. The sprawl
> of life, the weird . . .
> *Hannah:* Interconnectedness . . .
> *Louis:* Yes.
> *Belize:* Maybe the sheer size of the terrain.
> *Louis:* It's all too much to be encompassed by a single theory
> now.
>
> (2:146)

And yet, as Hannah notes, this impossibility does not obliterate the need: "You need an idea of the world to go out into the world. But it's the going into that makes the idea. You can't wait for a theory, but you have to have a theory" (2:147). This paradox is the central moment when *Angels in*

America connects with its own historic moment. Informed by the conflicted histories of Liberation Theory and civil rights, the partial end-point that marks the moment of the plays is one that demands more "theory" but which also suggests the inability of any *one* theory to offer *"More Life."* The plays do not offer a solution to this conundrum but, rather, ask that it be seen qua conundrum, as the inevitable condition of praxis, the necessary but impossible point at which theory and action merge, and it is with this recognition that the plays end and "The Great Work Begins" (2:148).[26]

NOTES

1. Steven Seidman's exploration of gay liberation and the new social movements of the 1960s contradicts this model. Seidman sees an "ethnic/essentialist" model in all the periods of gay politics I discuss, with its displacement only being effected in the 1990s. I perceive a certain fetishization of the present in Seidman's argument, but readers should consult his rewarding article and judge for themselves; see Steven Seidman, "Identity and Politics in a 'Postmodern' Gay Culture: Some Historical and Conceptual Notes," *Fear of a Queer Planet: Queer Politics and Social Theory,* ed. Michael Warner (Minneapolis and London: University of Minnesota Press, 1993), 105–42.

2. These origins are crisply outlined in Margaret W. Cruikshank, *The Gay and Lesbian Liberation Movement* (London: Routledge, 1992); a more analytical examination of them can be found in Toby Marotta, *The Politics of Homosexuality* (Boston: Houghton Mifflin, 1981).

3. Tony Kushner, *Angels in America: A Gay Fantasia on National Themes. Part Two: Perestroika* (New York: Theatre Communications Group, 1994), 154; emphasis mine. Further citations to this text will be given parenthetically.

4. The texts of this movement have been preserved in the important volume, *Out of the Closets: Voices of Gay Liberation,* ed. Karla Jay and Allen Young (New York: Douglas Communication, 1972); for a smaller taste of the period I examine here, see Neil Miller, *Out of the Past: Gay and Lesbian History from 1869 to the Present* (New York: Vintage Books, 1995), 363–88.

5. Gay Liberation Theatre, "Gay Liberation Theatre," *The Gay Liberation Book: Writings and Photographs on Gay (Men's) Liberation,* ed. Len Richmond and Gary Noguera (San Francisco: Ramparts Press, 1973), 102–3. Further references to this text will be cited parenthetically.

6. Carl Wittman, "Refugees from Amerika: A Gay Perspective," *Berkeley Tribe,* 26 December 1969: 12. Further references to this text will be cited parenthetically.

7. Chicago Third World Gay Revolution and Gay Liberation Front, "Gay Revolution and Sex Roles," in *Out of the Closets,* ed. Jay and Young, 254. Further references to this text will be cited parenthetically.

8. Charles P. Thorp, "I.D., Leadership and Violence," in *Out of the Closets,* ed. Jay and Young, 352. Further references to this text will be cited parenthetically.

9. For a fuller development of this idea, see Dennis Altman, *Homosexual Oppression and Liberation* (1971; reprint, New York: New York University Press, 1993). See also my exploration of liberation theory in Gregory W. Bredbeck, "The New Queer Narrative: Intervention and Critique," *Textual Practice* 9:3 (Winter 1995): 477–502.

10. It is interesting to note here the strong affinities between this conception of gay and the ways in which *queer* has begun to function in postmodern academic theory. In the disciplines of "queer theory" the term functions as a platform from which the concepts of male and female, as well as the biology that grounds them, can be viewed as effects of cultural power. As Eve Kosofsky Sedgwick has postulated, by way of a working understanding of *queer,* "that's one of the things that 'queer' can refer to: the open mesh of possibilities, gaps, overlaps, dissonances and resonances, lapses and excesses of meaning when the constituent elements of anyone's gender, of anyone's sexuality aren't made (or *can't be* made) to signify monolithically" (*Tendencies* [Durham: Duke University Press, 1993], 8). For Sedgwick *queer* designates instances when the descriptive powers of gender and gendered sexual identity (and thereby their *inscriptive* powers) fail. This idea is congruent with Sue-Ellen Case's advocacy of the term: "queer theory, unlike lesbian or gay male theory, is not gender specific. In fact, like the term 'homosexual,' queer foregrounds same-sex desire without designating which sex is desiring" ("Tracking the Vampire," *differences: A Journal of Feminist Cultural Studies* 3:2 [Summer 1991]: 2).

Case's formulation is helpful, for its crisp delineation indicates the debt queer theory owes to Gayle Rubin's germinal ruminations presented at the Barnard College Scholar and Feminist Ninth Conference, "Towards a Politics of Sexuality," in 1982: "Sex is a vector of oppression. The system of sexual oppression cuts across other modes of social inequality, sorting out individuals and groups according to its own intrinsic dynamics. It is not reducible to, or understandable in terms of, class, race, ethnicity, or gender" (Gayle Rubin, "Thinking Sex: Notes for a Radical Theory of the Politics of Sexuality," *Pleasure and Danger: Exploring Female Sexuality,* ed. Carole S. Vance [1984; reprint, London: Pandora Press, 1992], 293). Rubin later specifies this in relation to gender: "Gender affects the operation of the sexual system, and the sexual system has had gender-specific manifestations. But although sex and gender are related, they are not the same thing, and they form the basis of two distinct arenas of social practice" (308). Rubin's work provided terms for conceptualizing sex and gender as distinct areas of power and thereby set the stage for queer theory's skepticism of gender as a necessarily foundational language.

This view of gender, however important in its own right, points to a deeper concern in queer theory. At its heart is an intense unwillingness to privilege the logic of division and classification, the binary thinking that always attends the standard of "the normal." This aspect has been eloquently set forth by Teresa de Lauretis. In her introduction to the published proceedings of the 1990 Santa Cruz "Queer Theory" Conference she states, "The project of the conference was based on the speculative premise that homosexuality is no longer to be seen simply as marginal with regard to a dominant, stable form of sexuality (heterosexuality) against which it would be defined either by opposition or by homology" ("Queer

Theory: Lesbian and Gay Sexualities, An Introduction," *differences: A Journal of Feminist Cultural Studies* 3:2 [Summer 1991]: iii). The desire to escape comparison/contrast views of sexuality is also a desire to escape the idea of standardization, the process whereby discrete terms are held in binary opposition by both a comparison to each other and a comparison to a third, generally metaphysical, concept of value. This desire is also present in Judith Butler's analyses of *queer:* "The term . . . emerges as an interpellation that raises the question of the status of force and opposition, of stability and variability, *within* performativity" (*Bodies That Matter: On the Discursive Limits of "Sex"* [New York: Routledge, 1993], 226)—by which Butler means that *queer* potentially creates an identity (I *am* queer; you *are* queer) but does so in a way that does not necessarily reinscribe opposition (I am homosexual, *not* heterosexual).

11. The following section on Ludlam is derived from my article, Gregory W. Bredbeck, "The Ridiculous Sound of One Hand Clapping: Placing Ludlam's 'Gay' Theatre in Space and Time," *Modern Drama,* 39 (1996): 64–83.

12. Charles Ludlam, *Ridiculous Theatre, Scourge of Human Folly: The Essays and Opinions of Charles Ludlam,* ed. Steven Samuels (New York: Theatre Communications Group, 1992), 25. Further references to this text will be cited parenthetically with the designation *RT.* Because I deal with Ludlam in the highly specified context of liberation theory, my debts to other critics do not surface. But I acknowledge the help of two critics, Stefan Brecht, *Queer Theatre* (Frankfurt: Suhrkamp, 1978); and Kate Davy, "Reading Past the Heterosexual Imperative: *Dress Suits to Hire,*" *TDR: The Drama Review* 33:1 (1989): 153–70; and "Fe/Male Impersonation: The Discourse of Camp," in *The Politics and Poetics of Camp,* ed. Moe Meyer (London: Routledge, 1994), 130–48.

13. Charles Ludlam, *The Complete Plays* (New York: Harper and Row, 1989), 118. Further references to this text will be cited parenthetically with the designation *CP.*

14. My reading here has been inflected by Luce Irigaray, "Women on the Market," *This Sex Which Is Not One,* trans. Catherine Porter (Ithaca: Cornell University Press, 1985), 170–91, and her observation that, "by submitting women's bodies to a general equivalent, to a transcendent, super-natural value, men have drawn the social structure into an ever greater process of abstraction, to the point where they themselves are produced in it as pure concepts" (190). This is, I think, a more fully worked-out version of the point toward which Ludlam's notes converge.

15. I explore Wilde in more detail in Gregory W. Bredbeck, "Narcissus in the Wilde: Textual Cathexis and the Historical Origins of Queer Camp," in *The Politics and Poetics of Camp,* ed. Meyer, 51–74.

16. Tony Kushner, *Angels in America: A Gay Fantasia on National Themes. Part One: Millennium Approaches* (New York: Theatre Communications Group, 1993), 89–90. Further references to this text will be cited parenthetically.

17. Gay Liberation Theatre, "Gay Liberation Theatre," 104.

18. Chicago Third World Gay Liberation, "Gay Revolution and Sex Roles," 258.

19. Wittman, "Refugees from Amerika," 1.

20. "Declaration by the First National Congress on Education and Culture," in *Out of the Closets,* ed. Jay and Young, 249.

21. Harvey Fierstein, *Torch Song Trilogy* (New York: Gay Presses of New York, 1981), 15.

22. Urvashi Vaid, *Virtual Equality: The Mainstreaming of Gay and Lesbian Liberation* (New York: Doubleday, 1995), 36.

23. I am conscious that I appear antagonistic to civil rights, so let me stress here that I believe the strategy of civil rights to be *one* of the effective tools of power available in our culture; I simply disagree with its naturalization as an *inevitability* rather than its deployment as a *possibility*. This naturalization has effectively acted as a mode of censorship, one that stigmatizes alternative politics and modes of desire.

24. Antonio Gramsci's description of hegemony as a sort of floating equilibrium helps here; see Antonio Gramsci, *Selections from the Prison Notebooks,* ed. and trans. Quinton Hoare and Geoffrey Nowell Smith (New York: International Publishers, 1971). See also Ernesto Laclau, "Politics and the Limits of Modernity," *Universal Abandon? The Politics of Postmodernism,* ed. Andrew Ross (Minneapolis: University of Minnesota Press, 1988), 63–82, esp. 74–75.

25. This view of history recalls Linda Hutcheon's explanation of postmodernism as a stance that neither simply reiterates nor simply rejects the past; see Linda Hutcheon, *A Poetics of Postmodernism* (New York: Routledge, 1988). It also suggests that, even if *Angels* is not consciously espousing a postmodernity, it is certainly rejecting modernism, which, as Jean-François Lyotard has suggested, is constructed on a successive notion of history; see Jean-François Lyotard, *Le postmoderne expliqué aux enfants* (Paris: Galilée, 1979).

26. These ideas were rehearsed in talks at the Graduate Center of the City University of New York, the 1993 MLA Gay and Lesbian Caucus panel, the 1994 MLA Drama Division Panel, and the Gay, Lesbian and Bisexual Student Resource Center at the University of California, Riverside. I thank Michael Cadden, Steven Kruger, Steven Shum, Linnea Stenson, and Joseph Wittreich.

Contributors

Robert Altman has directed more than forty films, including *Brewster McCloud, MASH, McCabe and Mrs. Miller, The Long Goodbye, Welcome to L.A., Three Women, Nashville, A Wedding, Popeye, The Player, Short Cuts, Ready-to-Wear, Kansas City,* and a number of theatrical adaptations.

Arnold Aronson is author of *American Set Design* and *The History and Theory of Environmental Scenography* and served as Editor of *Theatre Design and Technology* for ten years. He is Chair of the Theatre Division of Columbia University's School of the Arts.

Art Borreca is Assistant Professor of Theatre History, Literature, and Dramaturgy at the University of Iowa, where he also serves as Dramaturg to the Iowa Playwrights Workshop. He has worked as a dramaturg on productions at the Yale Repertory Theatre, the New York Theatre Workshop, La Mama, E.T.C., and in the University of Iowa's Partnership-in-the-Arts program, which develops productions through professional residencies. He has published articles and reviews in *TDR, Modern Drama, Theatre Journal,* and in several collections.

Gregory W. Bredbeck teaches gay and lesbian studies in the English Department at the University of California, Riverside. He is the author of *Sodomy and Interpretation: Marlowe to Milton* and of essays that have appeared in *PMLA, Journal of Homosexuality, Modern Drama,* and a number of anthologies.

Michael Cadden is Director of the Program in Theater and Dance at Princeton University. He has written on many areas of dramatic literature and theory and is coeditor of *Engendering Men: The Question of Male Feminist Criticism.*

Nicholas de Jongh is theater critic for the London *Evening Standard.* He is author of *Not in Front of the Audience: Homosexuality on Stage.*

Allen J. Frantzen is Professor of English at Loyola University of Chicago. He is author of *The Literature of Penance in Anglo-Saxon England,*

Desire for Origins: New Language, Old English, and Teaching the Tradition, and *Troilus and Criseyde: The Poem and the Frame.* He has edited *Speaking Two Languages: Traditional Disciplines and Contemporary Theory in Medieval Studies* and coedited *The Work of Work: Servitude, Slavery, and Labor in Medieval England.*

Stanton B. Garner Jr. is Professor of English at the University of Tennessee. He has written articles on modern and contemporary drama and is the author of *The Absent Voice: Narrative Comprehension in the Theater* and *Bodied Spaces: Phenomenology and Performance in Contemporary Drama.* His current research interests include post–Cold War political theater, and he is presently writing a book on the British playwright Trevor Griffiths.

Deborah R. Geis is Associate Professor of English at Queens College, CUNY, where she teaches modern/contemporary drama, literature, and women's studies. She has published essays on feminist drama and performance art and other topics, and she is author of *Postmodern Theatric(k)s: Monologue in Contemporary American Drama.* She is currently writing a book on postmodern performance and the Holocaust.

Martin Harries, an Assistant Professor of English at Princeton University, has published in *New German Critique* and is working on "Scare Quotes and Reenchantment: Shakespeare, Marx, Keynes" and "Lot's Wife: Modern Drama and the Problem of Spectacle." His play *If You Can't Swim* was performed on the Edinburgh Fringe.

Steven F. Kruger teaches medieval studies and lesbian and gay studies at Queens College and the CUNY Graduate Center. He is author of *Dreaming in the Middle Ages* and *AIDS Narratives: Gender and Sexuality, Fiction and Science.* His current work involves an interrogation of medieval categories of race, religion, gender, and sexuality.

James Miller is Faculty of Arts Professor, University of Western Ontario. In 1988 he organized Canada's first interdisciplinary seminar on AIDS and the arts and curated "Visual AIDS," a traveling exhibition of AIDS posters from around the world. He is editor of the anthology *Fluid Exchanges: Artists and Critics in the AIDS Crisis* and author of *Measures of Wisdom: The Cosmic Dance in Classical and Christian Antiquity.*

Framji Minwalla is an independent scholar and writer. His essays on drama have appeared in *Theater, Theater Three, American Theater,* and various other publications. He is currently coediting, with Alisa Solomon, an anthology of essays on queer theater in America.

Janelle Reinelt is Chair of the Department of Dramatic Art and Dance at the University of California, Davis. She is the author of *After Brecht: British Epic Theatre* and the former editor of *Theatre Journal.* Her most recent book is an edited collection: *Crucibles of Crisis: Performance and Social Change*.

David Román is Assistant Professor in the Department of English at the University of Southern California. He is the author of *Acts of Intervention: Performance, Gay Culture, and AIDS*. His writings on theater and performance have also appeared in *Theatre Journal, Genders, American Literature, TDR*, and various anthologies.

David Savran is Professor of English at Brown University and the author of *Communists, Cowboys, and Queers: The Politics of Masculinity in the Work of Arthur Miller and Tennessee Williams*. His contribution to this volume won the Association for Theatre in Higher Education's 1996 Research Award for Outstanding Essay. A longer version of it appears in *Taking It like a Man: White Masculinity, Masochism, and U.S. Cultural Production*.

Ron Scapp is Director of the Graduate Program in Urban and Multicultural Education at the College of Mount Saint Vincent in the Bronx, New York, where he teaches education and philosophy. He has written on a variety of topics ranging from popular culture to education and from social and political philosophy to art criticism. He is coeditor of a cultural studies volume, *Eating Culture*, and is currently at work on a book, *A Question of Voice: The Search for Legitimacy*.

Alisa Solomon is an Associate Professor of English/Journalism at Baruch College, City University of New York, and a Staff Writer at the *Village Voice*, where she covers theater, politics, lesbian and gay issues, Jewish communities, and other matters. Her work has also appeared in the *New York Times, New York Newsday, Theater, American Theater, The Forward, Ms.*, as well as other magazines and several anthologies.

Index